er

The New Penguin World Atlas

The New Penguin World Atlas.

Edited by Peter Hall

Compiled and drawn by Oxford University Press

Allen Lane

Published in 1979 by The Viking Press
625 Madison Avenue
New York, N. Y. 10022

Library of Congress catalog card number: 79–65724

ISBN 0–670–78348–X

Made and printed in Great Britain
Compiled and drawn by Oxford University Press, Oxford
Colour maps printed by Cook Hammond and Kell Ltd., London
Monochrome printed by Cambridge University Press, Cambridge
Bound by William Clowes Ltd., Beccles

Contents

World Maps

1	World: Political	scale 1:163 million

Continental Maps

2,3	Eurasia: Physical	scale 1:44 million
	insets: Annual Rainfall, Build and Minerals	scale 1:110 million
4,5	North and South America: Physical	scale 1:44 million
	insets: Build, Minerals, Mean Annual Rainfall	scale 1:110 million
6	Australasia: Mean Annual Rainfall Physical	scale 1:44 million scale 1:132 million
	insets: Build, Minerals	
7	Africa: Physical	scale 1:44 million
	insets: Annual Rainfall, Build, Minerals	scale 1:190 million

Oceanic Maps

8	Atlantic Ocean	scale 1:63 million
33	Indian Ocean	scale 1:63 million
44,45	Pacific Ocean	scale 1:63 million

Topographic Maps

9	British Isles	scale 1:4.75 million scale 1:12.5 million
	insets: Population, Power	
10,11	Scotland	scale 1:1.5 million
12	Northern England	scale 1:1.5 million
13	Ireland	scale 1:1.8 million
14,15	Southern England and Wales	scale 1:1.5 million
16,17	Scandinavia and Iceland	scale 1:6.25 million
18,19	Western Europe	scale 1:6.25 million
20,21	Eastern Europe	scale 1:6.25 million
22,23	France	scale 1:3.15 million
24,25	Germany and the Alps	scale 1:3.15 million
26,27	U.S.S.R.	scale 1:25 million
28,29	Western U.S.S.R.	scale 1:12.5 million
30,31	Middle East, Pakistan and India	scale 1:19 million
32,33	India, Pakistan, Bangladesh and Sri Lanka	scale 1:12.5 million scale 1:7.75 million
	insets: Sri Lanka Rainfall during Summer Monsoon	
34,35	Far East	scale 1:19 million
36,37	Eastern China	scale 1:6.25 million
38	Mainland Southeast Asia	scale 1:12.5 million
39	Japan	scale 1:6.25 million
	insets: Tokyo Kobe-Nagoya	scale 1:2 million
40	Australasia	scale 1:22 million
41	New Zealand	scale 1:6.25 million
42,43	Eastern Australia	scale 1:6.25 million scale 1:6.25 million
	inset: South-West Australia	
46,47	Canada	scale 1:19 million
48,49	U.S.A. and Central America	scale 1:19 million scale 1:1.5 million
	inset: Panama Canal	
50,51	Eastern United States	scale 1:8 million
52,53	Western United States	scale 1:8 million
54,55	Northeastern United States	scale 1:2 million
56,57	Central Canada	scale 1:3.5 million
58,59	The Great Lakes	scale 1:6.25 million
60,61	Prairie Provinces	scale 1:5 million
62,63	Pacific Coast: Canada and U.S.A.	scale 1:6.25 million
64,65	South America	scale 1:25 million
66	Central South America	scale 1:7.85 million
67	Nigeria	scale 1:6.25 million
68,69	Africa: Cairo to Dakar	scale 1:19 million scale 1:1.5 million
	inset: Suez Canal	
70,71	Africa: Cape to Cairo	scale 1:19 million
72	South Africa	scale 1:12.5 million

COUNTRIES	CAPITAL CITY	AREA (10³ km²)	POPULATION (millions)	POPULATION DENSITY (/km²)	URBAN POPULATION (%)	BIRTH RATE (per 1 000)	DEATH RATE (per 1 000)	PER CAPITA GROSS NATIONAL PRODUCT ($US)	COUNTRIES	CAPITAL CITY
Afghanistan	Kabul	657	19.5	29	15	43	21	100	Guam	Agana
Albania	Tiranë	29	2.5	84	34	30	8	530	Guatemala	Guatemala City
Algeria	Algiers	2 383	17.3	7	50	49	15	650	Guiana, French	Cayenne
American Samoa	Fagatogo	0.2	0.03	155	n.a.	36	4	n.a.	Guinea	Conakry
Andorra	Andorra	0.5	0.03	49	n.a.	n.a.	n.a.	n.a.	Guinea-Bissau	Bissau
Angola	São Paulo de Luanda	1 247	6.4	3	15	47	24	580	Guyana	Georgetown
Antigua	St. John's	0.4	0.07	162	34	19	7	339	Haiti	Port-au-Prince
Antilles (Neth.)	The Hague*	1.0	0.2	248	32	25	7	1 530	Honduras	Tegucigalpa
Argentina	Buenos Aires	2 777	25.7	9	81	22	9	1 900	Hong Kong	Victoria
Australia	Canberra	7 687	13.8	2	86	18	9	4 760	Hungary	Budapest
Austria	Vienna	84	7.5	90	52	13	12	4 050	Iceland	Reyjavik
Bahamas, The	Nassau	14	0.2	14	58	22	6	2 460	India	New Delhi
Bahrain	Manama	0.6	0.2	391	78	44	15	2 250	Indonesia	Djakarta
Bangladesh	Dakar	143	76.1	521	9	47	20	100	Iran	Tehrán
Barbados	Bridgetown	0.4	0.2	566	4	21	9	1 110	Iraq	Baghdád
Belgium	Brussels	31	9.8	320	87	13	12	5 210	Ireland	Dublin
Belize	Belmopan	23	0.1	6	n.a.	39	5	n.a.	Israel	Jerusalem
Benin	Porto Novo	113	3.2	27	13	50	23	120	Italy	Rome
Bermuda	Hamilton	0.05	0.06	1 038	n.a.	21	8	n.a.	Ivory Coast	Abidjan
Bhutan	Timphu	50	1.2	24	3	44	21	70	Jamaica	Kingston
Bolivia	La Paz	1 099	5.8	5	35	44	18	250	Japan	Tokyo
Botswana	Gaborone	600	0.7	1	13	46	23	270	Jordan	Amman
Brazil	Brasília	8 512	110.2	12	58	37	9	900	Kampuchea	Phnom Penh
British Virgin Islands	Road Town	0.1	0.01	78	35	15	7	1 250	Kenya	Nairobi
Brunei	Bandar Seri Begawan	5.8	0.18	31	23	33	4	1 378	Korea, North	Pyongyang
Bulgaria	Sofiya	111	8.8	78	59	17	10	1 770	Korea, South	Seoul
Burma	Rangoon	678	31.2	45	19	40	16	90	Kuwait	Kuwait City
Burundi	Bujumbura	28	3.9	132	3	48	25	80	Laos	Vientiane
Cameroun	Yaoundé	475	6.5	13	20	40	22	260	Lebanon	Beirut
Canada	Ottawa	9 976	23.1	2	76	15	7	6 080	Lesotho	Maseru
Cape Verde Is.	São Vicente	4	0.3	72	6	33	10	340	Liberia	Monrovia
Cayman Is.	Georgetown	0.2	0.01	54	100	20	6	n.a.	Libya	Tarabulus
Central African Empire	Bangui	625	1.8	3	27	43	22	200	Liechtenstein	Vaduz
Chad	N'Djamena	1 284	4.1	3	12	44	24	90	Luxembourg	Luxembourg
Chile	Santiago	742	10.8	14	76	28	8	820	Macau (Port.)	Lisbon*
China	Peking	9 596	836.8	86	23	27	10	300	Malagasy Republic	Tananarive
Colombia	Bogotá	1 139	23.0	21	64	41	9	510	Malawi	Lilongwe
Comoro Is.	Moroni	2	0.3	135	5	44	20	170	Malaysia	Kuala Lumpur
Congo	Bangui	342	1.4	4	37	45	21	380	Maldives	Malé
Costa Rica	San José	51	2.0	38	41	28	5	790	Mali	Bamako
Cuba	Havana	115	9.4	79	60	25	6	640	Malta	Valletta
Cyprus	Nicosia	9	0.7	69	43	18	10	1 380	Martinique	Fort-de-France
Czechoslovakia	Prague	128	14.9	115	56	20	12	3 220	Mauritania	Nouakchott
Denmark	Copenhagen	43	5.1	117	80	14	10	5 820	Mauritius	Port Louis
Djibouti	Djibouti	23	0.1	5	n.a.	n.a.	n.a.	n.a.	Mexico	Mexico City
Dominica	Roseau	0.7	0.08	101	13	27	6	809	Monaco	Monte Carlo
Dominican Republic	Santo Domingo	48	4.8	94	40	46	11	590	Mongolia	Ulan Bator
Ecuador	Quito	284	6.9	25	39	42	10	460	Montserrat	Plymouth
Egypt	Cairo	1 002	38.1	36	43	38	15	280	Mozambique	Maputo
El Salvador	San Salvador	21	4.2	186	39	40	8	390	Namibia	Windhoek
Equatorial Guinea	Bata	28	0.3	11	9	37	20	260	Nauru	—
Ethiopia	Addis Ababa	1 222	28.6	22	11	49	26	90	Nepal	Katmandu
Faeroe Islands	Thorshavn	1.3	0.04	31	n.a.	18	7	n.a.	Netherlands, The	The Hague
Falkland Islands	Stanley	12.1	0.001	0.1	52	19	15	n.a.	New Caledonia	Noumea
Fiji	Suva	18	0.6	31	33	28	5	720	New Hebrides	Vila
Finland	Helsinki	337	4.7	14	58	13	10	4 130	New Zealand	Wellington
France	Paris	547	53.1	97	70	15	10	5 190	Nicaragua	Managua
Gabon	Libreville	265	0.5	2	17	32	22	1 560	Niger	Niamey
Gambia, The	Banjul	10	0.5	45	14	43	24	170	Nigeria	Lagos
Germany, Democratic Rep.	Berlin	105	16.8	157	75	11	14	3 430	Norway	Oslo
Germany, Federal Rep.	Bonn	248	62.1	250	88	10	12	5 890	Oman	Muscat
Ghana	Accra	239	10.1	40	29	49	22	350	Pakistan	Islamabad
Gilbert Is.	Tarawa	0.8	0.07	77	28	21	6	542	Panama	Panama City
Greece	Athens	131	9.0	68	53	16	8	1 970	Papua-New Guinea	Port Moresby
Greenland	Godthaab	2 176	0.05	v.s.	n.a.	n.a.	n.a.	n.a.	Paraguay	Asuncion
Grenada	Roseau	0.3	0.1	279	8	26	8	300	Peru	Lima
Guadeloupe	Pointe-à-Pitre	1.7	0.4	196	9	28	7	1 050	Pitcairn Is.	—

Population and Other Statistics

AREA (10³ km²)	POPULATION (millions)	POPULATION DENSITY (/km²)	URBAN POPULATION (%)	BIRTH RATE (per 1000)	DEATH RATE (per 1000)	PER CAPITA GROSS NATIONAL PRODUCT ($US)
0.4	0.1	187	25	33	5	n.a.
9	5.7	52	34	43	15	570
1	0.05	0.5	50	n.a.	n.a.	n.a.
6	4.5	18	16	47	23	120
6	0.5	14	20	40	25	330
5	0.8	4	40	36	6	470
8	4.6	163	20	36	16	140
2	2.8	26	28	49	14	340
1.0	4.4	4 066	90	19	5	1 540
3	10.6	114	49	18	12	2 140
3	0.2	2	86	20	7	5 550
7	620.7	189	20	35	15	130
9	135.4	86	18	38	17	150
8	34.1	20	43	45	16	1 060
4	11.4	25	61	48	15	970
9	3.1	44	52	22	11	2 370
1	3.5	159	86	28	7	3 380
1	56.3	184	53	16	10	2 770
2	6.8	15	28	46	21	420
1	2.1	182	37	31	7	1 140
2	112.3	295	72	19	6	3 880
7	2.8	27	43	48	15	400
1	8.3	44	19	47	19	n.a.
3	13.8	22	10	49	16	200
1	16.3	128	38	36	9	390
9	34.8	340	41	29	9	470
1	1.1	52	22	45	8	11 640
8	3.4	14	15	45	23	n.a.
6	2.7	268	61	40	10	1 080
0	1.1	33	5	39	20	120
1	1.6	15	28	50	21	330
0	2.5	1	29	45	15	3 360
0.2	0.02	151	n.a.	18	8	n.a.
2	0.4	137	68	11	12	5 690
0.02	0.3	16 625	97	25	7	270
7	7.7	13	14	50	21	170
9	5.1	41	4	48	24	130
2	12.4	35	27	39	10	660
0.3	0.1	393	11	50	23	90
4	5.8	4	12	50	26	70
0.3	0.3	1 024	94	18	9	1 060
1.0	0.3	325	33	22	7	1 330
1	1.3	1	10	39	25	230
2	0.9	426	44	28	7	480
3	62.3	29	61	46	8	1 000
s.	0.02	16 719	100	8	12	n.a.
5	1.5	1	46	40	10	620
0.1	0.01	133	11	17	10	500
6	9.3	12	10	43	20	420
4	0.9	1	23	46	23	n.a.
0.02	0.008	381	—	20	4	n.a.
	12.9	88	4	43	20	110
	13.8	337	77	14	8	4 880
	0.1	27	62	29	8	n.a.
.7	97	6	13	45	20	n.a.
	3.2	11	81	19	8	4 100
	2.2	17	49	48	14	650
	4.7	4	8	52	25	100
	64.7	66	16	49	23	240
	4.0	12	45	15	10	5 280
	0.8	4	n.a.	50	19	1 250
	72.5	90	26	44	15	130
	1.7	22	49	31	5	1 010
	2.8	6	11	41	17	440
	2.6	6	38	40	9	480
	16.0	12	60	41	12	710
	v.s.	n.a.	—	16	50	n.a.

COUNTRIES	CAPITAL CITY	AREA (10³ km²)	POPULATION (millions)	POPULATION DENSITY (/km²)	URBAN POPULATION (%)	BIRTH RATE (per 1000)	DEATH RATE (per 1000)	PER CAPITA GROSS NATIONAL PRODUCT ($US)
Philippines	Manila	300	44.0	138	32	41	11	310
Poland	Warsaw	312	34.4	108	55	18	8	2 450
Portugal	Lisbon	92	8.5	95	26	19	11	1 540
Puerto Rico	San Juan	9	3.2	341	58	23	6	2 400
Qatar	Doha	10	0.1	8	n.a.	50	19	5 830
Réunion	St.-Denis	3	0.5	195	43	28	7	1 210
Romania	Bucharest	237	21.5	89	42	20	9	n.a.
Rwanda	Kigali	26	4.4	157	3	50	24	80
St. Helena	Jamestown	0.1	v.s.	42	n.a.	24	8	n.a.
St. Kitts, Nevis and Anguilla	Basseterre	0.3	0.07	185	34	24	10	524
St. Lucia	Castries	0.6	0.1	185	39	35	7	345
St. Pierre and Miquelon	Paris*	0.2	v.s.	21	n.a.	16	9	n.a.
St. Vincent	Kingstown	0.4	0.1	258	22	33	10	234
São Tomé e Principe	São Tomé	1	0.1	82	23	45	11	470
Sa'udi Arabia	Riyadh	2 150	6.4	4	18	49	20	2 080
Senegal	Dakar	197	4.5	22	30	48	24	320
Seychelles	Victoria	0.3	0.06	209	n.a.	30	9	n.a.
Sierra Leone	Freetown	72	3.1	38	13	45	21	180
Singapore	Singapore	0.6	2.3	3 819	100	20	5	2 120
Solomon Is.	Honiara	29.7	0.2	6	9	36	13	326
Solami Republic	Mogadisco	638	3.2	5	26	47	22	80
South Africa	Pretoria	1 222	256	20	48	43	16	1 200
Spain	Madrid	505	36.0	70	61	19	8	1 960
Sri Lanka	Colombo	66	14.0	208	22	28	8	130
Sudan	Khartoum	2 506	18.2	7	13	48	18	150
Surinam	Paramaribo	163	0.4	3	49	41	7	870
Swaziland	Mbabane	17	0.5	28	8	49	22	400
Sweden	Stockholm	450	8.2	18	81	13	11	6 720
Switzerland	Bern	41	6.5	156	55	13	9	6 650
Syria	Damascus	185	7.6	38	44	45	15	490
Taiwan	Taipei	36	16.3	433	63	23	5	720
Tanzania	Dodoma	942	15.6	16	7	50	22	140
Thailand	Bangkok	514	43.3	80	13	36	11	300
Togo	Lomé	57	2.3	39	15	51	23	210
Tonga	Nuku'alofa	0.7	0.1	143	16	13	2	371
Trinidad & Tobago	Port-of-Spain	5	1.1	229	12	26	7	1 490
Tunisia	Tunis	164	5.9	34	40	38	13	550
Turkey	Ankara	781	40.2	49	39	39	12	690
Turks and Caicos Is.	Grand Turk	0.6	v.s.	14	—	26	9	401
Tuvalu	—	v.s.	v.s.	n.a.	n.a.	21	6	n.a.
Uganda	Kampala	236	11.9	47	8	45	16	160
Union of Soviet Socialist Republics	Moscow	22 402	257	12	60	18	9	2 300
United Arab Emirates	Abu Dhabi	84	0.2	3	65	50	19	13 500
United Kingdom	London	244	56.1	229	76	13	12	3 360
United States of America	Washington	9 363	215.3	23	74	15	9	6 640
Upper Volta	Ouagadougou	274	6.2	22	7	49	26	80
Uruguay	Montevideo	178	2.8	17	80	21	10	1 060
Venezuela	Caracas	912	12.3	13	75	36	7	1 710
Vietnam	Hanoi	336	46.4	138	16	37	15	150
Western Samoa	Apia	2.8	0.1	53	21	37	7	350
Yemen Arab Republic	San'a	195	6.9	33	7	50	21	120
Yemen, P.D.R.	Aden	287	1.7	6	26	50	21	120
Yugoslavia	Belgrade	256	21.5	83	39	18	8	1 250
Zaïre	Kinshasa	2 344	25.6	10	25	45	20	150
Zambia	Lusaka	753	5.1	6	34	51	20	480
Zimbabwe Rhodesia	Salisbury	389	6.5	17	19	48	14	480

n.a. not available.   v.s. very small.

* Centrally administered dependencies.

Sources: Based on the latest available United Nations figures.

Population of major urban areas in thousands

#	City	Pop	#	City	Pop	#	City	Pop	#	City	Pop
1	Tokyo	11 623	26	Manila	3 500	51	Pittsburgh	2 401	76	Nanking	1 750
2	New York	11 571	27	Karachi	3 499	52	Chungking	2 400	77	Clydeside	1 731
3	Mexico City	11 340	28	Lima	3 303	53	West Midlands	2 370	78	Milan	1 731
4	Shanghai	10 820	29	Rangoon	3 187	54	St. Louis	2 363	79	Dacca	1 730
5	Paris	8 424	30	Berlin	3 142	55	Alexandria	2 259	80	W. Yorkshire	1 730
6	São Paulo	8 050	31	Santiago	3 186	56	Singapore	2 250	81	Bucharest	1 707
7	Moscow	7 632	32	İstanbul	3 135	57	Kowloon	2 195	82	Harbin	1 670
8	Peking	7 570	33	San Francisco	3 109	58	Caracas	2 175	83	Lüta	1 650
9	London	7 168	34	Baghdad	2 969	59	Lahore	2 165	84	Bangalore	1 648
10	Los Angeles	7 032	35	Sydney	2 874	60	Athens	2 101	85	Monterrey	1 638
11	Calcutta	7 005	36	Rome	2 868	61	Nagoya	2 080	86	Lisbon	1 612
12	Rio de Janeiro	7 000	37	Washington	2 861	62	Baltimore	2 071	87	Sian	1 600
13	Chicago	6 979	38	Bogotá	2 855	63	Cleveland	2 064	88	Tashkent	1 595
14	Seoul	6 889	39	Toronto	2 803	64	Budapest	2 051	89	Ahmedabad	1 588
15	Bombay	5 969	40	Montréal	2 802	65	Kinshasa	2 008	90	Dallas	1 556
16	Cairo	5 715	41	Mukden	2 800	66	Houston	1 985	91	Surabaya	1 556
17	Philadelphia	4 818	42	Osaka	2 780	67	Guadalajara	1 963	92	Ankara	1 554
18	Djakarta	4 576	43	Boston	2 754	68	Kiev	1 947	93	Belo Horizonte	1 550
19	Leningrad	4 311	44	Greater Manchester	2 684	69	Taipei	1 922	94	Algiers	1 503
20	Tientsin	4 280	45	Yokohama	2 620	70	Vienna	1 859	95	Pyongyang	1 500
21	Detroit	4 200	46	Melbourne	2 584	71	Minneapolis. St. Paul	1 814	96	Lagos	1 477
22	Tehran	4 002	47	Wuhan	2 560	72	Barcelona	1 810	97	Kyoto	1 460
23	Bangkok	3 967	48	Canton	2 500	73	Hyderabad	1 799	98	Lanchow	1 450
24	Delhi	3 630	49	Madras	2 470	74	El Dar el Beida	1 753	99	Johannesburg	1 433
25	Madrid	3 520	50	Pusan	2 454	75	Hamburg	1 752	100	Seattle	1 422

Sources: Based on latest available United Nations figures

The Continents

	Africa	N. America	S. America	Antarctica	Asia	Europe	Oceania
Area (10³ km²)	30 319	24 386	17 834	15 540	44 518	9 933	8 942
Longest river (km)	Nile	Mississippi/ Missouri	Amazon		Yangtze	Volga	Murray/ Darling
	6 690	3 222	6 570	—	5 980	3 685	3 750
Highest peak (m)	Kilimanjaro	Mt. McKinley	Aconcagua	Vinson Massif	Mt. Everest	Mt. Elbrus	Mt. Jaya
	5 895	6 194	6 960	5 140	8 848	5 633	5 030
Largest lake (km²)	Victoria	Superior	Maracaibo		Caspian Sea	Ladoga	Torrens (dry)
	62 940	83 270	14 300	—	371 000	18 389	5 780

World : Political

© Oxford University Press

Scale 1:165 000 000

Modified Gall Projection

Map labels (geographic features and countries):

Date Line, 180°, 60°N, 30°N, Tropic of Cancer, Equator, Tropic of Capricorn, 30°S, 60°S, Antarctic Circle, Arctic Circle

Greenland, Alaska (U.S.A.), Canada, United States of America, Mexico, Bermuda, The Bahamas, Cuba, Jamaica, Haiti, Dom. Rep., Belize, Guatemala, El Salvador, Honduras, Nicaragua, Costa Rica, Panama, Colombia, Venezuela, Guyana, Su., French Guiana, Ecuador, Peru, Brazil, Bolivia, Paraguay, Chile, Argentina, Uruguay, Falkland Is. (U.K.), Galapagos Is. (Ec.), Hawaii (U.S.A.), Western Samoa, Tonga

Dominica, St. Lucia, Trinidad and Tobago, Grenada

Iceland, Ireland, U.K., Norway, Sweden, Finland, Denmark, Neth., Belg., G.F.R., G.D.R., Poland, Lux., France, Switz., Aust., Hun., Czech., Italy, Yugo., Alb., Greece, Bulgaria, Romania, Malta, Spain, Portugal, Gibraltar, Azores, Canary Is. (Sp.)

Union of Soviet Socialist Republics, Mongolia, China, N. Korea, S. Korea, Japan, Taiwan, Hong Kong, Philippines, Vietnam, Laos, Kam., Thai., Burma, Bangla-desh, Nepal, Bhutan, India, Sri Lanka, Pakistan, Afghanistan, Iran, Iraq, Kuwait, Syria, Leb., Is., Jor., Cyp., Turkey, Saudi Arabia, Yemen, Yemen P.D.R., Oman, U.A.E., Qatar, Maldives, Seychelles, Malagasy Rep., Réunion (Fr.), Mauritius

Morocco, Western Sahara, Mauritania, Senegal, The Gambia, Guinea Bissau, Gui., S.L., Liberia, Ivory Coast, Algeria, Mali Rep., Upper Volta, Ghana, Togo, Benin, Nigeria, Niger, Libya, Egypt, Chad, Sudan, Cen. Af. Emp., Cameroun, Eq. Gui., Gabon, Congo, Cabinda (Angola), Zaire, Angola, Namibia, Botswana, Rep. of South Africa, Lesotho, Swaziland, Mozambique, Zim., Zambia, Malawi, Tanzania, Burundi, Rwanda, Uganda, Kenya, Somali Rep., Ethiopia, Djibouti, Tunisia, Cape Verde Is.

Indonesia, Malaysia, Br., Papua New Guinea, Australia, New Zealand, New Guinea, Solomon Islands, Fiji, Tuvalu, Nauru, N.C.

Legend / Abbreviations:

Alb. Albania	G.F.R. German Federal Republic
Aust. Austria	Hun. Hungary
Belg. Belgium	Isr. Israel
Bh. Bhutan	Jor. Jordan
Br. Brunei	Kam. Kampuchea
Ca. Cameroun	Leb. Lebanon
Cen. Af. Emp. Central African Empire	Lux. Luxembourg
Cyp. Cyprus	Mal. Malawi
Czech. Czechoslovakia	N.C. New Caledonia
Dom. Rep. Dominican Republic	Neth. Netherlands
Eq. Gui. Equatorial Guinea	Q. Qatar
Gui. Guinea	R. Rwanda
G.D.R. German Democratic Republic	S. Singapore
	S.L. Sierra Leone
	Sur. Surinam
	Sw. Switzerland
	T. Togo
	Thai. Thailand
	U. A. E. United Arab Emirates
	U. K. United Kingdom
	Y. Yemen
	Yemen P. D. R. Yemen Peoples Democratic Republic
	Yugo. Yugoslavia
	Zim. Zimbabwe

1

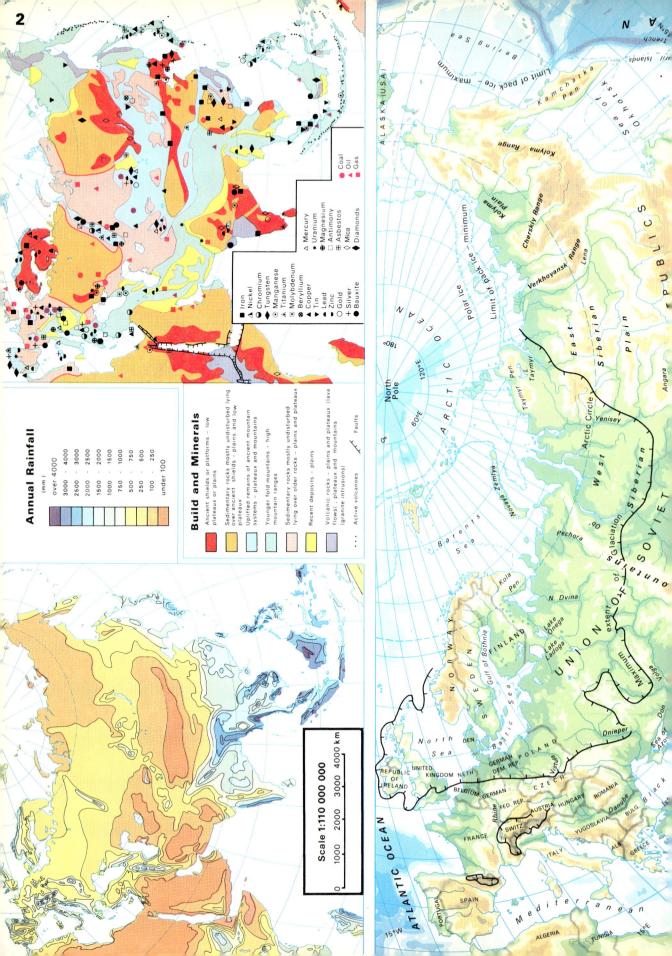

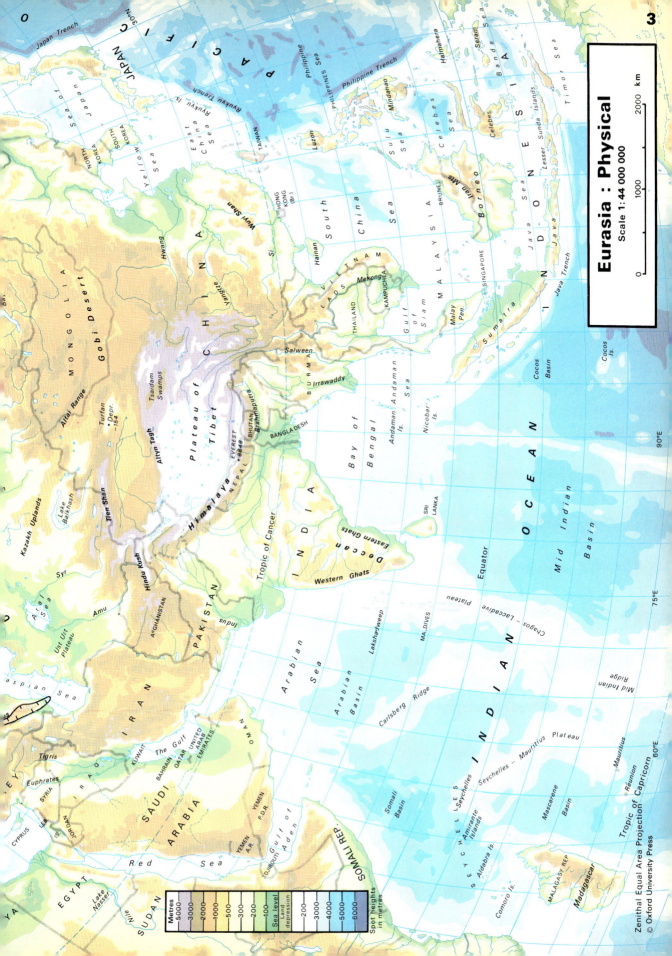

Eurasia : Physical

Scale 1: 44 000 000

0   1000   2000 km

Zenithal Equal Area Projection

Metres																
5000	3000	2000	1000	500	300	200	100	Sea level	Land depression	200	3000	4000	5000	6000		

Spot heights
in metres

JAPAN
Japan Trench
Sea of Japan
NORTH KOREA
SOUTH KOREA
Yellow Sea
East China Sea
Ryukyu Is.
Ryukyu Trench
TAIWAN
HONG KONG (Br.)
Hwang
Si
Yangtze
Wu-i Shan
CHINA
MONGOLIA
Gobi Desert
Altai Range
Tien Shan
Altyn Tagh
Tsaidam Swamps
Turfan Depr. -154
Plateau of Tibet
EVEREST 8848
NEPAL
BHUTAN
Brahmaputra
BANGLA DESH
BURMA
Irrawaddy
Salween
Mekong
LAOS
THAILAND
VIETNAM
KAMPUCHEA
Gulf of Siam
Malay Pen.
MALAYSIA
SINGAPORE
BRUNEI
Borneo
Iran Mts
Sumatra
Java Sea
Java
INDONESIA
Celebes
Celebes Sea
Sulu Sea
Mindanao
PHILIPPINES
Luzon
Philippine Sea
Philippine Trench
Hainan
South China Sea
Lesser Sunda Islands
Halmahera
Seram
Banda Sea
Timor Sea
PACIFIC OCEAN
Kazakh Uplands
Lake Balkhash
Syr
Aral Sea
Amu
Ust Urt Plateau
Caspian Sea
AFGHANISTAN
Hindu Kush
PAKISTAN
Indus
Himalaya
Tropic of Cancer
INDIA
Deccan
Western Ghats
Eastern Ghats
SRI LANKA
Bay of Bengal
Andaman Is.
Andaman Sea
Nicobar Is.
Cocos Is.
Cocos Basin
IRAN
IRAQ
Tigris
Euphrates
KUWAIT
BAHRAIN
QATAR
UNITED ARAB EMIRATES
The Gulf
OMAN
SAUDI ARABIA
YEMEN
YEMEN A.R.
YEMEN P.D.R.
Gulf of Aden
DJIBOUTI
SOMALI REP.
Red Sea
SUDAN
EGYPT
Lake Nasser
Nile
SYRIA
JORDAN
LEB.
CYPRUS
TURKEY
Arabian Sea
Arabian Basin
Carlsberg Ridge
Lakshadweep
MALDIVES
Chagos - Laccadive Plateau
Equator
Mid Indian Basin
INDIAN OCEAN
Somali Basin
SEYCHELLES
Amirante Islands
Aldabra Is.
Comoro Is.
MALAGASY REP.
Madagascar
Seychelles - Mauritius Plateau
Mascarene Basin
Réunion
Mauritius
Tropic of Capricorn
Mid Indian Ridge
90°E
75°E
60°E

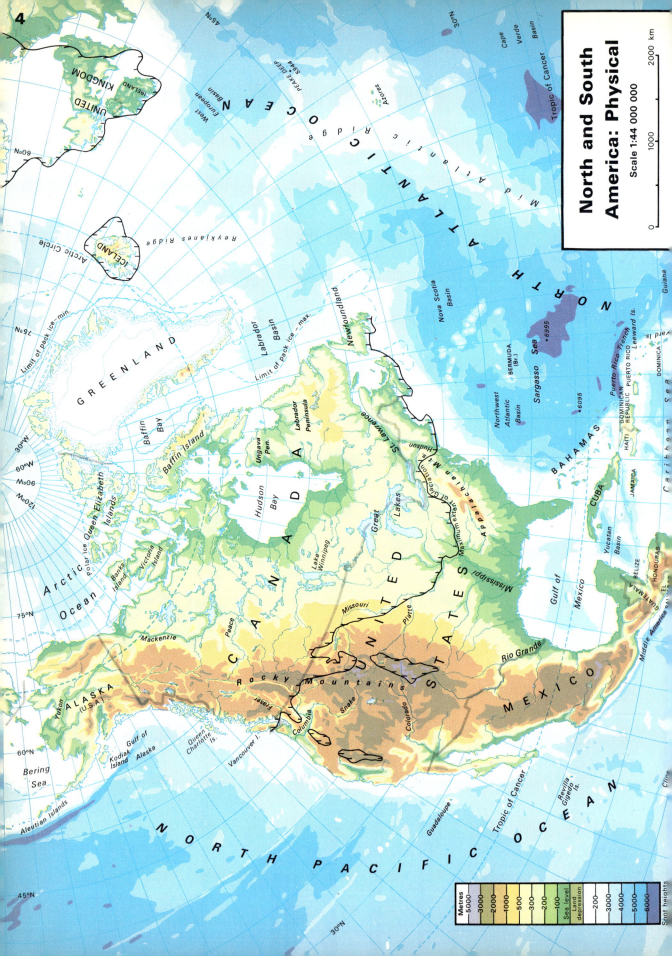

4

UNITED KINGDOM

IRELAND

ICELAND

Arctic Circle

Reykjanes Ridge

West European Basin

PEAKE DEEP

Azores

Mid Atlantic Ridge

GREENLAND

Baffin Bay

Limit of pack ice - min.

Baffin Island

Labrador Basin

Ungava Pen.

Labrador Peninsula

Limit of pack ice - max.

Newfoundland

Cape Verde Basin

Tropic of Cancer

NORTH ATLANTIC OCEAN

Nova Scotia Basin

BERMUDA (Br.)

Sargasso Sea 6995

Northwest Atlantic Basin

6096

Puerto Rico Trench

BAHAMAS

PUERTO RICO Leeward Is.

DOMINICAN REPUBLIC

HAITI

DOMINICA

Windward Is.

Caribbean Sea

Guiana

St. Lawrence

Great Lakes

extent of Glaciation

Appalachian Mts.

CUBA

JAMAICA

Yucatan Basin

Gulf of Mexico

Hudson

C A N A D A

Hudson Bay

Lake Winnipeg

U N I T E D S T A T E S

Mississippi

Missouri

Platte

Rio Grande

BELIZE

GUATEMALA

HONDURAS

EL

Middle America Trench

Arctic Ocean

Queen Elizabeth Islands

Polar ice

Banks Island

Victoria Island

Mackenzie

Peace

Rocky Mountains

Snake

Colorado

M E X I C O

ALASKA (U.S.A.)

Yukon

Fraser

Columbia

Maximum extent

Queen Charlotte Is.

Vancouver I.

Kodiak Island

Gulf of Alaska

Bering Sea

Aleutian Islands

Guadaloupe

Revilla Gigedo Is.

Tropic of Cancer

N O R T H   P A C I F I C   O C E A N

30°N

45°N

60°N

75°N

60°W

90°W

120°W

30°W

Metres
5000
3000
2000
1000
500
300
200
100
Sea level
Land depression
-200
-3000
-4000
-5000
-6000

Land heights

Spot heights

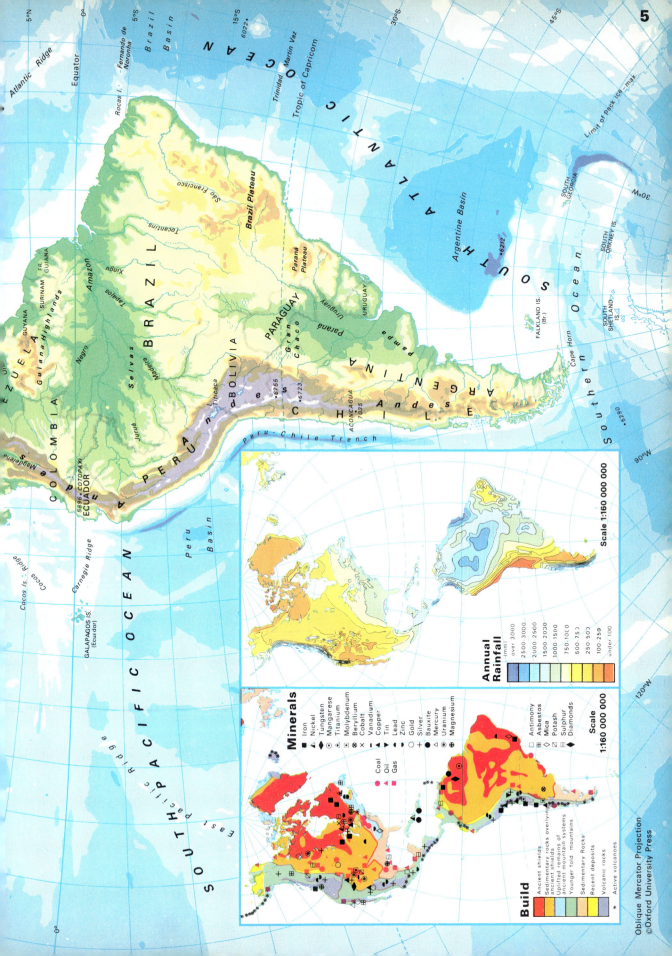

5

ATLANTIC OCEAN

Atlantic Ridge

Equator

Brazil Basin

Fernando de Noronha

Rocas I.

Trinidad Martin Vaz

Tropic of Capricorn

SOUTH ATLANTIC

Argentine Basin

SOUTH GEORGIA

SOUTH ORKNEY IS.

SOUTH SHETLAND IS.

Limit of pack ice max.

FALKLAND IS. (Br.)

Cape Horn

Southern Ocean

São Francisco

Brazil Plateau

Tocantins

BRAZIL

Xingu

Tapajós

Amazon

Negro

Madeira

Selvas

Guiana Highlands

GUYANA

SURINAM

FR. GUIANA

Juruá

Napo

Paraná Plateau

Uruguay

Paraná

URUGUAY

PARAGUAY

Gran Chaco

BOLIVIA

Titicaca

6755

6723

Pampa

ARGENTINA

Andes

ACONCAGUA 7035

CHILE

6755

VENEZUELA

COLOMBIA

Magdalena

ECUADOR

COTOPAXI 5896

Peru–Chile Trench

PERU

Galápagos Is. (Ecuador)

GALAPAGOS IS. (Ecuador)

Carnegie Ridge

Cocos Is.

Cocos Ridge

Peru Basin

SOUTH PACIFIC OCEAN

East Pacific Ridge

Annual Rainfall

(mm)
- over 3000
- 2500–3000
- 2000–2500
- 1500–2020
- 1000–1500
- 750–10C0
- 500–753
- 250–503
- 100–250
- under 100

Scale 1:160 000 000

Minerals

| Iron | Nickel | Tungsten | Mangarese | Titanium | Molybdenum | Beryllium | Cobalt | Vanadium | Copper | Tin | Lead | Zinc | Gold | Silver | Bauxite | Mercury | Uranium | Magnesium | Antimony | Asbestos | Mica | Potash | Sulphur | Diamonds |

Coal Oil Gas

Scale 1:160 000 000

Build

- Ancient shields
- Sedimentary rocks overlying ancient shields
- Uplifted remains of ancient mountain systems
- Younger fold mountains
- Sedimentary Rocks
- Recent deposits
- Volcanic rocks
- Active volcanoes

Oblique Mercator Projection
©Oxford University Press

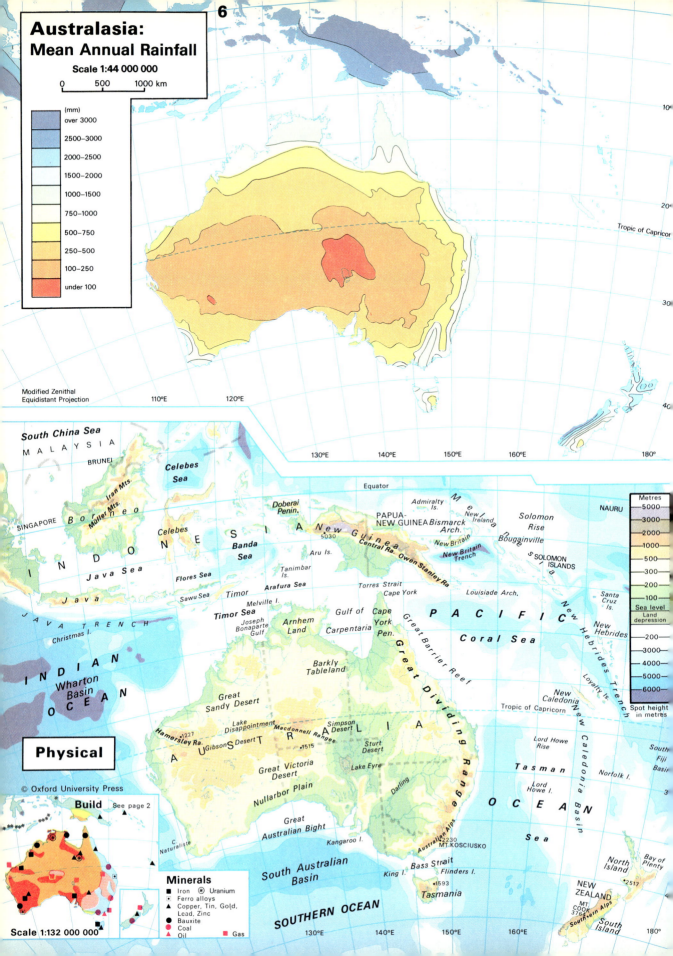

Australasia:
Mean Annual Rainfall
Scale 1:44 000 000

0   500   1000 km

(mm)
over 3000
2500–3000
2000–2500
1500–2000
1000–1500
750–1000
500–750
250–500
100–250
under 100

Modified Zenithal
Equidistant Projection

110°E   120°E

Tropic of Capricor

10°

20°

30°

40°

South China Sea

MALAYSIA

BRUNEI

SINGAPORE

Celebes Sea

B o r n e o

Iran Mts.

Müller Mts.

Celebes

Banda Sea

Java Sea

Flores Sea

Sawu Sea

J a v a

J A V A   T R E N C H

Christmas I.

I N D O N E S I A

Doberai Penin.

5030

New Guinea

Central Ra. Owen Stanley Ra.

PAPUA-
NEW GUINEA

Bismarck Arch.

Admiralty Is.

New Ireland

New Britain

New Britain Trench

M e l a n

Solomon Rise

Bougainville

S SOLOMON
ISLANDS

Coral Sea

NAURU

Equator

Aru Is.

Tanimbar Is.

Arafura Sea

Torres Strait

Cape York

Louisiade Arch.

Santa Cruz Is.

New Hebrides

New Hebrides Trench

Loyalty Is.

Timor

Timor Sea

Melville I.

Joseph
Bonaparte
Gulf

Arnhem
Land

Gulf of
Carpentaria

Cape
York
Pen.

Great Barrier Reef

Great Dividing Range

P A C I F I C

New
Caledonia

New Caledonia Basin

Lord Howe
Rise

New
Caledonia

Lord
Howe I.

Norfolk I.

South
Fiji
Basin

T a s m a n

S e a

*Wharton
Basin*

I N D I A N

O C E A N

*Great
Sandy Desert*

Hamersley Ra.

•1227

Lake
Disappointment

A U G i b s o n ' S   D E S E R T

Barkly
Tableland

Macdonnell Ranges

•1515

Simpson
Desert

Sturt
Desert

Lake Eyre

Darling

Tropic of Capricorn

Physical

© Oxford University Press

*Great Victoria
Desert*

Nullarbor Plain

*Great
Australian Bight*

Kangaroo I.

Australian Alps

•2230
MT.KOSCIUSKO

Bass Strait

King I.

Flinders I.

•1593

Tasmania

O C E A N

S e a

3

NEW
ZEALAND

North
Island

Bay of
Plenty

•2517

MT
COOK
3764

Southern Alps

South
Island

*South Australian
Basin*

SOUTHERN OCEAN

Build

See page 2

Minerals
■ Iron   ⊕ Uranium
⊡ Ferro alloys
▲ Copper, Tin, Gold,
   Lead, Zinc
● Bauxite
● Coal
▲ Oil   ■ Gas

Scale 1:132 000 000

Metres
5000
3000
2000
1000
500
300
200
100
Sea level
Land
depression
–200
–3000
–4000
–5000
–6000

•Spot height
in metres

C
Naturaliste

130°E   140°E   150°E   160°E   180°

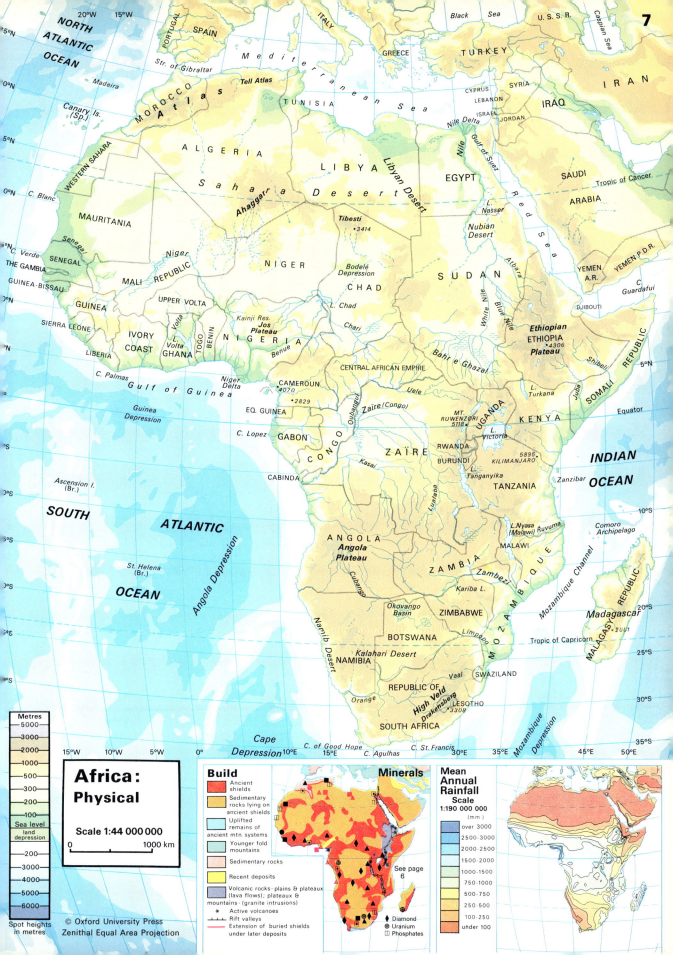

Africa:
Physical

Scale 1:44 000 000

0 ——————— 1000 km

© Oxford University Press
Zenithal Equal Area Projection

Metres
- 5000
- 3000
- 2000
- 1000
- 500
- 300
- 200
- 100

Sea level
land
depression

- 200
- 3000
- 4000
- 5000
- 6000

Spot heights
in metres

Build

- Ancient shields
- Sedimentary rocks lying on ancient shields
- Uplifted remains of ancient mtn. systems
- Younger fold mountains
- Sedimentary rocks
- Recent deposits
- Volcanic rocks - plains & plateaux (lava flows); plateaux & mountains - (granite intrusions)
- ✳ Active volcanoes
- Rift valleys
- Extension of buried shields under later deposits

Minerals

See page 6

- ◆ Diamond
- ⊕ Uranium
- ⊡ Phosphates

Mean Annual Rainfall
Scale 1:190 000 000
(mm)

- over 3000
- 2500-3000
- 2000-2500
- 1500-2000
- 1000-1500
- 750-1000
- 500-750
- 250-500
- 100-250
- under 100

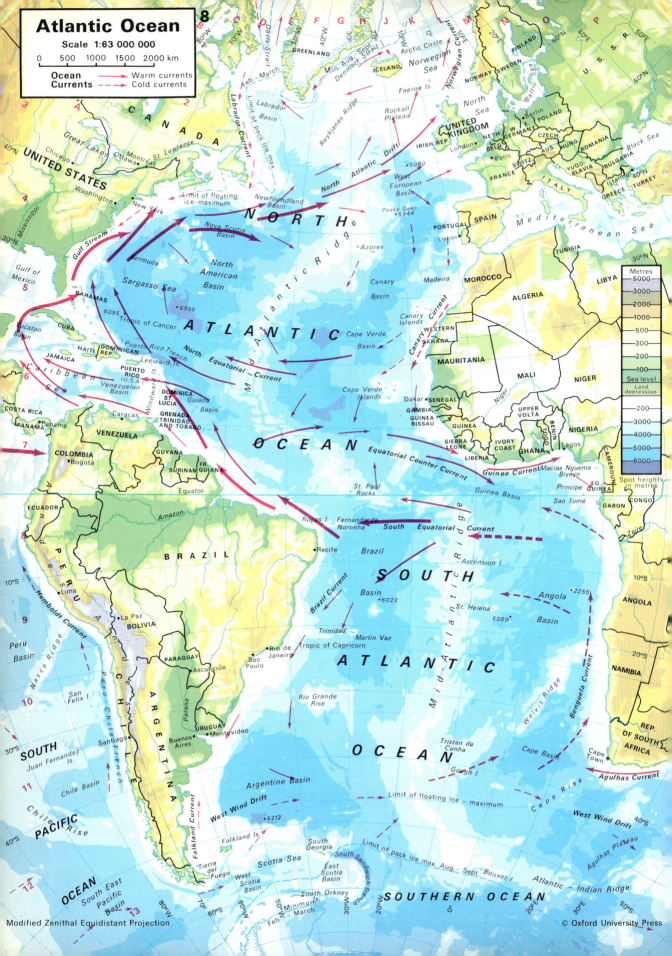

Population

Population Density

(/km²)

- over 700
- 100 - 700
- 10 - 100
- 1 - 9
- under 1

Glasgow

Dublin Manchester Leeds
Liverpool Sheffield

Birmingham

London

Scale 1:12 500 000

Cities
(million people)
- ■ over 2
- ● 1 - 2
- ○ 0.5 - 1

Power

Coalfield
- Coalfield
- Oil) fields,
- Gas) pipelines and pipelines under construction
- △ H.E.P. station
- ● Nuclear power station

British Isles

Scale 1:4 750 000

0   50   100   150 km

Metres
- 5000
- 3000
- 2000
- 1000
- 500
- 300
- 200
- 100
- Sea Level
- Land depression

Spot heights in metres

Boundaries International (in sea) (disputed)
Internal

Roads Motorways Other roads Tracks

Railways

Airports International Domestic

Canals Seasonal rivers, lakes

Marshes Salt pan Ice cap

Sand desert limits National Parks, etc.

Conical Orthomorphic Projection

© Oxford University Press

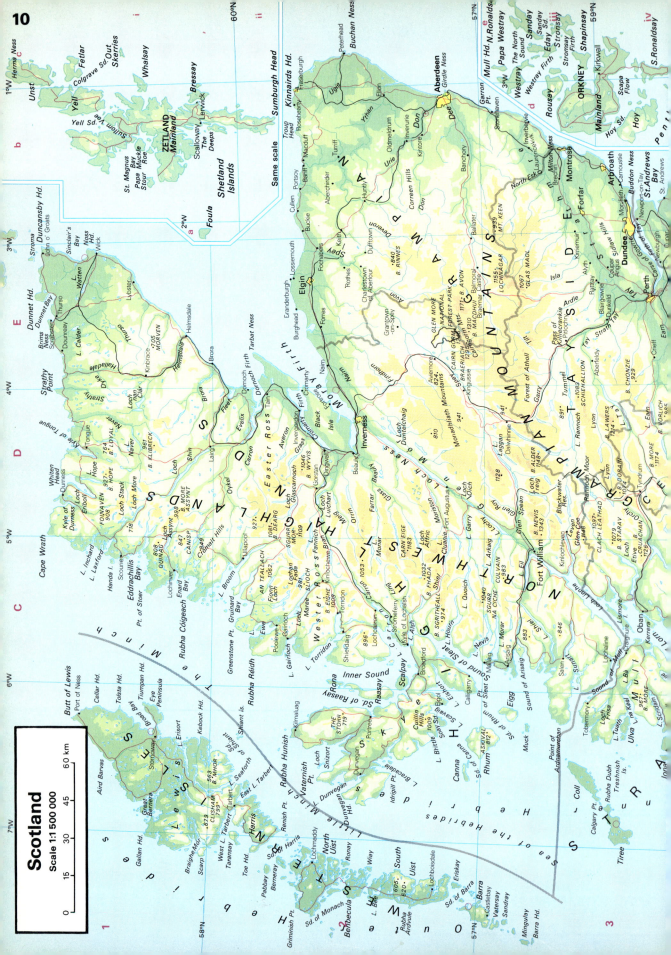

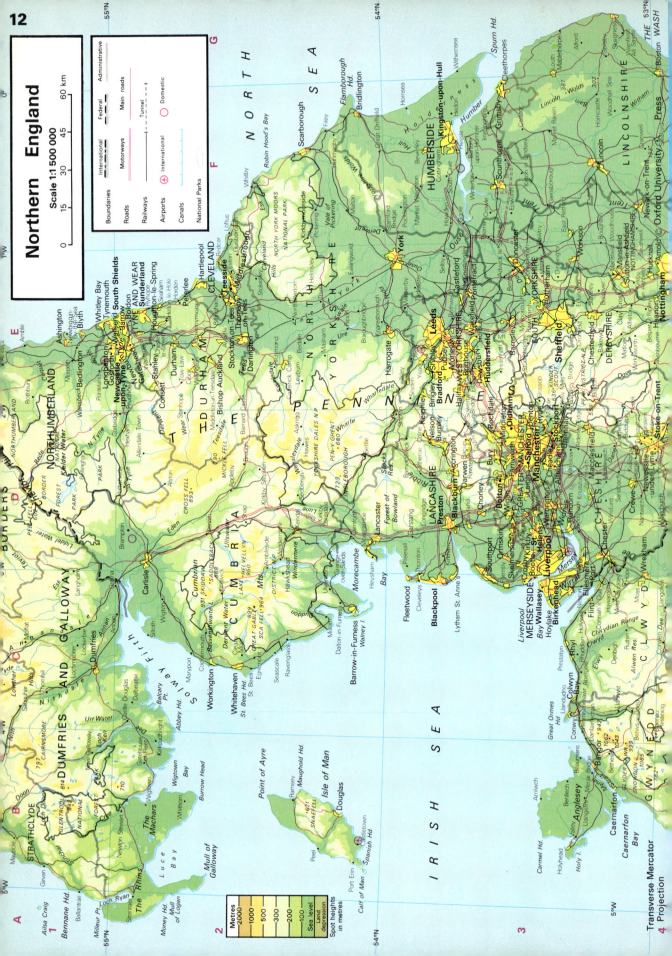

Ireland

Scale 1:1 800 000

0	15	30	45	60 km

Boundaries — International, Federal, Administrative

Roads — Motorways, Main roads

Railways — Tunnel

Airports — International, Domestic

Canals

National Parks

Metres
2000
1000
500
300
200
100
Sea level
Land depression

Spot heights in metres

Transverse Mercator Projection

© Oxford University Press

13

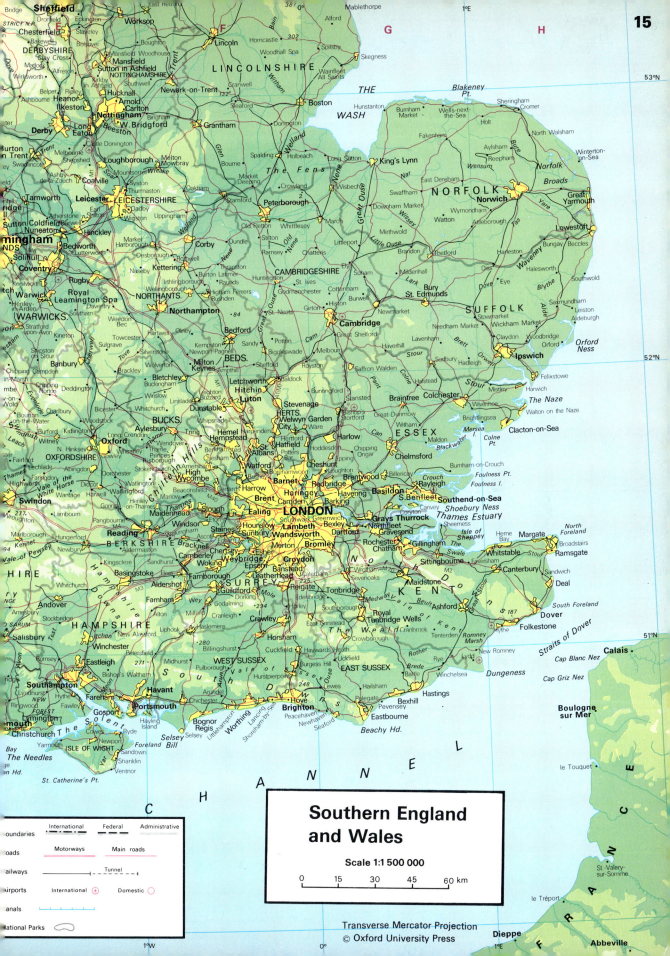

Southern England and Wales

Scale 1:1 500 000

0   15   30   45   60 km

Transverse Mercator Projection

© Oxford University Press

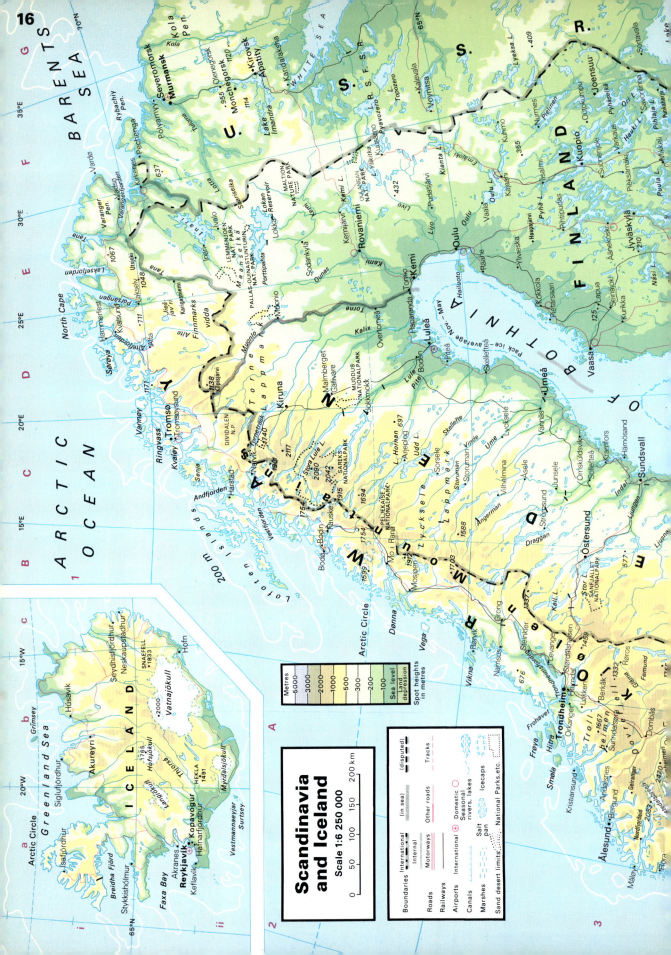

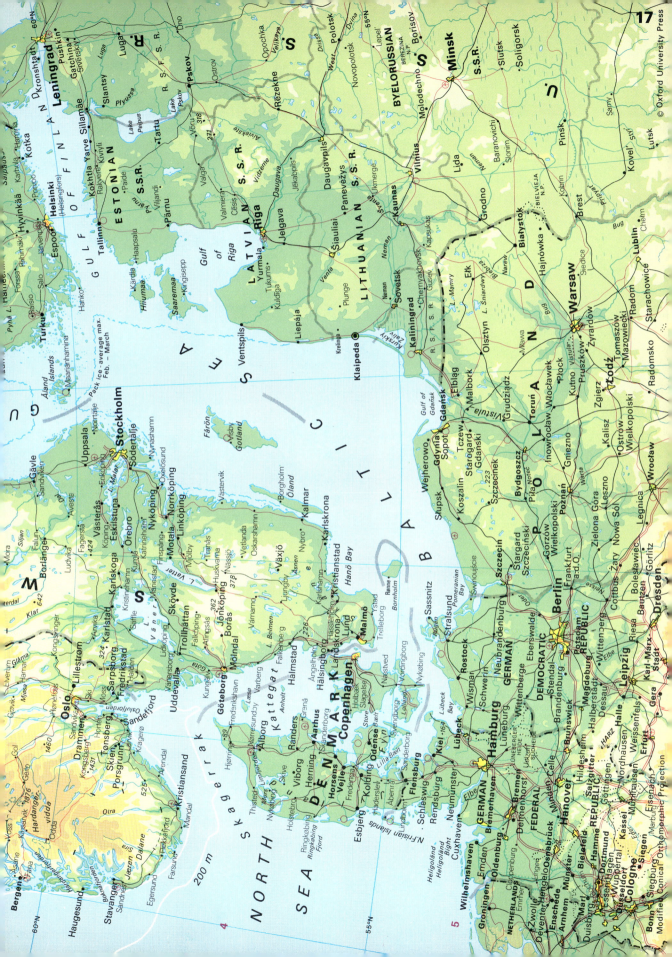

Western Europe

Scale 1:6 250 000

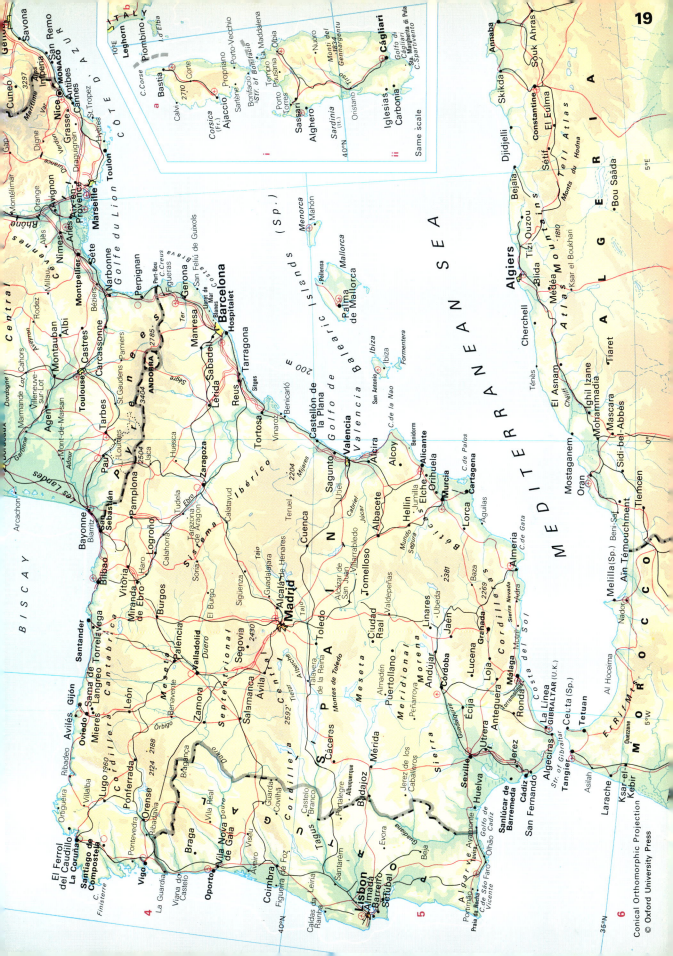

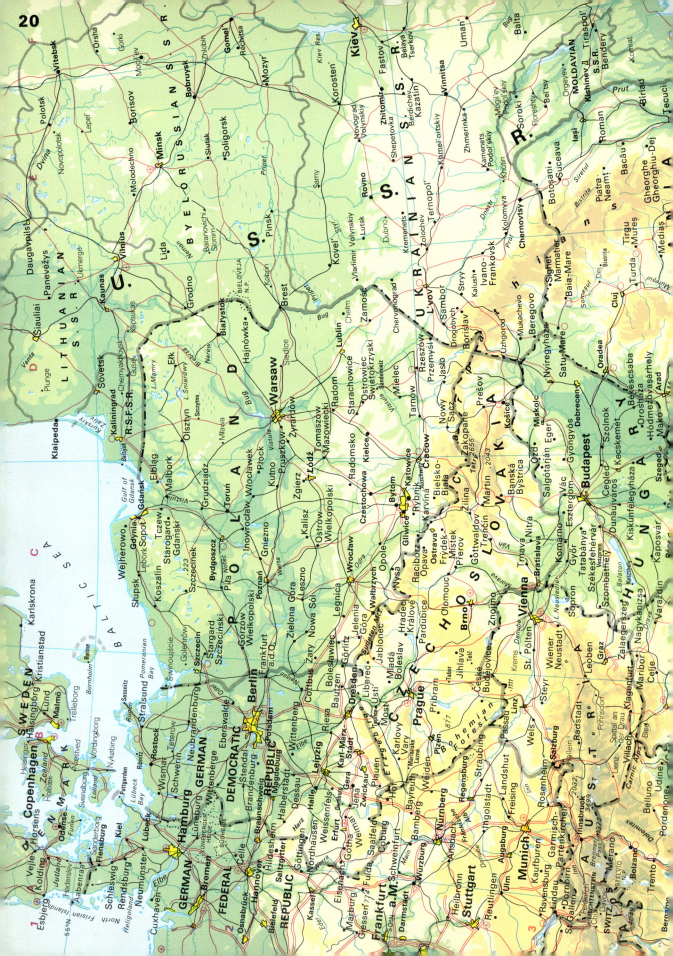

Eastern Europe

Scale 1:6 250 000

Conical Orthomorphic Projection

© Oxford University Press

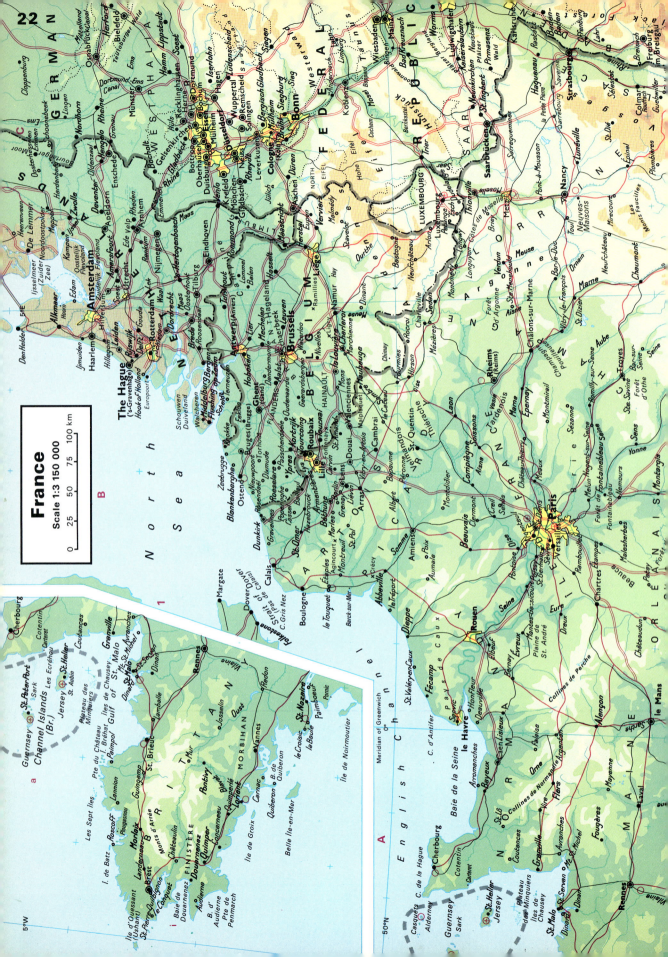

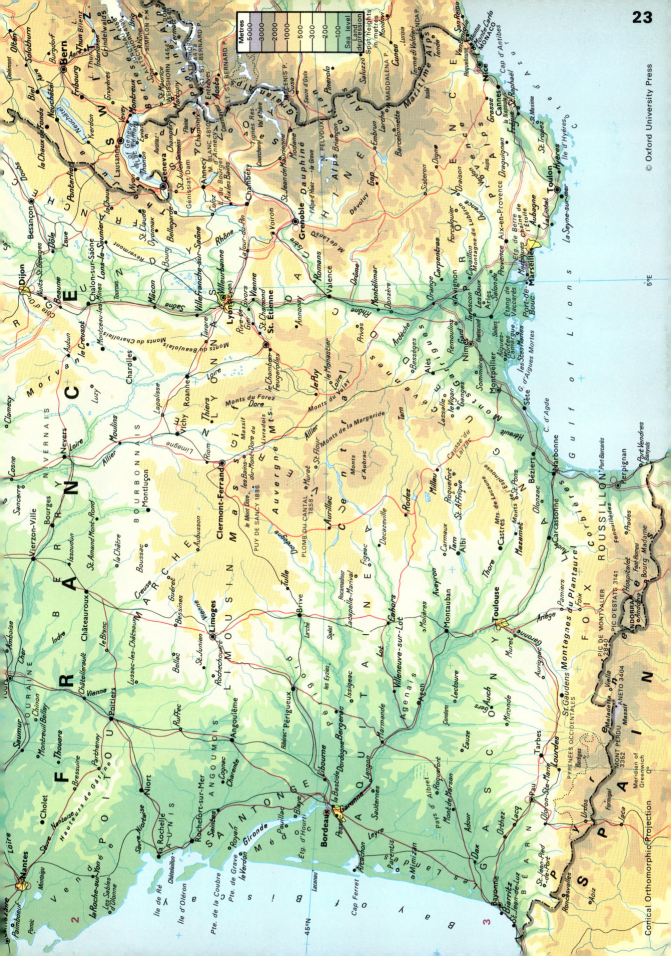

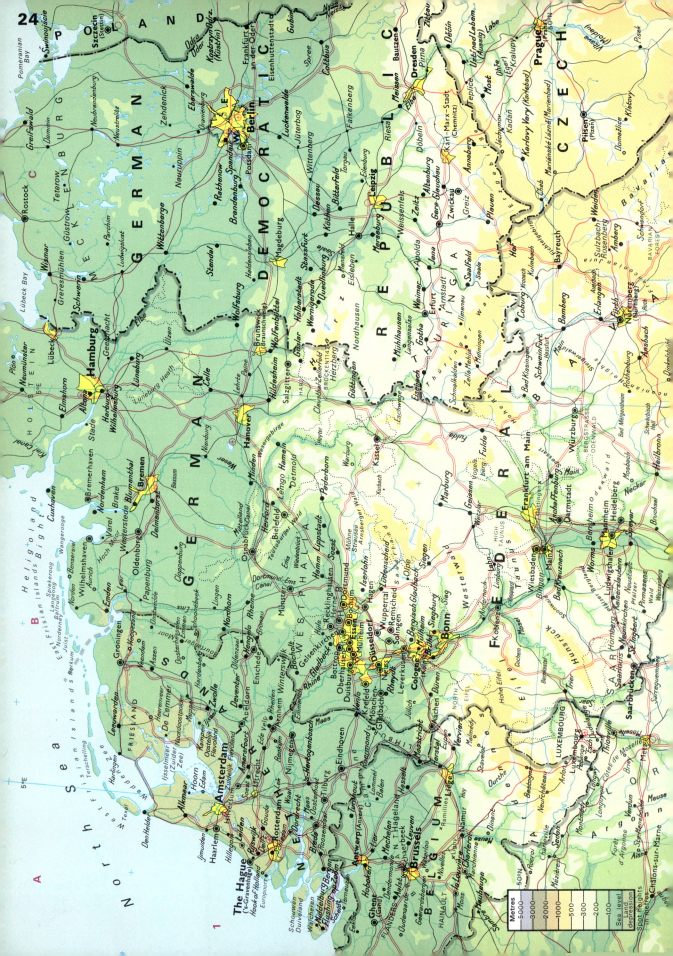

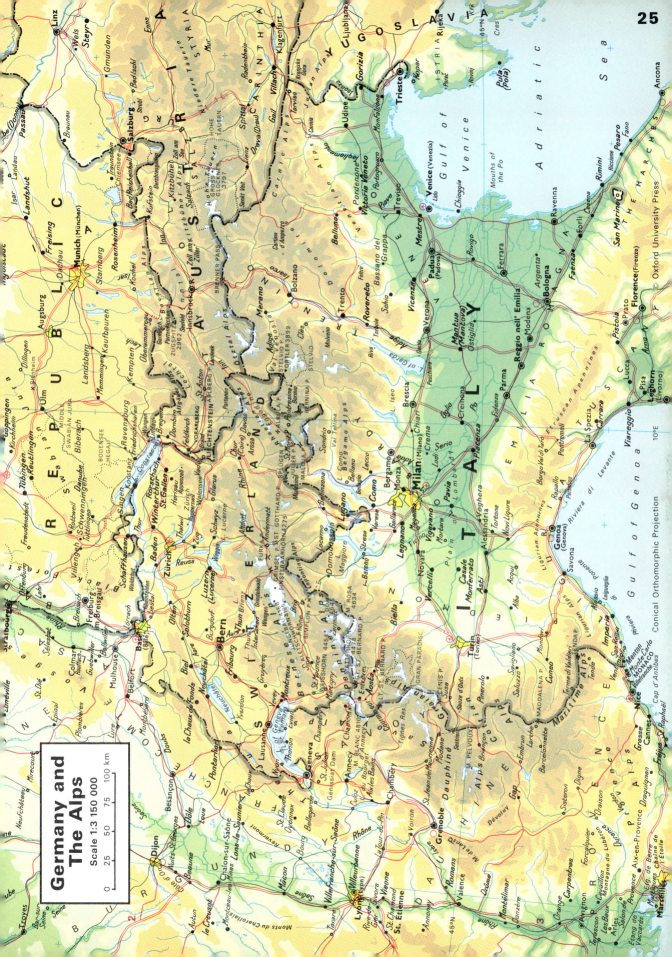

Germany and The Alps

Scale 1:3 150 000

0   25   50   75   100 km

© Oxford University Press

Conical Orthomorphic Projection

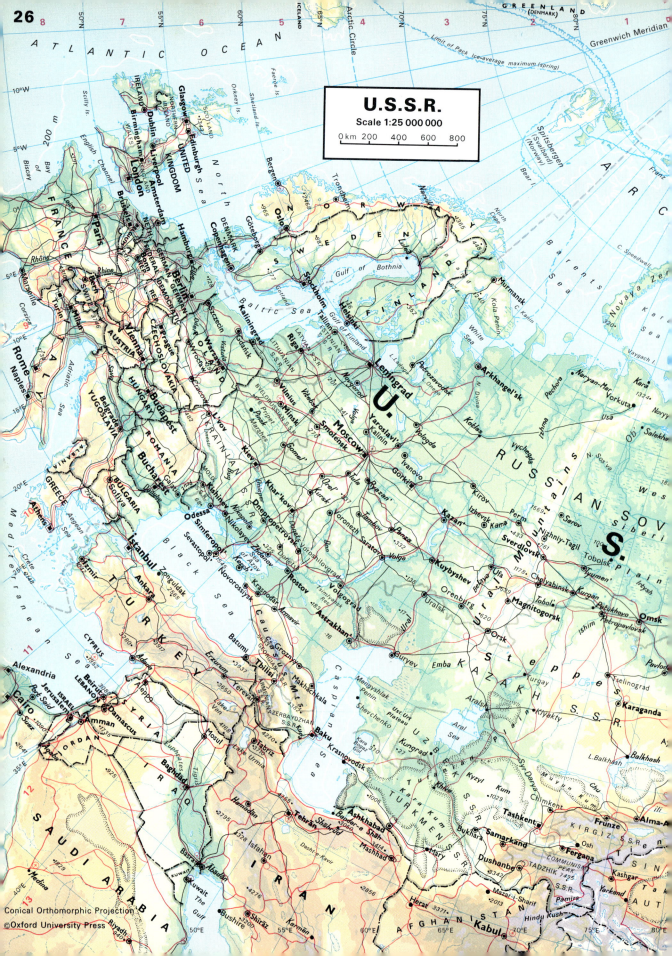

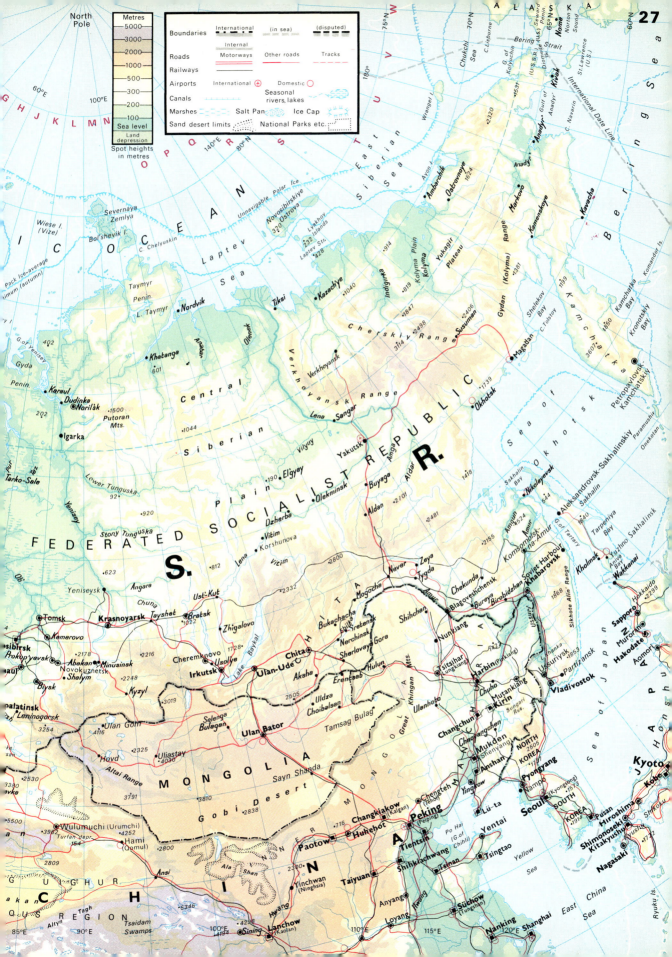

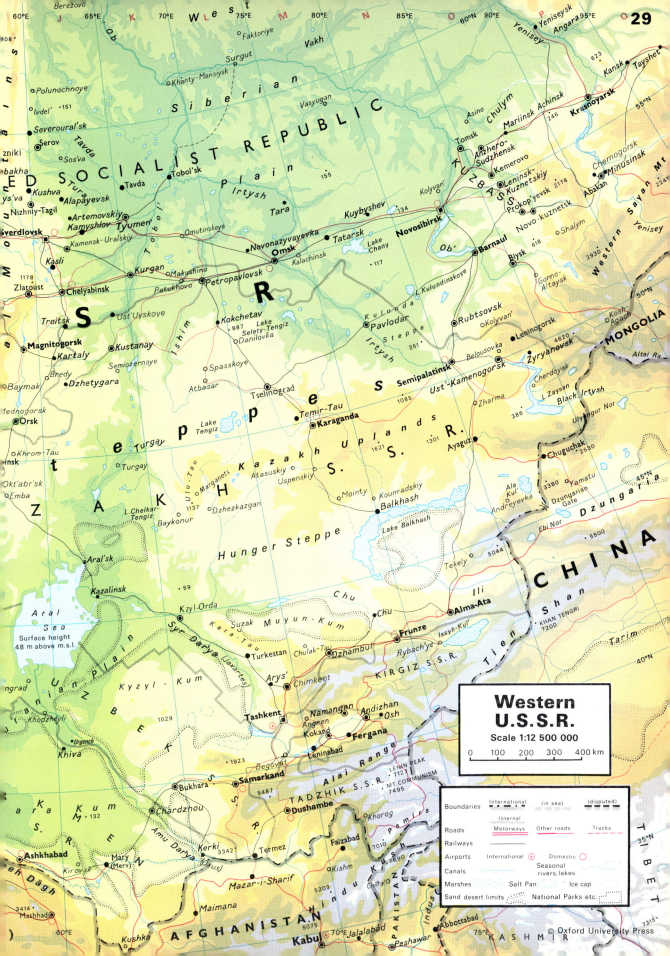

Western U.S.S.R.

Scale 1:12 500 000

0   100   200   300   400 km

Boundaries	International	(in sea)	(disputed)
	Internal		
Roads	Motorways	Other roads	Tracks
Railways			
Airports	International	Domestic	
Canals		Seasonal rivers, lakes	
Marshes		Salt Pan	Ice cap
Sand desert limits		National Parks etc.	

© Oxford University Press

India, Pakistan, Bangladesh and Sri Lanka

Scale 1:12 500 000

0   100   200   300   400 km

Sri Lanka

Scale 1:7 750 000

Boundaries	International	(in sea)	(disputed)
	Internal		
Roads	Roads	Tracks	
Railways	Metre	Broad	Narrow
Airports	International	Domestic	
Canals		Seasonal rivers, lakes	
Marshes	Salt pan	Ice cap	
Sand desert limits	National Parks, etc.		

Conical Orthomorphic Projection

Same scale

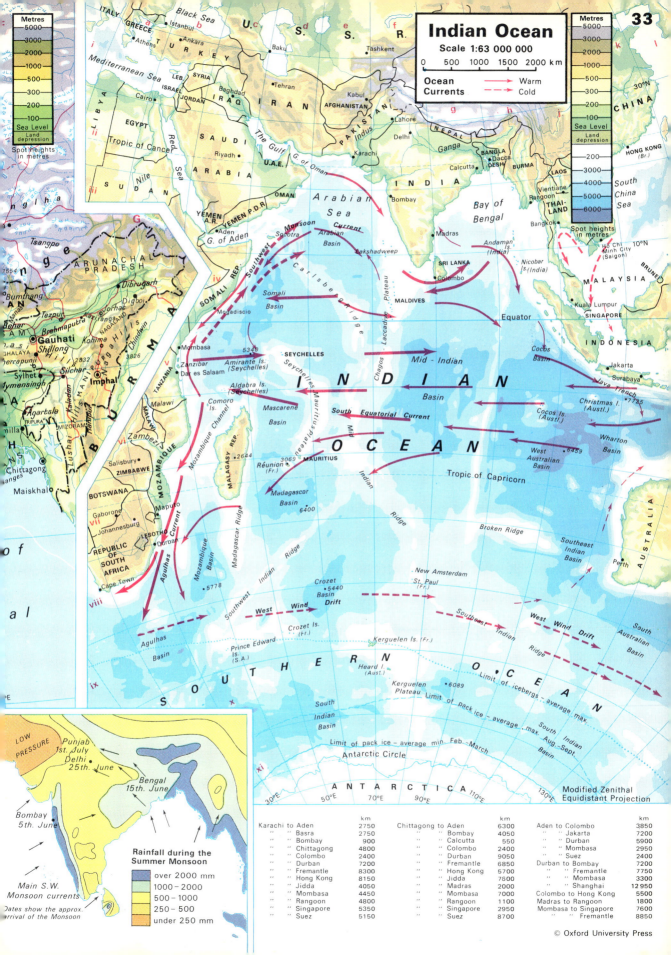

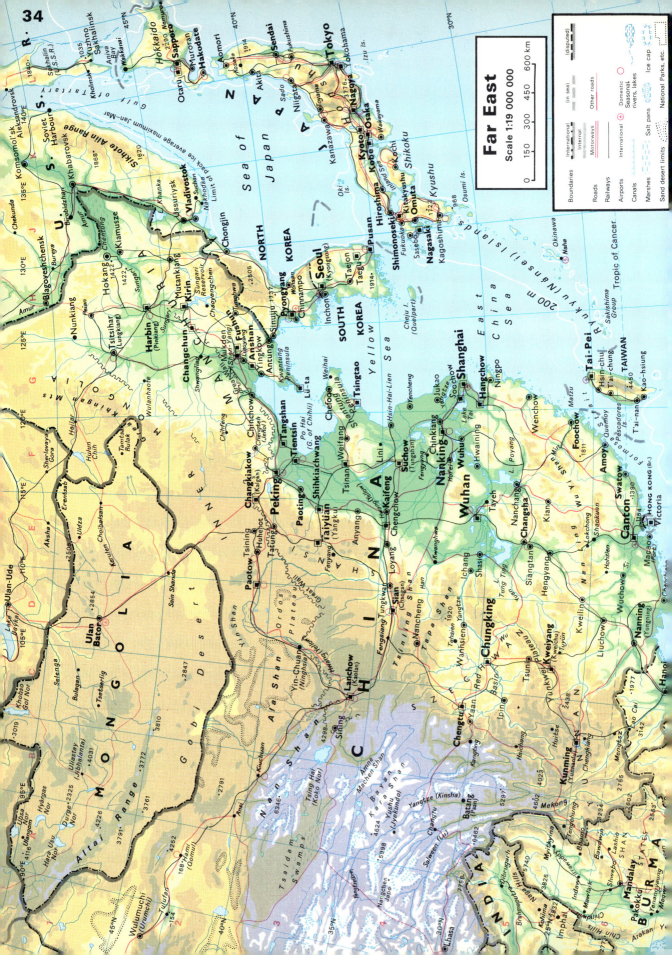

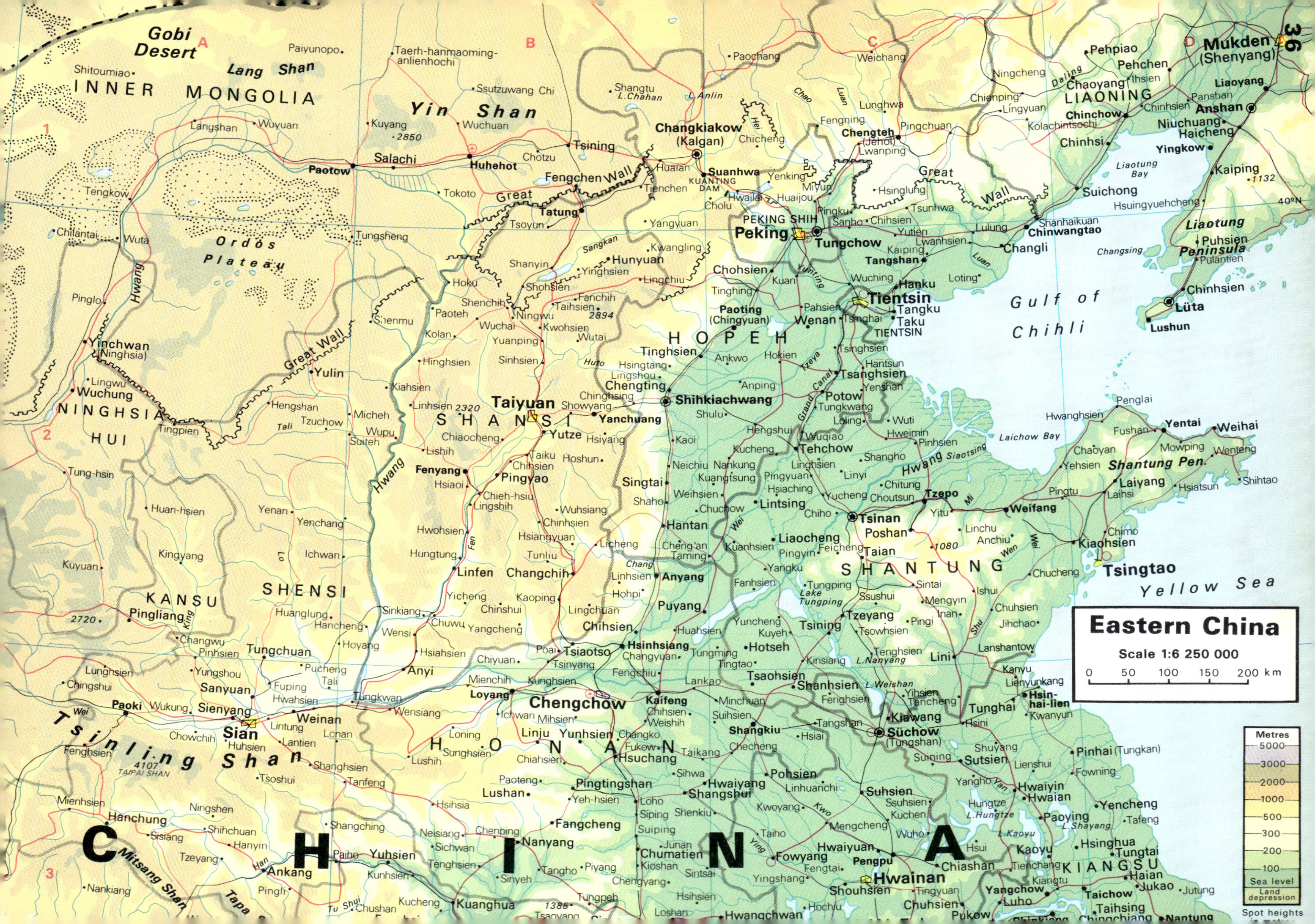

Eastern China

Scale 1:6 250 000

0 50 100 150 200 km

Metres		Sea level
5000	300	Land
3000	200	depression
2000	100	
1000	500	Spot heights

Yellow Sea

Gulf of Chihli

Liaotung Bay

Shantung Pen.

Liaotung Peninsula

Mukden (Shenyang)

Peking (Peiping)

Tientsin

Tsingtao

Taiyuan

Sian

LIAONING

HOPEH

SHANTUNG

SHANSI

SHENSI

KANSU

HONAN

ANHWAN

KIANGSU

NINGHSIA HUI

INNER MONGOLIA

Yin Shan

Lang Shan

Gobi Desert

Ordos Plateau

Great Wall

Tsinling Shan

CHINA

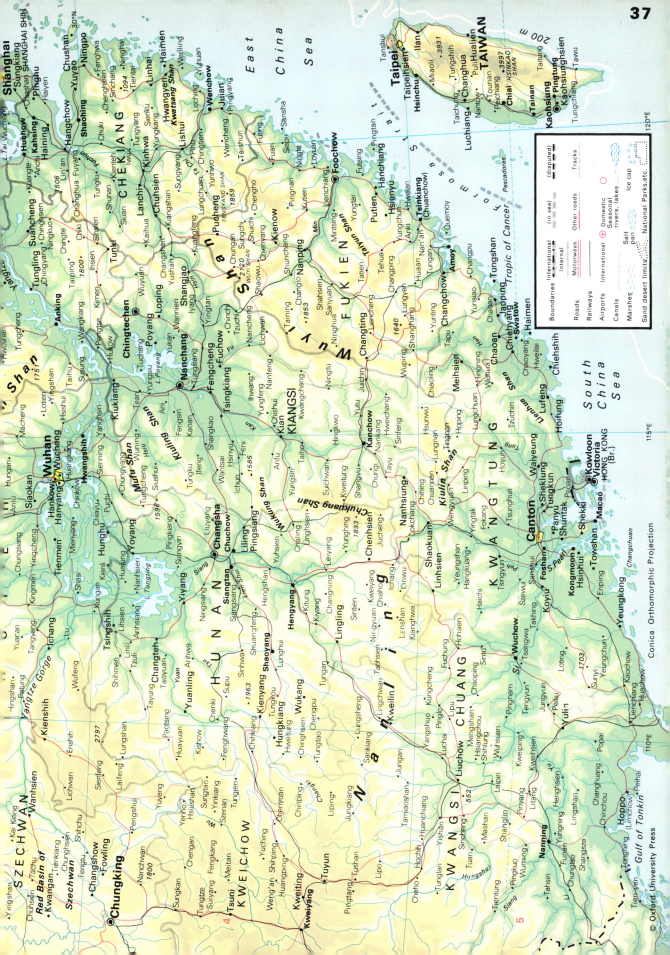

Japan

Scale 1:6 250 000

0   50   100   150   200 km

Scale 1:2 000 000

0   20   40   60 km

Boundaries	International	(in sea)	(disputed)
	Internal		
Roads	Motorways	Other roads	Tracks
Railways			
Airports	International	Domestic	
Canals		Seasonal rivers, lakes	
Marshes		Salt pans	Ice cap
Sand desert limits		National Parks, etc.	

Metres
5000
3000
2000
1000
500
300
200
100
Sea level
Land depression

Spot heights in metres

Zenithal Equidistant Projection   135°E ©Oxford University Press

SOUTH KOREA

Sea of Japan

PACIFIC OCEAN

Honshu

Hokkaido

Shikoku

Kyushu

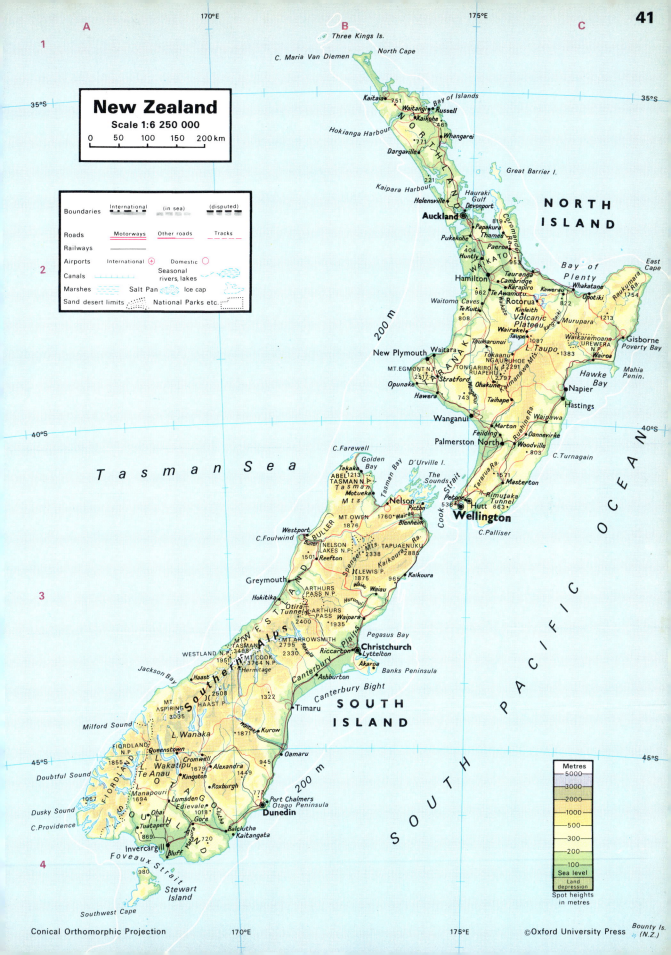

New Zealand

Scale 1:6 250 000

0   50   100   150   200 km

Boundaries
International | (in sea) | (disputed)

Roads
Motorways | Other roads | Tracks

Railways

Airports
International ⊕ | Domestic ○

Canals
Seasonal rivers, lakes

Marshes | Salt Pan | Ice cap

Sand desert limits | National Parks etc.

NORTH ISLAND

Three Kings Is.
C. Maria Van Diemen
North Cape
Kaitaia 751
Waitangi Russell
Kaikohe 461
Hokianga Harbour
Whangarei 771
Dargaville
Bay of Islands
Great Barrier I.
Kaipara Harbour 221
Helensville
Hauraki Gulf
Devonport
Auckland
Papakura 819
Pukekohe Thames
Paeroa
Huntly 404
Coromandel Ra.
Tauranga
Hamilton Cambridge
Karapiro 953
Te Awamutu Kawerau
962 Whakatane Opotiki
Waitomo Caves 822
Te Kuiti Rotorua Murupara 1213
808 Kinleith Volcanic Plateau
Wairakei Rangitaiki
Taupo UREWERA N.P.
New Plymouth Waitara 1087 L. Taupo Waikaremoana
Tokaanu 1383 Gisborne
MT. EGMONT N.P. NGAURUHOE Poverty Bay
2517 TONGARIRO N.P. 2291 Wairoa
Stratford RUAPEHU 2.797 Mahia Penin.
Opunake Ohakune Hawke Bay
Hawera 743 Taihape Napier
Raukumara Ra. 1754
East Cape
Kaimanawa Mts. Hastings
Wanganui Ruahine Ra. Waipawa
Marton Waipukurau
Feilding Dannevirke
Palmerston North 803 Woodville
C. Turnagain
Tararua Ra. 1671
Masterton
Petone 663 Rimutaka Tunnel
536 Hutt
Wellington
C. Palliser
Cook Strait

200 m

SOUTH ISLAND

C. Farewell
Golden Bay
Takaka 1213
ABEL TASMAN N.P.
Motueka Tasman Mts.
Tasman Bay D'Urville I.
The Sounds
Nelson
1760 Wairau Picton
Blenheim
Westport MT OWEN
C. Foulwind 1876
BULLER
Buller NELSON LAKES N.P.
1501 Spenser Mts. TAPUAENUKU
Reefton 2338 Kaikoura Ra. 2885
Greymouth LEWIS P.
1875 965 Kaikoura
Hokitika Waiau
ARTHURS PASS N.P. Hurunui
Otira Waiau
Tunnel ARTHURS PASS
2400 1935 Waipara
WESTLAND N.P. 3488 MT ARROWSMITH
MT TASMAN 2795 Pegasus Bay
1951 MT COOK 2330 Riccarton
3764 N.P. **Christchurch**
Hermitage Rakaia Lyttelton
Jackson Bay Akaroa
MT 2508 Banks Peninsula
ASPIRING HAAST Ashburton
3035 1322 Canterbury Bight
Milford Sound Timaru
L. Wanaka 1871 Kurow **SOUTH ISLAND**
FIORDLAND N.P. Queenstown Cromwell 945 Oamaru
1855 Alexandra
L. Wakatipu 1679 1449
Kingston
Te Anau Roxburgh
Manapouri 777
1694 Lumsden Edievale Port Chalmers
1087 Ohai 1018 Otago Peninsula
Dusky Sound Tuatapere Gore **Dunedin**
C. Providence 869 720 Balclutha
980 Invercargill Kaitangata
Bluff
Foveaux Strait
Stewart Island
Southwest Cape

Tasman Sea

SOUTH PACIFIC OCEAN

200 m

Metres
5000
3000
2000
1000
500
300
200
100
Sea level
Land depression

Spot heights in metres

Conical Orthomorphic Projection

©Oxford University Press

Bounty Is. (N.Z.)

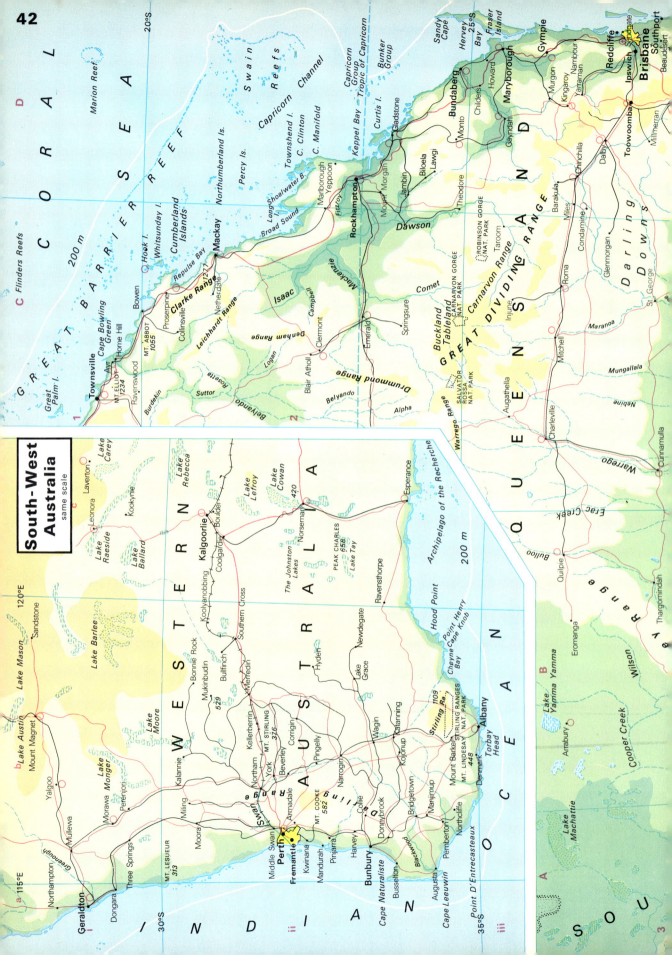

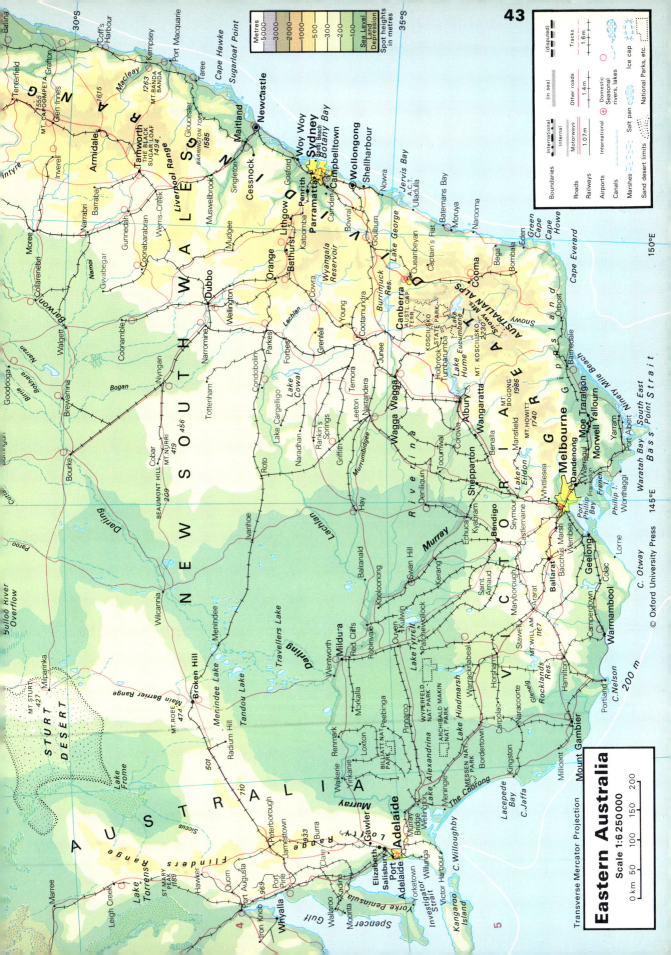

Eastern Australia

Scale 1:6 250 000

Transverse Mercator Projection

© Oxford University Press

43

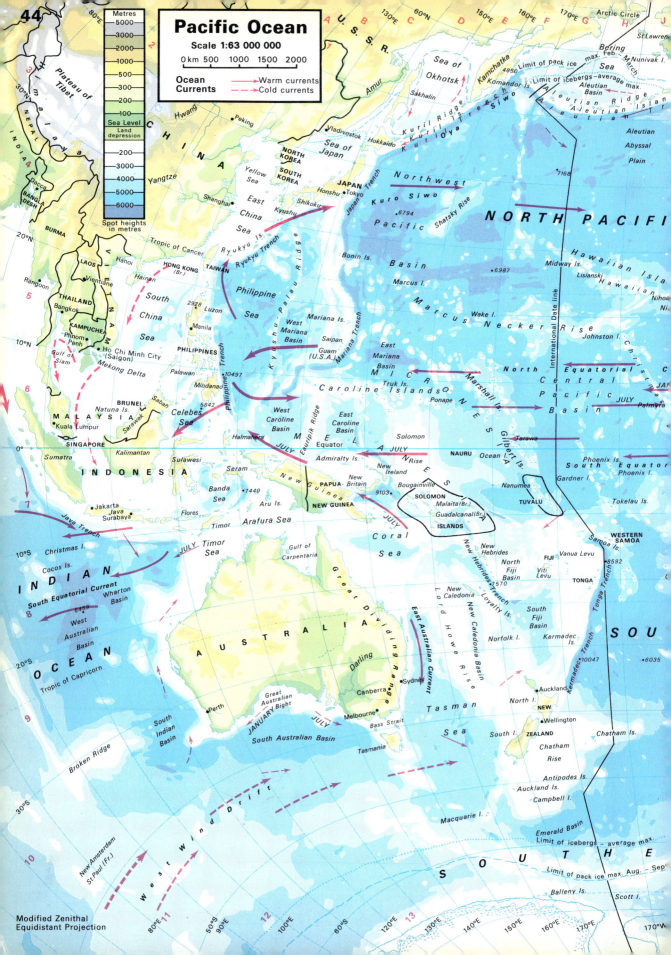

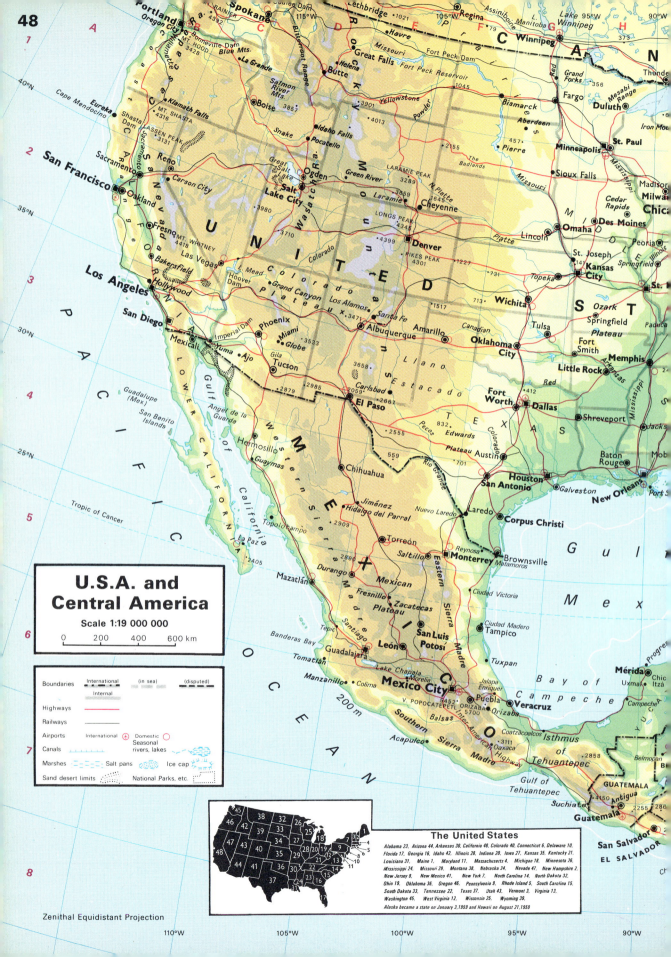

48

U.S.A. and Central America

Scale 1:19 000 000

0   200   400   600 km

Boundaries International (in sea) (disputed)
         Internal
Highways
Railways
Airports International Domestic
Canals   Seasonal rivers, lakes
Marshes   Salt pans   Ice cap
Sand desert limits   National Parks, etc.

The United States

Alabama 23, Arizona 44, Arkansas 30, California 48, Colorado 40, Connecticut 6, Delaware 10, Florida 17, Georgia 16, Idaho 42, Illinois 28, Indiana 20, Iowa 27, Kansas 35, Kentucky 21, Louisiana 31, Maine 1, Maryland 11, Massachusetts 4, Michigan 18, Minnesota 26, Mississippi 24, Missouri 29, Montana 38, Nebraska 34, Nevada 47, New Hampshire 2, New Jersey 8, New Mexico 41, New York 7, North Carolina 14, North Dakota 32, Ohio 19, Oklahoma 36, Oregon 46, Pennsylvania 9, Rhode Island 5, South Carolina 15, South Dakota 33, Tennessee 22, Texas 37, Utah 43, Vermont 3, Virginia 13, Washington 45, West Virginia 12, Wisconsin 25, Wyoming 39. Alaska became a state on January 3,1959 and Hawaii on August 21,1959

Zenithal Equidistant Projection

ATLANTIC OCEAN

Panama Canal
1 cm to 15 km approx.

Gaillard Cut (Culebra)
Maximum elevation 95 m

Minimum depth 12 m

Sea level

ATLANTIC | PACIFIC

Sea level

Gatun Locks	Pedro Miguel Locks	Miraflores Locks
3 pairs	1 pair	2 pairs
Length 305 m	Length 305 m	Length 305 m
Width 34 m	Width 34 m	Width 34 m
Total Lift 26 m	Total Lift 9·3 m	Total Lift 16·6 m

0 15 30 45 60 75 km

ATLANTIC OCEAN

80°W
●Colón
Gatun Locks
CANAL
Gatun Lake
ZONE
PANAMA
Pedro Miguel Locks
Miraflores Locks
Balboa● Panama ●
9°N
PACIFIC OCEAN

PANAMA: The canal, opened in 1914, is 80 km long, including approaches (actual canal 64 km). Minimum depth 12 m, minimum width 152 m (Gaillard Cut). Time of passage 8 hours. In 1976 12 157 vessels used the canal carrying 118 454 662 tonnes of cargo. In 1978 the Canal Zone became Panamanian territory but the U.S.A. will operate the Canal until 1999.

Metres
5000
3000
2000
1000
500
300
200
100
Sea level
Land depression
Spot heights in metres

ATLANTIC OCEAN

Caribbean Sea

Greater Antilles

Lesser Antilles

Windward Islands

Leeward Islands

THE BAHAMAS

CUBA

HAITI DOMINICAN REPUBLIC
Hispaniola

JAMAICA

PUERTO RICO

VENEZUELA

COLOMBIA

PANAMA

COSTA RICA

NICARAGUA

HONDURAS

GUYANA

TRINIDAD & TOBAGO

© Oxford University Press

Eastern
United States
Scale 1:8 000 000

0   100   200km

Boundaries	International	(in sea)	(disputed)
	Internal		
Roads	Limited access	Other highways	
Railways			
Airports	International ⊕	Domestic ○	
Canals		Seasonal rivers, lakes	
Marshes	Salt Pan	Ice cap	
Sand desert limits		National Parks etc.	

Conical Orthomorphic Projection

50

125°W 120°W 115°W 110°W

Cape Flattery Bellingham Castlegar Trail Lethbridge Cypress Hills

A Anacortes Mount Vernon NORTH CASCADES N.P. Tahk WATERTON LAKES N.P. B C D

Port Angeles Victoria Franklin D Roosevelt Lake Colville Eureka GLACIER INTERNATIONAL PEACE PARK Cut Bank Shelby

OLYMPIC NAT. PARK Seattle Everett Columbia Okanogan Pend Oreille Lake Sandpoint Libby Whitefish Kalispell Conrad Havre Malta Glasgow

Bremerton Grand Coulee Milk

1 Grays Harbor Hoquiam Aberdeen Tacoma Olympia Wenatchee Spokane Coeur d'Alene Flathead Lake Hungry Horse Res. Great Falls Winifred Fort Peck Reservoir

Willapa Bay Raymond MT. RAINIER 4392 Ellensburg Moses Lake Elk River 3069 Lewistown

200 m Longview Kelso Centralia Yakima Richland Colfax Puttman Moscow Snake Clearwater Missoula Deer Lodge Helena M O N T A N A

Astoria Saint Helens Prosser Kennewick Pasco Walla Walla Lewiston Grangeville Anaconda Butte Roundup

45°N Portland Vancouver Columbia Pendleton La Grande Ronde Salmon Bozeman Twin Bridges Dillon Billings Laurel Hardin

Oregon City The Dalles 3428 MT. HOOD Grande Warren 3142 Salmon River 3139 Livingston Forsyth

Corvallis Albany Lebanon Salem Silverton 3199 John Day Baker Salmon River Mountains Salmon 3232 YELLOWSTONE NATIONAL PARK 3860 Bighorn Mountains

Eugene Springfield B l u e M o u n t a i n s 2759 STRAWBERRY MT. Weiser Payette Cody YELLOWSTONE LAKE Powell Worland

2 North Bend Bend Burns Harney Basin Malheur Caldwell Nampa Boise Arrowrock Res. 3917 GRAND TETON N.P. Ashton Rexburg Thermopolis W Y O M I N G

Cape Blanco Roseburg Malheur L. Owyhee Res. CRATERS OF THE MOON N.M. Mountain Home Idaho Falls Lander Cass

Grants Pass CRATER LAKE NATIONAL PARK Upper Klamath L. Snake Big Wood Blackfoot American Falls Res. Pathfinder Res. Seminoe Res.

Medford Ashland Klamath Falls Owyhee IRON MTN 2386 Alameda Pocatello Green Rock Springs Rawlins

Crescent City Klamath Yreka Goose L. Twin Falls Burley Bear Lake Logan Evanston Green River Flaming Gorge Res. Little Snake

Weaverville MT. SHASTA 4316 Pit Alturas Brigham 2156 Ogden Green Vernal

40°N Arcata Eureka Redding Shasta L. LASSEN PEAK 3190 Westwood Winnemucca Humboldt Wells Lucin Great Salt Lake Salt Lake City DINOSAUR NAT. MONUMENT Yampa

Red Bluff Chico Willows Winnemucca Lake Battle Mountain Elko Palisade Wendover Great Salt Lake Desert Tooele Salt Lake UINTA MTS. Vernal

Ukiah Clear Lake Cloverdale Yuba City Pyramid Lake Sparks Reno Austin Eureka Desert 3502 Utah Lake Orem Provo Duchesne Price Glenwood Springs Rifle Asp

3 Healdsburg Santa Rosa Napa Vallejo Woodland Nevada City Roseville Sacramento Carson City Lake Tahoe Carson Sink N E V A D A U T A H M O U N T A I N S Grand Junction Delta Montrose

Point Reyes Berkeley Oakland Fairfield Lodi Stockton Walker Lake Hawthorne MT. GRANT 3445 Ely Richfield ARCHES NAT. MON. 3989 MT PEALE Gunnis

San Francisco Santa Clara Fremont Modesto Turlock YOSEMITE N.P. MT. RITTER 4009 Tonopah Pioche Caliente 3710 DELANO PEAK CAPITOL REEF N.M. CANYONLANDS N.P. Ophir Silverton

San Jose Gilroy Merced Madera Clovis KINGS CANYON N.P. MT. WHITNEY 4418 Cedar City St. George BRYCE CANYON N.P. Colorado Lake Powell San Juan MESA VERDE N.P. Durango

Santa Cruz Watsonville Fresno Visalia Hanford SEQUOIA N.P. DEATH VALLEY NATIONAL MONUMENT Owens L. 86 LION N.P. Virgin GRAND CANYON NATIONAL PARK Farmington

Monterey Bay Pacific Grove Monterey Salinas San Joaquin Tulare L. Delano Kern 3620 LAKE MEAD NATIONAL RECREATION AREA Lake Mead Grand Canyon

Big Sur C A L I F O R N I A Bakersfield S i e r r a N e v a d a Las Vegas Henderson Grand Canyon CANYON DE CHELLY NAT MON Los A

35°N Estero Bay San Luis Obispo Bay San Luis Obispo Aqueduct Mojave Devils Playground Boulder City Kingman Plateaux Flagstaff Winslow Zuni Gallup Albuquer

Point Arguello Point Conception Santa Maria Santa Barbara Santa Paula Mojave Desert Barstow Ludlow Needles Mogollon Plateau Little Colorado PETRIFIED FOREST N.P. San Jose Belen

Santa Ynez Santa Barbara Channel Oxnard Hollywood Pasadena Aqueduct Havasu Prescott Verde Socorro

Santa Cruz Santa Rosa San Miguel Los Angeles San Bernardino Riverside Blythe Colorado A R I Z O N A N E W

4 Santa Barbara Islands Long Beach Santa Ana JOSHUA TREE N.M. Phoenix Glendale Mesa Gila Globe Truth or Consequences

San Nicholas San Clemente Santa Catalina Oceanside Escondido ANZA-BORREGO DESERT S.P. Salton Sea Calipatria Gila Gila Bend Hayden San Pedro Caballo Res. El

Gulf of Santa Catalina San Diego Brawley El Centro Calexico Yuma Florence Safford Silver City WHITE SANDS El Pa

200 m Tijuana Mexicali San Luis Ajo ORGAN PIPE CACTUS N.P. Tucson Deming Ciuda Juare

Guadalupe Sierra de Juarez Puerto Penasco Sonoyta Bisbee

Ensenada 115°W 110°W

P A C I F I C   O C E A N

Conical Orthomorphic Projection

Metres
5000
3000
2000
1000
500
300
200
100
Sea level
Land depression

Spot heights in metres

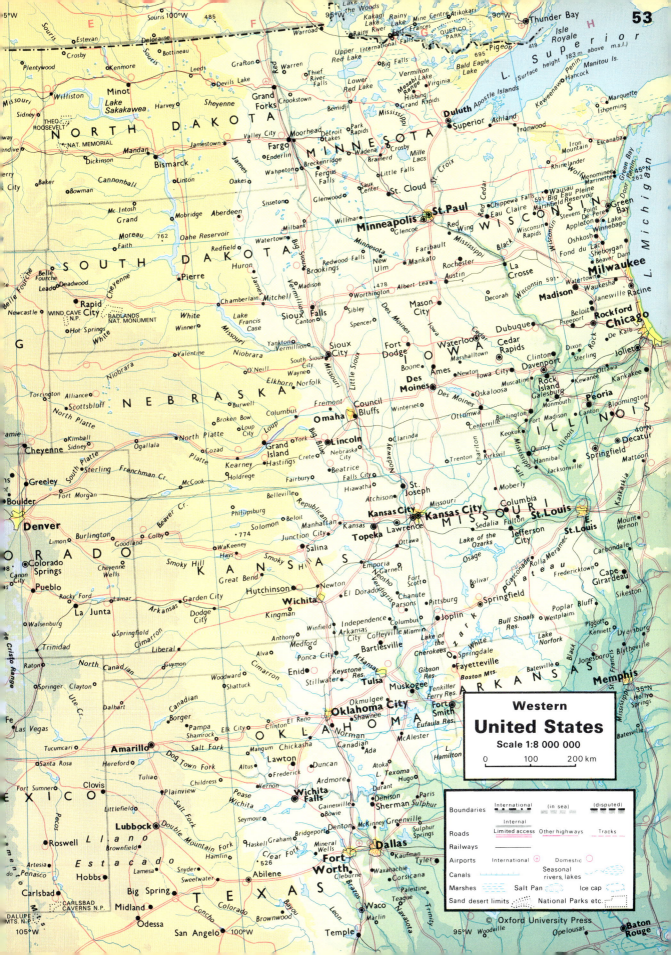

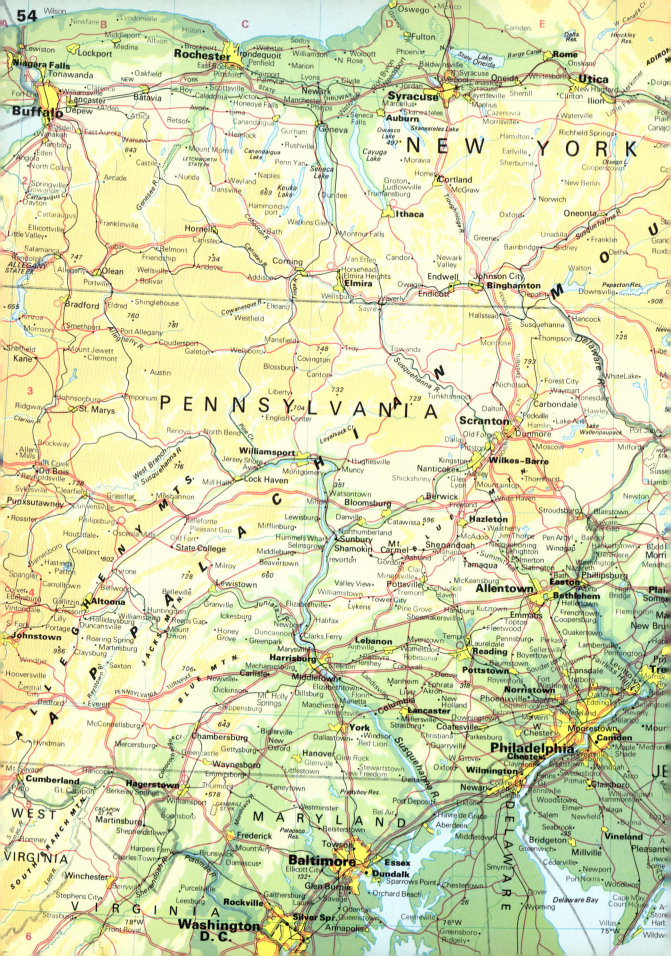

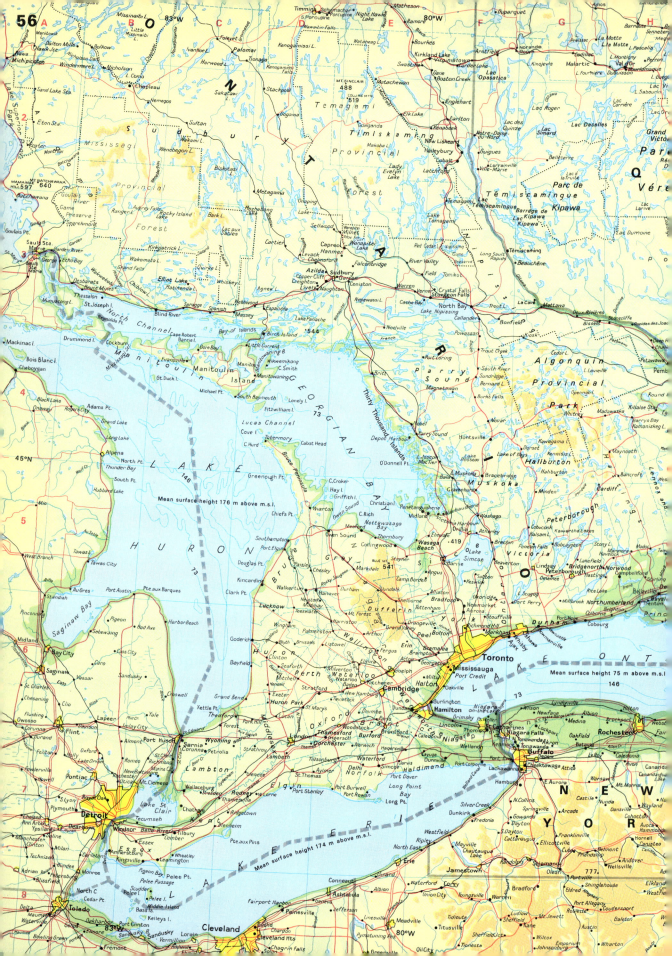

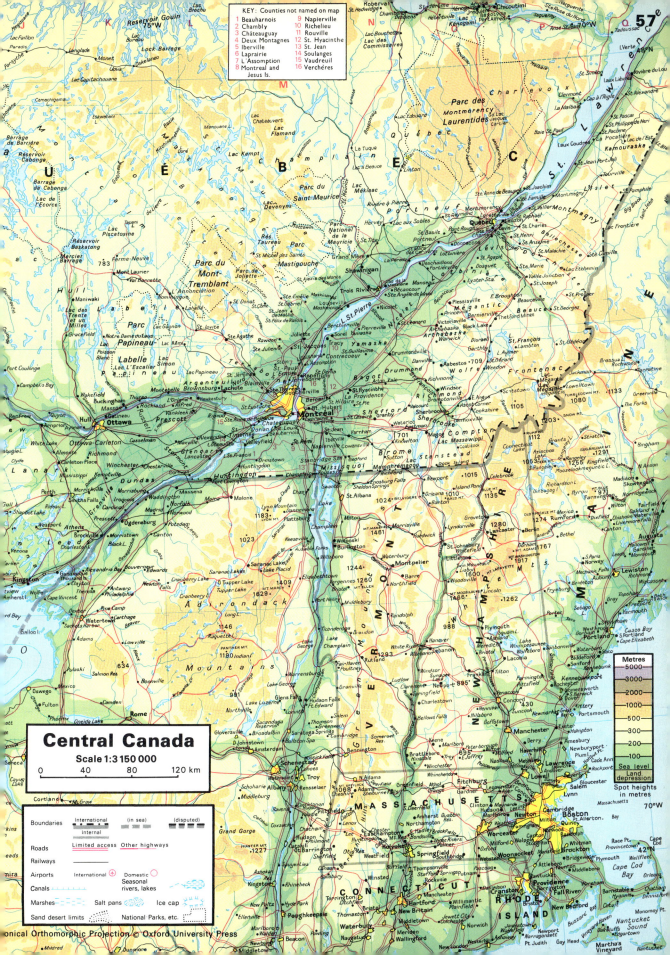

KEY: Counties not named on map

1 Beauharnois
2 Chambly
3 Châteauguay
4 Deux Montagnes
5 Iberville
6 Laprairie
7 L' Assomption
8 Montreal and Jesus Is.
9 Napierville
10 Richelieu
11 Rouville
12 St. Hyacinthe
13 St. Jean
14 Soulanges
15 Vaudreuil
16 Verchères

Central Canada

Scale 1:3 150 000

0   40   80   120 km

Boundaries
International
(in sea)
(disputed)
Internal

Roads   Limited access   Other highways

Railways

Airports   International ⊕   Domestic ○

Canals   Seasonal rivers, lakes

Marshes   Salt pans   Ice cap

Sand desert limits   National Parks, etc.

Metres
5000
3000
2000
1000
500
300
100
Sea level
Land depression

Spot heights in metres

onical Orthomorphic Projection © Oxford University Press

The Great Lakes

Scale 1:6 250 000

0   50   100   150   200 km

Metres
| 2000 |
| 1000 |
| 500 |
| 300 |
| 200 |
| 100 |
| Sea level |
| Land depression |

Spot heights in metres

Boundaries — International / Internal / (in sea) / (disputed)
Roads — Motorways / Other roads
Railways
Airports — International / Domestic
Canals — Seasonal rivers, lakes
Marshes — Salt pans — Ice cap
Sand desert limits — National Parks, etc.

Conical Orthomorphic Projection   © Oxford University Press

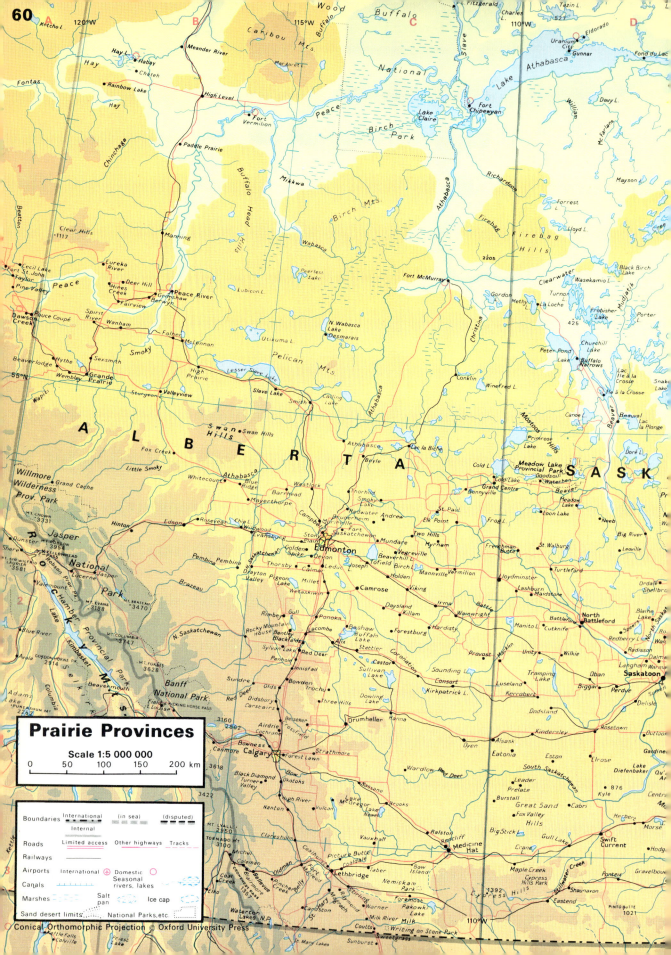

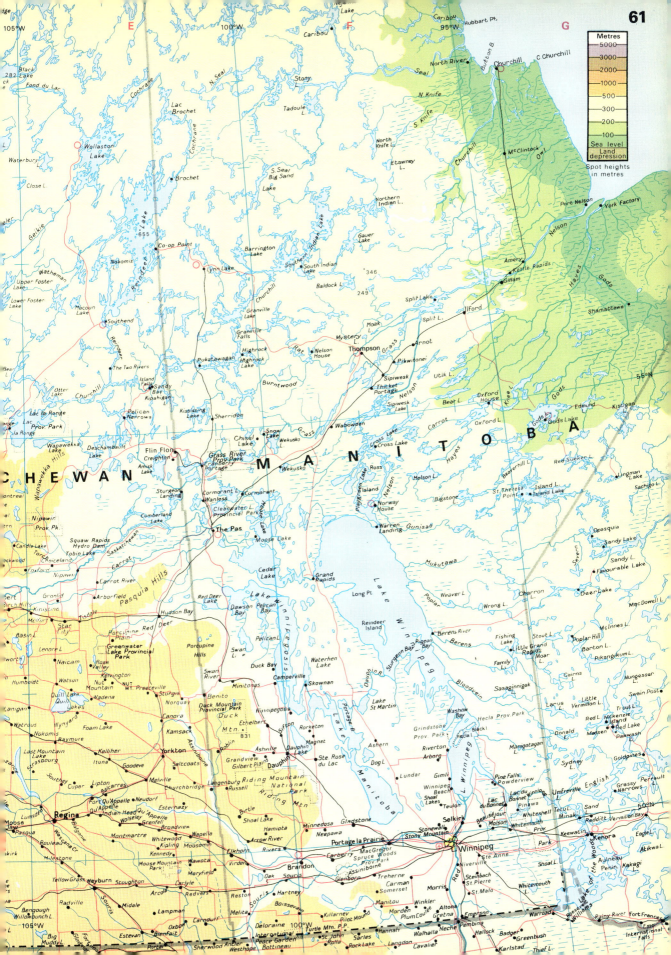

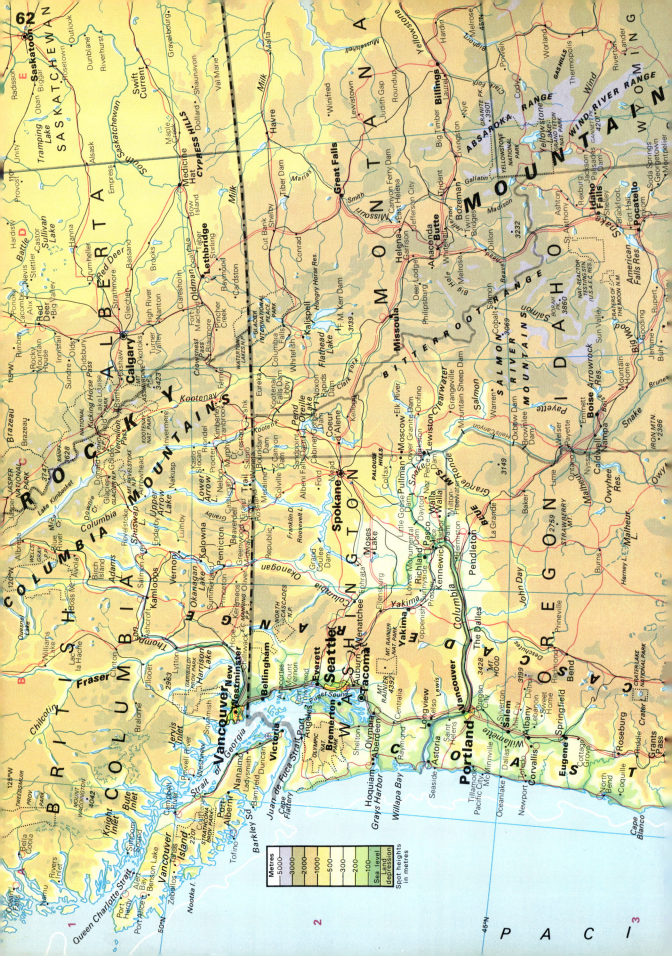

Pacific Coast: Canada & U.S.A.

Scale 1:6 250 000

0 50 100 150 200 km

Legend

Boundaries	International —————	(in sea) ————
	Internal —————	(disputed) - - - -
Roads	Limited Access —————	Other Highways —————
Railways		
Airports	⊕ International	🜨 Domestic
Canals	—————	Seasonal rivers, lakes
		Salt pans
		Ice cap
		National Parks, etc.
		Sand desert limits

© Oxford University Press

63

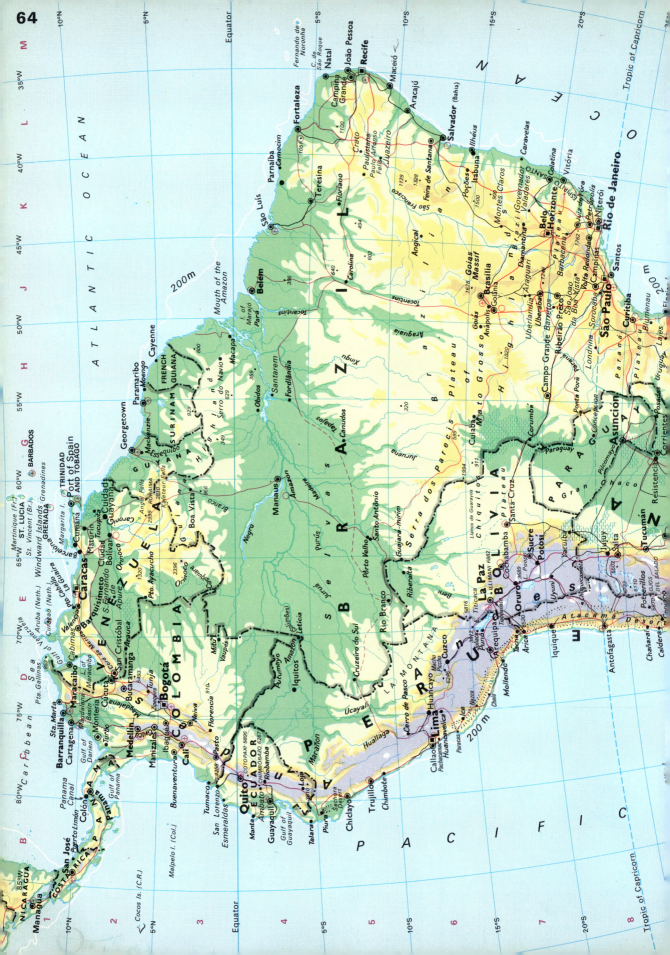

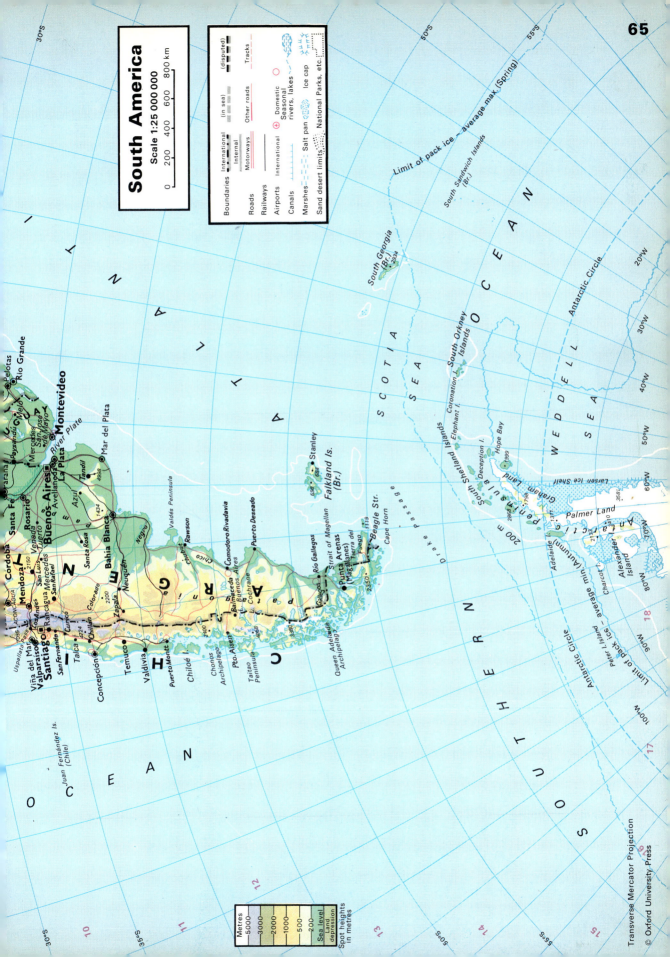

South America

Scale 1:25 000 000

0   200   400   600   800 km

Boundaries
International
Internal
(in sea)
(disputed)

Roads
Motorways
Other roads
Tracks

Railways
International

Airports

Canals

Marshes
Salt pan
Seasonal rivers, lakes
Ice cap

Sand desert limits
Domestic
National Parks, etc.

Limit of pack ice — average max (Spring)

South Sandwich Islands (Br.)

South Georgia (Br.) 2934

SCOTIA SEA

South Orkney Islands

Coronation I.

Elephant I.

South Shetland Islands

Deception I. 1999

Hope Bay

Graham Land

Larsen Ice Shelf

WEDDELL SEA

Palmer Land

Alexander Island 2713

Antarctic Circle

Adelaide I. (Autumn) — average min.

Charcot I.

Peter I. Island

Limit of pack ice

OCEAN

SOUTHERN

Pelotas
Rio Grande
Melo
G.
Montevideo
San José de Mayo
San José
Mercedes
La Plata
River Plate
Mar del Plata
Tacuarembó
Paraná
Santa Fe
Córdoba
Rosario
Buenos Aires
Avellaneda
Tandil
4992
Azul
1434
Bahía Blanca
Santa Rosa
Venado
San Luis
ACONCAGUA 7035
2150
Mendoza
San Rafael
Neuquén
Zapala
Colorado
200
Negro
Valdés Peninsula
Rawson
Chubut
Chico
Comodoro Rivadavia
Puerto Deseado
Río Gallegos
Gallegos
Strait of Magellan
Punta Arenas (Magallanes)
2350
Tierra del Fuego
Beagle Str.
1119
Cape Horn
Drake Passage
200

Andes
Uspallata Pass
Viña del Mar
Valparaíso
Santiago
San Fernando
Rancagua
Curicó
424
Talca
Chillán
Concepción
Temuco
Valdivia
Puerto Montt
Chiloé I.
Chonos Archipelago
Taitao Peninsula
Pto. Aisén
Balmaceda
Buenos Aires
Cochrane
Queen Adelaide Archipelago
2200
1468
380

Juan Fernández Is. (Chile)

OCEAN

Falkland Is. (Br.)
Stanley
834
698

ARGENTINA

PATAGONIA

CHILE

Transverse Mercator Projection

© Oxford University Press

Metres
5000
3000
2000
1000
500
200
Sea level
Land depression

Spot heights in metres

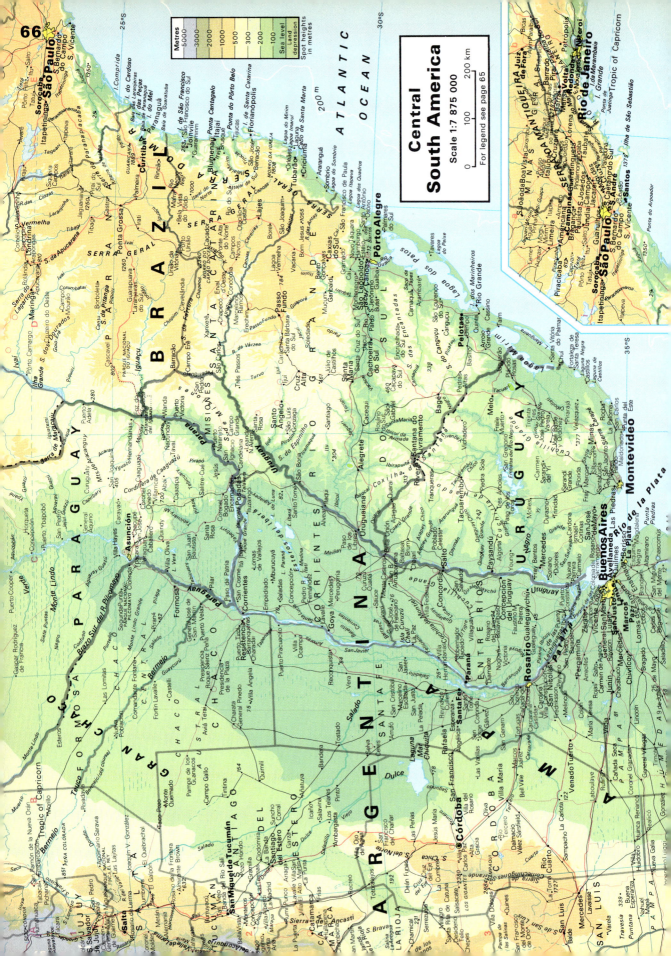

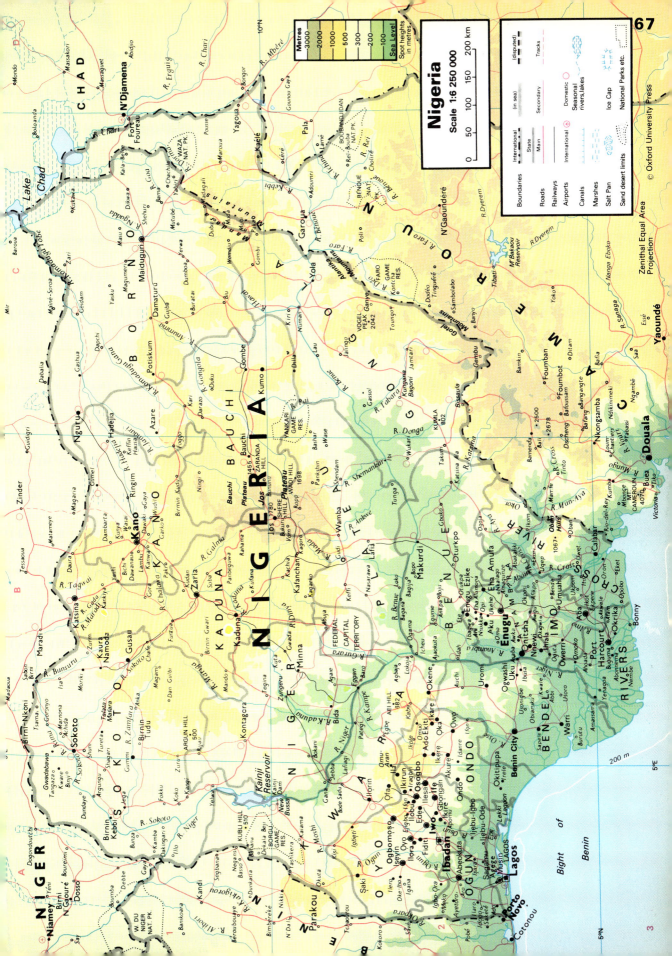

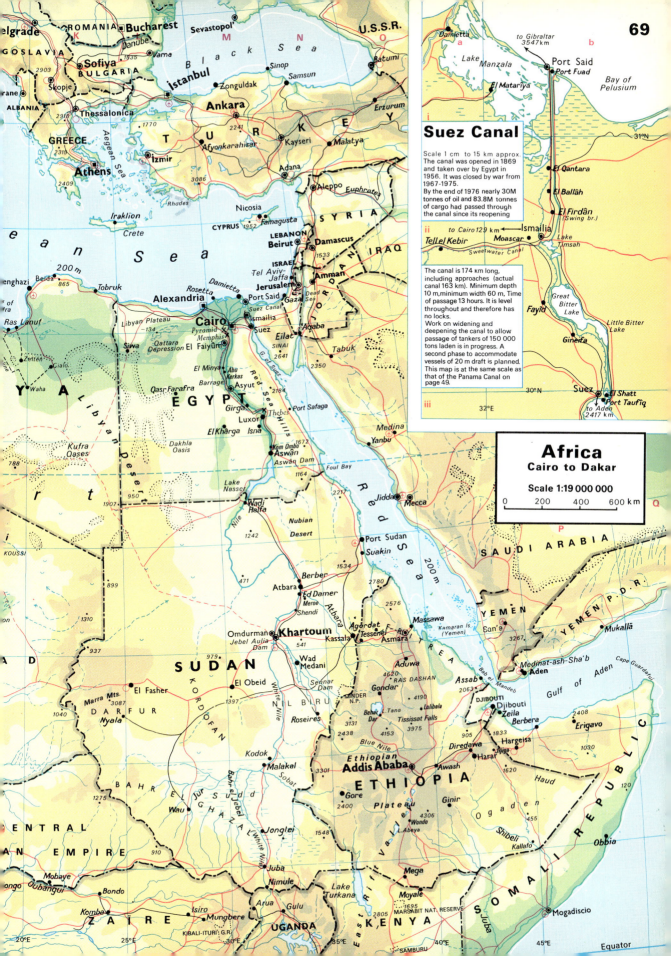

Suez Canal

Scale 1 cm to 15 km approx.
The canal was opened in 1869
and taken over by Egypt in
1956. It was closed by war from
1967-1975.
By the end of 1976 nearly 30M
tonnes of oil and 83.8M tonnes
of cargo had passed through
the canal since its reopening

The canal is 174 km long,
including approaches (actual
canal 163 km). Minimum depth
10 m, minimum width 60 m, Time
of passage 13 hours. It is level
throughout and therefore has
no locks.
Work on widening and
deepening the canal to allow
passage of tankers of 150 000
tons laden is in progress. A
second phase to accommodate
vessels of 20 m draft is planned.
This map is at the same scale as
that of the Panama Canal on
page 49.

Africa
Cairo to Dakar

Scale 1:19 000 000

| 0 | 200 | 400 | 600 km |

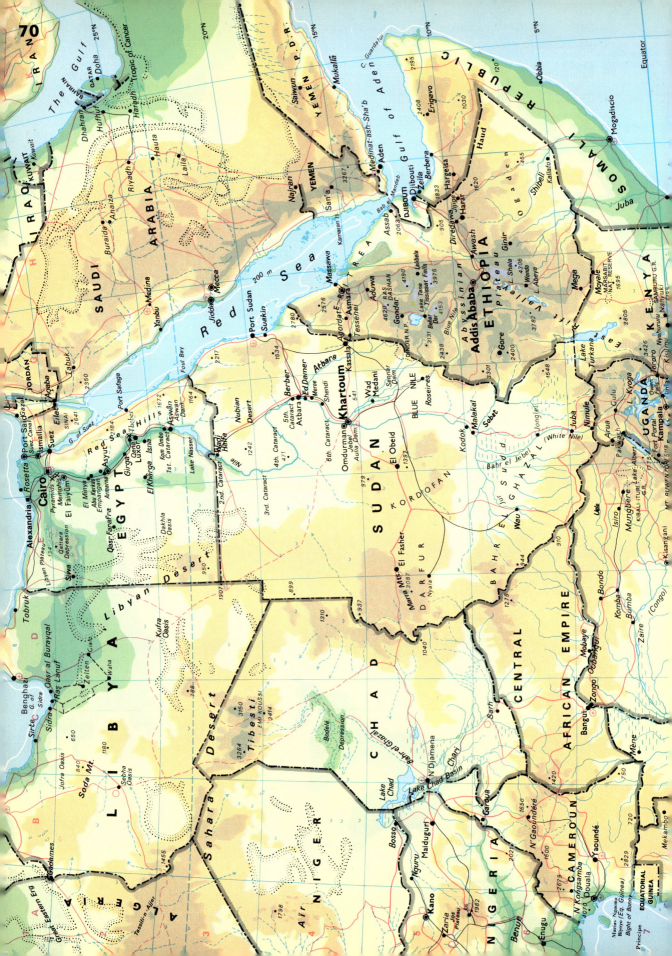

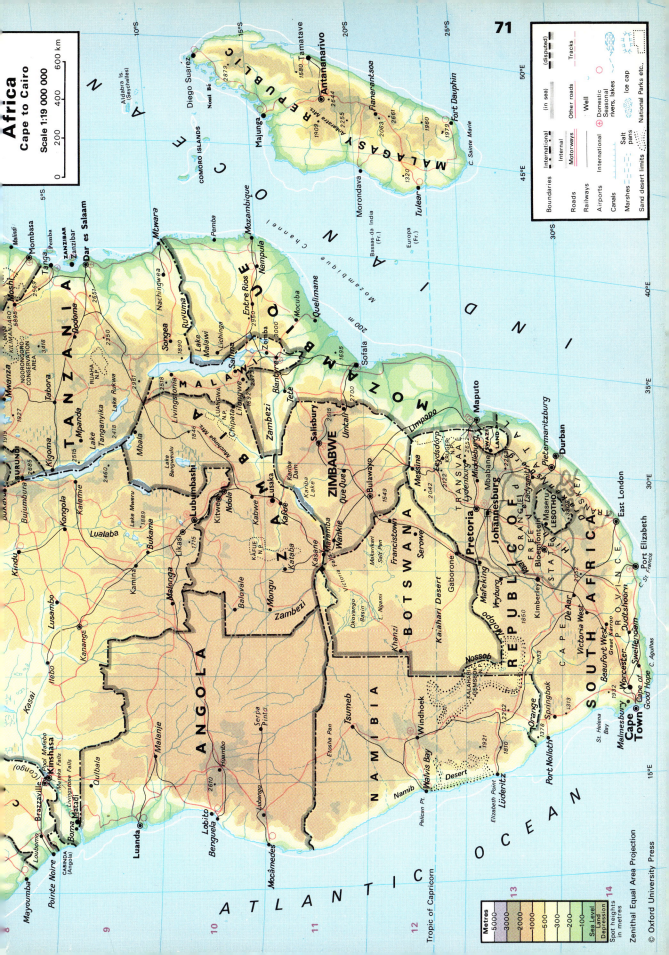

Africa
Cape to Cairo

Scale 1:19 000 000

0 200 400 600 km

71

ATLANTIC OCEAN

INDIAN OCEAN

Mozambique Channel

MALAGASY REPUBLIC

COMORO ISLANDS

Aldabra Is. (Seychelles)

Diego Suarez
Nossi Bé
Tamatave
Antananarivo
Majunga
Fianarantsoa
Fort Dauphin
Morondava
Tulear
C. Sainte Marie

Bassas da India (Fr.)
Europa (Fr.)

TANZANIA
Malindi
Mombasa
Tanga
Pemba
ZANZIBAR
Zanzibar
Dar es Salaam
Moshi
KILIMANJARO
NGORONGORO CONSERVATION AREA
Mwanza
Tabora
Mpanda
Kigoma
Lake Tanganyika
Lake Rukwa
RUAHA N.P.
Dodoma
Mtwara
Nachingwea
Songea
Ruvuma
Lichinga

MOZAMBIQUE
Pemba
Nampula
Mocuba
Quelimane
Entre Rios
Sofala
Tete
Zambezi
Blantyre
Zomba
Lilongwe
LUANGWA N.P.
Chipata
Lake Malawi

MALAWI

BURUNDI
Bujumbura
Kindu
Kalemie
Kongola
Kigoma
Lake Mweru
Lubumbashi
Likasi
Kamina
Kananga
Ilebo
Lusambo
Kasai
Lualaba
Lake Bangweulu
Kabwe
Kitwe
Ndola
Lusaka
Kafue
KAFUE N.P.
Mongu
Balovale
Zambezi

ZAMBIA

ZIMBABWE
Salisbury
Umtali
Que Que
Bulawayo
Wankie
Hwange
Kariba Dam
Kariba Lake
Kafue

ANGOLA
Luanda
Lobito
Benguela
Mocamedes
Malanje
Huambo
Quibala
Luena
Serpa Pinto

BOTSWANA
Francistown
Serowe
Gaborone
Maun
Orapa
L. Ngami
Lake Xau
Khanzi
Kalahari Desert
Okavango Basin

NAMIBIA
Windhoek
Walvis Bay
Swakopmund
Tsumeb
Etosha Pan
Namib Desert
Luderitz
Keetmanshoop

REPUBLIC OF SOUTH AFRICA
Pretoria
Johannesburg
Bloemfontein
Kimberley
Mafeking
Vryburg
CAPE PROVINCE
ORANGE FREE STATE
TRANSVAAL
Durban
Pietermaritzburg
East London
Port Elizabeth
Cape Town
Cape of Good Hope
C. Agulhas
Worcester
Malmesbury
Springbok
Port Nolloth
Oudtshoorn
Beaufort West
KALAHARI GEMSBOK N.P.
Nossob

LESOTHO
Maseru

SWAZILAND
Mbabane

Maputo
Limpopo
Messina
Leydsdorp
Lydenburg
KRUGER N.P.

St. Helena Bay
Pelican Pt.
Elizabeth Point

Brazzaville
Kinshasa
Pointe Noire
Pool Malebo
Matadi
Boma
CABINDA (Angola)
Livingstone Falls
Malebo Falls
Mayoumba
Louboma

Tropic of Capricorn

Metres
5000
3000
2000
1000
500
300
200
100
Sea Level
Land Depression

13
14

Spot heights in metres

Zenithal Equal Area Projection

© Oxford University Press

Boundaries: International, Internal, (disputed)
Roads: Motorways, Other roads, Tracks
Railways: International
Airports, Well
Canals: Domestic, International, Salt pans, Seasonal rivers, lakes, Ice cap
Marshes
Sand desert limits, National Parks etc.
(in sea)

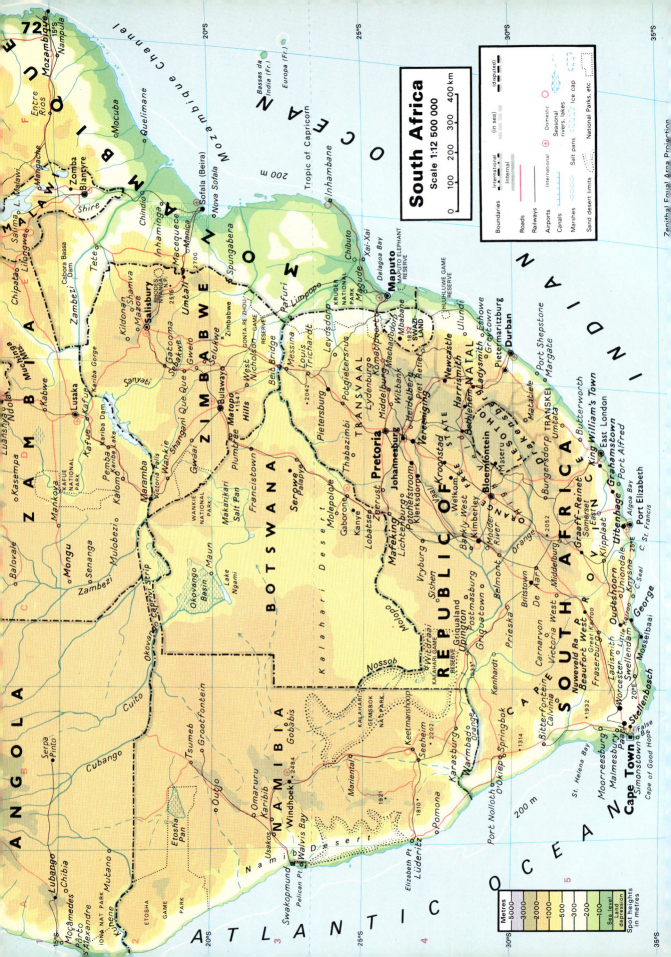

azetteer
Aachen/Atlantic City
73

Page ref
en: German F.R. 24 B1
: Belgium 22 B1
koski: Finland 16 E3
r., Switzerland 25 B2
us: Denmark 17 B4
Nigeria 67 B2
an: Iran 30 E4
la: Algeria 68 E2
Paraguay 66 C2
alık: Nigeria 67 B2
an: U.S.S.R. 29 P3
ville: France 22 B1
ville: U.S.A. 50 D3
yfeale: Irish Rep. 13 B4
y Head: Scot. 11 E5
yleix: Irish Rep. 13 D4
Nigeria 67 B2
t, Mt.: Austl. 42 C2
ttabad: Pak. 32 B2
l Kuri: i.,
abian Sea 30 F8
Tasman
t. Park: N.Z. 41 B3
rå: Denmark 17 A5
kuta: Nigeria 67 A2
aeron: Wales 14 B2
carn: Wales 14 C3
chirder: Scot. 10 F2
dare: Wales 14 C3
daron: Wales 14 B2
deen: Canada 60 D2
deen: Scotland 10 F2
deen: Md.,
S.A. 54 D5
deen: S. Dak.,
S.A. 53 F1
deen: Wash.,
S.A. 62 B2
dyfi: Wales 14 B2
feldy: Scotland 10 E3
gavenny: Wales 14 C3
gele: Wales 14 C1
soch: Wales 14 B2
illery: Wales 14 C3
ystwyth: Wales 14 B2
a, Lake: Ethiopia 69 N7
AN: Ivory Coast 68 E7
jio: Chad 67 D1
Hill: Nigeria 67 B2
ne: U.S.A. 50 C3
gdon: England 15 E3
gton: U.S.A. 55 K2
bi: r., Canada 59 D1
bi: Lake:
nada 59 E2
ne: r., Nigeria 67 B2
nnema: Nigeria 67 B3
zzo Nat. Park:
aly 21 B4
roka Range:
S.A. 62 E3
con: U.S.A. 54 F5
India 32 B4
DHABI: U.A.E. 30 F6
a: Nigeria 67 B2
Kerkas: Egypt 69 M3
ian N.P.: U.S.A. 59 G3
ulco: Mexico 48 G6
ay: r., Paraguay 66 C1
a: Ghana 68 E7
ngton: England 12 D3
l Is.: Irish Rep. 13 A3
n's Island
hamas 49 M5
acagua: mtn., Arg. 65 D10
nquija, Sierra del:
, Argentina 66 A2
ai: Italy 25 B3
n: Canada 56 E6
n Vale: town, Can. 57 N4
U.S.A. 50 C3
ms: Mass., U.S.A. 55 G2
ms: N.Y., U.S.A. 57 J6
ms, Lake: Canada 60 B2
n's Bridge:
, India/Sri Lanka 32 a ii
ms Lake: Canada 62 C1
ms Point: U.S.A. 56 B4
na: Turkey 28 D6
pazari: Turkey 28 C5
a: Italy 25 B2
s ABABA: Eth. 69 N7
son: U.S.A. 54 C2
ston: U.S.A. 58 D4
aide: Australia 43 A4
aide I.: Antarctica 65 E17
: Yemen P.D.R. 30 D8
, Gulf of:
abian Sea 30 E8
e: r., Italy 25 C2
ondack Mts.:
S.A. 57 L5
iralty Is.: arch.,
apua-New Guinea 40 H1
r., Japan 39 b i
Nigeria 67 A2
Ekiti: Nigeria 67 B2
gawa: Japan 39 c i
amri: Cameroun 67 C2
ur: r., France 23 A3
: Spain 19 B5
an: U.S.A. 56 A8
atic Sea: S. Europe 25 C3
wa: Ethiopia 69 N6
ick le Street: Eng. 12 E3
ean Sea:
Europe 21 D5
an: r., Wales 14 B2
n: Nigeria 67 B3
c, Loch: Scot. 10 D2
HANISTAN 30 H4
oo: Nigeria 67 B2
nkarahisar: Tur. 28 C6
dir: Morocco 68 D2
e: Nigeria 67 B2
no: Japan 39 f iv
rtala: India 33 F4
wam: U.S.A. 55 H2
aja: Nigeria 67 B2
e, Cap d': France 23 B3
ge: Nigeria 67 A2
n: France 23 B3
nais: old prov.,
ance 23 B3
o: Japan 39 f iv
court: hist., Fr. 22 B1
ew Lake: Canada 56 D3
Japan 39 c ii
rdat: Ethiopia 69 N5
: India 32 C3
gento: Sicily 21 B5
nion: Greece 24 D5
a Fria: r., U.S.A. 63 D5
ai: Brazil 66 a i
apey: r., Arg. 66 C2
a Prieta: Mexico 63 E5
aray Guazú: r., Par. 66 C1
aray Guazú: r., Par. 66 C1
las: Spain 19 B5
has Basin:
/Ind. O. 33 a ix
has Negras: Braz. 66 bi
ggar: mtns., Algeria 68 G4
adabad: India 32 B4
adnagar: India 32 B5

Page ref
Ahoada: Nigeria 67 B2
Ahwaz: Iran 30 E4
Aichi: Pref., Japan 39 d i
Aigues-Mortes,
Golfe d': France 23 B3
Aigues-Mortes
Camargue: France 23 B3
Aijal: India 38 A2
Aiken: U.S.A. 51 F3
Ailsa Craig: i., Scot. 11 C4
Ain Sefra: Algeria 68 E2
Ain Témouchent:
Algeria 19 B5
Air: mtns., Niger 68 G5
Aird Barvas:
bay, Scot. 10 B1
Airdrie: Canada 60 C2
Airdrie: Scotland 11 D4
Aire: r., England 12 E3
Aisne: r., France 22 B2
Aitape: Pap.-N.G. 40 G1
Aiviekste: r., U.S.S.R. 17 E4
Aix-en-Provence:
France 23 C3
Aix les Bains: France 23 C2
Aiyon: Greece 21 D5
Aizu-wakamatsu:
Japan 39 C2
Ajaccio: Corsica 19 a i
Ajaokuta: Nigeria 67 B2
Ajax: Canada 56 G6
Ajmer: India 32 B3
Ajo: U.S.A. 63 D5
Akabira: Japan 39 D1
Akaroa: N.Z. 41 B3
Akashi: Japan 39 a ii
Akhisar: Turkey 21 E5
Akijima: Japan 39 f iv
Akita: Japan 39 D2
Aklavik: Canada 46 H3
Akola: India 32 C4
Akosombo: Ghana 68 F7
Akranes: Iceland 16 a ii
Akritas, Cape: Greece 21 D5
Akron: N.Y., U.S.A. 56 G6
Akron: Ohio, U.S.A. 59 D3
Akron: Pa., U.S.A. 54 D4
Aksha: U.S.S.R. 27 O7
Aktyubinsk: U.S.S.R. 29 H3
Aku: Nigeria 67 B2
Akureyri: Iceland 16 b i
Akwele: Nigeria 67 B3
Akyab: Burma 38 A2
Alabama: State & r.,
U.S.A. 51 E3
Alai Range: U.S.S.R. 29 L6
Ala Kul': lake, U.S.S.R. 29 N4
Alamogordo: U.S.A. 53 D4
Alamosa: U.S.A. 53 D3
Åland Islands: Finland 17 D3
Alantika Mts.: Nig./
Cameroun 67 C2
Alapayevsk: U.S.S.R. 29 J2
Ala Shan: ra., China 34 C3
Alaska: State, U.S.A. 46 E3
Alaska, Gulf of:
Pacific Ocean 46 F5
Alaska Peninsula:
U.S.A. 46 C5
Alaska Range: U.S.A. 46 F4
Alassio: Italy 25 B3
Alaverdi: U.S.S.R. 28 E5
Alba: Italy 25 B3
Albacete: Spain 19 B5
ALBANIA 21 C4
Albany: Australia 42 b ii
Albany: Ga., U.S.A. 51 F3
Albany: N.Y., U.S.A. 55 G2
Albany: Oreg., U.S.A. 62 B3
Albeni Falls Dam:
U.S.A. 62 C2
Alberche: r., Spain 19 B4
Albermarle Sound:
U.S.A. 51 G2
Albert: France 22 B1
Albert, Lake: Ug./Zaire 70 F7
Alberta: Prov., Canada 60 B2
Albert Lea: U.S.A. 58 B3
Albert Nat. Park:
Zaire 71 E8
Albi: France 23 B3
Albion: N.Y., U.S.A. 56 G6
Albion: Pa., U.S.A. 56 E8
Albion: R.I., U.S.A. 55 J3
Alborg: Denmark 17 A4
Albreda: Canada 62 C1
Albula Pass: Switz. 25 B2
Albuquerque: Spain 19 A5
Albuquerque: U.S.A. 52 D3
Albury: Australia 43 C5
Alcalá de Henares:
Spain 19 B4
Alcázar de San Juan:
Spain 19 B5
Alcira: Spain 19 B5
Alcoy: Spain 19 B5
Aldabra Is.: Ind. O. 71 I9
Aldan: U.S.S.R. 27 P6
Aldan: r., U.S.S.R. 27 Q6
Alde: r., England 15 H2
Aldeburgh: England 15 H2
Alden: U.S.A. 54 B2
Alderley Edge: Eng. 14 D1
Aldermaston: Eng. 15 E3
Alderney:
i., Channel Is. 14 a i
Aldershot: England 15 F3
Aldridge: England 15 E2
Alegranza:
i., Canary Is. 68 C3
Alegrete: Brazil 66 C2
Aleksandrov Gay:
U.S.S.R. 28 F3
Aleksandrovsk-
Sakhalinsky:
U.S.S.R. 27 R7
Alemania: Arg. 66 A2
Alem Paraiba: Braz. 66 b i
Alençon: France 22 B2
Aleppo: Syria 28 D6
Alert: Canada 47 X0
Alert Bay:
town, Can. 62 A1
Alès: France 23 B3
Alessandria: It. 25 B3
Ålesund: Norway 16 A3
Aletschhorn: mtn.,
Switzerland 25 B2
Aleutian Abyssal
Plain: Pac. Ocean 44 J2
Aleutian Basin:
Pacific Ocean 44 H1
Aleutian Islands:
Pacific Ocean 44 H1
Aleutian Range:
U.S.A. 46 E5
Aleutian Ridge:
Pacific Ocean 44 H1
Aleutian Trench:
Pacific Ocean 44 H1
Alexander City: U.S.A. 51 E3
Alexander I.: Antarc. 65 D18
Alexandra: N.Z. 41 A4
Alexandria: Canada 57 L4
Alexandria: Egypt 69 L2

Page ref
Alexandria: Scot. 11 D4
Alexandria: U.S.A. 50 D3
Alexandria Bay:
sett., U.S.A. 57 K5
Alexandrina, Lake:
Australia 43 A5
Alford: England 15 G1
Alfred: Canada 57 L4
Alfreton: England 15 E1
Algarve: reg., Port. 19 A5
Algeciras: Spain 19 A5
ALGERIA 68 F3
Alghero: Sardinia 19 a i
Algoa Bay: S. Africa 72 D5
Algoma: Co., Canada 56 A2
Algonquin Provincial
Park: Canada 56 G4
Algorta: Uruguay 66 C3
Al Hoceima: Morocco 19 B5
Alicante: Spain 19 B5
Alice: U.S.A. 50 C4
Alice Springs:
town, Australia 40 E5
Aligarh: India 32 C3
Aling Kangri:
mtn., China 32 D2
Alingsås: Sweden 17 B4
Alix: Canada 60 C2
Alkmaar: Neth. 24 A1
Allagash: r., U.S.A. 57 Q3
Allahabad: India 32 D3
Allan: Canada 61 D2
Allard, Lac: Canada 47 X6
Allegany: U.S.A. 54 B2
Allegany State Park:
U.S.A. 54 B2
Allegheny: r., U.S.A. 54 B3
Allegheny Mts.: U.S.A. 59 E4
Allen, Lough:
Irish Rep. 13 C2
Allen Creek: U.S.A. 56 H6
Allendale Town:
England 12 D2
Allens Mills: U.S.A. 54 B3
Allentown: U.S.A. 54 E4
Alleppey: India 32 C7
Allgäuer Alps: mtns.,
Austria/German F.R. 25 C2
Alliance: Nebr.,
U.S.A. 53 E2
Alliance: Ohio, U.S.A. 59 D3
Allier: r., France 23 B2
Alliston: Canada 56 F5
Alloa: Scotland 11 E3
Alma: Canada 59 F2
Alma-Ata: U.S.S.R. 29 M5
Almada: Portugal 19 A5
Almadén: Spain 19 B5
Almeria: Spain 19 B5
Almirante Brown:
Argentina 66 B2
Almont: U.S.A. 56 B7
Almonte: Canada 57 J4
Aln: r., England 12 E1
Alnwick: England 12 E1
Alor: i., Indonesia 35 G12
Alor Setar: Malaysia 38 C5
Alpena: U.S.A. 56 B4
Alpha: U.S.A. 54 E4
Alpha: r., Australia 42 C2
Alsace: Old Prov.,
France 22 C2
Alsager: England 14 D1
Alsask: Canada 60 D2
Alsh, Loch: Scotland 10 C2
Alston: England 12 D2
Alta: Norway 16 D2
Alta Gracia: Arg. 66 B3
Altai Range: Mong. 34 A1
Altamaha: r., U.S.A. 51 F3
Altamirano: Arg. 66 C4
Altamont: U.S.A. 55 F2
Altamura: Italy 21 C4
Altdorf: Switz. 25 B2
Alte: r., Norway 16 D2
Altefjorden: fd.,
Norway 16 D1
Altenburg: Ger. D.R. 24 C1
Alton: England 15 F3
Alton: U.S.A. 58 B4
Altona: Canada 61 F3
Altona: German F.R. 24 B1
Altoona: U.S.A. 54 B4
Altrincham: Eng. 12 D3
Alturas: U.S.A. 63 B3
Altus: U.S.A. 50 C3
Altyn Tagh: ra., China 31 N3
Alva: Scotland 11 E3
Alva: U.S.A. 50 C2
Alvear: Argentina 66 C2
Alwar: India 32 C3
Alwen Res.: Wales 14 C1
Alyth: Scotland 10 E3
Amado: U.S.A. 63 D5
Amagansett: U.S.A. 55 H4
Amagasaki: Japan 39 b ii
Amagunze: Nigeria 67 B2
Amalfi: Italy 21 B4
Amarillo: U.S.A. 50 B2
Amassama: Nigeria 67 B2
Amazon: r.,
S. America 64 F4
Amazon, Mouth
of the: Brazil 64 H3
Ambala: India 32 C2
Ambalangoda:
Sri Lanka 32 b ii
Ambarchik: U.S.S.R. 27 T4
Ambargasta: Arg. 66 B2
Ambato: Ecuador 64 C4
Amberg: German F.R. 24 C2
Amble: England 12 E1
Ambleside: England 12 D2
Amboina: Indonesia 35 H11
Amboise: France 23 B2
Ambon: i., Indonesia 35 H11
Amboseli Game
Reserve: Kenya 71 G8
Americana: Brazil 66 a i
American Falls
Reservoir: U.S.A. 62 D3
American Fork:
U.S.A. 63 D3
Americus: U.S.A. 51 F3
Amersfoort: Neth. 24 B1
Amersham: England 15 F3
Amery: Canada 61 G1
Ames: U.S.A. 58 B3
Amesbury: England 15 E3
Amesbury: U.S.A. 55 K2
Amga: r., U.S.S.R. 27 Q5
Amgun: r., U.S.S.R. 27 Q7
Amherst: U.S.A. 55 H2
Amherstburg: Can. 56 B7
Amherst Island: Can. 57 J5
Amherstview: Canada 57 J5
Amhurst: U.S.A. 56 C8
Ami: Japan 39 g iii
Amiens: France 22 B2
Amirante Is.: Ind. O. 33 d v
Amisk Lake: Canada 61 E2
Amlwch: Wales 12 B3
AMMAN: Jordan 30 C4
Ammanford: Wales 14 B3

Page ref
Amne Machen
Shan: ra., China 34 B4
Amores: r., Arg. 66 C2
Amos: Canada 56 G1
Amoy: China 37 C5
Amparo: Brazil 66 a i
Ampthill: England 15 F2
Amraoti: India 32 C4
Amritsar: India 32 B2
Amsterdam: Neth. 24 A1
Amsterdam: U.S.A. 55 F2
Amu Dar'ya (Oxus):
r., U.S.S.R./Afg. 29 J6
Amur: r.,
U.S.S.R./China 27 Q7
Anabar: r., U.S.S.R. 27 O3
Anaconda: U.S.A. 62 D2
Anacortes: U.S.A. 62 B2
Anadyr': & r.,
U.S.S.R. 27 U5
Anadyr', Gulf of:
U.S.S.R. 27 V5
Anai Mudi: mtn.,
India 32 C6
Anambas Is.: Indon. 38 D6
Anambra: r. & State,
Nigeria 67 B2
Anan: Japan 39 B3
Anan'yev: U.S.S.R. 28 C4
Anápolis: Brazil 64 J7
Añatuya: Argentina 66 B2
Ancasti, Sierra de:
ra., Argentina 66 A2
Ancenis: France 23 A2
Anchi: China 37 C3
Anchiu: China 36 C2
Anchorage: U.S.A. 46 F4
Ancona: Italy 25 C3
Andalsnes: Norway 16 A3
Andalusia: U.S.A. 51 E3
Andaman Is.: Ind. O. 38 A4
Andaman Sea 38 B4
Andermatt: Switz. 25 B2
Andernach: Ger. F.R. 24 B1
Anderson: Ind.,
U.S.A. 58 C3
Anderson: S.C., U.S.A. 51 F3
Andfjorden: fd., Nor. 16 C2
Andhra Pradesh:
State, India 32 C6
Andizhan: U.S.S.R. 29 L5
ANDORRA: & city 23 B3
Andover: England 15 E3
Andover: Mass.,
U.S.A. 55 J2
Andover: N.Y., U.S.A. 56 H7
Andrew: Canada 60 C2
Andreyevka: U.S.S.R. 29 N4
Andros: i., Bahamas 51 G5
Andros: i., Greece 21 D5
Androscoggin:
r., U.S.A. 57 P5
Andújar: Spain 19 B5
Anegada:
i., Virgin Is. 49 O6
Anfu: China 37 B4
Angara: r., U.S.S.R. 27 M6
Angel de la Guarda:
i., Mexico 48 D4
Angel Falls: Ven. 64 F2
Ängelholm: Sweden 17 B4
Angélica: Argentina 66 B3
Angelina: r., U.S.A. 50 C3
Angelsey: i., Wales 14 B1
Angerman: r., Swed. 16 C3
Angers: France 23 A2
Angical: Brazil 64 K6
Angkor:
Kampuchea 38 C4
ANGOLA 71 C10
Angola: U.S.A. 54 A2
Angola Basin: Atl. O. 8 L9
Angoulême: France 23 B2
Angoumois: Old Prov.,
France 23 A2
Angren: U.S.S.R. 29 L5
Anguilla:
i., Leeward Is. 49 O6
Anholt: i., Denmark 17 B4
Anhsiang: China 37 B4
Anhui see Anhwei 36 C3
Anhwa: China 37 B4
Anhwei (Anhui):
Prov., China 36 C3
Ani: China 37 C4
Aniak: U.S.A. 46 D4
Aniva Bay: U.S.S.R. 27 R8
Anjou: Old Prov.,
France 23 A2
Anka: Nigeria 67 B1
Ankang: China 36 A3
ANKARA: Turkey 28 C6
Ankaratra Mts.:
Malagasy Rep. 71 I ii
Anki: China 37 C4
Anking: China 37 C3
Ankpa: Nigeria 67 B2
Ankwe: r., Nigeria 67 B2
Ankwo: China 36 C2
Anlin, Lake: China 36 B1
Anlu: China 37 B3
Ann, Cape: U.S.A. 55 K2
Annaberg: Ger. D.R. 24 C1
Annam Highlands:
Laos/Vietnam 38 –
Annan: & r., Scot. 11 E5
Annandale: val., Scot. 11 E4
Annapolis: U.S.A. 54 D6
Annapurna:
mtn., Nepal 32 D3
Ann Arbor: U.S.A. 56 B7
Annecy: & lake, Fr. 23 C2
An Nhon: Vietnam 38 D4
Anniston: U.S.A. 51 E3
Annonay: France 23 B2
Annville: U.S.A. 54 D4
Anoka: U.S.A. 58 B2
Anping: China 36 C2
Ansbach: Ger. F.R. 24 C2
Anse St. Jean: Canada 57 P1
Anshan: China 36 D1
Anshun: China 38 D1
Ansi: China 34 B2
Antakya (Antioch):
Syria 28 D6
ANTANANARIVO:
Malagasy Rep. 71 I ii
Antarctic Penin.:
Antarctica 65 –
Antas, Rio das:
r., Brazil 66 D2
An Teallach: mtn.,
Scotland 10 C2
Antequera: Spain 19 B5
Anthony: U.S.A. 50 C2
Antibes, Cap d': Fr. 23 C3
Anticosti, Île d': Can. 47 X7
Antifer, Cap d': Fr. 22 B2
Antigua: Guatemala 48 H7
Antigua: i.,
Leeward Is. 49 O6
Antioch see Antakya 28 D6
Antipodes Is.:
Southern Ocean 44 G11
Antler: U.S.A. 61 E3

Page ref
Antofagasta: Chile 64 D8
Antrim: & Co.,
N. Ireland 13 E2
Antrim Mts.: N. Ireland 13 E2
Antung: China 34 G2
Antwerp (Anvers):
Belgium 22 B1
Antwerp: U.S.A. 57 K5
Anumma: r., Nigeria 67 C1
Anvers see Antwerp 22 B1
Anyang: China 36 B2
Anyi: China 36 B3
Anza-Borrego Desert
State Park: U.S.A. 63 C5
Anzhero-Sudzhensk:
U.S.S.R. 29 O2
Anuradhapura: Sri
Lanka 32 b ii
Aomori: Japan 39 D1
Aosta: Italy 25 B2
Apalachee Bay: U.S.A. 51 F4
Apalachicola: r., U.S.A. 51 E3
Aparri: Philippines 35 G7
Apatity: U.S.S.R. 16 F2
Apeldorn: Netherlands 24 B1
Apennines: ra., Italy 21 B4
Apipé Grande,
Isla: i., Argentina 66 C2
Apolda: German D.R. 24 C1
Apolinario Saravia: Arg. 66 B1
Apomu: Nigeria 67 A2
Apostle Islands:
U.S.A. 58 B2
Appalachian Mts.:
U.S.A. 49 –
Appenzell: Switzerland 25 B2
Appleby: England 12 D2
Appleton: U.S.A. 58 C3
Apucarana: Brazil 66 D1
Aquidabán: r., Par. 66 C1
Aquitaine: Old Prov., Fr. 23 B3
Ara: r., Irish Rep. 13 C4
Arabian Basin: Ind. O. 33 e iii
Arabian Gulf see
Gulf, The 30 F5
Arabian Sea 30 H6
Aracajú: Brazil 64 L6
Aracanguy, Mts. de:
Paraguay 66 C1
Arad: Romania 20 D3
Araguaia: r., Brazil 64 H6
Araguari: Brazil 64 J7
Arakan: Divis., Burma 38 A2
Arakan Yoma:
mtns., Burma 38 A3
Araks (Araxes): r.,
U.S.S.R./Iran 28 F6
Aral Sea: U.S.S.R. 29 –
Aral'sk: U.S.S.R. 29 J4
Arambaré: Brazil 66 D3
Aran I.: Irish Rep. 13 C2
Aran Is.: Irish Rep. 13 B3
Arapey Chico: r., Uru. 66 C3
Arapey Grande: r., Uru. 66 C3
Arapongas: Brazil 66 D1
Araranguá: Brazil 66 E2
Araras: Brazil 66 a i
Ararat: Australia 43 B5
Ararat, Mt.: Turkey 28 E6
Arauca: Colombia 64 D2
Araxes: r., see Araks 28 F6
Arborfield: Canada 61 E2
Arborg: Canada 61 F2
Arbroath: Scotland 10 F3
Arcachon: France 23 A3
Arcade: U.S.A. 56 G7
Arcata: U.S.A. 63 B3
Arches Nat.
Monument: U.S.A. 63 E4
Archibald Makin Nat.
Park: Australia 43 B5
Arcola: Canada 61 E3
Arctic Ocean 26 –
Arctic Village: U.S.A. 46 F3
Ardara: Irish Rep. 13 C2
Ardbeg: Scotland 11 B4
Ardèche: France 23 B3
Ardee: Irish Rep. 13 E3
Ardennes: plat., Belg. 22 C1
Ardle: r., Scotland 10 E3
Ardmore: U.S.A. 50 C3
Ardmore Point: Scot. 11 C4
Ardnamurchan Point:
Scotland 10 B3
Ardrossan: Scotland 11 D4
Ards Peninsula: N. Irel. 13 F2
Arecibo: Puerto Rico 49 N6
Arena, Point: U.S.A. 63 B4
Arendal: Norway 17 A4
Arequipa: Peru 64 D7
Arerunguá: r., Uru. 66 C3
Arezzo: Italy 21 B4
Argenta: Italy 25 C3
Argentan: France 22 A2
Argenteuil: Co., Can. 57 L4
Argenteuil: France 22 B2
ARGENTINA 64 –
Argentine Basin: Atl. O. 8 F12
Arges: r., Romania 21 E4
Argonne: hills, France 22 C2
Argonne, Forêt d': Fr. 22 B2
Argos: Greece 21 D5
Arguello, Point: U.S.A. 63 B5
Argungu: Nigeria 67 A1
Argun Hill: Nigeria 67 B1
Argus: Canada 56 F5
Argyll Nat. Forest
Park: Scot. 11 D3
Arica: Chile 64 D7
Ariège: r., France 23 B3
Arisaig: & Sound,
Scotland 10 C3
Arizona: State, U.S.A. 63 D5
Arjanta: India 32 C4
Arjeplog: Sweden 16 C2
Arkaig, Loch: Scotland 10 C3
Arkansas: State & r.,
U.S.A. 50 D2
Arkansas City: U.S.A. 50 C2
Arkhangel'sk: U.S.S.R. 26 G5
Arklow: Irish Rep. 13 E4
Arkville: U.S.A. 54 F2
Arlberg Pass: Austria 25 C2
Arles: France 23 B3
Arlon: Belgium 22 C2
Armadale: Australia 42 b ii
Armadale: Scotland 11 E4
Armagh: & Co.,
N. Ireland 13 D2
Armavir: U.S.S.R. 28 E4
Armenian S.S.R.:
U.S.S.R. 28 E5
Armentières: France 22 B1
Armidale: Australia 43 D4
Armonk: U.S.A. 55 G3
Armstrong: Canada 58 C1
Arnhem: Netherlands 24 B1
Arnhem Land: geog.
reg., Australia 40 E3
Arno: r., Italy 25 C3
Arnold: England 15 E2
Arnot: Canada 61 F1
Arnprior: Canada 57 J4
Arnsberger Wald:
mtns., German F.R. 24 B1

Page ref
Arnstadt: Ger. D.R. 24 C1
Arntfield: Canada 56 F1
Aro: Nigeria 67 A2
Aroostook: r., U.S.A. 59 G2
Arosa: Switzerland 25 B2
Arpoador, Ponta do:
pt., Brazil 66 a i
Arrabury: Australia 42 B3
Arraga: Argentina 66 B2
Arran I.: Scotland 11 C4
Arras: France 22 B1
Arrecifes: Argentina 66 B3
Arrée, Monts d': Fr. 22 a i
Arroio Grande: Brazil 66 D3
Arromanches: France 22 A2
Arrow: r., England 14 D2
Arrow, Lough:
Irish Rep. 13 C2
Arrowhead: Canada 62 C1
Arrow River: town,
Canada 61 E2
Arrowrock Reservoir:
U.S.A. 62 C3
Arrowsmith, Mt.: N.Z. 41 B3
Arrufó: Argentina 66 B3
Arta: Greece 24 D5
Artemovskiy: U.S.S.R. 29 J2
Artesia: U.S.A. 53 E4
Arthabaska: & Co., Can. 57 O3
Arthur: Canada 56 E6
Arthur's Pass: & nat.
park, N.Z. 41 B3
Artigas: Uruguay 66 C3
Artois: Old Prov., Fr. 22 B1
Arua: Uganda 70 F7
Aruba: i., Neth.
Antilles 49 N7
Aru Is.: Indonesia 35 J12
Arun: r., England 15 F4
Arunachal Pradesh:
Union Territ., India 33 F3
Arundel: England 15 F4
Arvida: Canada 57 O1
Arvika: Sweden 17 B4
Arys': U.S.S.R. 29 K5
Arzamas: U.S.S.R. 28 E2
Arzew: Algeria 68 E1
Asaba: Nigeria 67 B2
Asahi: Japan 39 g iv
Asahigawa: Japan 39 D1
Åsane: Norway 17 A3
Asansol: India 32 E4
Asbestos: Canada 57 O4
Asbury Park:
town, U.S.A. 55 F4
Ascension Island:
Atlantic Ocean 8 J8
Aschaffenburg:
German F.R. 24 B2
Ascoli Piceno: Italy 21 B4
Ascot: England 15 F3
Ascot Corner: Canada 57 O4
Åsele: Sweden 16 C3
Ashbourne: England 15 E1
Asenovgrad: Bulgaria 21 D4
Ashburnham: U.S.A. 55 J2
Ashburton: England 14 C4
Ashburton: N.Z. 41 B3
Ashburton:
r., Australia 40 A5
Ashby-de-la-
Zouch: England 15 E2
Ashcroft: Canada 62 B1
Ashern: Canada 61 F2
Asheville: U.S.A. 51 F2
Ashford: England 15 G3
Ashikaga: Japan 39 C2
Ashington: England 12 E1
Ashizuri-zaki:
cape, Japan 39 B3
Ashkhabad: U.S.S.R. 29 H6
Ashland: Ky., U.S.A. 59 D4
Ashland: Mass., U.S.A. 55 J2
Ashland: N.H., U.S.A. 57 O6
Ashland: Oreg., U.S.A. 62 B3
Ashland: Pa., U.S.A. 54 D4
Ashland: Wis., U.S.A. 58 B2
Ashley: U.S.A. 54 E3
Ashokan Res.: U.S.A. 55 F3
Ashtabula: U.S.A. 56 E8
Ashton: U.S.A. 62 D3
Ashton-in-Makerfield:
England 12 D3
Ashuanipi Lake: Can. 47 X6
Ashville: Canada 61 E2
Asilah: Morocco 19 A5
Asino: U.S.S.R. 29 O2
Asir: geog. reg.,
Sau. Arab. 30 D7
Askeaton: Irish Rep. 13 C4
Askival: mtn., Scotland 10 B3
Askrigg: England 12 D2
Asmara: Ethiopia 69 N5
Åsnen: lake, Sweden 17 B4
Aspiring, Mt.: N.Z. 41 A3
Assab: Ethiopia 69 O6
Assam: State, India 33 F3
Assen: Netherlands 24 B1
Assiniboia: Canada 61 D3
Assiniboine: r., Can. 61 E2
Assisi: Italy 21 B4
Assynt, Loch: Scotland 10 D1
Astara: U.S.S.R. 28 F6
Asti: Italy 25 B3
Astipálaia: i., Greece 21 E5
Astoria: U.S.A. 62 B2
Astrakhan: U.S.S.R. 28 F4
ASUNCIÓN: Paraguay 66 C2
Aswân: & dam, Egypt 69 M4
Asyut: Egypt 69 M3
Atacama Desert:
Chile/Peru 64 E8
Atami: Japan 39 f iv
Atasuskiy: U.S.S.R. 29 L4
Atbara: Sudan 69 M5
Atbara: r., Sudan 69 N5
Atbasar: U.S.S.R. 29 K3
Atchafalaya: r.,
U.S.A. 50 D3
Atchafalaya Bay:
U.S.A. 50 D4
Atchison: U.S.A. 58 A4
Atco: U.S.A. 54 F5
Athabasca: & r., Can. 60 C2
Athabasca, Lake: Can. 60 D1
Athboy: Irish Rep. 13 E3
Athenry: Irish Rep. 13 C3
Athens: Canada 57 K5
ATHENS: Greece 21 D5
Athens: Ga., U.S.A. 51 F3
Athens: N.Y., U.S.A. 55 G2
Athens: Tenn., U.S.A. 51 F2
Atherley: Canada 56 F5
Atherstone: England 15 E2
Atherton: England 12 D3
Athlone: Irish Rep. 13 D3
Athol: U.S.A. 55 H2
Atholl, Forest of:
reg., Scotland 10 E3
Athos: r., Greece 21 D4
Athy: Irish Rep. 13 E4
Atikokan: Canada 58 B2
Atikwa Lake: Canada 61 G3
Atlanta: Ga., U.S.A. 51 F3
Atlantic City: U.S.A. 54 F5

Name	Page	ref
Atlantic-Indian Ridge: Atlantic Ocean	8	N13
Atlas Mts. Alg./Morocco	19	C5
Atoka: U.S.A.	50	C3
Atsugi: Japan	39	f iv
Atsumi-Hanto: penin., Japan	39	d ii
Atsumi-wan: bay, Japan	39	d ii
Attica: U.S.A.	54	B2
Attleboro: U.S.A.	55	J3
Attleborough: England	15	H2
Attopeu: Laos	38	D4
Aubagne: France	23	C3
Aube: r., France	22	B2
Aubrey Falls: Canada	56	B3
Auburn: Canada	51	E3
Auburn: Maine, U.S.A.	57	P5
Auburn: Nebr., U.S.A.	58	A3
Auburn: N.Y., U.S.A.	54	D2
Auburn: Wash., U.S.A.	62	B2
Aubusson: France	23	B2
Auch: France	23	B3
Auchi: Nigeria	67	B2
Auchterarder: Scotland	10	E3
Auckland: N.Z.	41	B2
Auckland Is.: Southern Ocean.	44	F12
Aude: r., France	23	B3
Auden: Canada	58	C1
Audierne: France	22	a i
Auerbach: German F.R.	24	C2
Augathella: Australia	42	C3
Augher: N. Ireland	13	D2
Aughnacloy: N. Ireland	13	E2
Au Gres: U.S.A.	56	B5
Augsburg: German F.R.	25	C2
Augusta: Australia	42	b ii
Augusta: Sicily	21	
Augusta: Ga., U.S.A.	51	F3
Augusta: Maine, U.S.A.	57	Q5
Auineau Peninsula: Canada	61	G3
Aumale: France	22	B2
Aunis: Old Prov., Fr.	23	A2
Aups: France	23	C3
Aurangabad: India	32	C5
Aurich: German F.R.	24	B1
Aurignac: France	23	B3
Aurillac: France	23	B3
Aurora: Canada	56	F5
Aurora: U.S.A.	58	C3
Ausable: r., U.S.A.	56	M5
Au Sable: r., U.S.A.	56	B5
Ausable, East Branch: r., U.S.A.	57	M5
Ausable, West Branch: r., U.S.A.	57	M5
Ausable Forks: sett., U.S.A.	57	M5
Auschwitz: Poland	20	C3
Austin: Minn., U.S.A.	58	B3
Austin: Nev., U.S.A.	63	C4
Austin: N.Y., U.S.A.	54	G8
Austin: Tex., U.S.A.	50	C3
Austin, Lake: Austl.	42	b i
AUSTRALIA:	40	–
Australian Alps: Austl.	43	C5
Australian Capital Territory: Australia	43	C5
AUSTRIA:	25	C2
Autun: France	23	B2
Auvergne: Old Prov., France	23	B2
Auvergne Mts.: France	23	B2
Auxerre: France	22	B2
Aux Sables: r., Ont., Canada	56	D6
Aux Sables: r., Ont., Canada	56	C3
aux Sables, Lac: Can.	56	C3
Avallon: France	23	B2
Avalon: U.S.A.	54	F5
Avaré: Brazil	66	E1
Avebury: England	15	F3
Avellaneda: Argentina	66	C3
Averill Park: U.S.A.	55	G2
Averon: r., Canada	10	D2
Avesta: Sweden	17	C3
Aveyron: r., France	23	B3
Avezzano: Italy	21	B4
Aviá Terai: Argentina	66	B2
Aviemore: Scotland	10	E3
Avignon: France	23	B3
Avila: Spain	19	B4
Avilés: Spain	19	A4
Avis: U.S.A.	54	C3
Avoca: r., Irish Rep.	13	E4
Avoca: U.S.A.	56	H7
Avola: Canada	60	G6
Avon: Co. & r., Eng.	14	D3
Avon: r., Hants., Eng.	15	E4
Avon: r., War., England	15	E4
Avon: r., Scotland	10	E3
Avon: r., N.Y., U.S.A.	55	H3
Avon: Conn., U.S.A.	55	J3
Avondale: U.S.A.	55	J3
Avonmouth: England	14	D3
Avoriaz: France	23	C2
Avranches: France	22	A2
Awaji: Japan	39	b ii
Awaji-shima: i., Japan	39	b ii
Awash: Ethiopia	69	N7
Awe, Loch: Scotland	10	C3
Awgu: Nigeria	67	B2
Awka: Nigeria	67	B2
Axe: r., England	14	D3
Axel Heiberg I.: Can.	47	R1
Axminster: England	14	D4
Aya: r., Nigeria	67	B2
Ayabe: Japan	39	b i
Ayaguz: U.S.S.R.	29	N4
Ayamonte: Spain	19	A5
Aycliffe: England	12	F2
Aydin: Turkey	21	E5
Ayer: U.S.A.	55	J2
Ayetoro: Nigeria	67	A2
Ayios Nikólaos: Crete	21	E5
Aylesbury: England	15	F3
Aylmer: Ont., Canada	56	E7
Aylmer, Qué.: Canada	57	K4
Aylmer, Lake: N.W.T., Canada	46	O4
Aylmer, Lake: Qué. Canada	57	O4
Aylsham: England	15	H2
Ayr: Australia	42	C1
Ayr: & r., Scotland	11	D1
Ayre, Point of: I. of Man	12	B2
Ayutthaya: Thailand	38	C4
Azare: Nigeria	67	C1
Azerbaydzhan S.S.R.:	28	F5
Azilda: Canada	56	D3
Azores: is., Atl. O.	8	H4
Azov, Sea of: U.S.S.R.	28	D4
Azul: Argentina	65	F11
Bà, Loch: Scotland	10	C3
Babana: Nigeria	67	A1

Name	Page	ref
Babar Is.: Indonesia	35	H12
Babbacombe Bay: Eng.	14	C4
Bab al Mandab: str., Africa/Asia	58	O6
Babine Lake: Canada	46	K6
Babylon: Iraq	30	E4
Bacău: Romania	20	E3
Bacchus Marsh: Austl.	43	B5
Bachelor Lake: Can.	59	E2
Bacolod: Philippines	35	G8
Bacup: England	12	D3
Badajoz: Spain	19	A5
Bad Axe: U.S.A.	56	C6
Baden: Canada	56	E6
Baden: Switzerland	25	B2
Baden: Old state, German F.R.	25	B2
Baden-Baden: Ger. F.R.	25	B2
Badger: U.S.A.	61	F3
Bad Ischl: Austria	25	C2
Bad Kissingen: Ger. F.R.	24	C1
Bad Kreuznach: Ger. F.R.	24	B2
Badlands Nat. Monument: U.S.A.	53	E2
Bad Mergentheim: German F.R.	24	B2
Bad Reichenhall: German F.R.	25	C2
Badulla: Sri Lanka	32	b ii
Bafang: Cameroun	67	C2
Baffin Bay: Canada	47	X2
Baffin Bay: U.S.A.	50	C4
Baffin I.: Canada	47	U2
Baffin I. Nat. Park: Canada	47	W4
Bafia: Cameroun	67	C2
Bafoussam: Cameroun	67	C2
Bagana: Nigeria	67	B2
Bagan-Siapiapi: Indon.	38	C6
Bagdad: U.S.A.	63	D5
Bagé: Brazil	66	D3
Bagenalstown: Irish Rep.	13	E4
Baggy Point: England	14	B3
BAGHDAD: Iraq	30	D4
Bagheria: Sicily	21	B5
Bagja: Nigeria	67	B2
Bagnell Dam: U.S.A.	58	B4
Bagot: Co., Canada	57	N4
Bagotville: Canada	57	P1
Baguio: Philippines	35	G7
BAHAMAS:	49	–
Bahawalpur: Pakistan	32	B3
Bahia see Salvador		L6
Bahía Samborombón: bay, Argentina	66	C4
Bahía Blanca: Argentina	65	F11
Bahraich: India	32	D3
BAHRAIN:	30	F5
Bahr el Ghazal: Prov., Sudan	69	L7
Bahr el Jebel (White Nile): r., Sudan	69	M7
Baía das Laranjeiras: bay, Brazil	66	E2
Baía de Guaratuba: bay, Brazil	66	E2
Baía de Paranaguá: bay, Brazil	66	E2
Baia-Mare: Romania	20	D3
Baie-Comeau: town, Canada	59	G2
Baie d'Audierne: bay, France	22	a i
Baie de Douarnenez: bay, France	22	a i
Baie de la Seine: bay, France	22	A2
Baie de Quiberon: bay, France	22	a i
Baie St.-Paul: sett. Canada	57	P2
Bailieborough: Irish Rep.	13	E3
Bailleul: France	22	B1
Bain: r., England	15	F1
Bainbridge: Ga., U.S.A.	51	F3
Bainbridge: N.Y., U.S.A.	54	E2
Bains, Lac du: Fr.	23	C2
Bairnsdale: Australia	43	C5
Baja: Hungary	20	C3
Baker: N. Dak., U.S.A.	53	E1
Baker: Oreg., U.S.A.	62	C3
Baker I.: U.S.A.	44	Q4
Baker Lake: sett. Can.	47	Q4
Bakersfield: U.S.A.	63	C4
Bakewell: England	12	E3
Baku: U.S.S.R.	28	F5
Bala: Canada	56	F4
Bala: & lake, Wales	14	C2
Balaghat: India	32	D4
Balaklava: U.S.S.R.	28	D5
Balashov: U.S.S.R.	28	E3
Balasore: India	32	E4
Balaton, Lake: Hungary	20	C3
Balboa: Panama	49	Ins.
Balbriggan: Irish Rep.	13	E3
Balcarces: Canada	61	F3
Balcary Point: Scot.	11	E5
Balclutha: N.Z.	41	A4
Balde: Argentina	66	A3
Bald Eagle Lake: U.S.A.		
Baldock: U.S.A.	53	G1
Baldock, Lake: Canada	61	F1
Baldwinsville: U.S.A.	54	D1
Bâle see Basel	25	B2
Balearic Is.: Med. Sea	19	C4
Balen: Belgium	22	C1
Balestrand: Norway	16	A3
Balgonie: Canada	61	E2
Bali: Cameroun	67	B2
Bali: i., Indonesia	35	E12
Balikesir: Turkey	21	E4
Balikpapan: Indonesia	35	F11
Bali Sea: Indonesia	35	F12
Balkhash: & lake, U.S.S.R.	29	M4
Ballantrae: Scotland	11	C1
Ballarat: Australia	43	B5
Ballard, Lake: Austl.	42	c i
Ballater: Scotland	10	E2
Balleny Is.: Antarctica	84	F13
Ballina: Australia	43	D3
Ballina: Irish Rep.	13	B2
Ballinamore: Irish Rep.	13	D2
Ballinasloe: Irish Rep.	13	C3
Ballincollig: Irish Rep.	13	C5
Ballinrobe: Irish Rep.	13	B3
Ballinskelligs Bay: Irish Rep.	13	A5
Ballston Spa: U.S.A.	55	G1
Ballybay: Irish Rep.	13	E2
Ballybofey: Irish Rep.	13	D2
Ballybunnion: Irish Rep.	13	B4
Ballycastle: N. Ireland	13	E1
Ballyclare: N. Ireland	13	E2
Ballydavid Head: pt., Irish Rep.	13	A4
Ballyhaunis: Irish Rep.	13	C3

Name	Page	ref
Ballyhoura Hills: Irish Rep.	13	C4
Ballyjamesduff: Irish Rep.	13	D3
Ballymahon: Irish Rep.	13	D3
Ballymena: N. Ireland	13	E2
Ballymoney: N. Ireland	13	E1
Ballymote: Irish Rep.	13	C2
Ballyshannon: Irish Republic	13	C2
Ballyteige Bay: Irish Rep.	13	E4
Balmaceda: Chile	65	D13
Balmoral Castle: Scot.	10	E2
Balonne: r., Australia	42	C3
Balovale: Zambia	72	C1
Balranald: Australia	43	B4
Balsam Lake: Canada	56	F5
Balsas: r., Mexico	48	G6
Balta: U.S.S.R.	20	E3
Baltasar Brum: Uru.	66	C3
Baltic Sea:	17	C4
Baltimore: U.S.A.	54	D5
Baltinglass: Irish Rep.	13	E4
Baltrum: i., Ger. F.R.	24	B1
Baluchistan: Prov., Pak.	32	A3
Bama: Nigeria	67	C1
BAMAKO: Mali	68	D6
Bamba: Mali	68	E5
Bamberg: German F.R.	24	C2
Bamfield: Canada	62	A2
Bamkin: Cameroun	67	C2
Bampton: England	14	C3
Banagher: Irish Rep.	13	D3
Banbridge: N. Ireland	13	E2
Banbury: England	15	F2
Banchory: Scotland	10	F2
Bancroft: Canada	56	H4
Banda Aceh: Indonesia	38	B5
Banda Banda, Mt.: Australia	43	D4
Banda del Rio Salí: Argentina	66	A2
Bandai-asahi-kokuritsu-kōen: N.P., Japan	39	C2
Bandar: India	32	D5
Bandar 'Abbās: Iran	30	G5
Bandar-e-Shāh: Iran	28	G6
Bandar-e-Shāhpūr: Iran	30	E4
BANDAR SERI BEGAWAN: Brunei	35	E10
Banda Sea: Indonesia	35	H12
Bandera: Argentina	66	B2
Banderas Bay: Mexico	48	E5
Bandirma: Turkey	21	E4
Bandjarmasin: Indon.	35	E11
Bandon: & r., Irish Rep.	13	C5
Bandra: India	32	B5
Bandung: Indonesia	35	D12
Banff: & nat. park, Can.	62	C1
Banff: Scotland	10	F2
Bangalore: India	32	C6
Bangante: Cameroun	67	C2
Bangka: i., Indon.	35	D11
BANGKOK: Thailand	38	C4
BANGLADESH:	32/3	
Bangor: N. Ireland	13	F2
Bangor: Maine, U.S.A.	59	G3
Bangor: Pa., U.S.A.	54	E4
Bangor: Wales	14	B1
Bang Saphan: Thailand	38	B4
Bangui: Cen. Afr. Emp.	69	J8
Bangweulu: Lake, Zambia	71	E10
Ban Houei Sai: Laos	38	C2
Baniyas: Syria	28	D6
Banja Luka: Yugoslavia	21	C4
Ban Kantang: Thailand	38	B5
Banks I.: Canada	46	L2
Banks Peninsula: N.Z.	41	B3
Ban Me Thuot: Vietnam	38	D4
Bann: r., N. Ireland	13	E1
Bannu: Pakistan	32	B2
Banská Bystrica: Czech.	20	C3
Bantry: & bay, Irish Republic	13	B5
Banstead: England	15	F3
Banwy: r., Wales	14	C2
Banyo: Cameroun	67	C2
Banyuls: France	23	B3
Baotou see Paotow	36	
Bapaume: France	22	B1
Baradero: Argentina	66	C3
Barakula: Australia	42	D3
Baranovichi [Slonim]: U.S.S.R.		E2
Barataria Bay: U.S.A.	50	E4
Barbacena: Brazil	64	K8
BARBADOS:	49	P7
Barbuda: i., Leeward Is.	49	O6
Barcellona: Sicily	21	C5
Barcelona: Spain	19	C4
Barcelona: Venezuela	49	O7
Barcelonnette: France	23	C3
Barcoo: r., Australia	40	G5
Bardsey I.: Wales	14	B2
Barèges: France	23	A3
Bareilly: India	32	C3
Barents Sea: Arctic O.	26	–
Bari: Italy	21	C4
Bark Lake: Canada	56	G4
Barletta: Italy	21	C4
Barking: England	15	G3
Barkley: r., U.S.A.	51	E2
Barkley Sound: Canada	62	A2
Barkly Tableland: Australia	40	F4
Barkly West: S. Africa	72	C2
Bar-le-Duc: France	22	C2
Barlee, Lake: Australia	42	b i
Barlin: France	22	B1
Barlow Haven: U.S.A.	51	F4
Barmouth: & bay, Wales	14	B2
Barnard Castle: England	12	E2
Barnaul: U.S.S.R.	29	N3
Barnesboro: U.S.A.	54	B4
Barnet: England	15	F3
Barnoldswick: England	12	D3
Barnsley: England	12	E3
Barnstable: U.S.A.	55	K3
Barnstaple: England	14	B3
Barnstaple (Bideford) Bay: England	14	B3
Baro: Nigeria	67	B2
Baroua: r., Niger	67	C1
Barques, Pointe aux: U.S.A.	56	C5
Barquisimeto: Ven.	56	N7
Barra: & Sound, Scot.	10	A2
Barraba: Australia	43	D3
Barracão: Brazil	66	D2
Barrackpore: India	32	E4
Barra do Piraí: Brazil	66	b i
Barrage de Barrière: dam, Canada	57	J2
Barra Head: pt., Scot.	10	A3
Barra Mansa: Brazil	66	b i
Barrancas: r., Argentina	66	A3
Barranco: r., Argentina	66	B3
Barranqueras: Arg	66	C2

Name	Page	ref
Barranquilla: Colombia	49	M7
Barraute: Canada	56	H1
Barre: U.S.A.	57	N5
Barreiro: Portugal	19	A5
Barretos: Brazil	64	J8
Barrhead: Canada	60	C2
Barrhead: Scotland	11	D4
Barrie: Canada	56	F5
Barrie Island: Canada	56	D4
Barrington: U.S.A.	55	J3
Barrington, Lake: Can.	61	E1
Barrington Tops: mtn., Australia	43	D4
Barrington: Australia	43	D4
Barro, Lago dos: Brazil	66	D2
Barrow: r., Irish Rep.	13	E4
Barrow, Point: U.S.A.	46	D2
Barrow-in-Furness: England	12	C2
Barrow Strait: Canada	47	R2
Barry: Wales	14	C3
Barrys Bay: sett., Can.	56	H4
Barstow: U.S.A.	63	C5
Bar-sur-Seine: France	22	B2
Barth: Wales	14	B2
Bartlesville: U.S.A.	58	A4
Barton: U.S.A.	57	N5
Barton, Lake: Canada	61	G2
Barton-upon-Humber: England	12	F3
Bārus: Indonesia	38	B6
Barwell: England	15	E2
Barwon: r., Australia	43	C3
Basavilbasco: Argentina	66	C3
Basel (Bâle): Switz.	25	B2
Bashaw: Canada	60	C2
Basilan: i., Phil.	35	G9
Basildon: England	15	G3
Basilio: Brazil	66	D3
Basingstoke: England	15	E3
Basin Lake: Canada	61	D2
Baskatong, Réservoir: Canada	57	K3
Baskunchak: U.S.S.R.	28	F4
Basra: Iraq	30	E4
Bassano: Canada	60	C2
Bassano del Grappa: Italy	25	C2
Bassas da India: Indian Ocean	72	F3
Bassein: Burma	38	A3
Bassenthwaite Lake: England	12	C2
Basse-Terre: Guadeloupe	49	O6
Bass Island: U.S.A.	56	C8
Bass Strait: Australia	43	C5
Bassum: German F.R.	24	B1
Bastia: Corsica	19	a i
Bastogne: Belgium	22	C1
Bataan Penn.: Phil.	35	G8
Batang (Paan): China	36	B5
Batangas: Phil.	35	G8
Batavia: U.S.A.	54	B2
Batchawana: r., Canada	56	A2
Batchawana, Mt.: Can.	56	A2
Batelito: r., Argentina	66	A2
Batemans Bay: Austl.	43	D5
Batesville: Ark., U.S.A.	50	D3
Batesville: Miss., U.S.A.	51	E3
Bath: England	14	D3
Bath: Maine, U.S.A.	57	Q6
Bath: N.Y., U.S.A.	54	C2
Bathgate: Scotland	11	E4
Bathurst: Australia	43	C4
Bathurst: Canada	46	W7
Bathurst, Cape: Can.	46	K2
Bathurst I.: Australia	40	E3
Bathurst I.: Canada	47	Q1
Batiscan: r., Canada	57	N2
Baton Rouge: U.S.A.	50	D3
Battambang: Kampuchea	38	C4
Batticaloa: Sri Lanka	32	b ii
Battle: England	15	G4
Battle: r., Canada	60	C2
Battle Creek: town, U.S.A.	56	A6
Battleford: Canada	60	D2
Battle Mountain: town, U.S.A.	63	C3
Batu Is.: Indonesia	38	B7
Batumi: U.S.S.R.	28	E5
Batu Pahat: Malaysia	38	C6
Bauchi: & State, Nig.	67	C1
Bauchi Plateau: Nigeria	67	B1
Baumstown: U.S.A.	54	D6
Bautzen: German D.R.	24	C1
Bavaria: State, German F.R.	25	C2
Bavarian Alps: Ger. F.R.	25	C2
Bavarian Forest: mtns. & nat. park, Ger. F.R.	24	C2
Bawdwin: Burma	38	A2
Bawtry: England	12	E3
Baxter State Park: U.S.A.	59	G2
Bayadh: Algeria	68	D1
Bayan Kara Shan: r., China	34	B4
Bay City: Mich., U.S.A.	56	C6
Bay City: Tex., U.S.A.	50	C4
Bayeux: France	22	A2
Bayfield: & r., Canada	56	D6
Baykal, Lake: U.S.S.R.	29	N7
Baymak: U.S.S.R.	28	H3
Baymore: Canada	61	E2
Bayonne: France	23	A3
Bayou: r., U.S.A.	50	C3
Bayreuth: German F.R.	24	C2
Bays, Lake of: Canada	56	F4
Bay Shore: town, U.S.A.	55	G4
Bayside: Canada	56	H5
Baza: Spain	19	B5
Bazn: r., Canada	56	L2
Beach Haven: U.S.A.	55	F5
Beachwood: U.S.A.	55	F5
Beachy Head: cape, England	15	G4
Beacon: U.S.A.	55	G2
Beacon Falls: town, U.S.A.	55	G3
Beacon Hill: Wales	14	C2
Beaconsfield: England	15	F3
Beagle Strait: Arg./Chile	65	E14
Beaminster: England	14	D4
Bear: r., U.S.A.	62	D3
Bear, Lake: U.S.A.	63	D3
Bear Brook State Park: U.S.A.	55	J1
Bear Island: Arctic O.	26	C7
Bear Island: Irish Rep.	13	B5
Bear Lake: U.S.A.	62	D3
Bear Mountain: U.S.A.	55	G2
Bearsden: Scotland	11	D4

Name	Page	ref
Béarn: Old Prov., Fr.	23	A3
Beas: r., India	32	C2
Beaton: r., Canada	60	C1
Beatrice: U.S.A.	58	A3
Beattyville: Canada	59	E2
Beaucaire: France	23	B3
Beauce: Co., Canada	57	P3
Beauce: geog. reg., Fr.	22	B2
Beauceville: Canada	57	P3
Beauchêne: Canada	56	G3
Beaudesert: Australia	43	D3
Beaufort: U.S.A.	51	F3
Beaufort Sea: Arctic Ocean	46	G2
Beaufort West: S. Africa	72	C5
Beauharnois: Canada	57	M4
Beaujolais, Monts du: hills, France	23	B2
Beaumaris: Wales	14	B1
Beaumont: U.S.A.	50	D3
Beaumont Hill: Austl.	43	C4
Beaune: France	23	F2
Beauséjour: Canada	61	F2
Beauvais: France	22	B2
Beauval: Canada	60	D1
Beaver: r., Canada	57	K6
Beaver Creek: town, Canada	50	D3
Beaver Dam: town, U.S.A.	58	C3
Beaverdell: Canada	62	C2
Beaverhead: r., U.S.A.	62	D2
Beaverhill Lake: Alberta, Canada	60	C2
Beaverhill Lake: Manitoba, Canada	61	G2
Beaver Island: U.S.A.	58	G2
Beaverlodge: Canada	60	B1
Beavermouth: Canada	60	C2
Beaverton: U.S.A.	56	F5
Beaverton: r., Canada	56	C4
Bécancour: Canada	57	N3
Bécancour: r., Canada	57	O3
Beccles: England	15	H2
Béchar: Algeria	68	D1
Beckemeyer: U.S.A.	58	C4
Beckley: U.S.A.	59	D4
Bedale: England	12	E2
Bedford: Canada	57	M4
Bedford: Ind., U.S.A.	51	F2
Bedford: Mass., U.S.A.	55	J2
Bedford: Pa., U.S.A.	54	B4
Bedfordshire: Co., Eng.	15	F2
Bedlington: England	12	E1
Bedworth: England	15	E2
Bee, Loch: Scotland	10	A2
Beeston: England	15	E2
Beeville: U.S.A.	50	C4
Bega: Australia	43	C5
Begovat: U.S.S.R.	29	K5
Behar see Bihar		
Beida: Libya	69	K2
Beijing see Peking	36	
Beijing Shih see Peking Shih	36	C1
Beira see Sofala	72	E2
BEIRUT: Lebanon	28	D7
Beiseker: Canada	60	C2
Beit Bridge: Zimbabwe	72	E3
Beja: Portugal	19	A5
Békéscaba: Hungary	20	D3
Bela: Pakistan	32	A3
Bel Air: U.S.A.	54	D5
Bela Vista do Tóldo: Brazil	66	D2
Belaya: r., U.S.S.R.	28	H3
Belaya Tserkov: U.S.S.R.	20	F3
Belcourt: Canada	56	H1
Belém: Brazil	64	J4
Belen: U.S.A.	53	C3
BELFAST: N. Ireland	13	F2
Belfast Lough: N. Ireland	13	F2
Belford: England	11	G4
Belfort: France	23	C2
Belgaum: India	32	B5
BELGIUM:	22	B1
Belgorod: U.S.S.R.	28	D3
BELGRADE: Yugoslavia	21	D4
Belitung (Billiton) i.: Indonesia	35	D11
BELIZE: Belize	48	J6
Belize: Belize	48	J6
Bellac: France	23	B2
Bella Coola: Canada	62	A1
Bellagio: Italy	25	B2
Bellary: India	32	C5
Bella Unión: Uruguay	66	C3
Bella Vista: Argentina	66	C2
Bellechasse: Co., Can.	57	P3
Belleek: N. Ireland	13	C2
Bellefonte: U.S.A.	54	C4
Belle Fourche: r., U.S.A.	53	E2
Bellegarde: France	23	C2
Belle Glade: U.S.A.	51	F4
Belle-Île-en-Mer: France	22	a i
Belle Isle, Strait of: Canada	47	Y6
Belle River: sett., Can.	56	C7
Belleterre: Canada	56	G2
Belleville: Canada	56	H5
Belleville: Pa., U.S.A.	54	C4
Bellevue: Canada	60	C2
Bellevue: U.S.A.	54	A4
Bellingham: England	12	D1
Bellingham: U.S.A.	62	B2
Bellinzona: Switz.	25	B2
Bellows Falls: town, U.S.A.	55	H1
Belluno: Italy	25	C2
Bell Ville: Argentina	66	B3
Bellwood: U.S.A.	54	B4
Belly: r., Canada	60	C2
Belmont: S. Africa	72	C2
Belmont: Canada	56	G4
Belmont: U.S.A.	54	C2
BELMOPAN: Belize	48	J6
Beloeil: Canada	57	M4
Belo Horizonte: Brazil	64	K7
Beloit: Kans., U.S.A.	58	A3
Beloit: Wis., U.S.A.	58	C3
Belorussia S.S.R.:	20	E2
Beltra, Lough: Irish Rep.	13	B3
Bel'tsy: U.S.S.R.	20	E3
Belturbet: Irish Rep.	13	D2
Belvidere: U.S.A.	58	C3
Belvidere Mt.: U.S.A.	57	M5
Belyando: r., Australia	42	C2
Bely Island: U.S.S.R.	29	K3
Bemidji: U.S.A.	58	B2
Ben Alder: mtn., Scot.	10	D3
Benalla: Australia	43	C5
Benbane Head: cape, N. Ireland	13	E1
Benbecula: i., Scotland	10	A2

Name	Page
Ben Chonzie: mtn., Scotland	10
Ben Cruachan: mtn., Scotland	10
Bend: U.S.A.	62
Bende: Nigeria	67
Ben Dearg: mtn., Scot.	10
Bendel: State, Nigeria	67
Bendery: U.S.S.R.	20
Bendigo: Australia	43
Ben Dorain: mtn., Scot.	10
Bengal, Bay of: Ind. O.	31
Benghazi: Libya	69
Bengough: Canada	61
Benguela: Angola	71
Ben Hope: mtn., Scot.	10
Beni: r., Bolivia	64
Benicarló: Spain	19
Benidorm: Spain	19
BENIN:	68
Benin, Bight of: Gulf of Guinea	68
Benin City: Nigeria	67
Beni Saf: Algeria	19
Benito: Canada	61
Ben Klibreck: mtn., Scotland	10
Ben Lawers: mtn., Scot.	10
Ben Ledi: mtn., Scot.	10
Benllech: Wales	14
Ben Lomond: mtn., Scotland	10
Ben Loyal: mtn., Scot.	10
Ben Macdhui: mtn., Scotland	10
Ben Mhor: mtn., Scotland	10
Ben More: mtn., Central, Scotland	10
Ben More: mtn., Mull., Scotland	10
Ben More Assynt: mtn., Scotland	10
Bennane Head: cape, Scotland	11
Ben Nevis: mtn., Scotland	10
Bennington: U.S.A.	57
Bénoué: r. & nat. park, Cameroun	67
Ben Rinnes: mtn., Scot.	10
Bensersiel: Ger. F.R.	24
Ben Sgritheall: mtn., Scotland	10
Bensheim: German F.R.	24
Benson: U.S.A.	63
Benson Lake: town, Canada	
Ben Starav: mtn., Scot.	10
Bentley: England	12
Bentley Blackfalds: Can.	60
Bento Gonçalves: Brazil	66
Benton: Ark., U.S.A.	50
Benton: Wis., U.S.A.	58
Benue: r. & State, Nigeria	67
Ben Vorlich: mtn., Scotland	10
Benwee Head: cape, Irish Rep.	13
Ben Wyvis: mtn., Scotland	10
Beppu: Japan	39
Berar: geog. reg., India	32
Berat: Albania	21
Berber: Sudan	69
Berbera: Somali Rep	69
Berchtesgaden: German F.R.	25
Berck-sur-Mer: France	22
Berdichev: U.S.S.R.	20
Beregovo: U.S.S.R.	20
Berens River: town & r., Canada	61
Berezniki: U.S.S.R.	29
Berezovo: U.S.S.R.	29
Bergama: Turkey	21
Bergamo: Italy	25
Bergamo Alps: Italy	25
Bergen: Norway	17
Bergen op Zoom: Neth.	24
Bergerac: France	23
Bergisch Gladbach: German F.R.	24
Bergstrasse Odenwald Nat. Park: Ger. F.R.	24
Berhampore: India	32
Berhampore: India	32
Beriso: Argentina	16
Berkåk: Norway	16
Berkeley: U.S.A.	63
Berkeley Springs: town, U.S.A.	54
Berkhamsted: England	15
Berkshire: Co., England	15
BERLIN: German D.R.	24
Berlin: German F.R.	24
Berlin: U.S.A.	57
Bermejo: r., Arg	66
Bermejo (old course): r., Argentina	66
BERMUDA:	49
BERN (Berne): Switz.	25
Bernard Lake: Canada	56
Berne see Bern	
Berneray: i., Scotland	10
Bernese Alps: Switz.	25
Bernierville: Canada	57
Bernina Pass: Switz.	25
Bernkastel: Ger. F.R.	24
Berry: Old Prov., Fr.	23
Berry Head: cape, Eng.	14
Berry Islands: Bahamas	51
Bersimis River: town, Canada	59
Berthier: Co., Canada	57
Berthierville: Canada	57
Bertraghboy Bay: Irish Rep.	13
Berwick-upon-Tweed: England	11
Berwyn: Canada	60
Berwyn: r., Wales	14
Besançon: France	23
Bessbrook: N. Ireland	13
Bessemer: U.S.A.	51
Bessines: France	23
Bethel: Alaska, U.S.A.	46
Bethel: Conn., U.S.A.	55
Bethel: U.S.A.	55
Bethesda: Wales	14
Bethlehem: S. Africa	72
Bethlehem: U.S.A.	54
Béthune: France	22
Betws y Coed: Wales	14
Beult: r., England	15
Beuvron: r., France	23
Beverley: Australia	12
Beverley: England	12

	Page	ref
…ly: Mass., U.S.A	55	K2
…ly: N.J., U.S.A	54	F4
…ley: England	14	D2
…l: England	15	G3
…rsa: U.S.S.R	28	C3
…s: France	23	B3
…alpur: India	32	E3
…am: Burma	38	B4
…agar: India	32	B4
…r.: India	32	C5
…aneswar: India	32	C4
…: India	32	B4
…AN	32/3	–
…a: Indonesia	35	K11
…stok: Poland	20	D2
…z: France	23	A3
…: Japan	39	D11
…ger: Ger. F.R.	25	B2
…: Brazil	66	b i
…ter: England	15	E3
…: Nigeria	67	B3
…: Nigeria	67	B2
…ford: U.S.A	57	P6
…ph: England	14	D1
…ord: England	14	B3
…ord (Barnstaple):		
…r: England	14	B3
…ra r.: Poland	20	D2
…: Switzerland	25	B2
…eld: Ger. F.R.	24	B1
…: Italy	25	B2
…eja Nat. Park: India	20	D2
…block: Pol.	20	C3
…at Canada	61	E3
…end Nat. Park: U.S.A	50	B4
…r.: Maine, U.S.A.	57	Q3
…ack r.: Miss., U.S.A	50	D3
…ue r.: U.S.A	53	F2
…Bay: England	14	C4
…au Pleine		
…: U.S.A	53	H2
…: town, U.S.A	58	B1
…servoir: U.S.A	58	B2
…ork: r., U.S.A	60	D1
…r: Scotland	10	E4
…r.: England	15	F2
…all Lake:		
…ada	57	J5
…ole: r., U.S.A	62	E2
…n: r., U.S.A	62	E2
…rn Mountains:		
…: U.S.A	52	D2
…ville: U.S.A	54	C5
…uddy Lake: Can.	61	E3
…ter: town, Can.	60	D2
…oux r.: U.S.A	61	F1
…: r., U.S.A	58	A3
…pring: town,		
…: U.S.A	50	B3
…ick Lake: Can.	60	D1
…one Lake: Can.	61	F2
…mber: U.S.A	61	E2
…alley town,		
…ada	62	D1
…ood: r., U.S.A	60	D3
…: Yugoslavia	21	C4
…State: India	32	C5
…: India	32	B4
…pur: India	32	D4
…ur: India	32	B4
…: Spain	19	B4
…cay: England	15	G3
…r Nat. Park:		
…tralia	43	B4
…ham: England	12	E2
…: Australia	42	B3
…rshurst: England	15	F3
…n i., see		
…: England	35	D11
…be: England	14	D4
…oe: Portland,		
…: Australia	42	D4
…bora: mtns.,		
…oslavia	20	C3
…: U.S.A	51	E3
…l Islands: The		
…hamas	51	G4
…enagh: mtn.,		
…rel. Rep	13	B1
…ter: Ger. F.R.	24	B2
…am: England	15	F2
…am: Maine, U.S.A	57	Q4
…am: Utah, U.S.A	63	D3
…amton: U.S.A	54	E2
…ey: England	12	E3
…: Indonesia	38	B6
…: Nigeria	67	A1
…: r., Indon.	35	C10
…u: Malaysia	38	C3
…: Tunisia	68	C1
…r.: Canada	60	C1
…Hills: town, Canada	61	D2
…Island: town, Canada	62	C1
…rio: Canada	56	D3
…Lake: Canada	60	C1
…Mts: Canada	60	C1
…: Australia	40	C4
…: Nepal	32	G4
…of Iran	30	G4
…head: England	12	C3
…: Romania	20	D3
…ngham: Eng	12	E2
…Kuda: Nigeria	67	B3
…Gwari: Nigeria	67	B3
…Kebbi: Nigeria	67	A1
…Nkoni: Nigeria	67	B3
…Tudu: Nigeria	67	B3
…dzhan: U.S.S.R	27	O8
…: Irish Rep	13	D3
…r.: Australia	43	C3
…: Canada	61	E2
…: Japan	39	c i
…a: U.S.A	57	Q4
…: Bay of: Fr./Sp	18/19	–
…Auckland: Eng	12	E2
…o's Castle: Scot.	11	D4
…o's Stortford: Eng	15	G3
…s Waltham: England	15	E4
…asi Lake: Can.	56	E4
…: Algeria	68	C3
…: U.S.A	53	E1
…rsk Archipelago:		
…ua-New Guinea	40	J1
…Guinea-Bissau	68	B6
…ala: Nigeria	67	C3
…: Canada	61	E2
…: Romania	20	D3
…: r., Rom	20	D3
…: Yugoslavia	21	D4
…ontein: S. Africa	72	B5
…Lake: Canada	61	D2

	Page	ref
Bitterroot Range: U.S.A	62	D2
Biu: Nigeria	67	C1
Biwa-ko: lake, Japan	39	C11
Biysk: U.S.S.R	29	O3
Black: r., Canada	56	F1
Black: r., U.S.A	50	D2
Black: r., Mich., U.S.A	56	A4
Black: r., Mich., U.S.A	56	C6
Black: r., N.Y., U.S.A	57	K6
Black: r., Wis., U.S.A	58	B3
Black Bear Island Lake: Canada	61	D1
Black Birch Lake: Canada	60	D1
Black Diamond: Canada	60	C2
Blackdown Hills: Eng	14	C4
Blackfoot: U.S.A	62	D3
Black Forest: Ger. F.R.	26	B2
Black Head: cape, England	14	A4
Black Head: cape, Irish Rep.	13	B3
Black Irtysh: r., Mong./U.S.S.R	29	O4
Black Island: Canada	61	D1
Black Isle: penin., Scotland	10	D1
Black Lake: Canada	61	D1
Black Lake: Sett. Quebec, Canada	57	O3
Black Lake: sett., Sask., Canada	61	D1
Black Lake: Mich., U.S.A	56	A4
Black Lake: N.Y., U.S.A	57	K5
Blackmoor, Vale of: Valley, England	14	D4
Black Mts: Wales	14	C3
Blackpool: England	12	C3
Black Rock Desert: U.S.A	63	C3
Black Sea	28	–
Blacksod Bay: Irish Republic	13	A4
Blackstairs Mt.: Irish Republic	13	E4
Black Sugar Loaf: The: mtn., Australia	43	D4
Blackwater: r., Eng	15	G3
Blackwater: r., Cork/Wat., Irish Rep.	13	C4
Blackwater: r., Meath: Irish Rep	13	E3
Blackwater Reservoir: Scotland	10	D3
Blackwood: r., Austl	42	b ii
Blaenau Ffestiniog: Wales	14	C2
Blagoveshchensk: U.S.S.R	27	P7
Blaine Lake: town, Canada	60	D1
Blainville: Canada	57	M4
Blair: U.S.A	58	A3
Blair Atholl: Australia	42	C2
Blairgowrie: Scotland	10	E3
Blairmore: Canada	60	C3
Blairstown: U.S.A	54	F4
Blakeney Point: Eng	15	H2
Blanc, Cape: Mauritania	68	B4
Blanc, Mont: France	23	B2
Blanco, Cape: U.S.A	62	B3
Blandford Forum: Eng	14	D4
Blanding: U.S.A	63	E4
Blanes: Spain	19	C4
Blankenberghe: Belg	22	B1
Blantyre: Malawi	72	F2
Blarney: Irish Rep	13	C5
Blasdell: U.S.A	54	B2
Blavet: r., France	22	a i
Blaye: France	23	A2
Bled: Yugoslavia	20	B3
Blenheim: Canada	56	C7
Blenheim: hist., Ger. F.R.	25	C2
Blenheim: N.Z	41	B3
Bletchley: England	15	F2
Blida: Algeria	19	C5
Blissfield: U.S.A	56	B3
Blitta: Togo	68	F7
Block Island: U.S.A	55	J3
Bloemfontein: South Africa	72	D4
Blois: France	23	B2
Bloodvein: r., Canada	61	F2
Bloody Foreland: cape, Irish Republic	13	C1
Bloomfield: U.S.A	55	H3
Bloomington: Ill., U.S.A	58	C3
Bloomington: Ind., U.S.A	58	C4
Bloomsburg: U.S.A	54	D3
Blossburg: U.S.A	54	C3
Bluefield: U.S.A	59	D4
Blue Mountain: Can.	57	L5
Blue Mountain: N.H., U.S.A	57	E5
Blue Mountain: r., U.S.A	54	D4
Blue Mountains: U.S.A	62	C2
Blue Nile: r., Ethiopia	69	N6
Blue Ridge: U.S.A	59	D4
Blue Ridge: U.S.A	51	F2
Blue River: town: Can	60	B2
Blue Stack Mts: Irish Republic	13	C2
Bluff: N.Z	41	A4
Blumenau: Brazil	66	E2
Blumenthal: Ger. F.R	24	B1
Blyth: r., England	12	E1
Blythe: r., England	15	H2
Blythe: U.S.A	63	D5
Blytheville: U.S.A	51	E3
Bo: Sierra Leone	68	C7
Boa Vista: Brazil	64	F3
Bobcaygeon: Canada	58	G5
Bobo Dioulasso: Upper Volta	68	E6
Bobruysk: U.S.S.R	20	E2
Bocholt: Ger. F.R	24	B1
Bochum: Ger. F.R	24	B1
Bodele Depression: Chad	69	J5
Boden: Sweden	16	D2
Bodensee: see Constance, Lake	25	B2
Bodensee Hegau: Nature Pk: Ger. F.R	25	B2
Boderg, Lough: Irish Republic	13	D3
Bodo Sadu: Nigeria	67	A2
Bodmin: England	14	B4
Bodmin Moor: England	14	B4
Bodø: Norway	16	C2
Bofin Lough: Irish Republic	13	D3

	Page	ref
Bogalusa: U.S.A	51	E3
Bogan: r., Austl	43	C4
Bogeragh Mts: Irish Republic	13	C4
Bognor Regis: England	15	F4
Bog of Allen: Irish Republic	13	D3
Bogong: Mt: Australia	43	C5
BOGOTÁ: Colombia	64	D3
Bohemian Forest: mtns. Czech./Ger. F.R	20	B3
Bohol: i.: Philippines	35	G9
Boise: r., U.S.A	62	C3
Boise: U.S.A	62	C3
Boissevain: Canada	61	E3
Bojador, Cape: W. Sahara	68	C3
Boju: Nigeria	67	B3
Bokani: Nigeria	67	B3
Bokaro: India	32	E4
Boké: Guinea	68	C6
Bokhara: r., Austl	43	C3
Boknafjorden: fd., Nor.	17	A4
Bokungu: Burma	38	B4
Bol: Yugoslavia	21	C4
Bolama: Guinea-Bissau	68	B6
Boland: r., Canada	56	D2
Bolan Pass: Pakistan	32	A3
Boldon: England	12	E2
Bolesławiec: Poland	20	C2
Bolivar: Mo., U.S.A	58	B4
Bolivar: N.Y., U.S.A	54	B2
BOLIVIA	64	F7
Bolkow: Canada	56	D2
Bollnäs: Sweden	17	C3
Bolmen: lake, Sweden	17	B4
Bolonda: Chad	67	C3
Bologna: Italy	25	C3
Bol'shevik: i., U.S.S.R	27	N2
Bolsover: England	15	F1
Bolt Head: cape, England	14	C4
Bolton: Canada	56	F6
Bolton: England	12	D3
Bolus Head: cape, Irish Republic	13	A5
Bolwiler: France	22	C2
Bolzano: Italy	25	C2
Boma: Zaire	71	B9
Bombala: Australia	43	C5
Bombay: India	32	B5
Bom Jesus: Brazil	66	D2
Bonaire: i., Neth. Antilles	49	N7
Bon, Cape: Tunisia	21	B5
Bondi Beach: Australia	43	E4
Bondo: Zaire	69	K8
Bondsville: U.S.A	55	H3
Bone, Gulf of: Indonesia	35	G11
Bo'ness: Scotland	11	E4
Bongor: Chad	67	D1
Bonifacio: Corsica	19	a i
Bonifacio, Strait of: Corsica/Sardinia	19	a i
Bonin Is: Pacific O.	44	D4
Bonn: Ger. F.R	24	B1
Bonner Springs: town, U.S.A	58	B4
Bonne Terre: U.S.A	58	B4
Bonnie Rock: Australia	42	b ii
Bonny: Nigeria	67	B3
Bonny, Bight of: Gulf of Guinea	68	G8
Bonnyville: Canada	60	C2
Boone: U.S.A	58	B3
Boonsboro: U.S.A	54	C5
Boonton: U.S.A	54	F4
Boonville: U.S.A	57	K6
Boothia Peninsula: Canada	47	R2
Bootle: England	12	C3
Boppard: German F.R	24	B1
Bopo: Nigeria	67	B3
Borah Peak: mtn., U.S.A	62	D3
Borås: Sweden	17	C4
Borboleta: Brazil	66	D1
Bordeaux: France	23	A3
Borden: i., Canada	46	N1
Border Forest Park: England	12	D1
Borden: Reg., Scot	11	F4
Bordertown: Australia	43	B5
Borehamwood: Eng	15	F3
Borel: Brazil	66	B2
Borger: U.S.A	50	B2
Borgholm: Sweden	17	C4
Borgo Valdi Taro: It.	25	B3
Borgu Game Reserve: Nigeria	67	A2
Borgund: Norway	16	A3
Borislav: U.S.S.R	20	D3
Borisoglebsk: U.S.S.R	28	E3
Borisov: U.S.S.R	20	E2
Borkum: i., Ger. F.R	24	B1
Borlänge: Sweden	17	C3
Bormio: Italy	25	B2
Borneo: i., S.E. Asia	35	E10
Bornholm: i., Den	17	B4
Borno: State, Nigeria	67	C1
Bornova: Turkey	21	E5
Boroughbridge: Eng	12	E2
Boscastle: England	14	B4
Boso-Hanto: penin., Japan	39	G iv
Bossier City: U.S.A	50	D3
Boss Mountain: town, Canada	60	B2
Bosso: Niger	68	H6
Boston: England	15	F2
Boston: U.S.A	55	K3
Boston Creek: sett., Canada	56	F1
Boston Mts: U.S.A	50	D2
Bostonnais: r., Canada	57	N2
Botany Bay: Australia	43	D4
Bothnia, Gulf of: Sweden/Finland	16/17	–
Botoşani: Romania	20	E3
BOTSWANA	72	–
Bottineau: U.S.A	61	E3
Bottrop: Ger. F.R	24	B1
Bouaké: Ivory Coast	68	E7
Boubandjian Nat Park: Cameroon	67	C2
Bouchemaine: France	22	a i
Boucherville: Canada	57	N1
Bougainville: i., Papua-New Guinea	40	J2
Boughton: England	15	F2
Boulder: Australia	42	e ii
Boulder: U.S.A	63	D4
Boulder City: U.S.A	63	D4
Boulogne: France	22	B1
Boundary Dam: U.S.A	62	C2
Boundary Peak: mtn.: U.S.A	63	C4
Bountiful: U.S.A	63	D3
Bounty Islands: N.Z	45	G8
Bourbonnais: Old Prov.: France	23	B2
Bourg: France	23	B2

	Page	ref
Bourges: France	23	B2
Bourg Madame: Fr	23	B3
Bourke: Australia	43	C4
Bourkes: Canada	56	F1
Bourlamaque: Can	56	H1
Bourne: England	15	F2
Bournemouth: England	15	E4
Bourntager Moor: Neth./Ger. F.R	24	B1
Bourton-on-the-Water: England	15	E3
Bou Saâda: Algeria	19	C5
Boussac: France	23	B2
Bouvet Island: Atl. O	8	L13
Bovey Tracey: England	14	C4
Bow: r., Canada	60	C2
Bowden: Canada	42	C2
Bowie: U.S.A	50	C3
Bow Island: town, Canada	60	C3
Bowland, Forest of: reg., England	12	D3
Bowling Green: Ky.: U.S.A	58	C4
Bowling Green: Ohio, U.S.A	56	B8
Bowling Green, Cape: Australia	42	C1
Bowman: U.S.A	53	E1
Bowmanville: Can	56	G6
Bowmore: Scotland	11	B4
Bowness: Canada	60	C2
Bowral: Australia	43	D4
Boyertown: U.S.A	54	E4
Boyle: Irish Rep	13	C3
Boyne: r., Irish Rep	13	E3
Boyne City: U.S.A	58	D2
Boyoma Falls: Zaire	70	E7
Bozeman: U.S.A	62	D2
Brabant: Prov.: Belgium	22	B1
Brač: i., Yugoslavia	21	C4
Bracadale, Loch: Scot	10	B2
Bracebridge: Canada	56	F5
Brackley: England	15	E2
Bracknell: England	15	F3
Bradenton: U.S.A	51	F4
Bradford: Canada	56	F5
Bradford: England	12	E3
Bradford: U.S.A	54	B3
Bradford-on-Avon: England	14	D3
Brady: U.S.A	50	C3
Braemar: Scotland	10	E2
Braemer: mtn.: Scot	10	E2
Braga: Portugal	19	A4
Bragado: Argentina	66	B4
Bragança: Brazil	66	a i
Bragança: Portugal	19	A4
Brahmani: r., India	32	D4
Brahmaputra (Tsangpo): r., India/China	33	F3
Braighe Mor: bay, Scotland	10	A1
Brăila: Romania	21	E3
Brainerd: U.S.A	58	B2
Braintree: England	15	G3
Brake: German F.R	24	B1
Bralorne: Canada	62	B1
Bramalea: Canada	56	F6
Bramhall: England	12	D3
Brampton: Canada	56	F6
Brampton: England	12	D2
Bran: r., Scotland	10	D2
Branco: r., Brazil	64	F3
Brandenburg: Ger. D.R	24	C1
Brandenburgh: Scot	10	E2
Brandon: Canada	61	E3
Brandon: England	15	G2
Brandon: U.S.A	55	M6
Brandon Bay: Irish Republic	13	A4
Brandon Mt.: Irish Republic	13	A4
Brandsen: Argentina	66	C4
Branford: U.S.A	55	H3
Brant: Co., Canada	56	E6
Brantford: Canada	56	E6
Brant Rock: town, U.S.A	55	K2
BRASÍLIA: Brazil	64	J7
Braşov: Romania	20	D3
Brasstown Bald: mtn., U.S.A	51	F3
Brassua Lake: U.S.A	57	Q4
Bratislava: Czech	20	C3
Bratsk: U.S.S.R	27	N6
Brattleboro: U.S.A	55	C2
Braunau: Austria	25	C2
Braunschweig, see Brunswick		
Braunton: England	14	B3
Brava, Sierra: ra., Argentina	66	A2
Brawley: U.S.A	63	C5
Bray: r., England	14	C3
Bray: Irish Rep	13	E3
Bray Head: cape, Irish Rep.	13	A5
Brazeau: Canada	62	C1
Brazeau: r., Canada	60	B2
Brazeau, Mt.: Canada	60	B2
BRAZIL	64	–
Brazil Basin: Atl. O	8	H9
Brazilian Highlands: Brazil	64	K7
Brazos: r., U.S.A	50	C4
Brazo Sur del Río Pilcomayo: r., Arg./Par	66	C1
BRAZZAVILLE: Congo	71	B8
Bream Down: penin., England	14	C3
Brechin: Scotland	10	F3
Breckenridge: U.S.A	58	A2
Brecon: Wales	14	C3
Brecon Beacons: mtns & nat park, Wales	14	C3
Breda: Netherlands	24	A1
Brede: r., England	15	G4
Bredy: U.S.S.R	29	K3
Bregenz: Austria	25	B2
Bréhat, Île: France	22	a i
Breidha Fjörd: Iceland	16	a i
Breisach: Ger. F.R	24	B2
Breiðafjörður, see Breidha Fjörd		
Bremen: German F.R	24	B1
Bremerhaven: Ger F.R	24	B1
Bremerton: U.S.A	62	B2
Brenner Pass: Italy/Austria	25	C2
Brent: Co., England	15	F3
Brentwood: U.S.A	55	G3
Brentwood: England	15	G3
Brescia: Italy	25	B2
Bressay: i., Shetland Is.	10	b i
Bressuire: France	22	A2
Brest: France	22	a i
Brest: U.S.S.R	20	D2

	Page	ref
Breton Sound: U.S.A	51	E4
Brett: r., England	15	G2
Brewarrina: Austl	43	C3
Brewster: U.S.A	55	G3
Brewton: U.S.A	51	E3
Briançon: France	23	C3
Briarcliffe: Canada	58	C1
Bride: r., Irish Rep	13	C4
Bridgehampton: U.S.A	55	H4
Bridgend: Wales	14	C3
Bridgenorth: Canada	56	G5
Bridge of Allan: Scot	11	E3
Bridgeport: Conn., U.S.A	55	G3
Bridgeport: Tex., U.S.A	50	C3
Bridgeton: U.S.A	54	E5
BRIDGETOWN: Barbados	49	P7
Bridgewater: U.S.A	55	K3
Bridgnorth: England	14	D2
Bridgton: U.S.A	57	P5
Bridgwater: England	14	C3
Bridgwater Bay: Eng	14	C3
Bridlington: England	12	F2
Bridport: England	14	D4
Brie: geog reg.: Fr	22	B2
Brienz: Lake: Switz	25	B2
Briey: France	22	C2
Brig: Switzerland	25	B2
Brigantine: U.S.A	55	F5
Brigg: England	12	F3
Brigham City: U.S.A	63	D3
Brighouse: England	12	E3
Brightlingsea: Eng	15	H3
Brighton: Canada	56	H5
Brighton: England	15	F4
Brims Ness: pt., Scot	10	E1
Brindisi: Italy	21	C4
Brisbane: Australia	42	D3
Bristol: England	14	D3
Bristol: Conn., U.S.A	55	H3
Bristol: N.H., U.S.A	57	O6
Bristol: N.Y., U.S.A	54	C2
Bristol: R.I., U.S.A	55	J3
Bristol: Tenn., U.S.A	51	F2
Bristol Bay: U.S.A	46	D5
Bristol Channel: est., England/Wales	14	C3
Britannia: Old Prov.: Fr	22	a i
British Columbia: Prov., Canada	46	K5
Britstown: S. Africa	72	C5
Britt: Canada	56	E4
Brittle, Loch: Scot	10	B2
Brive: France	23	B2
Brixham: England	14	C4
Brno: Czech	20	C3
Broadalbin: U.S.A	55	F1
Broadback: r., Can	56	E1
Broad Bay: Scotland	10	B1
Broadford: Scotland	10	C2
Broad Haven: bay, Irish Republic	13	B2
Broad Law: mtn., Scot	11	E4
Broad Sound: Australia	42	C2
Broadstairs: England	15	H3
Broadview: Canada	61	E2
Brochet: Canada	61	E1
Brochet, Lac: Canada	61	E1
Brochu: Canada	57	L1
Brocken: mtn., German D.R	24	C1
Brockport: U.S.A	54	C1
Brockton: U.S.A	55	J2
Brockville: Canada	57	K5
Brockway: Mont., U.S.A	53	D1
Brockway: Pa., U.S.A	54	C3
Brod: Yugoslavia	21	D4
Brodick: Scotland	11	C4
Broken Bow: U.S.A	53	F2
Broken Hill: town, Australia	43	B4
Broken Ridge: Ind. O	33	h viii
Brome: Canada	57	N4
Bromley: England	15	G3
Bromptonville: Canada	57	N4
Bromsgrove: England	14	D2
Bromyard: England	14	D2
Brookfield: U.S.A	55	H3
Brookhaven National Laboratory: U.S.A	55	H4
Brookings: Oreg., U.S.A	62	B3
Brookings: S. Dak., U.S.A	58	A3
Brooks: Canada	60	C2
Brooks Range: U.S.A	46	E3
Brooksville: Fla., U.S.A	51	F4
Broom, Loch: Scot	10	C1
Broome: Australia	40	C4
Brora: Scotland	10	E1
Brosna: r., Irish Rep	13	D3
Brothers: The: is., Arabian Sea	30	F8
Brough: England	12	D2
Brough Head: cape, Ork. Is	10	E1
Brown Clee Hill: Eng	14	D2
Brownfield: U.S.A	50	B3
Brownhills: England	15	E2
Brownlee Dam: U.S.A	62	C3
Brownsburg: Canada	57	L4
Brownsville: U.S.A	50	C5
Brown Willy: hill, England	14	B4
Brownwood: U.S.A	50	C3
Bruce: Co.: Canada	56	D5
Bruce Mines: Canada	56	D3
Bruce Peninsula: Can	56	D4
Bruchsal: Ger. F.R	24	B2
Bruderheim: Canada	60	C2
Brue: r., England	14	D3
Bruges (Brugge): Belgium	22	B1
Brühl: German F.R	24	B1
Bruneau: r., U.S.A	62	C3
BRUNEI	35	E10
Bruno: Canada	61	E2
Brunswick (Braunschweig): German F.R	24	C1
Brunswick: Ga., U.S.A	51	F3
Brunswick: Maine, U.S.A	57	Q6
Brunswick: Md., U.S.A	54	C5
Brusque: Brazil	66	E2
BRUSSELS: Belgium	22	B1
Bruton: England	14	D3
Bryansk: U.S.S.R	28	D3
Bryce Canyon Nat Park: U.S.A	63	D4
Bryher: i., Scilly Is	14	c iv
Brynmawr: Wales	14	C3
Bucaramanga: Colom	64	D2
Buchanan: Liberia	68	D7
Buchan Ness: pt., Scotland	10	G2
BUCHAREST: Romania	21	G2
Buckfastleigh: England	14	C4
Buckhaven: Scotland	11	E3
Buckie: Scotland	10	F2

	Page	ref
Buckingham: Canada	57	K4
Buckingham: England	15	F3
Buckinghamshire: Co., England	15	F3
Buckland Tableland: Australia	42	C2
Buckley: Wales	14	C1
BUDAPEST: Hungary	20	C3
Budd Lake: town, U.S.A	54	F4
Buddon Ness: pt.: Scot	10	F3
Bude: r., England	14	B4
Bude: England	14	B4
Budleigh Salterton: England	14	C4
Buea: Cameroon	67	B3
Buena Esperanza: Arg	66	A3
Buenaventura: Colom	64	C3
BUENOS AIRES: & Prov.: Argentina	66	C3
Buenos Aires: Lake: Argentina/Chile	65	D13
Buffalo: r., England	60	C1
Buffalo: N.Y., U.S.A	54	B2
Buffalo: Wyo., U.S.A	52	D2
Buffalo Head Hills: Canada	60	B1
Buffalo Lake: Canada	60	C2
Buffalo Narrows: Can	60	D1
Bug: r., Poland/U.S.S.R	20	D2
Bug: r., U.S.S.R	28	C4
Buguma: Nigeria	67	B3
Buhl: U.S.A	62	D3
Buie, Loch: Scotland	10	C3
Builth Wells: Wales	14	C2
BUJUMBURA: Burundi	71	E8
Bukachacha: U.S.S.R	27	O7
Bukama: Zaire	71	E9
Bukavu: U.S.S.R	29	J6
Bukittinggi: Indon	38	C7
Bukoba: Tanzania	71	F8
Bukuru: Nigeria	67	B2
Bulagan: Mongolia	34	C1
Bulawayo: Zimbabwe	72	D3
BULGARIA	25	D4
Buller: r. & Dist., N.Z	41	B3
Bullfinch: Australia	42	b ii
Bulloo: r. & lake	42	B3
Bull Point: England	14	B3
Bull Shoals Reservoir: U.S.A	58	B4
Bumba: Zaire	70	D7
Bumthang: Bhutan	33	F3
Bunbury: Australia	42	b ii
Buncrana: Irish Rep	13	D1
Bundaberg: Australia	42	D1
Bundoran: Irish Rep	13	C2
Bungay: England	15	H2
Bungersdorp: S. Africa	72	D5
Bungo-sudo: str.: Japan	39	B3
Bunker Group: is., Australia	42	D2
Bunnechere r.: Can	57	J4
Bunsuru: r., Nigeria	67	B1
Buntingford: England	15	F3
Bununu: Nigeria	67	B2
Bununu: Nigeria	67	A1
Buraimi: U.A.E	30	G6
Buratai: Nigeria	67	C1
Burdekin: r., Australia	42	C2
Bure: r., England	15	H2
Bureau, Lac: Canada	57	K1
Bureya: U.S.S.R	27	P8
Burford: Canada	56	E6
Burford: England	15	E3
Burgas: Bulgaria	21	E4
Burgdorf: Switz	25	B2
Burgess Hill: England	15	F4
Burghead: Scotland	10	E2
Burgos: Spain	19	B4
Burgundy: Old Prov.: Fr	23	B2
Burhou I.: Channel Is	14	a i
Burk's Falls: sett., Canada	56	F4
Burley: U.S.A	62	D3
Burlington: Canada	56	F6
Burlington: Colo., U.S.A	53	E3
Burlington Iowa, U.S.A	58	B3
Burlington: Mass., U.S.A	55	J2
Burlington N.J., U.S.A	54	F4
Burlington: N.C., U.S.A	51	G2
Burlington: Vt., U.S.A	55	G2
BURMA	38	–
Burnham Market: Eng	15	G2
Burnham-on-Crouch: England	15	G3
Burnham-on-Sea: Eng	14	C3
Burnie: Australia	40	b i
Burnley: England	12	D3
Burns: U.S.A	62	C3
Burntisland: Scot	11	E3
Burntwood: r., Can	61	F1
Burra: Australia	43	A4
Burrinjuck Reservoir: Australia	43	C4
Burrow Head: cape, Scotland	11	D5
Burry Port: Wales	14	B3
Burslem: England	14	D1
Burstall: Canada	60	D2
Burton Latimer: Eng	15	F2
Burton upon Trent: England	15	E2
Buru: i., Indonesia	35	H11
BURUNDI	71	E8
Burutu: Nigeria	67	B3
Burwell: England	15	G2
Burwell: U.S.A	58	A3
Bury: England	12	D3
Bury St Edmunds: Eng	15	G2
Bushey: England	15	F3
Bushire: Iran	30	F5
Busselton: Australia	42	b ii
Bute: i., Scotland	11	C4
Bute Inlet: Canada	60	A2
Butha Qi: China	34	G1
Butiaba: Uganda	71	F7
Butler: U.S.A	54	B4
Butte: U.S.A	62	D2
Butterworth: Malaysia	38	C5
Butterworth: S. Africa	72	D5
Butt of Lewis: hd., Scotland	10	B1
Button Bay: Canada	61	G1
Butung: i., India	35	G11
Buxton: England	15	E1
Buyaga: U.S.S.R	27	P6
Buzău: Romania	21	E4
Buzuluk: U.S.S.R	29	J3
Buzzards Bay: U.S.A	55	K3
Byam Martin I.: Can	46	P1
Bydgoszcz: Poland	20	C2
Byelorussian S.S.R: U.S.S.R	28	B3
Bylot I.: Canada	47	U2
Byron: U.S.A	57	P5
Bytom: Poland	20	C3

76 Caacupé/Chillicothe

	Page	ref.
Caacupé: Paraquay	66	C2
Caaguazú: Paraguay	66	C2
Caazapá: Paraguay	66	C2
Caballero: Paraguay	66	C2
Caballo Reservoir: U.S.A.	52	D4
Cabano: Canada	59	G2
Cabimas: Venezuela	49	M7
Cabinda: Angola	71	B8
Cabinet Gorge Dam: U.S.A.	62	C2
Cabo de Santa Marta: *cape*, Brazil	66	E2
Cabonga, Réservoir: Canada	57	J2
Cabora Bassa Dam: Mozambique	72	E2
Cabot Head: *pt.*, Can.	56	D4
Cabot Strait: Canada	47	Y7
Cabri: Canada	60	D2
Cabriel: *r.*, Spain	19	B5
Çaçador: Brazil	66	D2
Čačak: Yugoslavia	21	D4
Caçapava do Sul: Brazil	66	D3
Cacapon State Park: U.S.A.	54	B5
Cacequi: Brazil	66	D2
Cáceres: Spain	19	A5
Cache Bay: *sett.*, Can.	56	F3
Cachoeira do Sul: Brazil	66	D3
Cader Idris: *mtn.*, Wales	14	C2
Cadillac: Canada	56	G1
Cadillac: U.S.A.	58	C3
Cádiz: *& gulf*, Spain	19	A5
Caduna: Australia	40	E7
Caen: France	22	A2
Caerleon: Wales	14	D3
Caemarfon (Caernarvon): *& bay*, Wales	14	B1
Caerphilly: Wales	14	C3
Cafayate: Argentina	66	A2
Cagayan: Philippines	35	B9
Cágliari: *& gulf*, Sard.	19	a ii
Caha Mts.: Irish Rep.	13	B5
Caher I.: Irish Rep.	13	B3
Cahir: Irish Rep.	13	D4
Cahirciveen: Irish Rep.	13	A5
Cahore Point: Irish Rep.	13	E4
Cahors: France	23	B3
Caí: *& r.*, Brazil	66	D2
Caicos Is.: W. Indies	49	M5
Cairn Gorm: *mtn.*, Scotland	10	E2
Cairngorm Mts.: Scot.	10	E2
Cairns: Australia	40	H4
Cairns, Lake: Canada	61	G2
Cairnsmore: *mtn.*, Scot.	11	D4
CAIRO: Egypt	69	M2
Cairo: U.S.A.	56	B6
Caistor: England	12	F3
Calabar: Nigeria	67	B3
Calamian Group: *is.*, Phil.	35	F8
Calabozo: Venezuela	49	N8
Calabugie Lake: Can.	57	J4
Calahorra: Spain	19	B4
Calais: France	22	B1
Călărasi: Romania	21	E4
Calatayud: Spain	19	B4
Calcutta: India	32	E4
Caldas da Rainha: Port.	19	A5
Calder, Loch: Scotland	10	E1
Caldera: Chile	64	D9
Caldey I.: Wales	14	B3
Caldwell: U.S.A.	62	C3
Caledonia: Canada	56	F6
Caledonia: U.S.A.	54	C2
Calexico: U.S.A.	63	C5
Calf of Man: *i.*, I. of Man	12	B2
Calgary: Canada	60	C2
Calgary Point: Scot.	10	B3
Cali: Colombia	64	C3
Calicut: India	32	C6
Caliente: U.S.A.	63	D4
California: *State*, U.S.A.	63	–
California, Gulf of: Mex.	48	D4
Calipatria: U.S.A.	63	C5
Callan: Irish Rep.	13	D4
Callander: Canada	56	F3
Callander: Scotland	11	D3
Callao: Peru	64	C6
Calligary: Scotland	10	C2
Calling Lake: Canada	60	C1
Callington: England	14	B4
Calmar: Canada	60	C2
Calne: England	14	D3
Caltanissetta: Sicily	21	B5
Calvert City: U.S.A.	58	C4
Calvi: Corsica	19	a i
Calvinia: S. Africa	72	B5
Cam: *r.*, England	15	G2
Camaehigama, Lake: Canada	57	J2
Camagüey: Cuba	49	L5
Camaquã: *& r.*, Braz.	66	D3
Cambay: *& Gulf*, Ind.	32	B4
Camberley: England	15	F3
Cambourne: England	14	A4
Cambrai: France	22	B1
Cambrian Mts.: Wales	14	C2
Cambridge: Canada	56	E6
Cambridge: England	15	G2
Cambridge: N.Z.	41	C2
Cambridge: Md., U.S.A.	59	E4
Cambridge: Mass., U.S.A.	55	J2
Cambridge: N.Y., U.S.A.	55	G1
Cambridge Bay: Can.	46	O3
Cambridgeshire: *Co.*, England	15	G2
Camden: Australia	43	D4
Camden: England	15	F3
Camden: Ark., U.S.A.	50	D3
Camden: N.J., U.S.A.	54	E5
Camden: N.Y., U.S.A.	54	E1
Camdonagh: Irish Rep.	13	D1
Cameron: Ariz., U.S.A.	63	D4
Cameron: Tex., U.S.A.	50	C3
CAMEROUN	68	H8
Cameroun, Mt.: Cam.	67	B3
Camocim: Brazil	64	K4
Camooweal: Australia	40	F4
Camoustie: Scotland	10	F3
Campana: Argentina	66	C3
Campbell: *r.*, Austl.	42	C2
Campbell: *r.*, Canada	60	C2
Campbellford: Canada	56	H5
Campbell Is.: South O.	44	F12
Campbell River: *town*, Canada	62	A1
Campbells Bay: *sett.*, Canada	57	J4
Campbelltown: Austl.	43	D4
Campbelltown: Scot.	11	C4
Camp Borden: Canada	56	F5
Campeche: *& bay*, Mex.	48	H6
Camperdown: Australia	43	B5
Camperville: Canada	61	E2
Campina Grande: Brazil	64	L5
Campinas: Brazil	66	a i
Campine: *reg.*, Belg./Netherlands	22	C1
Campobasso: Italy	21	B4
Campo Erê: Brazil	66	D2
Campo Gallo: Argentina	66	B2
Campo Grande: Arg.	66	D2
Campo Grande: Brazil	64	H8
Campo Mourão: Brazil	66	D1
Campos do Jordão: Brazil	66	a i
Campos Novos: Brazil	66	D2
Campsie Fells: Scot.	11	D3
Camogne: *r.*, Irish Rep.	13	C4
Cam Ranh: Vietnam	38	D4
Camrose: Canada	60	C2
Can: *r.*, England	15	G3
Canaan: Conn., U.S.A.	55	G2
Canaan: N.Y., U.S.A.	55	G2
CANADA:	46/7	—
Canadaigua: *& lake*, U.S.A.	56	H7
Cañada de Gómez: Argentina	66	B3
Cañada Seca: Arg.	66	B3
Canadian: *r.*, U.S.A.	50	C3
Canajohane: U.S.A.	54	F2
Canakkale: Turkey	21	E4
Canandaigua: *& lake*, U.S.A.	54	C2
Canary Basin: Atl. O.	8	H5
Canary Islands: Atl. O.	68	C3
Canastota: U.S.A.	54	E1
CANBERRA: Australia	43	C5
Candelaria: Argentina	66	C2
Candle Lake: *sett.*, Canada	61	D2
Candlewood, Lake: U.S.A.	55	G3
Candor: U.S.A.	54	D2
Canelones: Uruguay	66	C3
Canguçu: Brazil	66	D3
Canisp: *mtn.*, Scotland	10	D1
Canisteo: *& r.*, U.S.A.	54	C2
Cankırı: Turkey	28	C5
Canmore: Canada	60	B2
Canna: *i & Sound*, Scotland	10	B2
Cannes: France	23	C3
Cannock: England	14	D2
Cannonball: *r.*, U.S.A.	53	E1
Canoas: *& r.*, Brazil	66	D2
Canoe Lake: Canada	60	D1
Canon City: U.S.A.	53	D3
Canora: Canada	61	E2
Cantagalo, Ponta: *pt.*, Brazil	66	E2
Canterbury: England	15	H3
Canterbury Bight: N.Z.	41	B3
Canterbury Plains: N.Z.	41	B3
Can Tho: Vietnam	38	D5
Canton (Guangzhou): China	37	B5
Canton: Ill., U.S.A.	58	B3
Canton: Maine, U.S.A.	57	P5
Canton: Mass., U.S.A.	55	J2
Canton: N.Y., U.S.A.	57	K5
Canton: Ohio, U.S.A.	59	D3
Canton: Pa., U.S.A.	54	D3
Canton: S. Dak., U.S.A.	58	A3
Cantu: *r.*, Brazil	66	D1
Cañuelas: Argentina	66	C4
Canudos: Brazil	64	G5
Canvey: England	15	G3
Canyon de Chelly Nat. Monument: U.S.A.	63	E4
Canyon Ferry Dam: U.S.A.	62	D2
Canyonlands Nat. Park: U.S.A.	63	E4
Cao Bang: Vietnam	38	D2
Cap à l'Aigle: *sett.*, Can.	57	P2
Cap de la Madeleine: *town*, Canada	57	N3
Cape Basin: Atl. O.	8	L11
Cape Breton I.: Can.	47	Y7
Cape Canaveral: *town*, U.S.A.	51	F4
Cape Charles: *town*, U.S.A.	59	E4
Cape Clear: Irish Rep.	13	B5
Cape Cod Bay: U.S.A.	55	K3
Cape Cod Canal: U.S.A.	55	K3
Cape Cod National Seashore: U.S.A.	55	K3
Cape Elizabeth: *sett.*, U.S.A.	57	P6
Cape Fear: *r.*, U.S.A.	51	G3
Cape Girardeau: *town*, U.S.A.	58	C4
Cape Hatteras National Seashore: U.S.A.	51	G2
Cape May Court House: *town*, U.S.A.	54	F5
Cape Parry: Canada	46	L2
Cape Province: S. Afr.	72	–
Capital Reef Nat. Monument: U.S.A.	63	D4
Cape Rise: Atl. O.	8	M12
Cape Town: S. Africa	72	B5
Cape Verde Basin: Atlantic Ocean	8	H5
CAPE VERDE:	8	H6
Cape York Peninsula: Australia	40	G3/4
Cape Wrath: Scotland	10	C1
Cap-Haïtien: Haiti	49	M6
Capiibary: *r.*, Paraguay	66	C1
Capitachouane: *r.*, Can.	57	J2
Capitachouane, Lac: Canada	57	K1
Capivari: Brazil	66	a i
Capoompeta, Mt.: Australia	43	D3
Capreol: Canada	56	E3
Capri: *i.*, Italy	21	B4
Capricorn Channel: Australia	42	D2
Capricorn Group: *is.*, Australia	42	D2
Caprivi Strip: *reg.*, Namibia	72	C2
Captain's Flat: Austl.	43	C5
CARACAS: Venezuela	49	N7
Caragh, Lough: Irish Republic	13	B4
Carapá: *r.*, Paraguay	66	C1
Carapé, Sierra: *ra.*, Uruguay	66	D3
Caravelas: Brazil	64	L7
Carayaó: Paraguay	66	C2
Caràzinho: Brazil	66	D2
Carberry: Canada	61	F3
Carbondale: Ill., U.S.A.	58	C4
Carbondale: Pa., U.S.A.	54	E3
Carbonia: Sardinia	19	a ii
Carcaraña: *& r.*, Arg.	66	B3
Carcassonne: France	23	B3
Cardamon Hills: India	32	C6
CARDIFF: Wales	14	C3
Cardigan: *& bay*, Wales	14	B2
Cardinal: Canada	57	K5
Cardona: Uruguay	66	C3
Cardoso, Ilha do: *i.*, Brazil	66	E2
Cardston: Canada	60	C3
Carey: *r.*, England	14	B4
Carey, Lake: Australia	42	c i
Caribbean Sea:	49	–
Cariboo: *& r.*, Canada	61	F1
Caribou Mts.: Canada	60	B1
Carinthia: *State*, Austria	25	C2
Carleton: U.S.A.	56	B7
Carleton Place: Canada	57	J4
Carlin: U.S.A.	63	C3
Carlingford Lough: N. Ireland/Irish Rep.	13	E2
Carlisle: England	12	D2
Carlisle: U.S.A.	54	C4
Carlos Beguerie: Arg.	66	C4
Carlow: *& Co.*, Irish Republic	13	E4
Carlsbad: U.S.A.	53	E4
Carlsbad Caverns Nat. Park: U.S.A.	53	E4
Carlsberg Ridge: Ind. O.	33	e iv
Carlton: England	15	E2
Carluke: Scotland	11	E4
Carlyle: Canada	61	E3
Carmacks: Canada	46	H4
Carman: Canada	61	F3
Carmarthen: *& bay*, Wales	14	B3
Carmaux: France	23	B3
Carmel Head: *cape*, Wales	12	B3
Carmelo: Uruguay	66	C3
Carmen: Uruguay	66	C3
Carmen de Areco: Arg.	66	B3
Carnac: France	22	a i
Carnarvon: Australia	40	A5
Carnarvon: S. Africa	72	C5
Carnarvon Gorge Nat. Park: Austl.	42	C2
Carnarvon Range: Australia	42	C3
Carnduff: Canada	61	E3
Carnegie Ridge: Pac. O.	45	R7
Carneige: *mtn.*, Scot.	10	C2
Carnforth: England	12	D2
Carnia: Italy	25	C2
Carnic Alps: Italy	25	C2
Carnsore Point: Irish Republic	13	E4
Carolina: Brazil	64	J5
Caroline Island: Pac. O.	45	L7
Caroline Is.: Pac. O.	45	K9
Caroni: *r.*, Venezuela	64	F2
Carpathians: *mts.*, Europe	20	D3
Carpentaria, Gulf of: Australia	40	F3
Carpentras: France	23	C3
Carpolac: Australia	43	B5
Carrabasset: *r.*, U.S.A.	57	P5
Carrara: Italy	25	C3
Carrauntouhil Reeks: *mtns.*, Irish Rep.	13	B5
Carre, Lough: Irish Rep.	13	B3
Carrickfergus: N. Irel.	13	F2
Carrickmacross: Irish Republic	13	E3
Carrick-on-Shannon: Irish Rep.	13	C3
Carrick-on-Suir: Irish Rep.	13	D4
Carrière, Lac: Canada	56	H2
Carrolltown: U.S.A.	54	B4
Carron: *r. & lake*, Scotland	10	C2
Carrot River: *town & r.*, Canada	61	E2
Carrowmore Lough: Irish Republic	13	B2
Carse of Gowrie: *geog. reg.*, Scot.	10	E3
Carson City: U.S.A.	63	C4
Carson Sink: *salt flat*, U.S.A.	63	C4
Carstairs: Canada	60	C2
Cartagena: Colom.	49	L7
Cartagena: Spain	19	B5
Carteret: France	22	a i
Carteret: U.S.A.	55	F4
Carthage: Mo., U.S.A.	58	B4
Carthage: N.Y., U.S.A.	57	K6
Carthage: Tex., U.S.A.	50	D3
Cartier: Canada	56	D3
Carvin: France	22	B1
Casablanca *see* El Dar el Beida	68	D2
Casa Grande: U.S.A.	63	D5
Casale Monferrato: It.	25	B2
Cascade Range: U.S.A./Canada	62	–
Cascavel: Brazil	66	D1
Casco Bay: U.S.A.	57	P6
Caserta: Italy	21	B4
Cashel: Irish Rep.	13	D4
Casilda: Argentina	66	B3
Casino: Australia	43	D3
Casiquiare: *r.*, Ven.	64	E3
Casper: U.S.A.	52	D2
Caspian Lowlands: U.S.S.R.	28	G4
Caspian Sea: U.S.S.R./Iran	28	–
Casquet Banks: Channel Islands	14	a i
Cass: *r.*, U.S.A.	56	B6
Cass City: U.S.A.	56	B6
Cassel: France	22	B1
Casselman: Canada	57	K4
Cassino: Brazil	66	D3
Cassino: Italy	21	B4
Castelli: Argentina	66	B2
Castellón de la Plana: Spain	19	B5
Castelo Branco: Port.	19	A5
Castile: U.S.A.	54	B2
Castillos: Uruguay	66	D3
Castillos, Laguna de: Uruguay	66	D3
Castlebar: Irish Rep.	13	B3
Castlebay: Scotland	10	A3
Castlebellingham: Irish Republic	13	E3
Castleblaney: Irish Rep.	13	E2
Castle Cary: England	14	D3
Castlecorner: Irish Republic	13	D4
Castlederg: N. Ireland	13	D2
Castle Donington: Eng.	15	E2
Castle Douglas: Scot.	11	E5
Castleford: England	12	E3
Castlegar: Canada	62	C2
Castleisland: Irish Rep.	13	B4
Castlemaine: Australia	43	B5
Castlepollard: Irish Republic	13	D3
Castlerea: Irish Rep.	13	C3
Castleton-on-Hudson: U.S.A.	55	G2
Castletown: I. of Man	12	B2
Castor: Canada	60	C2
Castres: France	23	B3
Castro: Brazil	66	D1
Catamarca: *& Prov.*, Argentina	66	A2
Catania: Sicily	21	C5
Catanzaro: Italy	21	C5
Cataratas del Iguazú: *falls*, Arg./Brazil	66	D2
Catastrophe, Cape: Australia	40	F8
Catawissa: U.S.A.	54	D4
Caterham: England	15	F3
Cat Island: The Bahamas	49	L5
Catoche, Cape: Mex.	49	J5
Catskill: U.S.A.	55	G2
Catskill Mountains: U.S.A.	55	F2
Catskill Forest Reserve: U.S.A.	54/5	F2
Cattaraugus: U.S.A.	54	B2
Cattaraugus Creek: U.S.A.	54	B2
Catterick Camp: Eng.	12	E2
Cauca: *r.*, Colombia	64	C2
Caucasus Mts.: U.S.S.R.	28	E5
Causse du Larzac: *plat.*, France	23	B3
Cauvery: *r.*, India	32	C6
Cavaillon: France	23	C2
Cavalier: U.S.A.	61	F3
Cavan: *& Co.*, Irish Republic	13	D3
Caveiras: *r.*, Brazil	66	D2
Caxambu: Brazil	66	b i
Caxias do Sul: Brazil	66	D2
Cayenne: Fr. Gu.	64	H2
Cayman Is.: W. Indies	49	K6
Cayuga: Canada	56	F7
Cayuga Lake: U.S.A.	54	D2
Cazenovia: U.S.A.	54	E2
Cebollatí: *r.*, Uru.	66	D3
Cebu: *& i.*, Philippines	35	G8
Cecil Lake: *sett.*, Can.	60	A1
Cedar: *r.*, Iowa, U.S.A.	58	B3
Cedar City: U.S.A.	63	D4
Cedar Falls: *town*, U.S.A.	58	B3
Cedar Lake: Man., Canada	61	E1
Cedar Lake: Ont., Can.	56	G2
Cedar Point: U.S.A.	56	B8
Cedar Rapids: *city*, U.S.A.	58	B3
Cedarville: U.S.A.	54	E5
Cegléd: Hungary	20	C3
Celebes (Sulawesi): *i.*, Indonesia	35	G11
Celebes Sea: Indon.	35	G10
Celje: Yugoslavia	20	C3
Cellar Head: *cape*, Scotland	10	B1
Celle: German F.R.	24	C1
Celyn, Llyn: *lake*, Wales	14	C2
Center: U.S.A.	55	G3
Center Moriches: U.S.A.	55	H4
Centerville: U.S.A.	58	B3
CENTRAL AFRICAN EMPIRE:	69	K7
Central Butte: Can.	60	D2
Central City: U.S.A.	54	B4
Centralia: Ill., U.S.A.	58	C4
Centralia: Wash., U.S.A.	62	B2
Central: *Reg.*, Scot.	10/11	D3
Central Pacific Basin: Pacific Ocean	44	H6
Central Range: Papua New Guinea	40	G2
Central Siberian Plain: U.S.S.R.	27	–
Central Village: U.S.A.	55	J3
Centreville: U.S.A.	54	D5
Cephalonia: *i.*, Greece	21	D5
Ceram: *i & sea*, Indon.	35	H11
Ceres: Argentina	66	B2
Cerro de Pasco: Peru	64	C6
Cesena: Italy	25	C3
Cēsis: U.S.S.R.	17	E4
České Budějovice: Czechoslovakia	20	B3
Cessnock: Australia	43	D4
Cetraro: Italy	21	C5
Ceuta: Spain	19	A5
Cévennes: *mtns.*, Fr.	23	B3
Chablis: France	22	B2
Chacabuco: Argentina	66	B3
Chachile: Nigeria	67	C1
Chachoengsao: Thai.	38	C4
Chaco: *Prov.*, Arg.	66	B2
Chaco Austral: *geog. reg.*, Argentina	66	B2
Chaco Central: *geog. reg.*, Argentina	66	C2
CHAD:	69	J6
Chad, Lake: Africa	68	H6
Chafe: Nigeria	67	B1
Chagos-Laccadive Plateau: Indian O.	33	f v
Chagrin Falls: *sett.*, U.S.A.	56	D8
Chahan, Lake: China	36	B1
Chaîne de l'Étoile: *hills*, France	23	C3
Chajarí: Argentina	66	C3
Chala: Peru	64	D7
Chalawa: *r.*, Nigeria	67	B1
Chaling: China	37	B4
Chalk River: *sett.*, Canada	56	H3
Châlons-sur-Marne: Fr.	22	B2
Chalon-sur-Saône: Fr.	23	B2
Chaman: Pakistan	32	A2
Chamba: India	32	C2
Chambal: *r.*, India	32	C3
Chamberlain: U.S.A.	53	F2
Chamberlain, Lake: U.S.A.	59	G2
Chambersburg: U.S.A.	54	C5
Chambéry: France	23	C2
Chamboro: Canada	57	N1
Chamical: Argentina	66	A3
Chamonix: France	23	C2
Chamouchouane: *r.*, Canada	59	F2
Champagne: *Old Prov.*, France	22	B2
Champagne Pouilleuse: *geog. reg.*, France	22	B2
Champaign: U.S.A.	58	C3
Champaqui: *mtn.*, Arg.	66	B3
Champlain: *Co.*, Can.	57	M2
Champlain, Lake: U.S.A.	57	M6
Champlain Canal: U.S.A.	57	M6
Chañaral: Chile	64	D9
Chandler: U.S.A.	63	D5
Chang: *r.*, China	36	B2
Changchih: China	36	B2
Changchow: Fukien, China	37	C5
Changchow: Kiangsu, China	36	C3
Changchuan: *i.*, China	37	B5
Changchun: China	34	H2
Changhua: China	37	C3
Changhua: Taiwan	37	D5
Chanhuang: China	37	A5
Changki: *r.*, China	37	A4
Changkiakow (Kalgan): China	36	B1
Changko: China	36	B3
Changli: China	36	C2
Changlo: China	37	C4
Changning: China	37	B4
Changping: China	37	C4
Changpu: China	37	C5
Changshan: China	37	C4
Changshow: China	37	A4
Changshu: China	37	D3
Changsing: *r.*, China	36	D2
Changteh: China	37	B4
Changting: China	37	C4
Changtu: China	34	B4
Changwu: China	36	A2
Changyuan: China	36	B2
Channel Islands: U.K.	14	a ii
Chanthaburi: Thailand	38	C4
Chanute: U.S.A.	58	A4
Chany, Lake: U.S.S.R.	29	M3
Chao: *r.*, China	36	C1
Chao, Lake: China	37	C3
Chaoan: China	37	C5
Chaoan: China	37	C5
Chaoping: China	37	B5
Chaotung: China	38	C1
Chaoyan: China	36	D2
Chaoyang: Kwangtung, China	37	C5
Chaoyang: Liaoning, China	36	D1
Chaoyangchen: China	34	H2
Chapala, Lake: Mex.	48	F5
Chapayevsk: U.S.S.R.	28	F3
Chapecó: *& r.*, Brazil	66	D2
Chapleau: Canada	56	B2
Chapleau: *r.*, Canada	56	B1
Chaplin Lake: Canada	60	D2
Chapra: India	32	D3
Charadai: Argentina	66	C2
Charata: Argentina	66	B2
Charcot I.: Antarc.	65	C17
Chard: England	14	D4
Chardon: U.S.A.	56	D8
Chardzhou: U.S.S.R.	29	J6
Charente: *r.*, France	23	A2
Chari: *r.*, Chad	68	J6
Chariton: *r.*, U.S.A.	58	B3
Charlbury: England	15	E3
Charleroi: Belgium	22	B1
Charles, Cape: U.S.A.	59	E4
Charles, Peak: *mtn.*, Austl.	42	c ii
Charles City: U.S.A.	58	B3
Charles Lake: Canada	60	C1
Charleston: Ill., U.S.A.	58	C4
Charleston: S.C., U.S.A.	51	F3
Charleston: W. Va., U.S.A.	59	D4
Charleston Lake: Can.	57	J5
Charles Town: U.S.A.	54	C5
Charlestown: U.S.A.	55	H1
Charlestown of Aberlour: Scotland	10	E2
Charleville: Australia	42	C3
Charleville: France	22	B2
Charlevoix: *Co.*, Can.	57	P2
Charlotte: U.S.A.	51	F2
Charlotte Harbour: U.S.A.	51	F4
Charlottesville: Va., U.S.A.	59	E4
Charlottetown: Can.	47	X7
Charny: Canada	57	O3
Charollais, Monts du: France	23	B2
Charolles: France	23	B2
Charron Lake: Canada	61	G2
Chartres: France	22	B2
Chascomús: Argentina	66	C4
Château, Pointe du: Fr.	22	a i
Châteaubriant: France	22	A2
Chateaudun: France	22	B2
Chateauguay: Canada	57	M4
Chateau Renault: Fr.	23	B2
Châteauroux: France	23	B2
Château-Thierry: Fr.	22	B2
Chateauvert, Lac: Can.	57	M2
Chateh: Canada	60	B1
Châtelaillon: France	23	A2
Chatellerault: France	23	B2
Chatham: Canada	56	C7
Chatham: England	15	G3
Chatham: Mass., U.S.A.	55	K3
Chatham: N.Y., U.S.A.	55	G2
Chatham Is.: Pac. O.	44	H11
Chatham Rise: Pac. O.	44	G11
Châtillon-sur-Seine: France	22	B2
Chatrapur: India	32	D5
Chattahoochee: *& r.*, U.S.A.	51	E3
Chattanooga: U.S.A.	51	E2
Chattens: England	15	G2
Chaudière: *r.*, Can.	57	O3
Chaumont: France	22	C2
Chausey, Îles de: Fr.	22	a i
Chautauqua Lake: U.S.A.	56	F7
Chazy: U.S.A.	57	M5
Cheadle: Gtr. Man., England	12	D3
Cheadle: Staffs., Eng.	15	E2
Cheaha Mt.: U.S.A.	51	E3
Cheb: Czech.	24	C1
Cheboksary: U.S.S.R.	28	F2
Cheboygan: U.S.A.	56	A4
Checheng: China	36	C3
Cheddar: England	14	D3
Cheektowaga: U.S.A.	56	G7
Cheho: China	37	A5
Cheju (Quelpart) I.: South Korea	34	H4
Chekiang (Zhejiang): *Prov.*, China	37	C4
Chekunda: U.S.S.R.	27	Q7
Cheleken: U.S.S.R.	28	G6
Cheli: China	38	C2
Chéliff: *r.*, Algeria	19	C5
Chelkar-Tengiz, Lake: U.S.S.R.	29	J4
Chelm: Poland	20	D2
Chelmsford: Canada	56	D3
Chelmsford: England	15	G3
Chelsea: U.S.A.	56	A7
Cheltenham: Eng.	14	D3
Chelyabinsk: U.S.S.R.	29	J2
Chelyuskin, Cape: U.S.S.R.	27	N2
Chemnitz *see* Karl-Marx-Stadt		
Chenab: *r.*, Ind./Pak.	32	C2
Chengan: China	37	A4
Cheng'an: China	36	B2
Chengchow (Zhengzhou): China	36	
Chengho: China	37	
Chenghsien: China	37	
Chengkiang: China	38	
Chengpu: China	37	
Chengteh (Jehol): China	36	
Chengting: China	36	
Chengtu (Chengdu): China	34	
Chengyang: China	36	
Chenhsien: China	37	
Chenki: China	37	
Chenping: China	36	
Chentung: China	34	
Chenyuan: China	37	
Chepes: Argentina	66	
Chepstow: Wales	14	
Cher: *r.*, France	23	
Cheraw: U.S.A.	51	
Cherbourg: France	22	
Cherchell: Algeria	19	
Cherdoyak: U.S.S.R.	29	
Cheremkhovo: U.S.S.R.	27	
Cherepovets: U.S.S.R.	28	
Chernogorsk: U.S.S.R.	29	
Chernovtsy: U.S.S.R.	20	
Chernyakhovsk: U.S.S.R.	17	
Cherokees, Lake of the: U.S.A.	58	
Cherrapunji: India	33	
Cherry Valley: *town*, U.S.A.	54	
Cherskiy Range: U.S.S.R.	27	
Chertsey: England	15	
Chervonograd: U.S.S.R.	20	
Cherwell: *r.*, England	15	
Chesaning: U.S.A.	56	
Chesapeake Bay: U.S.A.	59	
Chesham: England	15	
Cheshire: U.S.A.	55	
Cheshire: *Co.*, Eng.	14	
Cheshunt: England	15	
Chesil Beach: Eng.	14	
Chesire: Conn., U.S.A.	55	
Chesley: Canada	56	
Chester: England	14	
Chester: Mass., U.S.A.	55	
Chester: N.Y., U.S.A.	55	
Chester: Pa., U.S.A.	54	
Chesterfield: England	15	
Chesterfield Inlet: *sett.*, Canada	47	
Chesterfield Is.: Coral Sea	40	
Chester-le-Street: England	12	
Chestertown: U.S.A.	54	
Chesterville: Can.	57	
Chesuncook Lake: U.S.A.	59	
Cheviot: *mtn.*, Eng.	11	
Cheviot Hills: Eng./Scotland	11	
Chew Valley Lake: England	14	
Cheyenne: *& r.*, U.S.A.	53	
Cheyenne Wells: *town*, U.S.A.	53	
Cheyne Bay: Austl.	42	
Chhindwara: India	32	
Chi: *r.*, Thailand	38	
Chiaho: China	37	
Chiahsien: China	36	
Chiai: Taiwan	37	
Chiang Doa: Thailand	38	
Chiang Mai: Thailand	38	
Chiang Rai: Thailand	38	
Chiangyin: China	36	
Chiaocheng: China	36	
Chiaoling: China	37	
Chiari: Italy	25	
Chiashan: Anhwei, China	36	
Chiashan: Chekiang, China	37	
Chiayu: China	37	
Chiba: *& Pref.*, Japan	39	
Chibia: Angola	72	
Chiblow Lake: Can.	56	
Chibougamau: Can.	47	
Chibougamou Park: Canada	59	
Chibuto: Mozambique	72	
Chica, Sierra: *ra.*, Arg.	66	
Chicago: U.S.A.	58	
Chichagof I.: U.S.A.	46	
Chichén Itzá: Mex.	48	
Chicheng: China	36	
Chichester: England	15	
Chichibu: Japan	39	
Chichibu-tama-kokuritsu-kōen: *nat. park*, Japan	39	
Chickasha: U.S.A.	50	
Chiclayo: Peru	64	
Chico: *r.*, Chubut, Argentina	65	
Chico: *r.*, Tucuman, Argentina	66	
Chico: U.S.A.	63	
Chicopee: U.S.A.	55	
Chicoutimi: *& r.*, Can.	57	
Chicoutimi Park: Can.	59	
Chiefs Point: Can.	56	
Chieh-hsiu: China	36	
Chiehshih: China	37	
Chiehyang: China	37	
Chiemsee: *l.*, Ger. F.R.	25	
Chienping: China	36	
Chienyang: China	37	
Chieti: Italy	21	
Chigasaki: Japan	39	
Chihfeng: China	34	
Chihing: China	37	
Chihkiang: China	37	
Chihli, Gulf of: China	36	
Chiho: China	36	
Chihsien: Honan, China	36	
Chihsien: Honan, China	36	
Chihsien: Hopeh, China	36	
Chihsien: Shansi, China	36	
Chihuahua: Mexico	48	
Chiki: China	37	
Chilantai: China	36	
Chilaw: Sri Lanka	32	
Chilcotin: *r.*, Canada	62	
Childers: Australia	42	
Childress: U.S.A.	50	
CHILE	64/5	
Chile Basin: Pacific O.	45	
Chile Rise: Pacific O.	45	
Chillán: Chile	65	
Chillicothe: Mo., U.S.A.	58	

Name	Page	ref
...cothe: Ohio. U.S.A	58	D4
...wack: Canada	62	B2
...é Island: Chile	65	D12
...im Hills: Eng	15	F3
...ay: Belgium	24	B2
...borazo: volc. Ec	64	C4
...bote: Peru	64	C5
...kent: U.S.S.R	25	K5
...o: China	36	D2
...: China	34	—
...andega: Nicaragua	48	J7
...hago r.: Canada	60	B5
...hi: China	37	C4
...hilia: Australia	43	D3
...hou: China	37	A5
...chow: China	36	D1
...twin r.: China	38	B1
...ngchiang: China	36	D3
...o: China	37	C3
...hsien: Hunan, China	37	A4
...nghsing: China	36	B2
...gshu: China	36	A3
...g: China	37	C3
...ngdezhen): China	37	C4
...ngtien): China	37	D4
...ng: China	37	C3
...guyan see Paoting	36	C2
...Divis: Burma	38	A2
...ni: China	36	D1
...na: Liaoning, China	36	D1
...hsien: Liaoning, China	36	D2
...na: Shansi, China	36	B2
...iang: China	36	C3
...kow: China	37	B3
...hampo: N Korea	34	H3
...n: France	23	A4
...shui: China	37	A4
...shui: China	36	D4
...an Chn: China	36	C3
...wangtao: China	36	C2
...ngia: Italy	25	C2
...a: Zambia	72	E1
...enham: England	14	D3
...ewa r.: U.S.A (...ewa Falls n. U.S.A)	58	B3
...ing Camden: Eng	15	E2
...ing Ongar: Eng	15	G3
...ing Norton: Eng	15	E3
...ing Sodbury: Eng	14	D3
...jitos Plateau: Bol	64	F7
...: Japan	39	d ii
...: Lake: sett.: Can	61	E1
...olm: U.S.A	57	P5
...o: China	37	C4
...mao: Somali Rep	70	H8
...: Japan	39	c ii
...: China	27	O7
...Hanto: penin., an	39	c ii
...se: Japan	39	D1
...al: Pakistan	32	B1
...gong: Bangl	33	F4
...ang: Kiangsu, China	36	D3
...na: Shantung, China	36	C2
...coy: Argentina	66	B3
...an: China	36	B2
...awhatchee r. S.A	51	E3
...: Japan	39	f iv
...ma: China	36	C2
...alsan: Mongolia	34	E1
...eland: Canada	61	E2
...lomon:	40	K2
...t: France	23	A2
...é: Cameroon	67	C2
...n: Vietnam	38	D4
...: China	36	C1
...jin: N Korea	34	H2
...ungking	37	A4
...os Arch.: Chile	65	D12
...Thanh: Vietnam	38	D4
...ou: China	36	B1
...n: Brazil	66	D2
...ey: England	12	D3
...isun: China	36	C2
...rchih: China	36	A3
...n, Mt.: Canada	60	B4
...church: England	15	E4
...church: N.Z	41	B3
...iana: U.S.A	51	E3
...an Island: Can	56	E5
...ina r.: Canada	60	C1
...mas I.: Indian O	35	D13
...mas: Pac O	45	K6
...mas Ocean	44	J6
...r.: China	37	A3
...: r.: U.S.S.R	29	L5
...ing: China	37	C5
...iang: China	37	B5
...: China	37	C5
...park: Japan	39	C2
...r.: Argentina	66	E12
...na: China	36	C2
...how: China	36	D2
...eigh: England	14	C4
...es: Japan	39	B2
...uchak: China	29	N4
...sien: Anhwei, China	36	C3
...na: Chekiang, China	37	C4
...na: Shantung, China	36	C2
...na: Szechwan, China	37	A4
...Brazil	66	D3
...a: Malaysia	38	C6
...S.S.R./Alaska	27	V3
...ang: China	38	C1
...i-Tau: U.S.S.R	29	L5
...enham: England	14	C3
...m. r.: U.S.S.R	29	O2
...bicha: Argentina	66	B2
...nghsien: China	37	A3
...inhae: China	37	A3
...gming: China	36	D3

Name	Page	ref
Chungsiang: China	37	B3
Chungtso: China	37	A5
Chungyang: China	37	B4
Chuquicamata: Chile	64	C8
Chur (Coire): Switz	25	B2
Churchbridge: Canada	61	G2
Churchill: & cape, Can	61	G1
Churchill: r., Canada	61	E1
Churchill: r., Canada	61	E1
Churchill Falls: sett. Canada	47	X6
Churchill Lake: Canada	60	D1
Church Stretton: Eng	14	D2
Churn: r., England	15	E3
Chushan: Chekiang. China	37	D3
Chushan: Hupeh. China	36	B3
Chuwu: China	36	B2
Chuzu: Japan	39	c i
Cienfuegos: Cuba	49	K5
Cilician Gates: pass. Turkey	28	C6
Cincinnati: U.S.A	58	D4
Cimarron: r., U.S.A	50	C2
Cinzas: Rio das r.: Brazil	66	D1
Cirencester: England	15	E3
Ciudad Acuña: Mex	50	B4
Ciudad Bolívar: Ven	49	O8
Ciudad Guayana: Ven	49	O8
Ciudad Madero: Mex	48	G5
Ciudad Real: Spain	19	B5
Ciudad Victoria: Mex	48	G5
Civitavecchia: Italy	21	B4
Clach Leathad: mtn., Scotland	11	D3
Clacton-on-Sea: Eng	15	H3
Claerwen Res. Wales	14	C2
Claire, Lake: Canada	60	C1
Clamecy: France	23	B2
Clara: Irish Rep	13	D4
Clare: Australia	43	A4
Clare: Co., Irish Rep	13	B4
Clare: r., Irish Rep	13	B3
Clarecastle: Irish Rep	13	C4
Clare: r.: Irish Rep	13	A3
Claremont: U.S.A	54	C3
Claremorris: Irish Rep	13	C3
Clarence: U.S.A	54	E4
Clarence: r., N.Z	41	C3
Clarkdale: Ariz., U.S.A	63	D5
Clarke City: Canada	59	D1
Clarke Range: Austl	42	C2
Clark Fork: r., Mont., U.S.A	62	D1
Clark Fork: r., Wyo., U.S.A	62	E3
Clark Hill Reservoir: U.S.A	51	F3
Clark Point: Canada	56	D5
Clarksburg: U.S.A	58	E3
Clarksdale: U.S.A	50	D3
Clarks Ferry: U.S.A	54	D4
Clarkston: U.S.A	62	C2
Clarksville: U.S.A	51	E2
Clausthal-Zellerfeld: German F.R	24	C1
Clay Cross: England	15	E1
Claydon: England	15	H2
Claymont: U.S.A	54	E4
Claysburg: U.S.A	54	B4
Clayton: N. Mex., U.S.A	53	E3
Clayton: N.Y., U.S.A	57	J5
Clearfield: U.S.A	54	C4
Clear Fork: r., U.S.A	50	C3
Clear: Island: Irish Rep	13	B5
Clear Lake: U.S.A	63	B4
Clearwater: U.S.A	51	F4
Clearwater: r., Can	60	D1
Clearwater: r., U.S.A	62	C2
Clearwater Lake Provincial Park: Can	61	E2
Cleator Moor: England	12	C1
Cleburne: U.S.A	50	C3
Cleethorpes: England	12	F3
Clermont: Australia	42	C2
Clermont: Canada	57	P2
Clermont: France	22	A2
Clermont: France	23	A4
Clermont-Ferrand: Fr	23	B2
Clés: Italy	25	C2
Clevedon: England	14	D3
Cleveland: Co., Eng	12	E2
Cleveland: Miss., U.S.A	50	D3
Cleveland: Ohio, U.S.A	56	D8
Cleveland: Tenn., U.S.A	51	F2
Cleveland: Tex., U.S.A	50	D3
Cleveland Heights: town, U.S.A	56	D8
Cleveland Hills: England	12	E2
Clevelândia: Brazil	66	D2
Cleveleys: England	12	C2
Clew Bay: Irish Rep	13	B3
Clifden: Irish Rep	13	A3
Clifton: Ariz., U.S.A	63	E5
Clingmans Dome: mtn., U.S.A	51	F2
Clinton: B.C., Canada	62	B2
Clinton: Ont. Canada	56	D6
Clinton: Conn., U.S.A	55	H3
Clinton: Iowa, U.S.A	58	B3
Clinton: Mass., U.S.A	55	J2
Clinton: Mich., U.S.A	56	E1
Clinton: N.C., U.S.A	51	G3
Clinton: N.Y., U.S.A	54	E1
Clinton: Okla., U.S.A	50	C2
Clinton, Cape: Austl	42	D2
Clio: U.S.A	56	E6
Clipperton I.: Pacific O	45	P5
Clisham: mtn., Scot	10	B2
Clitheroe: England	12	D2
Clodomira: Argentina	66	B2
Cloghan: Irish Rep	13	D3
Clogher: Irish Rep	13	D2
Clogher Head: cape	13	E3
Clonakilty: Irish Rep	13	C5
Cloncurry: Australia	40	G5
Clondalkin: Irish Rep	13	E3
Clones: Irish Rep	13	D2
Clonmel: Irish Rep	13	D4
Clonmany: Irish Rep	13	D1
Cloonbannin: Irish Rep	13	C4
Cloppenburg: Ger F.R	24	B1
Cloquet: U.S.A	58	B2
Close Lake: Canada	61	E1
Clova: Canada	57	K1
Clovelly: England	14	B3
Cloverdale: U.S.A	63	B4
Clovis: Calif., U.S.A	63	C4
Clovis: N. Mex., U.S.A	53	E4
Cluanie, Loch: Scot	10	C2
Cluj: Romania	21	D4
Clun: r., England	14	D2
Clun Forest: England	14	D2
Clutha: r., N.Z	41	A4

Name	Page	ref
Clwyd: r. & Co., Wales	14	C1
Clwydian Range: Wales	14	C1
Clyde: U.S.A	54	D1
Clyde: r., Canada	57	J4
Clyde: r., Scotland	11	E4
Clyde, Firth of: est., Scotland	11	D4
Clydebank: Scotland	11	D4
Cnoc Moy: mtn., Scot	11	C4
Coal Creek: town, Canada	60	C3
Coaldale: Canada	60	C3
Coalhurst: Canada	60	C3
Coalisland: N. Ireland	13	E2
Coalport: U.S.A	54	B4
Coalville: England	15	E2
Coast Mts.: Can	46	J5
Coast Ranges: U.S.A	62/3	
Coatbridge: Scotland	11	E4
Coatesville: U.S.A	54	E5
Coaticook: Canada	57	O4
Coatzacoalcos: Mex	48	H6
Cobalt: Canada	56	F2
Cobalt: U.S.A	50	C2
Cobar: Australia	43	C4
Cobden: Canada	57	J4
Cobh: Irish Rep	13	C5
Cobourg: Canada	56	G6
Cobuconk: Canada	56	G5
Coburg: German F.R	24	C1
Cochabamba: Bolivia	64	E7
Cochem: German F.R	24	B1
Cochin: India	32	C6
Cochrane: Alta.: Can	60	C2
Cochrane: Ont.: Can	59	D2
Cochrane: r., Argentina/Chile	65	D13
Cochrane, Lake: Canada	60	C1
Cockburn Island: Can	56	B4
Cockermouth: England	12	C1
Cock of Arran: pt., Scotland	11	C4
Cocoa: U.S.A	51	F4
Coco Islands: Ind. O	38	A4
Cocos Islands: Ind. O	33	h v
Cocos Basin: Ind. O	33	h vi
Cocos Ridge: Pac O	45	R6
Cod, Cape: U.S.A	55	K2
Cody: U.S.A	62	E3
Coeur d'Alene: U.S.A	62	C1
Coffeyville: U.S.A	58	A4
Coff's Harbour: Austl	43	D4
Cognac: France	23	A2
Cohasset: U.S.A	55	K2
Cohocton: r., U.S.A	54	C3
Cohoes: U.S.A	55	G2
Coimbatore: India	32	C6
Coimbra: Portugal	19	A4
Coire: see Chur	25	B2
Colac: Australia	43	B5
Colatina: Brazil	66	H7
Colborne: Canada	56	H5
Colby: U.S.A	50	B2
Colchester: England	15	G3
Colchester: U.S.A	55	H3
Cold Lake: & town, Canada	60	D2
Cold Spring: town, U.S.A	55	G3
Coldstream: Scotland	11	F4
Colebrook: U.S.A	57	O5
Coleford: England	14	D3
Coleman: Canada	60	C3
Coleman: U.S.A	50	C3
Coleraine: N. Ireland	13	E1
Colfax: U.S.A	62	C2
Colgrave Sound: Shetland Islands	10	c i
Colima: Mexico	48	F6
Coll: r., Scotland	10	B3
Collarenebri: Austl	43	C4
Collie: Australia	42	b ii
Collines de Normandie: hills, France	22	A2
Collines de Perche: hills, France	22	A2
Collingwood: Canada	56	E5
Collins Mountain: Can	56	E2
Collins Park: town, U.S.A	54	E5
Collinsville: Australia	42	C2
Collinsville: U.S.A	55	H3
Colmar: France	22	C2
Coln: r., England	15	E3
Colne: England	12	D2
Colne: r., England	15	G3
Colne Point: England	15	H3
Cologne (Köln): German F.R	24	B1
COLOMBIA	64	—
Colombo: Sri Lanka	32	a ii
Colón: Argentina	66	B3
Colón: Panama	49	Ins.
Colonia del Rosario Sacramento: Uru	66	C3
ColorBay: Canada	61	D2
Colonsay: r., Scot	11	C3
Colorado: r., Argentina	65	E11
Colorado: State & r., U.S.A	52/3	D3
Colorado: r., Tex., U.S.A	50	C4
Colorado Nat. Monument: U.S.A	63	E4
Colorado Plateaus: U.S.A	63	D4
Colorado Springs: town, U.S.A	53	E3
Columbia: Mo., U.S.A	58	B3
Columbia: Pa., U.S.A	54	D4
Columbia: S.C., U.S.A	51	F3
Columbia: Tenn., U.S.A	51	E2
Columbia: r., Can./U.S.A	62	B2
Columbia, Cape: Can	47	VO
Columbia, Mt.: Canada	60	C2
Columbia Falls: town, U.S.A	62	D1
Columbus: Ga., U.S.A	51	F3
Columbus: Ind., U.S.A	58	C3
Columbus: Miss., U.S.A	51	E3
Columbus: Nebr., U.S.A	53	F2
Columbus: Ohio, U.S.A	58	D3
Colver: U.S.A	54	B4
Colville: U.S.A	62	C1
Colville: r., U.S.A	46	K3
Colwyn Bay: Wales	14	C1
Comandante Fontana: Argentina	66	C1
Combe Martin: England	14	B3
Comber: Canada	56	C6
Comber: N. Ireland	13	F2
Comechingones, Sierra de: ra., Argentina	66	B3
Comeragh Mts.: Irish Republic	13	D4
Comet: Australia	42	C2
Comilla: Bangladesh	33	F4
Commissaries, Lac des: Canada	57	N1

Name	Page	ref
Communism, Mt.: U.S.S.R	29	L6
Como: & lake, Italy	25	B2
Comox: Lake: Canada	56	B2
Comodoro Rivadavia: Argentina	65	E13
Comorin, Cape: India	32	C7
Comoro Is.: Indian O	71	H10
Compiègne: France	22	A2
Comprida, Ilha: r., Brazil	66	E2
Compton: Canada	57	O4
CONAKRY: Guinea	68	C7
Concarneau: France	22	a i
Concepción: Corrientes: Argentina	66	C2
Concepción: Tucumán, Argentina	66	B2
Concepción: Chile	65	D11
Concepción: Paraguay	66	C1
Concepción del Uruguay: Argentina	66	C3
Conception, Point: U.S.A	63	B5
Concho: r., U.S.A	50	C3
Concord: Mass. U.S.A	55	J2
Concord: N.C., U.S.A	51	F3
Concord: N.H., U.S.A	55	J1
Concordia: Argentina	66	C3
Concórdia: Brazil	66	D2
Condamine: Australia	42	D3
Condobolin: Australia	43	C4
Condom: France	23	B3
Condor: mtn., Arg	66	A1
Conestogo: r., Canada	56	E6
Confusto: r., Paraguay	66	C1
Congleton: England	14	D1
CONGO	71	D8
Congo (Zaire): r., Congo/Zaire	71	C8
Conisbrough: England	15	E3
Coniston: Canada	56	E3
Conklin: Canada	60	D2
Connah's Quay: Wales	14	C1
Conneaut: U.S.A	56	E8
Connecticut: State & r., U.S.A	55	H3
Connecticut Lake: U.S.A	57	O4
Connecticut Turnpike: hwy., U.S.A	55	G3
Connellsville: U.S.A	54	B4
Connemara: dist., Irish Rep	13	B3
Conococheague Creek: r., U.S.A	54	C5
Conrad: U.S.A	62	D1
Conroe: U.S.A	50	D3
Consett: England	12	E2
Conshohocken: U.S.A	54	E4
Consort: Canada	60	C2
Constance, Lake (Bodensee): Switz/German F.R	24	C2
Constanta: Romania	21	E4
Contact: U.S.A	63	D3
Contoocook: r., U.S.A	55	J2
Contrecoeur: Canada	57	M4
Conway: U.S.A	51	D3
Conwy: Wales	14	C1
Cooch Behar: India	33	F3
Cook, Mt. & N.P.: N.Z	41	B3
Cooke, Mt.: Australia	42	b ii
Cook Is.: Pacific O	44	K8
Cookshire: Canada	57	O4
Cookstown: N. Ireland	13	E2
Cook Strait: N.Z	41	B3
Coolangatta: Australia	42	D3
Coolgardie: Australia	42	c ii
Coolidge: U.S.A	63	D5
Coolidge Dam: U.S.A	63	D5
Cooma: Australia	43	C5
Coonabarabran: Austl	43	C4
Coonamble: Australia	43	C4
Cooper Creek: Austl	42	A3
Coopersburg: U.S.A	54	B3
Cooperstown: U.S.A	54	E3
Co-op Point: Canada	61	E1
Coorong, The: inlet, Australia	43	A5
Coosa: r., U.S.A	51	E3
Cootamundra: Australia	43	C4
Cootehill: Irish Rep	13	E2
Copake Falls: town, U.S.A	55	G3
Cozad: U.S.A	53	F2
COPENHAGEN: Denmark	17	B4
Copiapó: Chile	64	C8
Copper Cliff: Canada	56	D3
Coppermine: Canada	46	N3
Coquet: r., England	12	E1
Coral Gables: town, U.S.A	51	F4
Coral Rapids: town, Canada	59	D1
Coral Sea: Australia	42	C1
Corbières: mtns., Fr	23	B3
Corbridge: England	12	D2
Corby: England	15	F2
Cordele: U.S.A	51	F3
Cordillera Cantabrica: ra.: Spain	19	A4
Cordillera Central: ra.: Spain	19	A4
Cordillera de Caaguazú: ra.: Paraguay	66	C2
Cordillera de Mérida: ra.: Venezuela	49	M8
Cordilleras Béticas: ra.: Spain	19	B5
Córdoba: & Prov., Argentina	66	B3
Córdoba: Spain	19	B5
Cordova: Alaska, U.S.A	46	L3
Cordova: Ill., U.S.A	58	B3
Corinth: & gulf, Greece	21	D5
Corinth: Miss., U.S.A	51	E3
Corinth: N.Y., U.S.A	55	G1
Cork: & Co., Irish Republic	13	C5
Cork Harbour: Irish Republic	13	C5
Çorlu: Turkey	21	E4
Cormorant: & lake, Canada	61	E2
Cornélio Procópio: Brazil	66	D1
Corner Brook: Can	47	Y7
Corning: U.S.A	54	C3
Cornwall: England	14	B4
Cornwall: Co., England	14	B4
Cornwall: Canada	57	L4
Cornwall, Cape: U.K	14	A4
Cornwall I.: Can	47	R1
Cornwallis I.: Can	47	Q1
Coromandel Coast: India	32	D6
Coromandel Range: New Zealand	41	B2
Coronation: Canada	60	C2
Coronation Gulf: Can	46	N3
Coronation I.: S. Ork Is	65	J16
Coronda: Argentina	66	B3
Coronel Bogado: Par	66	C2
Coronel Granada: Arg	66	B3

Name	Page	ref
Coronel Moldes: Arg	66	A2
Coronel Oviedo: Par	66	C2
Corowa: Australia	43	C5
Corpus Christi: & bay, U.S.A	50	C4
Corraun Penin: Irish Republic	13	B3
Correen Hills: Scot	10	F2
Corrigin: Australia	42	b ii
Corrib, Lough: Irish Republic	13	B3
Corrientes: & Prov., Argentina	66	C2
Corrientes: r., Arg	66	C2
Corry: U.S.A	56	F8
Corse, Cap: Corsica	19	a i
Corse: Corsica	19	a i
Corsham: England	14	D3
Corsica: i., Med. Sea	19	a i
Corsicana: U.S.A	50	C3
Cortina d'Ampezzo: It	25	C2
Cortland: U.S.A	54	D2
Çorum: Turkey	28	C5
Corumbá: Brazil	64	G7
Corumbataí: r., Braz	66	D1
Coruna: Canada	56	C6
Coruña: Spain	19	A4
Corvallis: U.S.A	62	B2
Corve: r., England	14	D2
Corwen: Wales	14	C2
Coryton: England	15	G3
Cosenza: Italy	21	C5
Cosne: France	23	B2
Costa Brava: coast, Spain	19	C4
Costa del Sol: coast, Spain	19	B5
COSTA RICA	49	—
Côteau Station: Can	57	L4
Côte d'Azur: coast, France	23	C3
Côte d'Or: geog. reg., France	23	B2
Cotentin: geog. reg.: Fr	22	A2
Côtes de Moselle: hills, France	22	C2
Cothi: r., Wales	14	C3
Cotonou: Benin	68	F7
Cotopaxi: volc., Ec	64	C4
Cotswolds: hills, Eng	14	D3
Cottage Grove: U.S.A	62	B2
Cottbus: German D.R	24	C1
Cottenham: England	15	G2
Cottian Alps: Fr./It	23	C2
Cottingham: England	12	F3
Cotuit: U.S.A	55	K3
Cotulla: U.S.A	50	C4
Coubre, Pointe de la: Fr	23	A2
Coudersport: U.S.A	54	B3
Coudres: Ile aux: Canada	57	J3
Coulonge: r., Can	57	J3
Coulonge Est: r., Can	57	J3
Council Bluffs: U.S.A	58	A3
Coupar Angus: Scot	10	E3
Courchevel: France	23	C2
Courtenay: Canada	62	B2
Courtmacsherry Bay: Irish Republic	13	C5
Coutances: France	22	A2
Coutts: Canada	60	C3
Cove Island: Canada	56	D5
Coventry: England	15	E2
Coventry: Conn., U.S.A	55	H3
Coventry: R.I., U.S.A	55	J3
Covilhã: Portugal	19	A4
Covington: Ky., U.S.A	58	D4
Covington: Pa., U.S.A	54	C3
Cowal, Lake: Austl	43	C4
Cowan, Lake: Australia	42	c ii
Cowansque: r., U.S.A	54	C3
Cowansville: Canada	57	N4
Cowdenbeath: Scot	11	E3
Cowes: England	15	E4
Cowley: England	15	E3
Cowra: Australia	43	C4
Coxhila de Santana: hills: Braz./Uru	66	C3
Cozad: U.S.A	55	G2
Cracow: Poland	20	C3
Craignure: Scotland	10	C3
Craik: Canada	61	D2
Crail: Scotland	11	F3
Craiova: Romania	21	D4
Cranberry Lake: & sett., U.S.A	57	L5
Cranberry Portage: Can	61	E2
Cranbrook: Canada	60	C3
Cranbrook: England	15	G3
Crane Lake: Canada	60	D3
Cranleigh: England	15	F3
Cranston: U.S.A	55	J3
Crater Lake & nat. park: U.S.A	62	B3
Craters of the Moon Nat. Monument: U.S.A	62	D3
Crato: Brazil	64	L5
Crawfordsville: U.S.A	58	C3
Crawley: England	15	F3
Crécy: hist.: Fr	22	B1
Crediton: England	14	C4
Cree: r., Scotland	11	D5
Cree: r., Scotland	11	D5
Cree Lake: Canada	60	D1
Creighton: Ont., Can	56	D3
Creighton: Sask., Can	61	E2
Creil: France	22	B2
Crema: Italy	25	B2
Cremona: Italy	25	C2
Cres: i., Yugoslavia	21	B4
Crescent City: U.S.A	63	B3
Creston: Canada	62	C2
Creston: U.S.A	54	C2
Crestview: U.S.A	51	E3
Crete: i. & sea, Greece	21	D5
Creus, Cape: Spain	19	C4
Creuse: r., France	23	B2
Crewe: England	14	D1
Crewkerne: England	14	D4
Criccieth: Wales	14	B2
Criciúma: Brazil	66	E2
Cricklade: England	15	E3
Crieff: Scotland	11	E3
Crimea: penin., U.S.S.R	28	C4
Crna: r., Yugoslavia	21	D4
Croagh Patrick: mtn., Irish Republic	13	B3
Crocker: r., Canada	56	N2
Crockett: U.S.A	50	D3
Cromalt Hills: Scot	10	D1
Cromarty: & firth, Scot	10	D2
Cromer: England	15	H2
Cromwell: N.Z	41	A4
Crook: England	12	E2
Crookston: U.S.A	58	A2
Croom: Irish Rep	13	C4
Crosby: England	14	C1
Crosby: Minn., U.S.A	58	B2
Crosby: N. Dak., U.S.A	53	E1

Name	Page	ref
Cross: r., Nig./Cam	67	B2
Crosse, Ile à la: Can	60	D1
Cross Fell: Eng	12	D2
Crossfield: Canada	60	C2
Crosshaven: Irish Rep	13	C5
Cross Hill: N. Irel	13	E2
Crossmaglen: N. Irel	13	E2
Crossmolina: Irish Rep	13	B2
Cross River: State, Nigeria	67	B2
Croswell: U.S.A	56	C6
Crotone: Italy	21	C5
Crouch: r., England	15	G3
Crowborough: England	15	G3
Crowland: England	15	F2
Crowle: England	12	F2
Crowsnest Pass: Can	60	C3
Croydon: Australia	42	B1
Crozet Basin: Ind. O	33	d viii
Crozet Islands: Ind. O	33	d ix
Cruz Alta: Brazil	66	D2
Cruz del Eje: & r., Arg	66	B3
Cruzeiro: Brazil	66	a i
Cruzeiro do Oeste: Brazil	66	D1
Cruzeiro do Sul: Brazil	64	D5
Crystal City: U.S.A	50	C4
Crystal Falls: sett., Canada	56	F3
Cuaró Grande: r., Uru	66	C3
Cuarto: r., Argentina	66	B3
CUBA	49	—
Cuba: U.S.A	54	C2
Cubango: r., Angola	72	B2
Cubatão: Brazil	66	a i
Cuchilla de Haedo: hills, Uruguay	66	C3
Cuchilla de Montiel: hills, Argentina	66	C3
Cuchilla Grande: hills, Uruguay	66	C3
Cuckfield: England	15	F3
Cúcuta: Colombia	49	M8
Cuddalore: India	32	C6
Cuddapah: India	32	C6
Cudworth: Canada	61	D2
Cuenca: Spain	19	B4
Cuiabá: Brazil	64	G7
Cuillin Hills: Scot	10	B2
Cuito: r., Angola	72	B2
Culgoa: r., Australia	43	C3
Cullen: Scotland	10	F2
Cullin, Lough: Irish Republic	13	B3
Cullman: U.S.A	51	E3
Cullompton: England	14	C4
Culm: r., England	14	C4
Culoz: France	23	C2
Culter Fell: hill., Scotland	11	E4
Culvain: mtn., Scot	10	C2
Cumaná: Venezuela	49	O7
Cumberland: U.S.A	54	B5
Cumberland: r., Irish Republic	13	C5
Cumberland Gap: U.S.A	51	F2
Cumberland Is.: Austl	42	C2
Cumberland Lake: Can	61	E2
Cumberland Plateau: U.S.A	51	F2
Cumberland Sound: Canada	47	W3
Cumbernauld: Scot	11	E4
Cumbria: Co., England	12	C2
Cumnock: Scotland	11	D4
Cuneo: Italy	25	B3
Cunnamulla: Australia	42	C3
Cupar: Canada	61	D2
Cupar: Scotland	10	E3
Curaçao: i., Neth. Antilles	49	N7
Curicó: Chile	65	D11
Curitiba: Brazil	66	E2
Currane, Lough: Irish Republic	13	B5
Current: r., U.S.A	58	B4
Curtis I.: Australia	42	D2
Curuguay: Paraguay	66	C1
Curuzú Chalí: Isla: Argentina	66	C2
Curuzú Cuatiá: Arg	66	C2
Curwensville: U.S.A	54	B4
Cushendun: N. Ireland	13	E1
Cut Bank: U.S.A	62	D1
Cutre, Lough: Irish Republic	13	C3
Cuttaburra: r., Austl	43	C3
Cuttack: India	33	E4
Cuxhaven: Ger. F.R	24	B1
Cuyama Range: U.S.A	63	C4
Cuzco: Peru	64	D6
Cwmbran: Wales	14	C3
Cyclades: is., Greece	21	D5-6
Cypress Hills: & park, Canada	60	D3
CYPRUS	28	B4
Cywyn: r., Wales	14	B3
CZECHOSLOVAKIA	20	C3
Częstochowa: Poland	20	C2

Name	Page	ref
Dabalia: Niger	67	C1
DACCA: Bangladesh	33	F4
Dachau: German F.R	25	C2
Dadra and Nagar Haveli: Union Territ. India	32	B4
Dagupan: Phil	35	G7
Dahalak Archipelago: Red Sea	30	D7
Dahangri: Irish Rep	13	C3
Daio-zaki: cape, Japan	39	c ii
Dai-sen-oki-kokuritsu-kōen: N.P., Japan	39	B2
Dakar: Senegal	68	B6
Dakhla: W. Sahara	68	B4
Dakhla Oasis: Egypt	69	A1
Dakingari: Nigeria	67	A1
Dala: r., Sweden	17	C3
Dalane: geog. reg., Norway	17	A4
Da Lat: Vietnam	38	D4
Dalbandin: Pakistan	32	c iv
Dalbeattie: Scotland	11	E5
Dalby: England	12	D2
Dalby: Australia	42	D3
Dalhart: U.S.A	50	B2
Dalhousie: India	32	C2
Dalhousie, Cape: Can	46	L3
Daling: r., China	36	D2
Dalkeith: Scotland	11	E4
Dallas: Oreg., U.S.A	62	B2
Dallas: Pa., U.S.A	54	D3
Dallas: Tex., U.S.A	50	C3
Dalmatia: coast, Yugo	21	C4
Dalmacio Vélez Sarsfield: Argentina	66	B3
Dalmeny: Canada	60	D2

Dalton: Ga., U.S.A. 51 E3
Dalton: Mass., U.S.A. 55 G2
De Kalb: U.S.A. 54 E3
Dalton-in-Furness: Eng. 12 C2
Dalton Mills: sett., Canada 56 A1
Daltonganj: India 32 D4
Dalwhinnie: Scotland 10 D3
Daly: r., Australia 40 E4
Daly Waters: town, Australia 40 E4
Daman: Union Territ., India 32 B4
DAMASCUS: Syria 28 D7
Damascus: U.S.A. 54 C5
Damaturu: Nigeria 67 C1
Damavand: mtn., Iran 28 G6
Dambarta: Nigeria 67 B1
Dambulla: Sri Lanka 32 b ii
Damietta: Egypt 69 M2
Damodar: r., India 32 E4
Dampier: Australia 40 B5
Dampier Land: geog. reg., Australia 40 B5
Danai: Indonesia 38 C6
Da Nang: Vietnam 38 D3
Dandenong: Australia 43 C5
Dane: r., England 14 D1
Dan Gulbi: Nigeria 67 B1
Danielson: U.S.A. 55 J3
Danilovka: U.S.S.R. 29 L3
Dannemora: U.S.A. 57 M5
Dannevirke: N.Z. 41 C3
Dansville: U.S.A. 54 C2
Danube (Donau): r., Europe 21 E4
Danube Delta Nat. Park: Romania 21 E4
Danushkodi: India 32 C7
Danvers: U.S.A. 55 K2
Danville: Canada 57 N4
Danville: Ill., U.S.A. 58 C3
Danville: Pa., U.S.A. 54 C2
Danville: Va., U.S.A. 51 G2
Dapchi: Nigeria 67 C1
Darazo: Nigeria 67 C1
Dardanelles: str., Turk. 21 E4
Dar es Salaam: Tan. 71 G9
Darfur: Prov., Sudan 69 K6
Dargaville: N.Z. 41 B2
Darien: U.S.A. 55 G3
Darien, Gulf of: Colombia/Panama 49 L8
Darjeeling: India 32 E3
Darling: r., Australia 43 B4
Darling Downs: geog. reg., Austl. 42 C3
Darling Range: Austl. 42 b ii
Darlington: England 12 E2
Darmstadt: Ger. F.R. 24 C4
Darnall: U.S.A. 54 C4
Dartford: England 15 G3
Dartmoor Forest: Eng. 14 C4
Dartmoor Nat. Park: England 14 C4
Dartmouth: England 14 C4
Darvel: Scotland 11 D4
Darwen: England 12 D3
Darwin: Australia 40 E3
Dasht: r., Pakistan 32 c iv
Dasht-e-Kavir: des., Iran 30 C4
Dasht-e-Lut: des., Iran 30 G4
Date: Japan 39 D1
Daugava: r., U.S.S.R. 17 E4
Daugavpils: U.S.S.R. 17 E4
Dauphin: & lake, Can. 61 E2
Dauphin: r., Canada 61 F2
Dauphiné: Prov., Fr. 23 C2
Dauphiné Alps: France 23 C3
Daura: Nigeria 67 B1
Davao: Philippines 35 H9
Davenport: U.S.A. 58 B3
Daventry: England 15 E2
Davidson: Canada 61 D2
Davis Dam: U.S.A. 63 D4
Dawson: U.S.A. 56 B6
Davis Strait: Grnld./Canada 47 V3
Davos: Switzerland 25 B2
Davy Lake: Canada 60 D1
Dawaki: Nigeria 67 B1
Dawanau: Nigeria 67 B1
Dawley: England 14 D2
Dawlish: England 14 C4
Dawna Range: Burma 38 B3
Dawson: Canada 56 H4
Dawson: r., Australia 42 C2
Dawson Bay: Canada 61 E1
Dawson Creek: town, Canada 60 A1
Dax: France 22 A3
Daymán: r., Uruguay 66 C3
Daysland: Canada 60 C2
Dayton: N.Y., U.S.A. 54 B2
Dayton: Ohio, U.S.A. 58 D4
Dayton: Wash., U.S.A. 62 C2
Daytona Beach: city, U.S.A. 51 F4
De Aar: S. Africa 72 C5
Dead: r., U.S.A. 55 M4
Dead Sea: Israel/Jordan 30 C4
Deadwood: U.S.A. 53 E2
Deal: England 15 H3
Deán Funes: Argentina 66 B3
Dean Nat. Forest Park: England 14 D3
Dearborn: U.S.A. 56 B7
Death Valley: U.S.A. 63 C4
Death Valley Nat. Monument: U.S.A. 63 C4
Deauville: France 22 B2
Debrecen: Hungary 20 D3
Decatur: Ala., U.S.A. 51 E3
Decatur: Ill., U.S.A. 58 C4
Decazeville: France 23 B3
Deccan: geog. reg., India 32 C5
Deception Lac: Can. 56 G2
Deception I.: Shet. Islands 65
Děčín: Czechoslovakia 24 C1
Decorah: U.S.A. 58 B3
Deddington: England 15 F3
Dee: r., Dumf. & Gall. Scotland 11 E5
Dee: r., Grampian, Scotland 10 F2
Dee: r., Wales/Eng. 14 D1
Deel: r., Limerick, Irish Republic 13 C4
Deel: r., Westmeath Irish Republic 13 D3
Deep River: sett., Can. 56 H3
Deeps, The: bay, Shetland Islands 10 b i
Deerfield: U.S.A. 55 H2
Deer Hill: town, Can. 55 B1
Deer Lake: Canada 61 G2
Deer Lodge: U.S.A. 62 D2
Deer Mountain: U.S.A. 57 P4

Dehra Dun: India 32 C2
Dej: Romania 20 D3
De Kalb: U.S.A. 58 C3
Dekala Bay: Nigeria 67 A1
Delagoa Bay: Moz. 72 E4
Delano: U.S.A. 54 F4
Delano Peak: mtn., U.S.A. 63 D4
Delaware: State, U.S.A. 59 E4
Delaware: r., U.S.A. 54 E3
Delaware Bay: U.S.A. 59 E4
Delaware Water Gap: U.S.A. 54 E4
De Lemmer: Neth. 24 B1
Delft: Netherlands 24 A1
Delhi: Canada 56 E7
Delhi: & Union Territ., India 32 C3
Delisle: Canada 60 D2
Delmar: U.S.A. 54 F2
Delmenhorst: Ger. F.R. 24 B1
Deloraine: Canada 61 E2
Delphi: Greece 21 D5
Delray Beach: town, U.S.A. 51 F4
Del Rio: U.S.A. 50 B4
Delta: Colo., U.S.A. 52 D3
Delta: Ohio, U.S.A. 56 B8
Delta: Pa., U.S.A. 54 D5
Delta Reservoir: U.S.A. 54 E1
Demarcation Point: U.S.A. 46 G3
Deming: U.S.A. 52 D4
Demmin: German D.R. 24 C1
Denbigh: Wales 14 C1
Dendermonde: Belgium 22 B1
Denham Range: Austl. 42 C2
Den Helder: Neth. 24 A1
Deniliquin: Australia 43 C5
Denison: U.S.A. 50 B3
DENMARK: 17
Denmark: Australia 42 b ii
Denmark Strait: Grnld. 8 H1
Dennis Port: U.S.A. 55 K3
Denny: Scotland 11 E3
Denton: England 12 D3
Denton: U.S.A. 50 B3
D'Entrecasteaux Is.: Papua-New Guinea 40 J2
Denver: Colo., U.S.A. 53 E3
Denver: Pa., U.S.A. 54 D4
Déo: r., Cameroun 67 C2
De Pere: U.S.A. 58 C3
Depew: U.S.A. 54 B2
Deposit: U.S.A. 54 E2
Depot Harbour: Canada 56 F4
Deqing: U.S.A. 58 C3
Dera Ghazi Khan: Pak. 32 B2
Dera Ismail Khan: Pak. 32 B2
Derbent: U.S.S.R. 28 F5
Derby: Australia 40 C4
Derby: England 15 E2
Derby: U.S.A. 55 G3
Derbyshire: Co., Eng. 15 E1
Derg: r., N. Ireland 13 D2
Derg, Lough: Donegal, Irish Republic 13 D2
Derg: Lough: Tipperary Irish Republic 13 C4
Derravaragh, Lough: Irish Republic 13 D3
Derreen: r., Irish Rep. 13 E4
Derry: Lough: Irish Republic 13 B5
Derry: U.S.A. 55 J2
Derrynasaggart Mts.: Irish Republic 13 B5
Derryveagh Mts.: Irish Republic 13 C1
Derwent: r., Cumbria England 12 D2
Derwent: r., N. Yorks., England 12 F2
Derwent Water: Lake, England 12 C2
Desbarats: Canada 56 B3
Desbiens: Canada 57 N1
Desborough: England 15 F2
Deschaillons: Canada 57 N3
Deschambault Lake: Canada 61 D2
Deschutes: r., U.S.A. 62 B3
Deseronto: Canada 56 H5
Desderio Tello: Arg. 66 B3
Desmarais: Canada 60 C1
Des Moines: & r., U.S.A. 58 B3
Dessau: German D.R. 24 C1
D'estats, Pic: mtn., France 23 B3
Detmold: German F.R. 24 B1
Detroit: & r., Mich., U.S.A. 56 B7
Detroit: Oreg., U.S.A. 62 B3
Detroit Lakes: town, U.S.A. 58 A2
Dettingen: hist., Canada 24 B1
Deux Rivieres: sett., Canada 56 G3
Deva: Romania 20 D3
Deventer: Netherlands 24 B1
Devenyns, Lac: Canada 57 M2
Deveron: r., Scotland 10 F2
Devil's Bridge: Wales 14 C2
Devils Lake: town, U.S.A. 58 A2
Devil's Playground: desert, U.S.A. 52 D3
Devils Slide: U.S.A. 63 D3
Devizes: England 15 E3
Dévoluy: r., France 23 C3
Devon: Co., England 14 C4
Devon I.: Canada 47 S1
Devonport: England 14 B4
Devonport: N.Z. 41 B2
Dewa-Kyuryo: hills, Japan 39 D2
Dewsbury: England 12 E3
Dexter: Maine, U.S.A. 59 G2
Dexter: N.Y., U.S.A. 57 J5
Dezful: Iran 30 F3
Dezhneva, Mys: U.S.S.R. 31 U3
Dhahran: Saudi Arabia 30 F4
Dharwar: India 32 C5
Dhofar: Prov., Oman 30 F7
Dhulia: India 32 B4
Diamantina: Argentina 66 B4
Diamantina: Brazil 64 K7
Diamede Is.: U.S.A. 46 B3
Dibrugarh: India 33 F3
Dickinson: N. Dak., U.S.A. 53 F2
Dickinson: Pa., U.S.A. 54 C4
Didcot: England 15 F3
Didsbury: Canada 60 C2

Dieciocho de Marzo: Mexico 50 C4
Diefenbaker, Lake: Can. 60 D2
Diego Suarez: Malagasy Republic 71 I10
Dien Bien Phu: Vietnam 38 C2
Dieppe: France 22 B2
Digboi: India 33 G3
Digne: France 23 C3
Dijon: France 23 C2
Dikwa: Nigeria 67 C1
Dili: Indonesia 35 H12
Dilla: Nigeria 67 C2
Dillingen: German F.R. 25 C2
Dillon: U.S.A. 62 D2
Dillsburg: U.S.A. 54 C4
Dimitrovgrad: Bulgaria 21 E4
Dinajpur: Bangladesh 32 E3
Dinan: France 22 A i
Dinant: Belgium 22 B1
Dinard: France 22 A i
Dinaric Alps: Yugo. 21 C4
Dinas Head: cape, Wales 14 B2
Dinder Nat. Park: Eth. 69 N6
Dingle: & penin., Irish Republic 13 A4
Dingle Bay: Irish Rep. 13 A4
Dingwall: Scotland 10 D2
Dinkelsbühl: Ger. F.R. 24 C2
Dinnington: England 12 E3
Dinorwic: Canada 58 B2
Dinosaur Nat. Monument: U.S.A. 63 E3
Dinya: r., Nigeria 67 B2
Dir: Pakistan 32 B1
Diredawa: Ethiopia 69 O7
Dirk Hartog I.: Austl. 40 A4
Dirrandandi: Australia 42 C3
Disappointment, Lake: Australia 40 C5
Disko: r., Greenland 47 Z3
Disraeli: Canada 57 O4
Diss: England 15 H2
Ditam: Cameroun 67 C2
Dividalen Nat. Park: Norway 16 C2
Divinópolis: Turkey 28 D6
Dixfield: U.S.A. 57 P5
Dixmude: Belgium 22 B1
Dixon: U.S.A. 58 C3
Diyarbakir: Turkey 28 E6
Dizzard Point: England 14 B4
DJAKARTA: Indon. 35 D12
Djallop: Guinea 68 C6
Djambi: Indonesia 35 C11
Djawa: r., see Java 35 D12
Djaya Pura: Indon. 40 G1
Djaya Pura: see Indonesia
Djelfa: Algeria 68 F2
Djerba I.: Tunisia 68 H2
DJIBOUTI: 69 O6
Djibouti: Djibouti 69 O6
Djidjelli: Algeria 19 D5
Dneprodzerzhinsk: U.S.S.R. 28 C4
Dnepropetrovsk: U.S.S.R. 28 D4
Dnestr: r., U.S.S.R. 20 E3
Dno: U.S.S.R. 17 E4
Döbeln: German D.R. 24 C1
Doberai Peninsula: Indonesia 35 J11
Dodecanese: is., Greece 21 E5
Dodo: Cameroun 67 C2
Dodge City: U.S.A. 50 B1
DODOMA: Tanzania 71 G9
Dodsland: Canada 60 D2
Dog Island: Canada 61 F2
Dog Town Fork: r., U.S.A. 50 B3
Doha: Qatar 30 F5
Dokai I.: Indonesia 40 F5
Dolbeau: Canada 59 F2
Dôle: France 23 C2
Dolgellau: Wales 14 C2
Dolgeville: U.S.A. 54 F1
Dollar: Scotland 11 E3
Dollard: Canada 62 E2
Dolomites: mtns., Italy 25 C2
Dolores: Uruguay 66 C3
Dolores: r., U.S.A. 63 E4
Dom: mtn., Switz. 25 B2
Domažlice: Czech. 24 C2
DOMINICA: 49 O6
DOMINICAN REP.: 49 N6
Domodossola: Italy 25 B2
Don: r., Scotland 10 F2
Don: r., U.S.S.R. 28 E3
Don: r., England 13 F2
Donaghadee: N. Irel. 13 F2
Donald: r., Yugoslavia 21 C4
Donald Lake: Canada 61 G2
Donau: r., see Danube 21 B4
Donauwörth: Ger. F.R. 25 C2
Donbass: geog. reg.: U.S.S.R. 28 D4
Doncaster: England 12 E3
Dondra Head: cape, Sri Lanka 32 b iii
Donegal: & Co., Irish Republic 13 C2
Donegal Bay: Irish Republic 13 C2
Donegal Point: Irish Republic 13 B4
Donets: r., U.S.S.R. 28 D4
Donetsk: U.S.S.R. 28 D4
Donga: r., Nigeria 67 C2
Dongara: Australia 42 a i
Dong Hoi: Vietnam 38 D3
Donington: England 15 F2
Dønna: r., Norway 16 C2
Donnybrook: Australia 42 b ii
Donzère: France 23 B3
Dooish Mt.: N. Irel. 13 D2
Doon: r. & loch, Scot. 11 D4
Doornik: see Tournai
Door Peninsula: U.S.A. 58 C2
Dorado: r., Argentina 66 B4
Dorchester: Canada 57 P3
Dorchester: Dorset, England 14 D4
Dorchester: Oxon., England 15 E3
Dordogne: r., France 23 A3
Dordrecht: Neth. 24 A1
Dore: r., England 14 D2
Dore: r., France 23 B2
Doré Lake: Canada 60 D1
Dorian: Canada 58 C2
Dorking: England 15 F3
Dormaa: r., Cam./Nig. 67 C2
Dornbirn: Austria 25 B2
Dornburg: German D.R. 20 B3
Dornoch: & firth, Scot. 10 E2
Dorset: Co., England 14 D4
Dorset, Cape: Can. 47 U4

Dortmund: Ger. F.R. 24 B1
Dortmund-Ems Canal: German F.R. 24 B1
Dosquet: Canada 57 O3
Dothan: U.S.A. 51 E3
Douai: France 22 B1
Douala: Cameroun 67 B3
Double Mountain Fork: r., U.S.A. 50 B3
Doubtful Sound: N.Z. 41 A4
Doubs: r., France 23 C2
DOUGLAS: I. of Man 12 B2
Douglas: U.S.A. 63 E5
Douglas Point: Canada 56 D5
Dounreay: Scotland 10 E1
Douro (Duero): r., Port./Spain 19 A4
Dove: r., Derby/Staffs. England 15 E1
Dove Creek: town, U.S.A. 63 E4
Dover: England 15 H3
Dover: Del., U.S.A. 54 E5
Dover: N.H., U.S.A. 55 K1
Doverfell: mtn., Nor. 16 A3
Dowling Lake: Canada 60 C2
Down: Co., N. Irel. 13 E2
Downham Market: Eng. 15 G2
Downie Creek: Can. 62 C1
Downpatrick: N. Irel. 13 F2
Downpatrick Head: cape, Irish Rep. 13 B2
Downside: U.S.A. 54 B3
Doylestown: U.S.A. 54 E4
Dozois, Réservoir: Can. 56 H2
Dra: r., Morocco 68 D3
Draggan: lake, Sweden 16 C3
Draguignan: France 23 C3
Drakensberg: mtns., Lesotho/S. Africa 72 D4
Drake Passage: Southern Ocean 65 F15
Dráma: Greece 21 D4
Drammen: Norway 17 B4
Drau (Drava): r., Europe 25 C2
Drayton Valley: town, Canada 60 C2
Dresden: Canada 56 C7
Dresden: German D.R. 24 C1
Dreux: France 22 B2
Drina: r., Yugoslavia 21 C4
Drissa: r., U.S.S.R. 17 E4
Drogheda: Irish Rep. 13 E3
Drogobych: U.S.S.R. 20 D3
Droichead Nua: Irish Republic 13 E3
Droitwich: England 14 D2
Drôme: r., France 23 C3
Dromore: Down, N. Ireland 13 E2
Dromore: Tyrone, N. Ireland 13 D2
Dronfield: England 15 E1
Drumbo: Canada 56 E6
Drumheller: Canada 60 C2
Drummond: Co., Can. 57 N4
Drummond Island: U.S.A. 56 B4
Drummond Range: Australia 42 C2
Drummondville: Can. 57 N4
Drygarn Fawr: pk., Wales 14 C2
Dschang: Cameroun 67 C2
Dubai: U.A.E. 30 G5
Dubawnt Lake: Canada 46 P4
Dubbo: Australia 43 C4
DUBLIN: & Co., Irish Republic 13 E3
Dublin: Irish Rep. 51 F3
Dubno: U.S.S.R. 20 E2
Du Bois: U.S.A. 54 B3
Dubrovnik: Yugoslavia 21 C4
Dubu: Nigeria 67 C1
Dubuisson: Canada 56 H1
Dubuque: U.S.A. 58 B3
Duchesne: U.S.A. 63 D3
Duck Bay: Canada 61 E1
Duck Lake: town, Can. 60 D2
Duck Mt.: Canada 61 E2
Duck Mountain Prov. Park: Canada 61 E2
Duddon: r., England 12 C2
Dudelange: Lux. 22 C2
Dudinka: U.S.S.R. 27 L4
Dudley: England 14 D2
Duero (Douro): r., Spain/Port. 19 A4
Dufferin: Co., Can. 56 E5
Dufftown: Scotland 10 E2
Dugi: r., Yugoslavia 21 B4
Duisburg: Ger. F.R. 24 B1
Duku: Nigeria 67 C1
Dulce: r., Argentina 66 B3
Duluth: U.S.A. 58 B2
Dulverton: England 14 C3
Dumaresq: r., Australia 43 D3
Dumbarton: Scotland 11 D4
Dumbleyung: Australia 42 b ii
Dumfries: Scotland 11 E4
Dumfries and Galloway: Reg., Scotland 11 E4
Dumoine: r., Can. 56 H3
Dunaújváros: Hungary 20 C3
Dunbar: Scotland 11 F3
Dunblane: Canada 62 E1
Dunblane: Scotland 11 E3
Dunboyne: Irish Rep. 13 E3
Duncan: Canada 62 B2
Duncan: U.S.A. 50 B3
Duncannon: Irish Rep. 13 E4
Duncansby Head: cape, Scotland 10 E1
Dundalk: Canada 56 E5
Dundalk: Irish Rep. 13 E2
Dundalk: U.S.A. 54 D4
Dundalk Bay: Irish Rep. 13 E3
Dundas: Canada 56 F6
Dundas: Co., Can. 57 K4
Dundaye: Nigeria 67 A1
Dundee: Scotland 11 F3
Dundee: N.Y., U.S.A. 54 C2
Dundonald: N. Irel. 13 F2
Dunedin: N.Z. 41 B4
Dunfermline: Scotland 11 E3
Dungannon: N. Irel. 13 D2
Dungannon: r. & harbour, Irish Republic 13 D4
Dungeness: penin., England 15 G3
Dungiven: Irish Rep. 13 D2
Dunglow: Irish Rep. 13 C1
Dunipace: Scotland 11 E3
Dunkeld: Scotland 10 E3
Dunkellin: r., Irish Republic 13 C3
Dunkerque: France 22 B1
Dunkery Beacon: hill, England 14 C3

Dunkirk: Canada 61 D2
Dunkirk: France 22 B1
Dunkirk: U.S.A. 56 F7
Dun Laoghaire: Irish Republic 13 E3
Dunmanway: Irish Rep. 13 B5
Dunmore: U.S.A. 54 E3
Dunmurry: N. Irel. 13 E2
Dunnet Bay: Scotland 10 E1
Dunnet Head: cape, Scotland 10 E1
Dunnville: Canada 56 F7
Dunoon: Scotland 11 D4
Duns: Scotland 11 F4
Dunstable: England 15 F3
Dunster: Canada 60 B3
Duntelchaig, Loch: Scotland 10 D2
Dunvegan: & head & loch, Scotland 10 B2
Duparquet: Canada 56 F1
Durance: r., France 23 C3
Durand: U.S.A. 56 B7
Durango: Mexico 48 B6
Durango: U.S.A. 52 D3
Durant: U.S.A. 50 C3
Durazno: Uruguay 66 C3
Durban: S. Africa 72 E4
Düren: German F.R. 24 B1
Durgapur: India 32 E4
Durham: & Co., Eng. 12 E2
Durham: Canada 56 E5
Durham: Conn., U.S.A. 55 H3
Durham: N.C., U.S.A. 51 G2
Durham: Co., Canada 56 G6
Durlston Head: cape, England 15 E4
Durness: & loch, Scot. 10 D1
Durres: Albania 21 C4
Durrow: Irish Rep. 13 D4
Dursey I.: Irish Rep. 13 A5
Dursley: England 14 D3
D'Urville Island: N.Z. 41 B3
Dushanbe: U.S.S.R. 29 K6
Dusky Sound: N.Z. 41 A4
Düsseldorf: Ger. F.R. 24 B1
Duxbury: U.S.A. 55 K2
Dvina: r., U.S.S.R. 28 E2
Dwight: U.S.A. 58 C3
Dyer: U.S.A. 63 C4
Dyerem: r., Cameroun 67 C2
Dyersburg: U.S.A. 51 E2
Dyfed: Co., Wales 14 B3
Dyfi: r., Wales 14 C2
Dyke: r., Scotland 10 E1
Dysynni: r., Wales 14 C2
Dzerzhinsk: U.S.S.R. 28 E2
Dzhambul: U.S.S.R. 29 L5
Dzherba: U.S.S.R. 29 O4
Dzhetygara: U.S.S.R. 29 J3
Dzhezkazgan: U.S.S.R. 29 K4
Dzungaria: geog. reg., China 29 O5
Dzungarian Gate: pass., China/U.S.S.R. 29 N4

Eckington: England 15
E.C. Manning Prov. Park: Canada 62
Ecorce, Lac de l': Can. 57
ECUADOR: 64
Edam: Netherlands 24
Eday: r., Orkney Is. 10
Ed Damer: Sudan 69
Eddrachillis Bay: Scot. 10
Eddystone Rocks: Eng. 14
Ede: Netherlands 24
Ede: Nigeria 67
Eden: Australia 43
Eden: r., England 12
Eden: r., Scotland 10
Eden: r., Wales 14
Edenbridge: England 15
Edenderry: Irish Rep. 13
Edessa: Greece 21
Édhessa: Greece 21
Edievale: N.Z. 41
EDINBURGH: Scot. 11
Edirne: Greece 21
Edjelé: Algeria 68
Edmonton: Canada 60
Edmund Lake: Can. 61
Edmundston: Canada 59
Edna: U.S.A. 50
Edo: r., Japan 39
Edosaki: Japan 39
Edremit: Turkey 21
Edson: Canada 60
Edward, Lake: Ug. 71
Edwards: U.S.A. 57
Edwards Plateau: U.S.A. 50
Eeklo: Belgium 22
Eel: r., U.S.A. 63
Efate: r., New Hebrides 40
Egan: U.S.A. 56
Eganville: Can. 56
Egbe: Nigeria 67
Eger: Hungary 20
Eger: r., see Ohře 24
Egersund: Norway 17
Egg Harbor City: U.S.A. 54
Egham: England 15
Egremont: England 12
EGYPT: 69
Eha Alumona: Nigeria 67
Eha Amufa: Nigeria 67
Eifel: mtns., Ger. F.R. 24
Eigg: r., Scotland 10
80 Mile Beach: Austl. 40
Eilat: Israel 30
Eildon, Lake: Austl. 43
Eilenburg: Ger. D.R. 24
Eindhoven: Neth. 24
Eisenach: Ger. D.R. 24
Eisenhuttenstadt: German D.R. 24
Eishort, Loch: Scot. 10
Eisleben: Ger. D.R. 24
Ejido: Nigeria 67
Eket: Nigeria 67
Ekuru: Nigeria 67
El Aaiun: W. Sahara 68
El Asnam: Algeria 19
Ealing: England 15
Earlsferry: Scotland 11
Elba: r., Italy 21
Elbe: r., German Dem. R. & F.R. 24
Elbert, Mount: U.S.A. 52
Elbeuf: France 22
Elblag: Poland 20
El'brus: mtn., U.S.S.R. 28
El Burgo: Spain 19
Elburz Mts.: Iran 28
El Carmen: Argentina 66
El Centro: U.S.A. 63
Elche: Spain 19
Elda: Spain 19
El Darel Beida (Casablanca): Mor. 68
Eldorado: Canada 60
El Dorado: Ark., U.S.A. 50
El Dorado: Kans., U.S.A. 50
Eldred: U.S.A. 54
Elephant Butte Reservoir: U.S.A. 52
Elephant I.: Shet. Is. 65
El Eulma: Algeria 19
Eleuthera I.: Bahamas 51
El Faiyum: Egypt 69
El Fasher: Sudan 69
El Ferrol del Caudillo: Spain 19
El Firdân: Egypt 69
El Gâlon: Argentina 66
Elgin: Scotland 10
Elgin: Co., Canada 56
Elgol: Scotland 10
El giay: U.S.S.R. 27
Elizabeth: Australia 43
Elizabeth: U.S.A. 55
Elizabeth City: U.S.A. 51
Elizabeth Islands: U.S.A. 55
Elizabeth Point: Namibia 72
Elizabethton: U.S.A. 51
Elizabethtown: Ky., U.S.A. 58
Elizabethtown: N.Y., U.S.A. 54
Elizabethtown: Pa., U.S.A. 54
Elk: r., Canada 54
Elkhart: U.S.A. 58
Elkhorn: r., U.S.A. 53
Elkins: U.S.A. 54
Elk Lake: sett., Can. 56
Elkland: U.S.A. 54
Elko: Canada 54
Elko: U.S.A. 62
Elk Point: town, U.S.A. 60
Elk River: town, U.S.A. 62
Elkton: U.S.A. 54
Ellef Ringnes I.: Can. 46
Ellen, Mount: U.S.A. 63
Ellensburg: U.S.A. 62
Ellenville: U.S.A. 54
Ellesmere: England 14
Ellesmere I.: Canada 47
Ellesmere Port: Eng. 14
Ellice: r., Canada 46
Ellicott City: U.S.A. 54
Ellicottville: U.S.A. 54
Elliot, Mt.: Austl. 42
Elliot Lake: town, Can. 56
Ellon: Scotland 10

	Page	ref.
India	32	C4
worth: U.S.A.	59	G3
er: U.S.A.	54	E5
linya: Egypt	69	M3
ra: Canada	56	C6
ra: U.S.A.	54	D2
na Heights: U.S.A.	54	D2
ore: U.S.A.	56	B8
horn: Ger. F.R.	24	C4
ebul: Sudan	56	M6
.: U.S.A.	63	D5
abed: Sudan	52	D4
SALVADOR	48	J7
: Canada	56	C1
att: Egypt	69	Ins.
gre: r., Arg	23	B3
run: Norway	17	A3
ood: U.S.A.	58	C3
England	15	G2
Minn.: U.S.A.	58	B2
Nev.: U.S.A.	63	C4
joki: r., Finland	16	E8
a: U.S.S.R.	29	H4
alse del Río Negro: s. Uruguay	66	C3
arcación: Arg	66	B1
run: Canada	23	B3
rald: Australia	24	B1
rald: Australia	42	C2
rald Basin: outhern Ocean	44	G12
rson: Canada	61	F3
Koussi: mtn. Chad	69	J4
la Romagna: Reg.		
s. Uruguay	25	C3
en: Netherlands	24	E4
en: Netherlands	24	B1
nerich: Ger. F.R.	24	B1
nett: U.S.A.	62	C3
nitsburg: U.S.A.	54	C5
a: International		
alls: Canada	61	G3
ry Peak: mtn.: U.S.A.	50	B4
ehart: Canada	56	F2
t: Canada	61	C4
ash Center: U.S.A.	54	C3
ish Channel: ngland/France	9	C2
: U.S.A.	50	C2
pping: Sweden	17	B4
Sicily	21	B5
ell, Lough: Irish epublic	13	D3
scorthy: Irish Rep.	13	C4
skerry: Irish Rep.	13	E3
skillen: N Irel	13	C4
styman: Irish Rep.	13	B4
s.: r., Austria	25	C3
ng: China	37	N5
chede: Netherlands	24	B1
anada: Argentina	66	C3
anada: Mexico	63	C5
bih: China	37	A3
rprise: U.S.A.	54	F7
becasteaux, Point: Australia	42	b ii
e Ríos: Prov.: Arg	66	C3
e Ríos: Moz.	72	F1
eves: Italy	25	B2
gu: Nigeria	67	B2
gu Ezike: Nigeria	67	B2
m: Japan	39	e iv
Nigeria	67	A2
nay: France	22	B2
esus: Turkey	21	E4
Pa.: U.S.A.	54	D4
ata: Wash.: U.S.A.	62	C2
ata: U.S.A.	22	C2
ng: England	15	G3
m: England	15	F3
nt: England	15	F3
ATORIAL GUINEA	70	B7
Creek: Austl.	42	C2
rim: Brazil	66	D2
tsab: Mongolia	34	F1
: German D.R.	24	C1
no: r., Greece/rkey	21	E4
Lough: Scot.	10	D1
Loch: Scot.	10	B1
: U.S.A.	10	E7
Lake: Can / Canada	56	—
vo: Somali Rep.	56	P6
Canada	56	E6
: r., Scot.	10	A2
rt: Loch: Scot.	10	B1
ta: Prov.: Eth.	69	O6
r., Irish epublic	13	D4
gen: Ger. F.R.	24	C2
anga: Australia	42	B3
f Mts.: Mor	68	C2
l mtn.: Irish public	13	C1
Head: cape. Irish Republic	13	A2
manga: i., New Hebrides	40	M4
d'Oeste: Braz.	66	D2
abridge: mtns. Ger. R./Czech.	24	C1
rum: Turkey	28	E6
berg: Denmark	17	A4
bjer, Lac: U.		
		K4
: U.S.A.	58	B3
: Luxembourg	24	C2
wege: Ger. F.R.	24	C1
er: England	15	F3
s: S. Africa	72	C4
t., England	11	E4
t., Scotland	11	C4
stuna: Sweden	17	C4

	Page	ref.
Eskimo Point: town, Canada	47	R4
Eskişehir: Turkey	28	C6
Eskwehani, Lac: Can.	57	K2
Esla: r., Spain	19	A4
Espalion: Ec	56	C4
Espanola: Can.	56	D3
Esperance: Australia	42	c ii
Esperanza: Argentina	66	B3
Espírito Santo: i., New Hebrides	40	M4
Espírito Santo: State, Brazil	64	K8
Espoo: Finland	17	D3
Esquina Negra: Arg	68	C6
Essaouira: Morocco	68	D2
Essé: Cameroun	67	C3
Essen: Ger. F.R.	24	B1
Esssequibo: r., Guyana	64	G3
Essex: & Co.: Canada	56	C7
Essex: Conn.: U.S.A.	55	H3
Essex: Mkt.: U.S.A.	54	D5
Essex: Co.: England	15	G2
Esslingen: Ger. F.R.	25	B2
Esteio: Brazil	66	D2
Esterhazy: Canada	61	E2
Estero Bay: U.S.A.	63	B4
Esteros: Paraguay	66	B1
Esteros del Iberá: swamps, Argentina	66	C2
Estevan: Canada	61	E3
Estherville: U.S.A.	58	B3
Eston: Canada	60	D2
Eston: England	12	E2
Estonian S.S.R.	17	E4
Esztergom: Hungary	20	C3
Étampes: France	22	B2
Étang de Berre: lag., France	23	C3
Étang de Vaccarès: lag., France	23	B3
Étang d'Hourti: lag., France	23	A2
Étaples: France	22	B1
Etawah: India	32	C3
Etawney Lake: Can.	61	F1
Ete: Nigeria	67	B2
Ethelbert: Canada	61	E2
ETHIOPIA	69	N7
Ethiopian Plateau: Eth.	69	N7
Etive, Loch: Scotland	10	C3
Etna: Mt.: volc., Sicily	21	B5
Eton: England	15	F3
Eton Station: Canada	56	F3
Etosha Game Park: Namibia	72	A2
Etosha Pan: salt lake, Namibia	72	B2
Etruscan Apennines: mtns., Italy	25	C3
Euboea: i., Greece	21	D5
Eucla: Australia	40	D7
Euclid: U.S.A.	56	D8
Eucumbene, Lake: Australia	43	C5
Eudora: U.S.A.	50	D3
Eufaula: U.S.A.	51	E3
Eufaula Reservoir: U.S.A.	50	C2
Eugene: U.S.A.	62	B3
Eunice: U.S.A.	50	D3
Eupen: Belgium	22	C1
Euphrates: r., Asia	30	B2
Eure: r., France	22	B2
Eureka: Calif.: U.S.A.	63	B3
Eureka: Mont.: U.S.A.	62	C2
Eureka: Nev.: U.S.A.	63	C4
Eureka River: town, Canada	60	B1
Europe: i., Indian O.	72	F3
Europoort: Neth.	24	A1
Evans, Mt.: Canada	60	B2
Evansburg: Canada	60	C2
Evanston: U.S.A.	63	D3
Evansville: Canada	56	C6
Evansville: U.S.A.	58	C4
Evelix: r., Scotland	10	D2
Evenlode: r., England	15	E3
Everard, Cape: Austl.	43	C5
Everest, Mt.: China/Nepal	32	D3
Everett: r., U.S.A.	56	A3
Everett: Wash.: U.S.A.	62	B2
Everglades, The: swamps, U.S.A.	51	F4
Everglades Nat. Park: U.S.A.	51	F4
Evesham: England	15	E2
Evian: France	23	C2
Évora: Portugal	19	A5
Evreux: France	22	B2
Exe: r., England	14	D2
Exeter: Canada	56	D6
Exeter: England	14	D2
Exeter: U.S.A.	55	K2
Exmoor Forest: reg., England	14	C3
Exmoor Nat. Park: Eng.	14	C3
Exmouth: England	14	D2
Exmouth Gulf: Austl.	40	A5
Exshaw: Canada	60	C2
Exton: U.S.A.	54	E4
Eye: England	15	H2
Eyemouth: Scotland	11	F4
Eyo Peninsula: Scot.	10	B1
Eyre, Lake: Australia	40	F6
Ezike: Nigeria	67	B2
Fåberg: Norway	17	B3
Fada: Chad	69	J5
Faenza: Italy	25	C3
Faeroe Is.: Atl. O.	8	K1
Fagernes: Norway	17	A3
Fagersta: Sweden	17	C4
Faguibine, Lake: Mali	68	E5
Faillon, Lac: Canada	57	J1
Fairbanks: U.S.A.	46	P4
Fairborn: U.S.A.	56	C8
Fairbury: U.S.A.	53	D4
Fairfield: U.S.A.	56	Q5
Fairford: England	15	E3
Fair Haven: U.S.A.	55	M6
Fair Head: cape, N. Ireland	13	C1
Fair Isle: Scot.	10	c i
Fairlie: N.Z.	41	c ii
Farless Hills: town, U.S.A.	54	F4
Fairmont: Minn.: U.S.A.	58	B3
Fairmont: W. Va.: U.S.A.	59	D4
Fairport: N.Y.: U.S.A.	54	G1
Fairport Harbor: U.S.A.	56	D7
Fairview: Canada	60	C1
Faith: U.S.A.	53	E1
Faizabad: Afghanistan	31	L6
Fakenham: England	15	G2
Faktovyo: U.S.S.R.	29	L1
Fal: r., England	14	B4
Falaise: France	22	A2
Falconbridge: Canada	24	C1

	Page	ref.
Falkenberg: Sweden	17	B4
Falkirk: Scotland	11	E4
Falkland Is.: Atlantic O.	65	G14
Falköping: Sweden	17	B4
Fallon: U.S.A.	63	C4
Fall River: city, U.S.A.	55	J3
Falls: sett.: U.S.A.	57	K5
Falls City: U.S.A.	58	A3
Falls Village: U.S.A.	55	G3
Falmouth: & bay, Eng.	14	A4
Falmouth: U.S.A.	55	K3
False Bay: S. Afr.	72	B5
Falun: Sweden	17	B4
Famagusta: Cyprus	30	C2
Family Lake: Can.	61	F2
Fana: Norway	17	A3
Fanchih: China	36	B3
Fangcheng: China	36	B3
Fanghsien: China	36	C2
Fanhsien: China	36	C2
Fannich, Loch: Scot.	10	C2
Fanning I.: Pacific O.	44	K6
Fano: Italy	25	C3
Farah: Afghanistan	30	H4
Farasan Is.: Red Sea	30	D7
Fareham: England	15	F4
Farewell: Canada	61	F2
Farewell, Cape: Grnld.	47	BB5
Farewell, Cape: N.Z.	41	B3
Faribault: U.S.A.	58	B3
Farndon: England	15	E3
Farmington: r., U.S.A.	57	P5
Farmington: N.H.: U.S.A.	55	J1
Farmington: N. Mex.: U.S.A.	52	D3
Farmington: r., U.S.A.	55	H4
Farnborough: England	15	F3
Farnham: Canada	57	N4
Farnham: England	15	F3
Farnworth: England	12	D3
Faro: r., Cameroun	67	C2
Faro: Portugal	19	A5
Faro Game Reserve: Cameroun	67	C2
Fårön: i., Sweden	17	C4
Farrar: r., Scot.	10	D2
Farsund: Norway	17	A4
Fastov: U.S.S.R.	20	F2
Father: Canada	60	D1
Fauske: Norway	16	C2
Faustino M. Parera: Argentina	66	C3
Faversham: England	15	G3
Favourable Lake: Can.	61	G2
Fawley: England	15	F4
Faxa Bay: Iceland	16	a ii
Fayette: U.S.A.	51	E3
Fayetteville: Ark.: U.S.A.	50	D2
Fayetteville: N.C.: U.S.A.	51	G2
Fayetteville: N.Y.: U.S.A.	54	D1
Fayid: Egypt	69	Ins.
F'Derik: Mauritania	68	C4
Feale: r., Irish Rep.	13	B4
Fear, Cape: U.S.A.	51	G3
Fecagh, Lough: Irish Republic	13	B4
Fécamp: France	22	B2
Federal Capital Territory: Nigeria	67	B2
Feicheng: China	36	B2
Feihsi: China	37	C3
Fielding: N.Z.	41	C3
Feira de Santana: Brazil	64	L6
Feldkirch: Austria	25	B2
Feliciano: r., Arg.	66	C3
Felixstowe: England	15	H3
Feltre: Italy	25	C2
Femund: lake, Norway	17	B3
Fen: r., China	36	B2
Fenelon Falls: sett.: Canada	56	G5
Fengcheng: China	36	B3
Fengcheng: China	37	C4
Fengchieng: China	38	B2
Fenghsien: Kiangsu: China	36	C3
Fenghsien: Shensi: China	36	A3
Fenghwa: China	37	D4
Fenghwang: China	37	A4
Fengkang: China	37	A4
Fenglo: China	37	B3
Fenning: China	37	C1
Fengsiang: China	36	A3
Fengsin: China	37	B3
Fengtai: China	36	B2
Fengtai: China	37	A4
Fengyang Shan: mtn. China	37	C4
Feni: China	37	C4
Fenouillèdes: r., Fr.	23	B3
Fens, The: reg., Eng.	15	F2
Fenton: U.S.A.	56	D6
Fenyang: China	36	B2
Feolin Ferry: Scot.	11	C4
Ferbane: Irish Rep.	13	C3
Ferdows: U.S.S.R.	20	L5
Fergana: U.S.S.R.	28	L5
Fergus: Canada	56	D6
Fergus Falls: town, U.S.A.	58	A2
Fermanagh: Co., N. Ireland	13	C2
Ferme-Neuve: Canada	57	K3
Fermoy: Irish Rep.	13	B4
Fernando de Noronha: i., Brazil	64	M4
Fernie: Canada	62	C2
Ferrara: Italy	25	C3
Ferret, Cap: France	23	A3
Fès: Morocco	68	E2
Fethard: Irish Rep.	13	C4
Fetlar: i., Shetland Is.	10	c i
Ffestiniog: Wales	14	C2
Ffloest Fawr: hills, Wales	14	C3
Fianarantsoa: Malagasy Republic	71	I12
Fichtelgebirge: mtns., German F.R.	25	C2
Fidenza: Italy	25	C3
Field: Scotland	11	E3
Field: B.C.: Canada	60	C2
Field: Ont.: Canada	56	D5
Fier: Albania	21	C3
Fife: Reg.: Scotland	11	E3
Fife Lake: Canada	61	E3
Fife Ness: pt.: Scot.	11	F3
Figeac: France	23	B3
Figile: r., Irish Rep.	13	C3
Figueira da Foz: Port.	19	A4
Figueras: Spain	19	C4
Filey: England	12	F2
Filton: England	14	D3
Finca el Rey, Parque Nacional: Argentina	66	B1

	Page	ref.
Findhorn: Scotland	10	E2
Findlay: U.S.A.	58	D3
Finistère: Dept.: France	22	a i
Finisterre, Cape: Spain	19	A4
FINLAND	16/17	–
Finland, Gulf of: Finland/U.S.S.R.	17	D3
Finnmarksvidda: plat., Norway	16	D2
Finschhafen: Papua-New Guinea	40	H2
Finspång: Sweden	17	C4
Finsteraarhorn: mtn. Switzerland	25	B2
Fintona: N. Ireland	13	C2
Fionn, Loch: Scotland	10	C2
Fionnphort: Scotland	11	C3
Fiordland: Dist. & nat. park, N.Z.	41	A4
Firebag: r., Canada	60	C1
Firebag Hills: Canada	60	C1
Fire Island National Seashore: U.S.A.	55	H4
Firenze see Florence	25	C3
Fishers Island: U.S.A.	55	J3
Fishguard: Wales	14	B3
Fishhall: U.S.A.	55	J3
Fitchburg: U.S.A.	55	J1
Fitzroy: r., Australia	42	D2
Fitzroy: r., Australia	40	C4
Fitzwilliam Island: Can.	56	D4
Flagstaff: U.S.A.	63	D5
Flame: France	23	C2
Flåm: Norway	17	A3
Flammand, Lac: Can.	57	M2
Flambeau: r., U.S.A.	58	B2
Flamborough Head: cape, England	12	F2
Flaming George Reservoir: U.S.A.	63	D4
Flanders: Prov.: Belg.	22	B1
Flathead Lake: U.S.A.	62	C2
Flattery, Cape: U.S.A.	62	B2
Fleet: England	15	F3
Fleet: r., Scotland	10	D2
Fleetwood: England	12	C3
Fleetwood: U.S.A.	54	E4
Flekkefjord: Norway	17	A4
Flemington: r., U.S.A.	54	F4
Flers: France	22	A2
Flinders: r., Australia	40	G4
Flinders Range: Austl.	43	A3
Flinders Reef: Austl.	42	C1
Flin Flon: Canada	61	E2
Flint: r., Ga.: U.S.A.	51	E3
Flint: r., Mich.: U.S.A.	56	D6
Flint: Wales	14	C1
Flint: U.S.A.	56	D6
Flora: Norway	16	A3
Florence (Firenze): It.	25	C3
Florence: Ala.: U.S.A.	51	E2
Florence: Oreg.: U.S.A.	63	B3
Florence: S.C.: U.S.A.	51	G2
Florencia: Colombia	64	C3
Flores: i. & sea, Indon.	35	G12
Floreshty: U.S.S.R.	20	E3
Florianópolis: Brazil	64	K8
Florianópolis: Brazil	66	C1
Florida: Uruguay	66	C3
Florida: State, U.S.A.	51	F4
Florida Bay: U.S.A.	51	F4
Florida Keys: is., U.S.A.	51	F4
Florida, Straits of: The Bahamas/U.S.A.	51	G4
Florin: U.S.A.	63	C4
Florina: Greece	21	D4
Flushing: Netherlands	24	A1
Flushing: U.S.A.	56	D6
Fly: r., Papua-New Guinea	40	G2
Fontainebleau: & for.: France	22	B2
F. M. Kerr Dam: U.S.A.	62	C2
Foam Lake: Canada	61	E2
Fochabers: Scotland	10	E2
Foel Wen: mtn., Wales	14	C2
Foggia: Italy	21	B4
Foggo: Nigeria	67	B1
Fohnsdorf: Austria	25	C2
Foinaven: mtn., Scot.	10	D1
Foix & Prov.: France	23	B3
Fokang: China	37	B4
Fokku: Nigeria	67	A1
Foleyet: Canada	56	C1
Foligno: Italy	21	B4
Folkestone: England	15	H3
Fond-du-I.: U.S.A.	55	F1
Fond du Lac: Can.	61	D1
Fond du Lac: r., Can.	58	B2
Fond du Lac: r., Canada	60	E1
Fontas: r., Canada	60	E1
Fontenay: Inst., Belg.	22	B2
Font Romeu: France	23	B3
Foochow (Fuzhou): China	37	C4
Forbes: Australia	43	C4
Forbes, Mt.: Canada	60	C2
Forcalquier: France	23	C3
Ford: r., Scotland	11	C3
Fordingbridge: England	15	F4
Foreland: pt.: England	15	F4
Foreland Point: Eng.	14	C3
Foremost: Canada	60	D2
Forest: Canada	56	D6
Forestburg: Canada	60	D2
Forest City: U.S.A.	54	E4
Forest Lawn: Canada	59	C2
Forestville: Canada	60	C4
Forez, Monts du: Fr.	23	B2
Forfar: Scotland	11	F3
Forget: Canada	57	J1
Forlì: Italy	25	C3
Formby: England	12	C3
Formentera: i., Balearic Is.	19	C5
Formosa: Prov., Arg.	66	C1
Formosa Strait: China/Taiwan	37	C4
Forres: Scotland	10	E2
Forrest: Australia	40	D6
Forrest City: U.S.A.	50	D2
Forsayth: Australia	40	G4
Forst: Germany	24	D1
Fort Albany: Canada	47	T6
Fortaleza: Brazil	64	L4
Fortaleza de Santa Teresa: Uruguay	66	D3
Fort Ann: U.S.A.	55	G1
Fort Augustus: Scot.	10	D2
Fort Bragg: U.S.A.	63	B4
Fort Chimo: Canada	47	W5
Fort Chipewyan: Can.	60	D1
Fort Collins: U.S.A.	52	D3
Fort Coulonge: Canada	57	J2
Fort Dauphin: Malagasy Republic	71	I12
FORT DE FRANCE: Martinique	49	O7

	Page	ref.
Fort Dodge: U.S.A.	58	B3
Fort Edward: U.S.A.	55	G1
Fort Erie: Canada	56	E6
Fort Erie: U.S.A.	54	G1
Fortescue: r., Austl.	40	B5
Fort Fitzgerald: Can.	60	C1
Fort Foureau: Chad	67	C1
Fort Frances: Canada	61	F2
Forth: r., Scotland	11	D3
Forth, Firth of: est., Scotland	11	F3
Fort Hall: U.S.A.	62	D3
Fortierville: Canada	57	N3
Fortín Lavalle: Arg.	66	B2
Fort Lauderdale: U.S.A.	51	F4
Fort Liard: Canada	46	L4
Fort Macleod: Canada	60	C3
Fort McMurray: Can.	60	C1
Fort McPherson: Can.	46	H3
Fort Madison: U.S.A.	58	B3
Fort Morgan: U.S.A.	53	E3
Fort Myers: U.S.A.	51	F4
Fort Nelson: Can.	46	L5
Fort Norman: Canada	46	L4
Fort Peck Reservoir: U.S.A.	52	D1
Fort Pierce: U.S.A.	51	F4
Fort Plain: town, U.S.A.	54	F2
Fort Portal: Uganda	70	F7
Fort Providence: Can.	60	C1
Fort Qu'Appelle: Can.	61	E2
Fort Resolution: Can.	46	N4
Fortrose: Scotland	10	D2
Fort Royal: Scotland	54	B6
Fort St. John: Can.	60	A1
Fort Sandeman: Pak.	32	A2
Fort Saskatchewan: Canada	60	C2
Fort Scott: U.S.A.	58	B4
Fort Shevchenko: U.S.S.R.	28	C5
Fort Simpson: Canada	46	L4
Fort Smith: Canada	46	N4
Fort Smith: U.S.A.	50	D2
Fort Sumner: U.S.A.	53	E4
Fortuna: Canada	60	B1
Fort Vermilion: Can.	60	B1
Fort Washington: U.S.A.	54	E4
Fort Wayne: U.S.A.	58	C3
Fort William: Scot.	10	C3
Fort William: see Thunder Bay		
Fort Worth: U.S.A.	50	C3
Fort Yukon: U.S.A.	46	F3
Forssa: Finland	17	D3
Forsyth: U.S.A.	52	D1
Forsythe: Canada	57	J1
Foshan: China	37	B5
Foster: r., Canada	61	D1
Fougères: France	22	A2
Foula: i., Shetland Is.	10	c i
Foulness I. & cape: England	15	G3
Foul Bay: Red Sea	69	N4
Foulwind, Cape: N.Z.	41	B3
Foumban: Cameroun	67	C2
Foumbot: Cameroun	67	C2
Fourmies, Lac: Canada	56	G1
Fourmies: France	22	B1
Foveaux Strait: N.Z.	41	A4
Fowey: & r.: England	14	B4
Fowlerville: U.S.A.	56	D6
Fowling: China	37	A4
Fowning: China	36	C3
Fowyang: China	36	C3
Foxboro: U.S.A.	55	J1
Fox Creek: town, Canada	60	D2
Foxe Basin: Canada	47	U3
Foxford: Canada	61	E2
Foxford: Irish Rep.	13	B3
Fox Valley: town, Canada	60	D2
Foyle, Lough: N. Irel	13	C1
Foynes: Irish Rep.	13	B4
Foz do Iguaçu: Brazil	66	C1
Fraile Muerto: Uru	66	D3
Fraças: r., Romania	20	E3
Framingham: U.S.A.	55	J2
FRANCE	22/3	–
France, Île de: geog. reg., France	22	B2
Franche Comté: Old Prov., France	22	C2
Francis Case, Lake: U.S.A.	53	F2
Francistown: Botswana	72	D3
Franconian Heights: hills, Germany	24	C2
Franconian Jura: mtns., German F.R.	24	C2
Frankfort: Ind.: U.S.A.	58	C3
Frankfort: Ky.: U.S.A.	58	D4
Frankfurt am Main: German F.R.	24	B1
Frankfurt an der Oder: German D.R.	24	D1
Franklin: Mass.: U.S.A.	55	J2
Franklin: N.H.: U.S.A.	55	J1
Franklin: N.J.: U.S.A.	54	F3
Franklin D. Roosevelt Lake: U.S.A.	62	C2
Franklinville: U.S.A.	54	E1
Frankston: Austl.	43	C5
Franz Josef Land: is., Arctic Ocean	26/7	H1
Fraserburg: S. Africa	72	C5
Fraserburgh: Scotland	10	F2
Fraser: r., Australia	56	A2
Frater: Canada	56	A2
Fray Bentos: Uru.	66	C3
Fray Marcos: Uru.	66	C3
Fredericia: Denmark	17	A4
Frederick: Md.: U.S.A.	54	D4
Frederick: Okla.: U.S.A.	50	C2
Fredericksburg: U.S.A.	59	E4
Fredericktown: U.S.A.	58	B4
Fredericton: Canada	47	W7
Frederikshavn: Den.	17	B4
Fredonia: U.S.A.	54	E1
Fredriksson: Argentina	66	B3
Fredrikstad: Norway	17	B4
Freehold: U.S.A.	54	F3
Freeland: U.S.A.	54	E3
Freel Peak: U.S.A.	63	C4
Freeport: Ill.: U.S.A.	58	C3
Freeport: Maine: U.S.A.	57	P6
Freeport: Tex.: U.S.A.	50	D4
FREETOWN: Sierra Leone	68	C7
Freiburg im Breisgau: German F.R.	25	B2
Freising: Ger. F.R.	25	C2
Fréjus: France	23	C3
Fremantle: Australia	42	b ii
Fremont: Nebr.: U.S.A.	58	A3
Fremont: Ohio: U.S.A.	56	D7
French Creek: U.S.A.	54	E1
FRENCH GUIANA	64	H3
French I.: Australia	43	C5
Frenchman Butte: Can.	60	D2
Frenchman Creek: U.S.A.	53	E2

	Page	ref.
Frenchtown: U.S.A.	54	E4
Fresnillo: Mexico	48	F5
Fresno: U.S.A.	63	C4
Freudenstadt: Ger.	25	B2
Frías: Argentina	66	A2
Fribourg: Switzerland	25	B2
Friedrichshafen: German F.R.	25	B2
Friendship: U.S.A.	54	B2
Friesland: Prov., Neth.	24	B1
Frio: r., U.S.A.	50	C4
Frisa, Loch: Scotland	10	B3
Frobisher Bay: town & bay, Canada	47	W4
Frobisher Lake: Can.	60	D1
Frodsham: England	14	D1
Frog Lake: Canada	60	D2
Frohavet: bay, Norway	16	A3
Frome: England	14	D3
Frome: r., Dorset Eng.	14	D4
Frome: r., Here & Worcs. England	14	D2
Frome, Lake: Austl.	43	B4
Frontenac: Co., Ont., Canada	57	J5
Frontenac: Que.	57	P4
Frosinone: Italy	21	B4
Frostburg: U.S.A.	59	E4
Frøya: r., Norway	16	A3
Frunze: U.S.S.R.	29	L5
Frýdek-Místek: Czech.	20	D3
Fryeburg: U.S.A.	57	P5
Fu: r., China	37	C4
Fuan: China	37	C4
Fuchow: China	36	B3
Fuchun: r., China	37	C4
Fuchung: China	37	B5
Fuerteventura: i., Canary Islands	68	C3
Fujian see Fukien		
Fuji-hakone-izu-kokuritsu-kōen: nat. park, Japan	39	C3
Fujioka: Japan	39	f iii
Fuji-san (Fujiyama): mtn., Japan	39	e iv
Fujishiro: Japan	39	f iv
Fujiyama see Fuji-san	39	g iv
Fuiyoshida: Japan	39	e iv
Fukaya: Japan	39	f iii
Fukien (Fujian): Prov., China	37	C4
Fukow: China	36	B3
Fukuchiyama: Japan	39	C3
Fukuoka: Japan	39	B3
Fukushima: Japan	39	D2
Fukuyama: Japan	39	a ii
Fukuzaki: Japan	39	C3
Fulda: r., Ger. F.R.	24	B1
Fulo: China	38	B3
Fulton: Mo.: U.S.A.	58	B4
Fulton: N.Y.: U.S.A.	54	F1
Fultonville: U.S.A.	55	F2
Funabashi: Japan	39	f iv
Funan: China	37	A4
Funchal: Madeira	68	A5
Fundy, Bay of: Can.	47	W8
Funtua: Nigeria	67	B1
Fuping: China	36	B3
Furka Pass: Switz.	25	B2
Fürth: German F.R.	25	C2
Fushan: China	36	C2
Fushun: China	34	G2
Futing: China	37	C4
Fuyang: China	37	C3
Fuzhou see Foochow		
Fyn: i., Denmark	17	B4
Fyne, Loch: Scot.	11	C3
Gabès: & gulf, Tunisia	68	H2
GABON:	71	B8
GABORONE: Botswana	72	D3
Gabrovo: Bulgaria	21	E3
Gaçar: r., Romania	67	B1
Gadames: Libya	68	G2
Gadsden: U.S.A.	51	E3
Gaeta: Italy	21	B4
Gaffney: U.S.A.	51	F2
Gafsa: Tunisia	68	G2
Gagnon: Canada	47	W6
Gagnon, Lac: Canada	57	K3
Gail: r., Austria	25	C2
Gailey: r., Irish Rep.	13	B4
Gainsborough: England	12	F3
Gainesville: Fla.: U.S.A.	51	F4
Gainesville: Ga.: U.S.A.	51	F3
Gainesville: Tex.: U.S.A.	50	C3
Gairdner, L.: Austl.	40	F7
Gairloch: & loch, Scotland	10	C2
Gaithersburg: U.S.A.	54	D4
Galapagos Is.: Pac. O.	45	Q7
Galashiels: Scotland	11	F4
Galati: Romania	20	E3
Galax: U.S.A.	51	F2
Galena: Ill.: U.S.A.	58	B3
Galena: Kans.: U.S.A.	58	B4
Galesburg: U.S.A.	58	B3
Gallipoli: Italy	21	C4
Gallan Head: cape, Scotland	10	A1
Gallarate: Italy	25	B2
Gallatin: r., U.S.A.	62	D2
Galle: Sri Lanka	32	b ii
Gallegos: r., Arg	65	D14
Galley Head: cape, Irish Republic	13	C5
Gallinas, Punta: c., Colombia	49	M7
Gallitzin: U.S.A.	54	D3
Galloo Island: U.S.A.	57	J6
Galloway, Mull of: penin. Scotland	11	D4
Gal Oya: Sri Lanka	32	b ii
Galston: Scotland	11	D4
Galtee Mts.: Irish Republic	13	C4
Galtymore: mtn. Irish Republic	13	C4
Galup: U.S.A.	53	D3
Galveston: & bay, U.S.A.	50	D4
Gálvez: Argentina	66	B3
Galway: & Co.: Irish Republic	13	B3
Galway Bay: Irish	13	B3
Gamagori: Japan	39	d ii
GAMBIA, THE:	68	B6
Gambia: r., The Gambia/Senegal	68	C6
Gambier Islands: Pacific Ocean	45	M9

Name	Page	ref
Gambrill State Park: U.S.A.	54	C5
Gampola: Sri Lanka	32	b ii
Gana: Nigeria	67	A2
Gananoque Thousand Islands: sett., Can.	57	J5
Gand see Ghent	22	B1
Gandak: r., India	32	D3
Gander: Canada	47	Z7
Ganga (Ganges): r., India/Bangladesh	32	E3
Ganges: France	23	B3
Ganges: r., see Ganga	32	E3
Ganges, Mouths of the: Bangladesh/India	32/3	E4
Gannett Peak: mtn., U.S.A.	62	E3
Ganongga: i., Solomon Islands	40	K2
Gansu see Kansu	36	A2
Ganye: Nigeria	67	C2
Ganzhou see Kanchow	37	B4
Gap: France	23	C3
Gard: r., France	23	B3
Gardelegen: Ger. D.R.	24	C3
Garden: r., Canada	56	B3
Garden City: U.S.A.	50	B2
Garden River: sett., Canada	56	A3
Garden State Parkway: hwy., U.S.A.	55	F5
Gardez: Afghanistan	32	A2
Gardiner: U.S.A.	57	Q5
Gardiner Dam: Canada	60	D2
Gardiner: U.S.A.	55	H2
Gardiner I.: Phoenix Is.	44	H7
Gare, Lough: Irish Rep	13	C2
Garfield: U.S.A.	63	D3
Gargano, Cape: Italy	21	C4
Garian: Libya	68	H2
Garibaldi: Brazil	66	D2
Garibaldi Prov. Park: Canada	62	B2
Garko: Nigeria	67	B1
Garmisch: Ger. F.R.	25	C2
Garnett: U.S.A.	58	A4
Garonne: r., France	23	B3
Garoua: Cameroun	67	C2
Garrigues, Monts: Fr.	23	B3
Garrison: N. Ireland	13	C2
Garrison: U.S.A.	62	D2
Garrock Head: cape, Scotland	11	C4
Garronne: r., France	23	A3
Garron Point: N. Irel	13	F1
Garron Point: Scot.	10	D3
Garry: r., Scotland	10	D3
Garry Lake: Canada	46	P4
Garry, Loch: Scot.	10	D2
Garson: Canada	56	E3
Garstang: England	12	D3
Garthby: Canada	57	O4
Gartok: China	32	D2
Garvagh: N. Ireland	13	D2
Gary: U.S.A.	58	C3
Garza: Argentina	66	B2
Gasconade: r., ...	58	B4
Gasherbrum: mtn., India	32	C1
Gas Hills: U.S.A.	62	E3
Gashua: Nigeria	67	C1
Gaspar Rodríguez de Francia: Paraguay	66	C1
Gaspé: & penin., Can.	47	X7
Gas-san: mtn., Japan	39	C2
Gassol: Nigeria	67	C2
Gastonia: U.S.A.	51	F2
Gata, Cabo de: cape, Spain	19	B5
Gatchina: U.S.S.R	17	F4
Gateshead: England	12	E2
Gatehouse of Fleet: Scotland	11	D5
Gatineau: r., Can.	57	K4
Gatooma: Zimbabwe	72	D2
Gatun Lake: & locks, Panama	49	Ins.
Gauer Lake: Canada	61	F1
Gauhati: India	33	F4
Gävle: Sweden	17	C3
Gawler: Australia	43	A4
Gaya: India	32	E3
Gaya: Niger	66	B1
Gaya: Nigeria	67	B1
Gayndah: Australia	42	D3
Gaziantep: Turkey	28	D6
Gboko: Nigeria	67	B2
Gbongan: Nigeria	67	B2
Gdańsk: & gulf, Pol.	20	C2
Gdynia: Poland	20	C2
Gediz: r., Turkey	21	E5
Geelong: Australia	43	B5
Geeraardsbergen: Belg	22	B3
Geesthacht: Ger. F.R.	24	C1
Geidam: Nigeria	67	C1
Geilo: Norway	17	A3
Geikie: r., Canada	61	E1
Geiranger: Norway	16	A3
Giessen: German F.R.	24	B2
Gela: Sicily	21	B5
Gelibolu: Turkey	21	E4
Gelligaer: Wales	14	C3
Gelsenkirchen: Ger. F.R.	24	B1
Gemas: Malaysia	38	C6
Gembu: Nigeria	67	C2
General Alvear: Arg	66	C4
General Aquino: Par.	66	C1
General José de San Martín: Argentina	66	C2
General Martín Miguel de Güemes: Arg	66	A1
General Pico: Arg.	66	B4
General Pinedo: Arg	66	B2
General San Martín: Argentina	66	C3
General Villegas: Arg	66	B4
Genesee: r., U.S.A.	54	D2
Geneva: Switzerland	25	B2
Geneva: N.Y., U.S.A.	54	D2
Geneva: Ohio, U.S.A.	54	E8
Geneva: Utah, U.S.A.	63	D3
Geneva, Lake of (Léman, Lac): Switz./France	25	B2
Genissiat Dam: France	23	C2
Genoa (Genova): & gulf, Italy	25	B3
Genoa: U.S.A.	56	B8
George: S. Africa	72	C5
George, Lake: Australia	43	C5
George, Lake: Canada	57	M8
George, Lake: U.S.A.	57	M6
Georgetown: Canada	56	F6
GEORGETOWN: Guyana	49	P8
George Town: Malaysia	38	C5
Georgetown: Conn., U.S.A.	55	G3
Georgetown: Idaho, U.S.A.	62	D3
Georgetown: Mass., U.S.A.	55	K2
Georgetown: S.C., U.S.A.	51	G3
Georgia: State, U.S.A.	51	F3
Georgia, Strait of: Can.	62	B2
Georgian S.S.R.: U.S.S.R.	28	E5
Georgiu-Dezh: U.S.S.R.	28	D3
Gera: German D.R.	24	C1
Geraldton: Australia	42	a i
Geraldton: Canada	58	C2
GERMAN DEMOCRATIC REPUBLIC	24	—
GERMAN FEDERAL REPUBLIC	24	
Gerona: Spain	19	C4
Gerrards Cross: Eng	15	F3
Gers: r., France	23	B3
Gettysburg: U.S.A.	54	C5
Ghaghara: r., India	32	D3
GHANA	68	E7
Ghardaia: Algeria	68	F2
Ghazipur: India	32	D3
Ghent (Gand): Belg	22	B1
Gheorghe Gheorghiu-Dej: Romania	20	E3
Giako: Libya	69	K3
Giant's Causeway: rocks, N. Ireland	13	E1
Gibbstown: U.S.A.	54	E5
GIBRALTAR	19	A5
Gibraltar, Strait of: Africa/Europe	19	A5
Gibson Desert: Austl	40	C/D5
Gibson Reservoir: U.S.A.	50	C2
Giddings: U.S.A.	50	C2
Gien: France	23	B2
Gifu: Japan	39	C2
Gigha I.: Scotland	11	C4
Gijón: Spain	19	A4
Gila: r., U.S.A.	52	C4
Gila Bend: town, U.S.A.	63	D5
Gilbert: r., Austl	40	G4
Gilbert Is.: Pac. O.	44	G7
Gilbert Plains: town, Canada	61	E2
Gilbertville: U.S.A.	55	H2
Gifford Park: town, U.S.A.	55	F5
Gilgit: India	32	B1
Gill, Lough: Irish Republic	13	C2
Gillam: Canada	61	G1
Gillette: U.S.A.	53	D2
Gillingham: Kent, Eng.	15	G3
Gillingham: Wilts., Eng	14	D3
Gilroy: U.S.A.	63	B4
Gimli: Canada	61	F2
Ginebra: Egypt	69	Ins.
Ginir: Ethiopia	69	O7
Gippsland: geog. reg., Australia	43	C5
Girard: U.S.A.	56	E8
Girdle Ness: pt., Scotland	10	F2
Girga: Egypt	69	M3
Gir Hills: India	32	B4
Gironde: est., France	23	A2
Girton: England	15	G2
Girvan: Scotland	11	D4
Gisborne: N.Z.	41	C2
Giurgiu: Bulgaria	21	E4
Givors: France	23	B2
Gjinokastër: Albania	21	D4
Gjøvik: Norway	17	B3
Glace Bay: town, Canada	47	Y7
Glacier: & N.P., Can	62	C1
Glacier International Peace Park	62	D2
Gladbeck: German F.R.	24	B1
Gladmar: Canada	61	E3
Gladstone: Australia	42	D2
Gladstone: Canada	61	F2
Glåma: r., Norway	17	B3
Glasco: U.S.A.	55	G1
Glascarnoch, Loch: Scotland	10	D2
Glasgow: Scotland	11	D4
Glasgow: Ky., U.S.A.	58	C4
Glasgow: Mont., U.S.A.	52	E1
Glas Maol: mtn., Scot.	10	E3
Glassboro: U.S.A.	54	E5
Glass: r., Scotland	10	D2
Glastonbury: England	14	D3
Glastonbury: U.S.A.	55	H3
Glauchau: Ger. D.R.	24	C1
Glazov: U.S.S.R.	28	G2
Gleichen: Canada	61	D2
Glen: r., England	15	F2
Glenboro: Canada	61	F3
Glen Burnie: U.S.A.	54	D5
Glen Canyon Dam: U.S.A.	63	D4
Glencoe: Canada	56	D7
Glen Coe: valley, Scotland	10	D3
Glencoe: U.S.A.	58	B3
Glencolumbkille: Irish Republic	13	C2
Glendale: Ariz., U.S.A.	63	D5
Glendale: Calif., U.S.A.	63	C5
Glendive: U.S.A.	53	E1
Glenelg: r., Australia	43	B5
Glengad Head: cape, Irish Republic	13	D1
Glengarry: Co., Can	57	L4
Glen Innes: Austl	43	D3
Glen Lyon: U.S.A.	54	D3
Glen Mór: valley, Scotland	10	D2
Glen More: hat., Forest Park: Scot	10	E2
Glenmorgan: Austl	42	C3
Glen Rock: U.S.A.	54	D5
Glenrothes: Scotland	11	E3
Glen Roy: valley: Scot	10	D3
Glens Falls: town, U.S.A.	55	G1
Glen Spean: valley, Scotland	10	D3
Glenties: Irish Rep	13	C2
Glentrool har. Forest Park: Scotland	11	D4
Glenwood: U.S.A.	58	A2
Glenwood Springs: town, U.S.A.	53	D4
Glin: Irish Rep	13	B4
Gliwice: Poland	20	D3
Globe: U.S.A.	63	D5
Glossop: England	12	D3
Gloucester: Australia	43	D4
Gloucester: England	14	D3
Gloucester: U.S.A.	55	K2
Gloucestershire: Co., England	14	D3
Gloversville: U.S.A.	55	F1
Glyder Fawr: mtn., Wales	14	B1
Gmunden: Austria	20	C3
Gniezno: Poland	20	D2
Goa: Union Territ., India	32	B5
Goat Fell: mtn., Scot	11	C4
Gobabis: Namibia	72	B3
Gobernador Racedo: Argentina	66	B3
Gobi Desert: China/Mongolia	34	C2
Godalming: England	15	F3
Godavari: r., India	32	C5
Goderich: Canada	56	D6
Godmanchester: Eng.	15	F2
Gods: r., Canada	61	G1
God's Lake: town & lake, Canada	61	G2
GODTHAAB: Greenland	47	AA4
Goffstown: U.S.A	55	J1
Gogorna: Canada	56	D2
Goiânia: Brazil	64	J7
Goiás: Brazil	64	H7
Goiás Massif: Brazil	64	J7
Goio-Erê: r., Brazil	66	D1
Gojo: Japan	39	b ii
Gol: Norway	17	A3
Golaghat: India	33	A1
Golden: Canada	62	C1
Golden Bay: N.Z.	41	B3
Golden Spike: Canada	60	C2
Goldpines: Canada	61	G2
Gomati: r., India	32	D3
Gombe: Nigeria	67	C1
Gombi: Nigeria	67	C1
Gomel': U.S.S.R.	28	D3
Gondar: Ethiopia	69	N6
Gongola: r., Nigeria	67	C1
Gongola: State, Nigeria	67	C2
Gonta-Re-Zhou Game Reserve: Zimbabwe	72	E3
González Moreno: Arg	66	B4
Goodeve: Canada	61	E2
Good Hope, Cape of: S. Africa	72	B5
Gooding: U.S.A.	62	D3
Goodland: U.S.A.	50	B2
Goodooga: Australia	43	C3
Goodsoil: Canada	60	D2
Goole: England	12	F3
Goondiwindi: Austl.	42	D3
Goose: r., N. Dak., ...	58	A2
Goose: r., Utah, U.S.A.	63	D3
Goose Bay: town, Canada	47	X6
Goose Lake: U.S.A.	63	B3
Göppingen: Ger. F.R.	25	B2
Gora: Nigeria	67	B1
Gorakhpur: India	32	D3
Gorda Rise: Pacific O.	45	M2
Gordes: U.S.A.	54	D4
Gordonhorne Peak: mtn., Canada	60	B2
Gordon Lake: Canada	60	C1
Gore: Ethiopia	69	N7
Gore: New Zealand	41	B3
Gore Bay: sett., Can	56	C4
Gorey: Irish Rep.	13	E4
Gorgãn: Iran	28	G6
Gorham: Maine, U.S.A.	57	P6
Gorham: N.H., U.S.A.	57	O5
Gorham: N.Y., U.S.A.	54	D2
Goring: England	15	E3
Gorizia: Italy	25	C2
Gorki: U.S.S.R.	28	F2
Gor'kiy: U.S.S.R.	28	E2
Görlitz: Poland	20	C2
Gorno-Altaysk: U.S.S.R.	29	O3
Goronyo: Nigeria	67	B1
Gort: Irish Rep.	13	C3
Gorzow Wielkopolski: Poland	20	C2
Gose: Japan	39	b ii
Gosford: Australia	43	D4
Gosforth: England	12	E1
Goshen: Ind., U.S.A.	58	C3
Goshen: N.Y., U.S.A.	55	F2
Goslar: German F.R.	24	C1
Gosport: England	15	E4
Göta: r., Sweden	17	B4
Göteborg: Sweden	17	B4
Gotel Mts.: Nig./Cam.	67	C2
Gotenba: Japan	39	e iv
Gotha: German D.R.	24	C1
Gotland: i., Sweden	17	C4
Göttingen: Ger. F.R.	24	C1
Gottwaldov: Czech.	20	D3
Gouda: Netherlands	24	A1
Gouin, Réservoir: Can.	57	K1
Goulais: r., Canada	56	D3
Goulais Point: Canada	56	A3
Goulais River Game Preserve: Canada	56	B3
Goulburn: Australia	43	C4
Gounou Gaya: Chad	67	D2
Gourock: Scotland	11	D4
Gouverneur: U.S.A.	57	K5
Governador Valadares: Brazil	64	K7
Gowanda: U.S.A.	54	D2
Gower: penin., Wales	14	B3
Gowganda: Canada	56	D3
Goya: Argentina	66	C2
Gozo: i., Malta	21	B5
Graaff-Reinet: S. Afr.	72	C5
Gracefield: Canada	57	K3
Gracias a Dios, Cape: Nicaragua	49	K7
Grafton: Australia	43	D3
Grafton: U.S.A.	58	A2
Graham: U.S.A.	50	C3
Graham Land: reg., Antarctica	65	F17
Grahamstown: S. Africa	72	D5
Graian Alps: Fr./Italy	23	C2
Gramado: Brazil	66	D2
Gramilla: Argentina	66	B2
Grampian: reg., Scot.	10	E2
Grampian Mts.: Scot	10	D3
Granada: Spain	19	B5
Granard: Irish Rep	13	D3
Granby: Canada	57	N4
Granby: r., Canada	62	C2
Granby: U.S.A.	55	H3
Gran Canaria: i., Canary Islands	68	B3
Gran Chaco: geog. reg., Argentina/Paraguay	66	B2
Grand: r., Ont., Can	56	E6
Grand: r., Mich., U.S.A.	58	C3
Grand: r., Mo., U.S.A.	58	B3
Grand: r., Ohio, U.S.A.	56	D3
Grand: r., S. Dak., U.S.A.	53	E1
Grand Bahama: i., The Bahamas	51	G4
Grand Banks: Atl. O.	47	Z7
Grand Bend: sett., Can	56	D6
Grand Canal: China	36	C2
Grand Canyon Nat. Park: U.S.A.	63	D4
Grand Centre: Canada	60	D2
Grand Coulee Dam: U.S.A.	62	C2
Grande: r., Brazil	66	b i
Grande: r., Uruguay	66	C3
Grande, Ilha: i., Parana, Brazil	66	D1
Grande, Ilha: i., R. de J., Brazil	66	b i
Grande, Sierra: ra., Argentina	66	B3
Grande Cache: Canada	60	B2
Grande Prairie: town, Canada	60	B1
Grande Ronde: r., ...	62	C2
Grand Falls: Canada	56	B3
Grand Falls: town, N.B., Canada	59	G2
Grand Falls: town, Nfld. Canada	47	Y7
Grand Forks: Canada	62	C2
Grand Forks: U.S.A.	58	A2
Grand Gorge: town, U.S.A.	54	F2
Grand Haven: U.S.A.	58	C3
Grand Island: city, U.S.A.	53	F2
Grand Junction: U.S.A.	63	E4
Grand Lake: Canada	56	B4
Grand Mère: Canada	57	N3
Grand Rapids: town, Canada	61	F2
Grand Rapids: city, Mich., U.S.A.	58	C3
Grand Rapids: town, Minn., U.S.A.	58	B2
Grand Teton Nat. Park: U.S.A.	62	D3
Grand Valley: sett., Can	56	E6
Grandview: Canada	61	E3
Granet, Lac: Can	56	H2
Graney, Lough: Irish Republic	13	C4
Grangemouth: Scotland	11	E3
Grange-over-Sands: England	12	D2
Grangeville: U.S.A.	62	C2
Granite Peak: mtn., U.S.A.	62	E2
Graniel: Canada	61	E2
Gran Paradiso Nat. Park: Italy	25	B3
Grantham: England	15	F2
Grantown-on-Spey: Scotland	10	E2
Grants: U.S.A.	57	P4
Grants Pass: town, U.S.A.	62	B3
Granville: France	22	A2
Granville: N.Y., U.S.A.	55	G1
Granville: Pa., U.S.A.	54	C4
Granville Falls: Can	61	E1
Granville Lake: Can	61	E1
Grass: r., Canada	61	F1
Grass: r., U.S.A.	57	K5
Grasse: France	23	C3
Grassflat: U.S.A.	54	B3
Grass River Provincial Park: Canada	61	E2
Grassy Narrows: Can.	61	G2
Grave, Pointe de: Fr.	23	A2
Gravelbourg: Canada	60	D3
Gravelines: France	22	B1
Gravesend: England	15	G3
Gray: U.S.A.	58	D3
Grayling: U.S.A.	58	D3
Grays Harbor: U.S.A.	62	B2
Grays Thurrock: Eng.	15	G3
Graz: Austria	20	C3
Great Abaco i.: The Bahamas	51	G4
Great Australia Bight: Australia	40	D/E7
Great Barrier I.: N.Z.	41	C2
Great Barrier Reef: Australia	40	—
Great Barrington: U.S.A.	55	G2
Great Basin: U.S.A.	52	C3
Great Bear Lake: Canada	46	L3
Great Bend: U.S.A.	50	C2
Great Bernera: i., Scot.	10	B1
Great Bitter Lake: Egypt	69	Ins.
Great Blasket I.: Irish Republic	13	A4
Great Cacapon: U.S.A.	54	B5
Great Chazy: r., U.S.A.	57	M5
Great Cumbrael: Scot.	11	D4
Great Dividing Range: Australia	42/3	
Great Driffield: England	12	F2
Great Duck Island: Can.	56	C4
Great Dunmow: Eng.	15	G3
Great Eastern Erg: des., Algeria	68	G3
Greater Antilles: is., West Indies	49	—
Greater Manchester: Met. Co., England	12	D3
Great Falls: city, Mont., U.S.A.	62	D2
Great Himalaya Range: Asia	32/3	A2
Great Inagua: i., The Bahamas	49	M5
Great Karroo: plat., S. Africa	72	C5
Great Malvern: England	14	D2
Great Mis Tor: hill, Eng.	14	B4
Great Nicobar: i., Nicobar Is.	38	A5
Great Ormes Head: cape, Wales	14	C2
Great Ouse: r., Eng.	15	G2
Great Palm I.: Austl	42	C1
Great St. Bernard Pass: Switz./Italy	25	B3
Great Salt Lake: U.S.A.	63	D3
Great Salt Lake Desert: U.S.A.	63	D3
Great Sand Hills: Can	60	D2
Great Sandy Desert: Australia	40	C5
Great Shelford: Eng.	15	G2
Great Slave Lake: Can	46	N4
Great Smoky Mts. Nat. Park: U.S.A.	51	F2
Great Stour: r., Eng.	15	H3
Great Torrington: Eng.	14	C4
Great Victoria Desert: Australia	40	D/E6
Great Western Erg: des., Algeria	68	F2
Great Wall: China	34	D2
Great Yarmouth: Eng	15	H2
GREECE	21	L5
Greeley: U.S.A.	53	E3
Green: r., Ky., U.S.A.	58	C4
Green: r., Utah, U.S.A.	63	D3
Green Bay: & city, U.S.A.	58	C3
Green Cape: Australia	43	D5
Greencastle: N. Irel.	13	E2
Greencastle: U.S.A.	54	C5
Greene: U.S.A.	54	E2
Greenfield: Mass., U.S.A.	55	H2
Greenfield: Tenn., U.S.A.	51	E2
Greenhough Point: Can.	56	D5
GREENLAND	47	B2
Greenland Sea	16	—
Green Mountains: U.S.A.	55	N6
Greenmouth: Scotland	11	F4
Greenock: Scotland	11	D4
Greenore Point: Irish Republic	13	E4
Greenough: r., Austl	42	b i
Greenpark: U.S.A.	54	C4
Greenport: U.S.A.	55	H3
Green River: town, U.S.A.	63	E3
Greensboro: Md. U.S.A.	54	E6
Greensboro: N.C., U.S.A.	51	G2
Greenstone Point: Scot	10	C2
Greenville: Ala., U.S.A.	51	E3
Greenville: Maine, U.S.A.	57	Q4
Greenville: Miss. U.S.A.	50	D3
Greenville: N.H., U.S.A.	55	J2
Greenville: Pa., U.S.A.	56	E8
Greenville: S.C., U.S.A.	51	F3
Greenville: Tenn. U.S.A.	51	F2
Greenville: Tex. U.S.A.	50	C3
Greenwater Lake Prov. Park: Canada	61	E2
Greenwich: England	15	G3
Greenwich: Conn., U.S.A.	55	G3
Greenwich: N.J., U.S.A.	54	E5
Greenwich: N.Y., U.S.A.	55	G1
Greenwood: Canada	62	C2
Greenwood: Miss., U.S.A.	50	D3
Greenwood: S.C., U.S.A.	51	F3
Greenwood Lake: town, U.S.A.	55	F3
Greese: r., Irish Rep	13	E4
Greifswald: Ger. D.R.	24	C1
Greiz: German D.R.	24	C1
Grenå: Denmark	17	B4
Grenville: Pa., U.S.A.	54	C4
GRENADA	49	O7
Grenadines: is., Windward Islands	49	O7
Grenay: France	22	B1
Grenfell: Australia	43	C4
Grenfell: Canada	61	E2
Grenoble: France	23	C2
Grenville: Co., Can	57	K5
Gresmanitten: Ger. D.R.	24	C1
Gretna: Canada	61	F3
Gretna: Scotland	11	E5
Grey: Co., Canada	56	E6
Greymouth: N.Z.	41	B3
Grey Range: Austl	42	B3
Greystones: Irish Rep	13	E3
Greytown: S. Africa	72	E4
Griffin: U.S.A.	51	F3
Griffith: Australia	43	C4
Griffith Island: Can	56	E5
Griminish Point: Scot	10	A2
Grimsby: Canada	56	F6
Grimsby: England	12	F3
Grimsel Pass: Switz	25	B3
Grimsey: i., Iceland	16	b i
Grinshaw: Canada	60	B1
Grindelwald: Switz	25	B3
Grindstone Provincial Park: Canada	61	F2
Griqualand: reg., S. Afr	72	C4
Griquatown: S. Africa	72	C4
Gris Nez, Cap: Fr.	22	B1
Grodno: U.S.S.R.	20	E2
Groix, Île de: France	22	a i
Gronau: Ger. F.R.	24	B1
Grong: Norway	16	B3
Groningen: Neth	24	B1
Groote Eylandt: i., Australia	40	F3
Grootfontein: Namibia	72	B2
Grosnez Point: Jersey	23	a ii
Grosseto: Italy	21	B4
Gross Glockner: mtn., Austria	25	C2
Groton: Conn., U.S.A.	55	H3
Groton: N.Y., U.S.A.	54	D2
Groundhog: r., Can	59	D2
Groveton: U.S.A.	57	O5
Grozny: U.S.S.R.	28	F5
Grudziadz: Poland	20	D2
Gruinard Bay: Scot	10	C2
Gruyères: Switz	25	B3
Guadalajara: Mexico	48	B3
Guadalajara: Spain	19	B4
Guadalcanal: i., Solomon Islands	40	K2
Guadalquivir: r., Spain	19	A5
Guadalupe: i., Pac O	45	O4
Guadalupe: r., Mex.	63	C5
Guadalupe: r., U.S.A.	50	C4
Guadalupe Mts. Nat Park: U.S.A.	53	E4
Guadeloupe: i., Leeward Islands	49	O6
Guadiana: r., Port.	19	A5
Guaíba: & r., Braz	66	D3
Guajará-mirim: Brazil	64	E6
Gualeguay: & r., Arg	66	C3
Gualeguaychú: & r., Argentina	66	C3
Guam: i., Pacific O.	44	D5
Guangdong see Kwangtung	37	
Guangzhou see Canton	37	B5
Guantánamo: Cuba	49	L5
Guanxi Zhuang see Kwangsi Chuang	37	A5
Guaporé: Brazil	66	D2
Guarabira: Brazil	66	b i
Guarapuava: Brazil	66	D1
Guaratinguetá: Brazil	66	a ii
Guarda: Portugal	19	A4
Guardafui, C. see Asir, Somali Rep	69	Q6
Guarulhos: mtn., Braz	66	b i
Guatemala: Guat	48	H6
GUATEMALA	48	H7
Guatemala Basin: Pacific Ocean	45	Q5
Guayabal: & gulf, Cu	49	L5
Guayabero, Laguna de: lake, Argentina	66	A1
Guaycurú: r., Arg	66	B2
Guayguiraró: r., Arg	66	C3
Guaymas: Mexico	48	B2
Guazú: r., Paraguay	66	C2
Gubakha: U.S.S.R.	29	
Gubin: Poland	24	
Gudi: Nigeria	67	
Guebwiller: France	22	
Gruequen, Lac: Can	56	
Guelph: Canada	56	
Guéret: France	23	
Guernsey: i., Chan. Is	14	
Guiana Basin: Atl. O	8	
Guiana Highlands: S. America	64	
Guidigni: Niger	67	
Guigues: Canada	56	
Guildford: England	15	
Guilford: U.S.A	55	
GUINEA	68	
Guinea, Gulf of: W Afr	68	
Guinea Basin: Atl O	8	
GUINEA-BISSAU	68	
Guingamp: France	22	
Guisborough: England	12	
Guiyang see Kweiyang	37	
Guizhou see Kweichow	37	
Gujba: Nigeria	67	
Gujranwala: Pakistan	32	
Guntur: India	32	
Gunungsitoli: Indon	38	
Gurara: r., Nigeria	67	
Gurnard's Head: cape, England	14	
Gur'yev: U.S.S.R	28	
Gusau: Nigeria	67	
Gusev: U.S.S.R.	17	
Güstrow: Ger. D.R	24	
GUYANA	64	
Guymon: U.S.A	50	
Gwabe: Zimbabwe	72	
Gwabegar: Australia	43	
Gwada: Nigeria	67	
Gwadabawa: Nigeria	67	
Gwadar: Pakistan	32	
Gwalior: India	32	
Gweebarra Bay: Irish Republic	13	
Gwelo: Zimbabwe	72	
Gwennap Head: cape, England	14	
Gwent: Co., Wales	14	
Gwynedd: Co., Wales	14	
Gyangtse: China	32	
Gyda Peninsula: U.S.S.R.	27	
Gydan Range (Kolyma Ra.): U.S.S.R	27	
Gympie: Australia	42	
Gyoda: Japan	39	
Gyöngyös: Hungary	20	
Győr: Hungary	20	

Name	Page	ref.
-lock: U.S.A.	61	F3
-owell: U.S.A.	57	Q5
-s Greek: sett., Australia	40	D4
-mahera: i., Indon.	35	H10
-lstead: U.S.A.	54	E3
-mstad: Sweden	17	B4
-singborg: Sweden	17	B4
-lstead: England	15	G3
-ton: Co., Canada	56	F6
-twhistle: England	12	D2
-nada: Japan	39	B3
-madan: Iran	30	E4
-mamatsu: Japan	39	C3
-nar: Norway	17	B3
-mbantota: Sri Lanka	32	b ii
-mber Prov.: see Canada	60	B2
-mburg: Ger. F.R.	24	C1
-mburg: N.J., U.S.A.	54	F3
-mburg: N.Y., U.S.A.	54	B2
-mburg: Pa., U.S.A.	54	D4
-meenlinna: Finland	17	D3
-met: German F.R.	24	B1
-mersley Range: Australia	40	B5
-mi (Qomul): China	34	A2
-milton: Australia	43	B5
-milton: Canada	56	F6
-milton: N.Z.	41	C2
-milton: Scotland	11	D4
-milton: N.Y., U.S.A.	54	E2
-milton: Ohio, U.S.A.	54	B2
-milton, Lake: U.S.A.	50	D3
-mina: Finland	17	E3
-miota: Canada	61	E2
-mlin: Pa., U.S.A.	54	E3
-mlin: Tex., U.S.A.	50	F4
-mm: German F.R.	24	B1
-mmond: U.S.A.	55	K2
-mmond: Va., U.S.A.	59	E4
-mun-Helmand: Afghanistan	30	H4
-r., Kwangtung, China	37	C5
-n: Shensi, China	36	A3
-ncheng: China	36	A3
-nchung: China	37	C4
-nchung: China	36	A3
-ncock: Md., U.S.A.	54	B5
-ncock: Mich, U.S.A.	53	C1
-ncock: N.Y., U.S.A.	54	E3
-nda: Japan	39	c ii
-nda I.: Scotland	10	C1
-nford: U.S.A.	63	C4
-ngchow: China	37	D3
-ngkuang: China	36	D4
-ng: Finland	17	D4
-nkow: China	37	B3
-nku: China	36	C2
-nley: England	14	D1
-nna: Canada	60	D4
-nnibal: U.S.A.	61	F3
-nnibal: U.S.A.	58	B4
-nno: Japan	39	f iv
-no Bay: Sweden	17	B4
-noi: Vietnam	38	D2
-nover: German F.R.	24	B1
-nover: Canada	56	D5
-nover: N.H., U.S.A.	57	N6
-nover: Pa., U.S.A.	54	D5
-nshan: China	36	C3
-ntan: China	36	B2
-ntsun: China	38	B2
-nyang: China	37	B3
-nyin: China	36	B2
-nyu: China	39	f iii
-ogoundou, Lake: Mali	68	E5
-paranda: Sweden	16	D1
-ppy Valley: town, Canada	47	X6
-ra: Ethiopia	69	D7
-ra Usu Nor: lake, Mongolia	34	A1
-rbin (Pinkiang): China	34	H1
-rbor Beach: sett., U.S.A.	56	C6
-burg-Wilhelmsburg: German F.R.	24	B1
-rdangerfjorden: fd., Norway	17	A3
-rdangervidda: plat., Norway	17	A3
-rdenberg: Neth	24	A4
-rdin: U.S.A.	62	E2
-rdisty: Canada	60	C2
-rdwick: St.	57	N5
-rgeisa: Somali Rep.	69	O7
-ringey: England	15	H2
-riryana: State, India	32	C3
-rlech: Wales	14	B2
-rleston: England	15	H2
-rlingen: Neth	24	B1
-rlingen: U.S.A.	50	C4
-rlow: England	15	F3
-rmsnand: Sweden	16	C3
-ro: Spain	19	B4
-rpenden: England	15	F3
-rpers Ferry: U.S.A.	54	C5
-rricana: r., Can	59	E1
-rriman State Park: U.S.A.	55	F3
-rris: r., Scotland	10	B2
-rrisburg: U.S.A.	54	D4
-rismith: S. Africa	72	D4
-risonburg: U.S.A.	59	E4
-rrison Lake: Can	62	B2
-rris Sound: Scot	10	A2
-rrogate: England	12	E3
-rrow: England	15	F3
-rstad: Norway	16	C2
-rtford: England	55	H3
-rtland: England	14	B3
-rtland Point: Eng.	14	B3
-rtlepool: England	12	E2
-rtwell: Canada	61	E3
-rtwell: England	15	F2
-rvey: Australia	42	b ii
-rwell: England	15	E3
-rwich: England	15	H3
-rz: mtns. German F.R./D.R.	24	C1
-rz Nature Park: German F.R.	24	B1
-ssa: geog. reg., Saudi Arabia	30	E5
-sasaki: Japan	39	g iv
-shima: Japan	39	b ii
-shimoto: Japan	39	c i
-askell: U.S.A.	50	C3
-skovo: Bulgaria	21	E4
-slemere: England	15	F3

Name	Page	ref.
Hassan: India	32	C6
Hasselt: Belgium	22	C1
Hassfurt: Ger. F.R.	24	C1
Hassi Messaoud: Alg.	68	G2
Hässleholm: Sweden	17	B4
Hastings & Co., Can.	56	H5
Hastings: England	15	G3
Hastings: N.Z.	41	C2
Hastings: Nebr., U.S.A.	53	F2
Hatboro: U.S.A.	54	E4
Hatfield: England	15	F3
Hatherleigh: England	14	B4
Hatteras, Cape: U.S.A.	51	G2
Hattiesburg: U.S.A.	51	E3
Hatiman-zaki: cape, Japan	39	g iv
Ha Tinh: Vietnam	38	D2
Hat Yai: Thailand	38	C5
Haud: reg. Ethiopia	69	P7
Haugesund: Norway	17	A4
Hauki Lake: Finland	16	E3
Hauraki Gulf: N.Z.	41	C2
Hauteurs de Gâtine: hills, France	23	A2
HAVANA: Cuba	49	K5
Havant: England	15	E4
Havelock: Canada	56	H5
Haverfordwest: Wales	14	B3
Haverhill: England	15	G3
Haverhill: U.S.A.	55	J2
Havering: England	15	G3
Havre: Canada	14	D5
Havre de Grace: U.S.A.	54	D5
Hawarden: Wales	14	C1
Hawaii: i., Hawaiian Is.	45	K5
Hawaiian Is.: State, U.S.A.	44/5	J4
Hawaiian Ridge: Pacific Ocean	44	J4
Hawal: r., Nigeria	67	C1
Hawera: N.Z.	41	B2
Hawes: England	12	D2
Hawke, Cape: Australia	43	D4
Hawke Bay: N.Z.	41	C2
Hawker: Australia	43	A3
Hawkesbury: Canada	57	L4
Hawk Junction: Canada	56	F1
Hawkshead: England	12	C2
Hawksnest I.: U.S.A.	58	E3
Hawthorne: U.S.A.	63	C4
Hay: Australia	43	B4
Hay: Belgium	22	C1
Hay: r & lake, Can	60	B1
Hayden: U.S.A.	63	D5
Hayes: r., Canada	61	F2
Hay Island: Canada	56	E5
Hayle: England	14	A4
Hayling Island: England	15	F4
Hay River: town, Canada	46	M4
Hays: U.S.A.	50	C2
Haywards Heath: Eng.	15	F3
Hazardville: U.S.A.	55	H3
Hazaribagh: India	32	D4
Hazebrouck: France	22	B1
Hazleton: U.S.A.	54	E4
Healdsburg: U.S.A.	63	B4
Heanor: England	15	E1
Heard I.: Southern O	33	f x
Hearst: Canada	58	D2
Heber: Prov. see Hopeh	36	
Heber: U.S.A.	63	D3
Hébertville: Canada	57	O1
Hecla Island: Can	61	D2
Hecla Prov. Park: Canada	61	F2
Hedon: England	12	F3
Heerenveen: Neth	24	B1
Hei: r., China	36	
Heidelberg: Ger F.R.	24	B1
Heidelberg: S. Africa	72	
Heilbronn: Ger. F.R.	24	B1
Heimdal: Norway	16	B3
Heinola: Finland	17	E3
Hekinan: Japan	39	d ii
Hekla: volc. Iceland	16	b ii
Helena: Ark., U.S.A.	50	D3
Helena: Mont., U.S.A.	62	D2
Helensburgh: Scot.	11	D3
Helensville: N.Z.	41	B2
Heligoland Bight: bay, German F.R.	24	B1
Hellertown: U.S.A.	54	E4
Hellin: Spain	19	B5
Hells Canyon: U.S.A.	62	C2
Helmsdale: r., Scot.	10	E1
Helmsley: England	12	E2
HELSINKI (Helsingfors): Finland	17	D3
Helston: England	14	A4
Helvellyn: mtn., Eng	12	C2
Helvick Head: cape, Irish Republic	13	D4
Hemel Hempstead: England	15	F3
Hemlock: U.S.A.	54	C2
Henan: Prov. see Honan	36	
Henderson: Ky., U.S.A.	54	B5
Henderson N.C.: U.S.A.	51	G2
Henderson: Nev., U.S.A.	63	D4
Hengelo: Netherlands	24	B1
Hengshien: China	37	A5
Hengnan: Hunan, China	37	B4
Hengshan: Shensi, China	36	A2
Hengshui: China	36	C2
Hengyang: China	37	B4
Henley-in-Arden: Eng.	15	E2
Henley-on-Thames: England	15	F3
Henlopen, Cape: U.S.A.	54	E5
Henlow: U.S.A.	54	
Henry, Point Austl	42	b ii
Hensall: Canada	56	D6
Henzada: Burma	38	B3
Herat: Afghanistan	30	H4
Hérault: r., France	23	B3
Herbert: Canada	60	D2
Herberton: Australia	40	G4
Herculaneum: U.S.A.	58	D4
Hereford: England	14	D2
Hereford: U.S.A.	50	B3
Hereford & Worcester: U.S.A.	14	D2
Herford: Ger. F.R.	24	B1
Hensau: Switz	25	B2
Herm: i., Chan Is	14	a ii
Herma Ness: cape, Shetland Islands	10	c i
Hermiston: U.S.A.	62	C2
Hermitage: N.Z.	41	B3
Hermosillo: Mexico	48	B4
Hernandarias: Par	66	C2
Herne: Ger. F.R.	24	B1
Herne Bay: England	15	H3

Name	Page	ref.
Herney Lake: U.S.A.	62	C3
Herning: Denmark	17	A4
Herschel I.: Canada	46	H3
Hershey: U.S.A.	54	D4
Herstal: Belgium	22	C1
Hertford: England	15	F3
Hertfordshire: Co., Eng.	15	F3
Hervey: England	57	N3
Hervey Bay: Austl	43	D3
Herzberg: German F.R.	24	C1
Hessle: England	12	F3
Heta: Japan	39	e v
Hetton-le-Hole: Eng	12	E2
Hexham: England	12	D2
Heysham: England	12	D2
Hiawatha: U.S.A.	58	A4
Hibbing: U.S.A.	58	B3
Hibiki-nada: sea, Japan	39	B3
Hidalgo del Parral: Mexico	48	E4
Higashiosaka: Japan	39	b ii
Higganum: U.S.A.	55	H3
Higham Ferrers: Eng.	15	F2
High Atlas: mts, Mor.	68	D2
High Bridge: U.S.A.	54	F4
Highlands: Reg., Scot.	10	C2
High Level: Canada	60	B1
High Point: town, U.S.A.	51	G2
Highpoint State Park: U.S.A.	54	F3
High Prairie: town, Canada	60	B1
High River: town, Can.	60	C2
Highrock: r & lake: Can.	61	E1
High Taunus Nature Park: German F.R.	24	B1
High Veld: geog reg., S. Africa	72	D4
Highworth: England	15	E3
High Wycombe: England	15	F3
Hiiumaa: i., U.S.S.R.	17	D4
Hijaz: geog. reg., Saudi Arabia	30	C6
Hikone: Japan	39	c i
Hilla: Iraq	30	D4
Hildesheim: German F.R.	24	C1
Hillegom: Neth.	24	A1
Hillsboro: Ill., U.S.A.	58	C4
Hillsboro N.H., U.S.A.	55	J1
Hilton: U.S.A.	54	C1
Hilversum: Neth	24	B1
Himachal Pradesh: State, India	32	C2
Himalayas see Great Himalayan Range	32/3	-
Himeji: Japan	39	a ii
Himi: Japan	39	c ii
Hinckley: England	15	E2
Hinckley Reservoir: U.S.A.	54	F2
Hindmarsh, Lake: Austl	43	B5
Hindu Kush: ra., Asia	29	L6
Hines Creek: town, Canada	60	B1
Hingham: U.S.A.	55	J2
Hingkwo: China	37	C4
Hingning: China	37	C5
Hingshan: China	37	C4
Hino: & r., Japan	39	c i
Hinton: Canada	55	H2
Hirakata: Japan	39	b ii
Hiratsuka: Japan	39	f iv
Hirosaki: Japan	39	B3
Hiroshima: Japan	39	B3
Hirson: France	22	C1
Hisai: Japan	39	c ii
Hispaniola: i., W. Indies	49	M6
Histon: England	15	G2
Hitachi: Japan	39	D2
Hitchin: England	15	F3
Hitra: i., Norway	16	A3
Hizuoka: Pref. Japan	39	e iv
Hjørring: Denmark	17	A4
Hluhluwe Game Reserve: S. Africa	72	E4
Hobbs: U.S.A.	50	B3
Hobart: Australia	40	b i
Hoboken: Belgium	22	B1
Hochih: China	37	A5
Ho Chi Minh City (Saigon): Vietnam	38	D2
Hochiu: China	36	C3
Hoch Moor: reg., German F.R.	24	B1
Hockessin: U.S.A.	54	E5
Hodeida: Yemen	30	D8
Hodgeville: Canada	60	D2
Hódmezővásárhely: Hungary	20	D3
Hoding, Monts du: Alg	68	F1
Hof: German F.R.	24	C1
Hofei: China	36	C3
Hofn: Iceland	16	b ii
Hofsjökull: ice-cap, Ice.	16	b ii
Hohe Eifel: mtns, German F.R.	24	B1
Hohe Rhön: mtns., German F.R.	24	B1
Hohhot: China	36	B2
Hohe Tauern: mtns., Austria	25	C2
Hohe Tauern Nature Park: Austria	25	C2
Hohpi: China	37	B5
Hohsien: China	37	B5
Hoifung: China	37	B5
Hokang: China	34	J1
Hokianga Harbour: N.Z.	41	B2
Hoken: China	36	C2
Hokitika: N.Z.	41	B3
Hokkaido: i., Japan	39	a iii
Hokota: Japan	39	g iii
Hokudan: Japan	39	a ii
Holbæk: Denmark	17	B4
Holbeach: England	15	F2
Holbrook: Australia	43	C5
Holden: Canada	60	C2
Holderness: penin., England	12	F3
Holdrege: U.S.A.	53	F2
Holguín: Cuba	49	L5
Holland: U.S.A.	58	B4
Hollidaysburg: U.S.A.	54	B4
Holliston: U.S.A.	55	J2
Holly: U.S.A.	56	B7
Holly Springs: town, U.S.A.	51	
Hollywood: Calif., U.S.A.	52	B4
Hollywood: Fla., U.S.A.	51	F4
Holmfirth: England	12	E1
Holmhead: Scotland	11	D4
Holstebro: Denmark	17	A4
Holstein: Old State: German F.R.	24	C1
Holsworthy: England	14	B4
Holt: England	15	H2
Holyhead: Wales	14	B1
Holy I.: England	12	E1
Holy I.: Scotland	11	C4
Holy I.: Wales	14	B1

Name	Page	ref.
Holyoke: U.S.A.	55	H2
Holywell: Wales	14	C1
Holywood N. Irel.	13	F2
Homalin: Burma	38	B2
Homberg: German F.R.	24	B2
Homb: town, Australia	42	C1
Homer: Alaska, U.S.A.	46	E5
Homer: N.Y., U.S.A.	54	D2
Homerville: U.S.A.	51	F4
Homestead: U.S.A.	51	F4
Homs: Libya	68	H1
Homs: Syria	28	D7
Honan (Henan): Prov., China	36	B3
HONDURAS:	48/9	-
Hønefoss: Norway	17	B3
Honeoye Falls: U.S.A.	54	C2
Honesdale: U.S.A.	54	C3
Honey Grove: U.S.A.	54	C4
Honfleur: France	22	B2
HONG KONG:	37	B5
HONIARA: Solomon Is.	40	K2
Honiton: England	14	C4
Honjo: Japan	39	f iii
Honshu: i., Japan	39	C2
Hood, Mount: U.S.A.	62	B2
Hood Point: Austl	42	b ii
Hoogezand: Neth	24	B1
Hooghly: r., India	32	E4
Hook Head: cape, Irish Republic	13	
Hook I.: Australia	42	C1
Hook of Holland: Netherlands	24	A1
Hoorn: Netherlands	24	B1
Hoosic: r., U.S.A.	55	G2
Hoosick Falls: town, U.S.A.	55	G2
Hoover Dam: U.S.A.	63	D4
Hope: Canada	62	B3
Hope: Wales	14	C1
Hope: U.S.A.	50	D3
Hope, Loch: Scot.	10	D1
Hope Bay: Antarc	65	G16
Hope (Hebei): Prov., China	36	C2
Hope's Nose: pt., England	14	C4
Hopewell: N.J.		
Hopewell: Va., U.S.A.	54	F4
Hoping: China	37	B5
Hopkinsville: U.S.A.	51	E2
Hoppo (Limchow): China	37	A5
Hoquiam: U.S.A.	62	B2
Horbury: England	12	E1
Horcones: r., Arg	66	B4
Horden: England	12	E2
Horley: England	15	F3
Hormuz, Strait of: Iran/U.A.E.	30	G5
Horn, Cape: Chile	65	E15
Hornan, Lake: Swed.	16	C3
Horncastle: England	15	F1
Hornell: U.S.A.	54	C2
Horn Head: cape, Irish Republic	13	D1
Hornsea: England	12	F3
Horqueta: Paraguay	66	C2
Horseheads: U.S.A.	54	D2
Horsens: Denmark	17	A4
Horsham: Australia	43	B5
Horsham: England	15	F3
Horten: Norway	17	B4
Horwood Lake: Can.	56	F1
Hosanagad: India	32	C4
Hoshun: China	36	B2
Hospitalet: Spain	19	C4
Hotsieh: China	36	B2
Hot Springs: town, U.S.A.	50	D3
Houghton Lake: U.S.A.	58	D3
Houghton-le-Spring: England	12	E2
Houma: U.S.A.	50	D4
Hounslow: England	15	F3
Hourn, Loch: Scot.	10	C2
Housatonic: r., U.S.A.	55	G3
Houston: Miss., U.S.A.	51	E3
Houston: Tex., U.S.A.	50	C4
Houtzdale: U.S.A.	54	B4
Hove: England	15	F4
Howard: Australia	42	D3
Howden: England	12	F3
Howe, Cape: Austl	43	D5
Howell: U.S.A.	54	F3
Howitt, Mt.: Austl	43	C5
Howrah: India	32	E4
Howth: Irish Rep	13	E3
Hoy: i. & sound, Orkney Islands	10	d iv
Hoyang: China	36	B2
Høyanger: Norway	16	A3
Hoylake: England	12	C1
Hoyt: Ger. F.R.	24	B1
Hoyun: China	37	B5
Hradec Králové: Czech	20	C3
Hsiaching: China	36	C3
Hsiahsien: China	36	B3
Hsiangchou: China	37	A5
Hsiangyüan: China	36	B3
Hsianhsien: China	36	C2
Hsiatsun: China	36	D5
Hsichang: China	36	
Hsingi: China	36	
Hsingkuo: China	37	C4
Hsinghua: China	36	C3
Hsingtang: China	36	C3
Hsin-hai-lien: China	36	C3
Hsinhsien: China	36	A4
Hsinhui: China	37	B5
Hsinü: China	37	C4
Hsinkao Shan: mtn., Taiwan	37	D5
Hsinyu: China	37	C4
Hsipaw: Burma	38	B2
Hsishui: China	36	
Hsuan: China	36	C3
Hsuchang: China	36	B3
Hsüchow: China	36	C3
Hsüi: China	36	C3
Hydas Nor: lake, Mongolia	34	A1
Hyde: England	12	D1
Hyden: Australia	42	b ii
Hyde Park: town, U.S.A.	55	G3
Hyderabad & State: India	32	C3
Hyderabad: Pak	32	A3
Hyères: France	23	D3
Hyndman: U.S.A.	54	C5
Hythe: Canada	60	B1
Hythe: Hants., Eng	15	E4
Hythe: Kent, Eng.	15	H3
Hyuga: Japan	39	B3
Hyvinkää: Finland	17	D3

Name	Page	ref.
Hualaga: r., Peru	64	C5
Huambo: Angola	71	C10
Huancavelica: Peru	64	C6
Huancayo: Peru	64	D6
Huanching: China	37	A5
Hungkang: China	37	B3
Hungliung: China	36	A2
Hungpeng: China	37	A4
Huan-hsien: China	37	A4
Hubbard Lake: U.S.A.	56	B5
Hubbard Point: Can	61	G1
Hubbell: U.S.A.	58	C2
Hubei: Prov., see China	37	
Hubli: India	32	C5
Huchow: China	37	D3
Hucknall: England	15	E1
Huddersfield: Eng	12	E1
Hudiksvall: Sweden	16	C3
Hudson: Canada	58	B1
Hudson: Mass., U.S.A.	55	J2
Hudson: N.Y., U.S.A.	55	G2
Hudson: r., U.S.A.	59	F3
Hudson Bay: town	47	T5
Hudson Falls: town, U.S.A.	55	G1
Hué: Vietnam	38	D3
Huelva: Spain	19	A5
Huesca: Spain	19	B4
Hufuh: Saudi Arabia	30	E6
Hughenden: Austl	40	G5
Hughesville: U.S.A.	54	D3
Hugo Town: Scilly Is	14	c iv
Hugo: U.S.A.	50	C3
Huhehot: China	36	B2
Huhsien: China	36	A3
Huillapima: Arg	66	B3
Huinca Renancó: Arg.	66	B3
Hukow: China	37	C4
Hukow: China	37	C4
Hull: Canada	57	K4
Hull: r., England	12	F3
Hull: Co., Canada	57	K4
Huls: Ger. F.R.	24	B1
Hulun Chih: lake, China	34	F1
Humahuaca: Argentina	66	B2
Humber: r., Canada	56	F6
Humber, est.: Eng	12	F3
Humberside: Co., Eng	12	F3
Humboldt: Canada	61	D2
Humboldt: r., U.S.A.	63	C3
Hume, Lake: Austl	43	C5
Hummels Wharf: U.S.A.	54	D4
Hunan: Prov., China	37	B3
Hunedoara: Rom.	20	B4
Hungan: China	37	
HUNGARY:	20	C3
Hungerford: England	15	E3
Hunger Steppe: U.S.S.R.	29	L4
Hunghu: China	37	B4
Hunghu: China	37	A4
Hungry Horse Reservoir: U.S.A.	62	D2
Hungshui: r., China	37	A5
Hungtung: China	36	B2
Hungtze: & lake, China	36	C3
Hummanby: England	12	F2
Hunsrück: mtns., German F.R.	24	B1
Hunstanton: Eng	15	G2
Huntingdon: England	15	F2
Huntingdon: U.S.A.	54	B4
Huntington: Canada	57	L4
Huntington: England	15	F2
Huntington: U.S.A.	54	C1
Huntington: N.Y., U.S.A.	55	G4
Huntington: W. Va., U.S.A.	59	E4
Huntly: N.Z.	41	C2
Huntly: Scotland	10	E2
Huntsville: Canada	57	L4
Huntsville: Ala., U.S.A.	51	E3
Huntsville: Tex., U.S.A.	54	C4
Huntzan: China	36	B2
Hupeh (Hubei): Prov., China	37	B3
Hurd, Cape: Can	56	B3
Huron: U.S.A.	53	F2
Huron: Co., Canada	56	D6
Huron, Lake: Canada/U.S.A.	58	D3
Hurricane: U.S.A.	63	D4
Hurstpierpoint: Eng	15	F3
Hurunui: r., N.Z.	41	B3
Húsavik: Iceland	16	b i
Huskvarna: Sweden	17	B4
Hutchinson: U.S.A.	50	C3
Huto: r., China	36	B2
Hutt: N.Z.	41	C3
Hwashsien: China	37	A5
Hwaian: China	36	C3
Hwailai: China	36	C1
Hwainan (Huainan): China	36	C3
Hwang (Yellow): r., China	34	C3
Hwangchwan: China	36	B3
Hwanghsien: China	36	D2
Hwangshih: China	37	C4
Hwangyen: China	37	D4
Hweian: China	37	C4
Hweichang: China	37	C4
Hweilai: China	37	C5
Hweiting: China	36	A4
Hwohsien: China	36	B2
Hyannis: U.S.A.	55	K3

Name	Page	ref.
Ibagué: Colombia	64	C3
Ibagwa Ani: Nig	67	B2
Ibaraki: Japan	39	b ii
Ibaraki: Pref. Japan	39	g iii
Iberá, Lago: Argentina	66	C3
Iberville: Canada	57	M4
Ibi: Nigeria	67	B2
Ibicuí: r., Brazil	66	C3
Ibicuí da Armada: r., Brazil	66	C3
Ibiraputiã: r., Braz	66	C3
Ibirocaí: r., Brazil	66	C2
Ibiza: & i., Balearic Islands	19	C5
Ibusa: Nigeria	67	B2
Ica: Peru	64	C6
Içamaquá: r., Braz	66	C2
Icatu: Argentina	66	B2
Ice Harbor Dam: U.S.A.	62	C2
ICELAND:	16	-
Ichang: Hunan, China	37	
Ichang: Hupeh, China	37	B3
Icheng: China	37	B3
Icheu: Nigeria	67	B2
Ichi: r., Japan	39	a ii
Ichihara: Japan	39	g iv
Ichikawa: Chiba, Japan	39	f iv
Ichikawa: Hyogo, Japan	39	a ii
Ichinomiya: Aichi, Japan	39	c i
Ichinomiya: Chiba, Japan	39	g iv
Ichinoseki: Japan	39	D2
Ichun: China	37	B4
Ichwan: Honan, China	36	B3
Ichwan: Shensi, China	36	B3
Ickseburg: U.S.A.	54	C4
Idabel: U.S.A.	50	D3
Idaho: State, U.S.A.	63	D3
Idaho Falls: city, U.S.A.	62	D3
Idanre: Nigeria	67	B2
Idogo: Nigeria	67	A2
Idrigill Pt.: Scot	10	B2
Ife: Nigeria	67	A2
Ifeng: China	37	B4
Ifon: Nigeria	67	B2
Iganga: Nigeria	67	
Igarka: U.S.S.R.	27	L4
Igbetti: Nigeria	67	A2
Igbo-Ora: Nigeria	67	A2
Ighil Izane: Algeria	19	C5
Iglesias: Sardinia	18	
Iglook: Canada	47	T3
Iguaçu: r., Brazil	66	C2
Iguaçu, Parque Nac. do: Brazil	66	D2
Iguatemi: r., Brazil	66	D2
Ihala: Nigeria	67	B2
Ihsien: Liaoning, China	36	D1
Ihsien: Anhwei, China	37	C4
Ihwang: China	37	C4
Iida: Japan	39	C2
Iisalmi: Finland	16	E3
Iizuka: Japan	39	B3
Ikare: Nigeria	67	B2
Ikaria: i., Greece	21	E5
Ikeja: Nigeria	67	A2
Ikire: Nigeria	67	B2
Ikirun: Nigeria	67	B2
Ikole: Nigeria	67	B2
Ikom: Nigeria	67	B2
Ikot Ekpene: Nig	67	B2
Ikuno: Japan	39	a ii
Ila: Nigeria	67	A2
Ilan: Taiwan	37	D5
Ilaro: Nigeria	67	A2
Ilchester: England	14	D4
Ilebo: Zaire	71	D8
Île de France: Old Prov. France	22	B2
Ilero: Nigeria	67	A2
Ilesa: Nigeria	67	B2
Ilford: Canada	61	F1
Ilfracombe: Eng	14	B3
Ilha Grande: r., Brazil	66	D1
Ilhéus: Brazil	65	L6
Ili: r., China/U.S.S.R.	29	M5
Iliamna Lake: U.S.A.	46	D5
Ilion: U.S.A.	54	E2
Ilkeston: England	15	E2
Ilkley: England	12	E3
Illimani: mtn. Bol	64	D7
Illinois: State & r., U.S.A.	53	C3
Illo: Nigeria	67	A1
Ilmen, Lake: U.S.S.R.	26	E4
Ilmenau: Ger. D.R.	24	C1
Ilminster: England	14	D4
Ilobu: Nigeria	67	B2
Iloilo: Philippines	35	G8
Ilora: Nigeria	67	A2
Ilorin: Nigeria	67	B2
Imaban: Japan	39	B3
Imandra, Lake: U.S.S.R.	16	F2
Imari: Japan	39	B3
Imatú Lagoa: Braz	16	E3
Imatra: Finland	16	E3
Imbanuma: r., Japan	39	g iv
Imlay City: U.S.A.	56	B6
Immingham: England	12	F3
Imo: r & State: Nigeria	67	B2
Imperia: Italy	18	B2
Imperial Dam: U.S.A.	63	D4
Imphal: India	33	F4
Inagawa: Japan	39	b ii
Inari: China	36	
Inari: & l., Finland	16	E2
Inazawa: Japan	39	c i
Inchard, Loch: Scot	10	C1
Inch'on: S. Korea	36	D2
Indal: r., Sweden	16	C3
Independence: U.S.A.	58	A4
INDIA:	32/3	-
Indiana: State, U.S.A.	58	C4
Indianapolis: U.S.A.	58	
Indian Head: sett.: Canada	61	D2
Indian Lake: U.S.A.	57	L6
Indian Ocean:	5	
Indio: U.S.A.	63	C4
Indira: r., U.S.S.R.	27	R3
INDONESIA:	35	-
Indore: India	32	C4
Indre: r., France	23	B2
Indus: r., India/Pak	32	A3
Indus, Mouths of the: Pakistan	32	A4
Ingenico Luggi: Arg	66	A2
Ingenio Santa Ana: Argentina	66	A2
Ingersoll: Canada	56	E6
Ingleborough: mtn.: England	12	D2
Ingolstadt: Ger. F.R.	25	C2
Inhambane: Moz	72	E3
Inhaminga: Moz	72	E2

Name	Page	ref
Inisbofin: i., Irish Rep.	13	A3
Inishark: i., Irish Rep.	13	A3
Inisheer: i., Irish Rep.	13	B3
Inishmaan: i., Irish Rep.	13	B3
Inishmore: i., Irish Rep.	13	B3
Inishmurray: i., Irish Republic	13	C2
Inishowen Peninsula: Irish Republic	13	D1
Inisturk: i., Irish Republic	13	A3
Ijebu-Ode: Nigeria	67	A2
Ijebu-Igbo: Nigeria	67	A2
Ijmuiden: Neth.	24	A1
Ijssel: r., Neth.	24	B1
Ijsselmeer (Zuider Zee): Neth.	24	B1
Ijui: & r., Brazil	66	D2
Injune: Australia	42	C3
Inkerman: U.S.S.R.	28	C5
Inkom: U.S.A.	62	D3
Inland Sea see Seto-naikai		
Inn: r., Austria	25	C2
Inner Hebrides: is., Scot.		B3
Innerleithen: Scot	11	E4
International Falls: town, U.S.A.	58	B2
Inner Mongolia: Aut. Reg., China	34	F2
Inner Sound: Scot	10	C2
Innisfail: Canada	62	D1
Innishowen Hd.: N. Ireland	13	E1
Innsbruck: Austria	25	C2
Inntal: val., Aus.	25	C2
Inny: r., England	14	B4
Inny: r., Kerry, Irish Republic	13	A5
Inny: r., Longford, Irish Republic	13	D3
Inowrocław: Poland	20	C2
Inspiration: U.S.A.	63	D5
Inter-American Highway: Mexico	48	G6
Interlaken: Switz	25	B2
International Falls: town, U.S.A.	58	B2
International Peace Garden: Canada	61	E3
Intracoastal Waterway: U.S.A.	55	F5
Inubo-saki: cape, Japan	39	g iv
Inuvik: Canada	46	H3
Inuyama: Japan	39	c i
Inveraray: Scot.	11	C3
Inverbervie: Scot	10	F3
Invercargill: N.Z.	41	A4
Inverell: Austl.	43	D3
Invergordon: Scot	10	D2
Inverkeithing: Scot	11	E3
Invermere: Canada	62	C1
Inverness: Scot	10	D2
Inverurie: Scot	10	F2
Investigator Strait: Australia	43	A5
Inzai: Japan	39	g iv
Iola: U.S.A.	58	A4
Iona: i., Scotland	10	B3
Iona Nat. Park: Angola	72	A2
Ionian Is.: Greece	21	D5
Ionian Sea: Med. Sea	21	C5
Ioninna: Greece	21	D5
Ios: i., Greece	21	E5
Iowa: State & r., U.S.A.	58	B3
Iowa City: U.S.A.	58	B3
Ipin: China	34	C5
Ipoh: Malaysia	38	C6
Ipswich: Australia	42	D3
Ipswich: England	15	H2
Ipswich: U.S.A.	55	K2
Iquique: Chile	64	B2
Iquitos: Peru	64	D4
Iragbiji: Nigeria	67	A2
Irago-suido: str., Japan	39	c ii
Iráklion: Crete	21	E5
IRAN:	30	F4
'IRAQ:	30	D4
Irati: Brazil	66	D2
Irbil: Iraq	28	E6
Irele: Nigeria	67	A2
Irfon: r., Wales	14	C2
IRISH REPUBLIC:	13	—
Irish Sea: Irel./Eng	14	A2
Irkutsk: U.S.S.R.	27	N7
Irma: Canada	60	C2
Iron: Lough, Irish Republic	13	D3
Iron Bridge: England	14	D2
Irondale: r., Can.	56	G5
Irondequoit: U.S.A.	54	C1
Iron Gates: gorge, Rom./Yugo.	21	D4
Iron Knob: Austl.	43	A4
Iron Mountain: Idaho, U.S.A.	62	C2
Iron Mountain: town, Mich., U.S.A.	58	C2
Iron Springs: town, U.S.A.	63	D4
Ironton: U.S.A.	63	D3
Ironwood: U.S.A.	58	B2
Iroquois: Canada	57	K5
Irrawaddy: r. & Divis., Burma	38	B3
Irrawaddy Delta: Burma	38	A3
Irthlingborough: Eng	15	F2
Irtysh: r., U.S.S.R.	29	L2
Irvine: Scotland	11	D4
Irvinestown: N. Irel	13	D2
Iruya: r., Arg	66	B1
Isa: Nigeria	67	B1
Isaac: r., Austl	42	C3
Isafjördhur: Ice.	16	a i
Isanzo: r., Italy/Yugoslavia	25	C2
Isar: r., Ger. F.R	25	C2
Isara: Nigeria	67	A2
Isarco: r., Italy	25	C2
Ise: Japan	39	c ii
Iseo, Lake: Italy	25	C2
Isère: r., France	23	D4
Iserlohn: Ger. F.R	24	B1
Ise-shima-kokuritsu-köen: nat. park, Japan	39	c ii
Ise-wan: bay, Japan	39	c ii
Iseyin: Nigeria	67	A2
Isfahan: Iran	30	F4
Ishikari-wan: bay, Japan	39	D1
Ishim: r., U.S.S.R.	29	K3
Ishimbay: U.S.S.R.	28	H3
Ishinomaki: Japan	39	D2
Ishioka: Japan	39	g iii
Ishpeming: U.S.A.	58	C2
Ishui: China	36	C2
Isiro: Zaire	70	E7

Name	Page	ref
Iskâr: r., Bulg	21	D4
Iskenderun: Turkey	28	D6
Isla: r., Scot	10	E3
ISLAMABAD: Pak	32	B2
Island Beach State Park: U.S.A.	55	F5
Island Falls: town, Ont., Canada	59	D2
Island Falls: town, Sask., Canada	61	E1
Island Lake: sett. & l., Canada	61	G2
Island Pond: sett. U.S.A.	57	O5
Islands, Bay of: Can.	56	C3
Islands, Bay of: N.Z.	41	B2
Islay: i., Scotland	11	B4
Isle: r., England	14	D4
Isle Royale: i. & Nat. park, U.S.A.	58	C2
Ismael Cortinas: Uru.	66	C3
Ismailia: Egypt	69	M2
Isna: Egypt	69	M3
Isola: France	23	C3
ISRAEL:	30	B4
Issigeac: France	23	B3
Issoudun: France	23	B3
Issyk-Kul': U.S.S.R.	29	M5
Istanbul: Turkey	21	E4
Istra (Istria): penin., Yugoslavia	21	B3
Itabuna: Brazil	64	L6
Ita Ibaté: Argentina	66	C2
Itajaí: Brazil	66	E2
Itajaí do Norte: r., Brazil	66	E2
Itajaí do Sul: r., Brazil	66	E2
Itajaí Mirim: r., Brazil	66	E2
Itajubá: Brazil	66	a i
Itako: Japan	39	g iv
ITALY:	25	C2
Itami: Japan	39	b ii
Itapetininga: & r., Brazil	66	a i
Itapetinga: r., Brazil	66	a i
Itapeva: Brazil	66	a i
Itapeva, Lagoa: Brazil	66	E2
Itapira: Brazil	66	a i
Itaqui: Brazil	66	C2
Itararé: & r., Brazil	66	E1
Itati, Lago: Arg	66	C2
Itatiaia, Parque Nacional do: Brazil	66	b i
Itchen: r., England	15	E3
Ithaca: U.S.A.	54	D2
Ithon: r., Wales	14	C2
Ito: Japan	39	f v
Itu: Brazil	66	a i
Itu: Nigeria	67	B3
Itu: Brazil	67	B2
Itu: r., Brazil	66	E2
Ituim: r., Brazil	66	D2
Ituna: Canada	61	D2
Ituzaingó: Arg.	66	C2
Ivalo: Finland	16	E2
Ivanhoe: Australia	43	B4
Ivanhoe Lake: Can.	56	C1
Ivano-Frankovsk: U.S.S.R.	20	D3
Ivanovo: U.S.S.R.	28	E2
Ivdel': U.S.S.R.	29	J1
IVORY COAST:	68	D7
Ivoryton: U.S.A.	55	H3
Ivybridge: England	14	C4
Iwade: Japan	39	b ii
Iwaki: Japan	39	D1
Iwakuni: Japan	39	B3
Iwanai: Japan	39	D1
Iwanuma: Japan	39	D2
Iwate-san: mtn., Japan	39	D2
Iwo: Nigeria	67	A2
Iyang: China	37	C4
Iyo-nada: sea, Japan	39	B3
Izhevsk: U.S.S.R.	28	H2
Izhma: r., U.S.S.R.	26	H5
Izmir: Turkey	21	E5
Izumi: Japan	39	b ii
Izumi-otsu: Japan	39	b ii
Izumi-sano: Japan	39	b ii
Izu-Shoto: arch., Japan	39	C3

Name	Page	ref
Jamestown: N.Y., U.S.A.	56	F7
Jamestown: R.I., U.S.A.	55	J3
Jammu: India	32	B2
Jammu and Kashmir: State, disputed between India & Pak.	32	C2
Jamnagar: India	32	B4
Jamshedpur: India	32	E4
Jamtari: Nigeria	67	C2
Janesville: U.S.A.	58	C3
Jaoping: China	37	C5
JAPAN:	39	—
Japan, Sea of: Japan	34	J3
Japen: i., Indon	35	K11
Jarrow: England	12	F1
Järvenpää: Finland	17	E3
Jarvis: Canada	56	E7
Jaslo: Poland	20	D3
Jasper: & Nat. park, Canada	60	D2
Jasper: U.S.A.	51	E3
Jauf: Saudi Arabia	30	C5
Java: i., Indon.	35	D12
Java Sea: Indon.	35	E12
Java Trench: Ind. O	33	j v
Jebba: Nigeria	67	A2
Jebel Aulia Dam: Sudan	69	M5
Jedburgh: Scot.	11	F4
Jefferson: r., U.S.A.	56	E8
Jefferson: r., U.S.A.	62	D2
Jefferson City: Mo., U.S.A.	58	B4
Jefferson City, Mont.: U.S.A.	62	D2
Jeffersonville: U.S.A.	54	B4
Jega: Nigeria	67	A1
Jehol: see Chengteh	36	C1
Jejui Guazú: r., Par	66	C1
Jékabpils: U.S.S.R.	17	E4
Jelenia Góra: Pol	20	C2
Jelgava: U.S.S.R.	17	D4
Jena: German D.R	24	C1
Jerez: Spain	19	A5
Jerez de los Caballeros: Spain	19	A5
Jerome: U.S.A.	62	D3
Jersey: i., Chan. Is	14	a ii
Jersey City: U.S.A.	55	F4
Jersey Shore: city, U.S.A.	54	C3
JERUSALEM: Israel	30	B4
Jervis Bay: Austl	43	D5
Jervis Inlet: Canada	62	B1
Jessore: Bangladesh	32	F4
Jesup: U.S.A.	51	F3
Jesús: Paraguay	66	C2
Jesús Maria: Arg	66	B3
Jethou: i., Chan. Is	14	a ii
Jhansi: India	32	C3
Jhelum: r., Pak	32	B2
Jiangsu: Prov. see Kiangsu		
Jiangxi: Prov. see Kiangsi		
Jibhalanta see Uliastay		
Jidda: Saudi Arabia	30	C6
Jichiao: China	36	B2
Jihlava: Czech	20	C3
Jijiga: Ethiopia	69	O7
Jiménez: Mexico	48	E4
Jim Thorpe: U.S.A.	54	E4
Jinan see Tsinan	36	C2
Jingdezhen see Chingtechen	37	C4
Jinja: Uganda	70	F7
João Pessoa: Brazil	64	L5
Joaquin V. González: Argentina	66	B1
Jodhpur: India	32	B3
Joensuu: Finland	16	E3
Jofra Oasis: Libya	68	H3
Joggakarta: Indon.	35	E12
Johannesburg: S. Afr	72	D4
John Day: r., U.S.A.	62	C2
John o'Groats: Scot	10	E1
Johnsonburg: U.S.A.	54	B3
Johnson City: N.Y., U.S.A.	54	E2
Johnson City: Tenn., U.S.A.	51	F2
Johnston: i., Pac. O	11	D4
Johnston Lakes: Austl	42	b ii
Johnston's Point: Scotland	11	C4
Johnstown: N.Y., U.S.A.	55	F1
Johnstown: Pa., U.S.A.	54	B4
Johor Bahru: Mal.	38	C6
Joinvile: Brazil	66	E2
Jokkmokk: Sweden	16	C2
Joliet: U.S.A.	58	C3
Joliette: Can.	57	L3
Joliette, Parc du: Canada	57	L3
Jolo: i., Philippines	35	G9
Jonesboro: U.S.A.	50	D2
Jones Sound: Can	47	M2
Jonglei: Sudan	69	M7
Jönköping: Sweden	17	B4
Jonquière: Canada	57	O1
Joplin: U.S.A.	58	B4
JORDAN:	30	C4
Jordan: U.S.A.	54	D1
Jordão: r., Brazil	66	D1
Jorhat: India	33	F3
Jos: Nigeria	67	B2
José Battle y Ordóñez: Uru	66	C3
José Pedro Varela: Uruguay	66	D3
Joseph: U.S.A.	56	F4
Joseph Bonaparte Gulf: Austl.	40	C2
Joseph Lake: Can	60	C2
Joshua Tree Nat. Monument: U.S.A.	63	D4
Jos Plateau: Nig	67	B2
Josselin: France	22	a i
Jostedalsbreen: ice-cap, Norway	16	A3
Jotunheimen: mtns., Norway	16	A3
Joyces Country: dist., Irish Republic	13	B3
Joyo: Japan	39	b ii
Juan B. Arruabarrena: Argentina	66	C2
Juan de Fuca Strait: Can./U.S.A.	62	B2
Juan Fernández Is.: Pacific Ocean	65	C10
Juárez, Sierra de: Mexico	48	C5
Juatinga, Ponta de: pt., Brazil	66	b i

Name	Page	ref
Juazeiro: Brazil	64	K5
Juba: Sudan	69	M8
Juba: r., Somali Rep	69	O8
Juby, Cape: Canary Is.	68	C3
Júcar: r., Spain	19	B5
Jucheng: China	37	B4
Judith, Point: U.S.A.	55	J3
Judith Gap: town, U.S.A.	62	E2
Juichin: China	37	D4
Juist: r., Ger. F.R	24	B1
Juiz de Fora: Braz	66	b i
Jujuy: Prov., Arg	66	A1
Jukao: China	36	D3
Juliaca: Peru	64	D7
Julian Alps: Italy/Yugoslavia	25	C2
Jülich: Ger. F.R	24	B1
Julier Pass: Switz.	25	C2
Júlio de Castilhos: Brazil	66	D2
Jullundur: India	32	C2
Jumilla: Spain	19	B5
Junan: China	36	B3
Junction City: U.S.A.	58	a i
Jundiaí: Brazil	66	a i
Juneau: U.S.A.	46	J5
Junee: Australia	43	C4
Jungan: China	37	A4
Jungfrau: mtn., Switzerland	25	B2
Jungkang: China	37	A4
Jungyun: China	37	B5
Juniata: r., U.S.A.	54	C4
Junín: Argentina	66	B3
Junsele: Sweden	16	C3
Juquiá: r., Brazil	66	a i
Jur: r., Sudan	69	L7
Jura: i & sound, Scotland	11	C4
Jura, The: mtns. Fr./Switz	25	B2
Juruá: r., Brazil	64	E5
Juruena: r., Brazil	64	G6
Jussey: France	22	C2
Jüterbog: Ger. D.R	24	C1
Jutland: penin., see Jylland	17	A4
Jutung: China	36	D3
Jyekundo: see Yushu	34	B4
Jylland (Jutland): penin., Denmark	17	A4
Jyväskylä: Finland	16	E3
Kaba: Nigeria	67	B2
Kabaena: i., Indon.	35	G12
KABUL: Afghanistan	32	A2
Kabwe: Zambia	72	D1
Kachia: Nigeria	67	B2
Kachin: State, Burma	38	B1
Kadah: Czechoslovakia	24	C1
Kadina: Australia	43	A4
Kadoma: Japan	39	b ii
Kaduna: & State, Nigeria	67	B1
Kaduna: r., Nig	67	B2
Kaélé: Cameroun	67	C1
Kafanchan: Nigeria	67	B2
Kafue: & r., Zambia	72	D1
Kafue Nat. Park: Zambia	72	D1
Kaga: Nigeria	67	B1
Kagoro: Nigeria	67	B2
Kagoshima: Japan	39	B3
Kahing: China	37	D3
Kaiama: Nigeria	67	b i
Kaibara: Japan	39	b ii
Kaieteur Falls: Guyana	64	G2
Kaifeng: China	36	B3
Kaihua: China	37	C4
Kai Is.: Indonesia	35	J12
Kai Kung Chow: China	37	A3
Kaikohe: N.Z.	41	A1
Kaikoura: & range, New Zealand	41	B3
Kailas Range: China	32	D1
Kaimanawa Mts.: N.Z.	41	C2
Kainji Reservoir: Nigeria	67	A1
Kainji Dam: Nigeria	67	A1
Kaipara Harbour: N.Z.	41	B2
Kaiping: Liaoning, China	36	D1
Kairouen: Tunisia	68	H1
Kaiserslautern: German F.R	24	B2
Kaitaia: N.Z.	41	B1
Kaitangata: N.Z.	41	A4
Kaizuka: Japan	39	b ii
Kajaani: Finland	16	E3
Kakagi, Lake: Can.	58	A2
Kakinada: India	32	D5
Kako: r., Japan	39	a ii
Kakogawa: Japan	39	b ii
Kaktovik: U.S.A.	46	G2
Kala-Belge: Nigeria	67	C1
Kalachinsk: U.S.S.R.	29	L2
Kalahari Desert: Botswana/Namibia	72	C3
Kalahari Game Reserve: S. Afr.	72	C3
Kalahari Gemsbok Nat. Park: S. Africa	72	C4
Kalámai: Greece	21	D5
Kalamazoo: & r., U.S.A.	58	C3
Kalannie: Australia	42	b ii
Kalat: Pakistan	32	A3
Kale: r., Turkey	21	F2
Kalgansee: Changkiakow	36	C6
Kalgoorlie: Australia	42	c ii
Kaliningrad: U.S.S.R.	17	D5
Kalinin: U.S.S.R.	28	D2
Kalispell: U.S.A.	62	D2
Kalisz: Poland	20	C2
Kalix: r., Sweden	16	D2
Kalimantan: Prov., Indonesia	35	E11
Kallo: Ethiopia	69	O7
Kall Lake: Sweden	16	B3
Kalmar: Sweden	17	C4
Kalmunai: Sri Lanka	32	b ii
Kalomo: Zambia	72	D2
Kalush: U.S.S.R.	20	D3
Kaluga: U.S.S.R.	28	D2
Kama: r., U.S.S.R.	28	G2
Kamaishi: Japan	39	D2
Kamakura: Japan	39	f iv
Kamaran Is.: Yemen P.D.R	30	D7
Kamba: Nigeria	67	A1
Kamchatka: penin., U.S.S.R.	27	S6
Kamchatka Bay: U.S.S.R.	27	S6
Kamenets Podol'skiy: U.S.S.R.	20	E3

Name	Page	ref
Kamenskoye: U.S.S.R.	27	T5
Kamensk-Uralskiy: U.S.S.R.	29	J2
Kameoka: Japan	39	b i
Kamet: mtn., India	32	C2
Kamisato: Japan	39	c ii
Kamloops: Canada	62	B1
Kamogawa: Japan	39	g iv
Kamouraska: Co., Canada	57	Q2
KAMPALA: Uganda	70	F7
Kampe: r., Nigeria	67	B2
Kampen: Neth	24	B1
Kampot: Kampuchea	38	C4
KAMPUCHEA (Cambodia):	38	—
Kamsack: Canada	61	E2
Kamyshin: U.S.S.R.	28	F3
Kamyshlov: U.S.S.R.	29	J2
Kan: r., China	37	C4
Kanagawa: Pref., Japan	39	f iv
Kananga: Zaire	71	D9
Kanazawa: Japan	39	C2
Kanchow (Gangzhou): China	37	B4
Kandahar: Afghanistan	32	A2
Kanchanaburi: Thai	38	B4
Kandalaksha: U.S.S.R.	16	F2
Kandi: Benin	68	F6
Kandla: India	32	B4
Kandy: Sri Lanka	32	b ii
Kane Basin: Canada	54	V1
Kangar: Malaysia	38	C5
Kangaroo I.: Australia	43	A5
Kangchenjunga: mtn., India/Nepal	32	E3
Kangean Is.: Indon.	35	F12
Kangi: Nigeria	67	A1
Kangting: China	34	C5
Kanin: Cape: U.S.S.R.	26	E5
Kankaanpää: Finland	16	D3
Kankakee: U.S.A.	58	C3
Kankan: Guinea	68	D6
Kankiya: Nigeria	67	B1
Kannapolis: U.S.A.	51	F2
Kano: Nigeria	67	B1
Kanonji: Japan	39	B3
Kanoya: Japan	39	B3
Kanpur: India	32	D3
Kansas: State, U.S.A.	50	C2
Kansas City: r., U.S.A.	58	B4
Kansas City: Mo., U.S.A.	58	B4
Kansas Turnpike: hwy., U.S.A.	58	A4
Kansk: U.S.S.R.	29	Q2
Kansu (Gansu): Prov., China	36	A2
Kanto Heiya: plain, Japan	39	e iii
Kanto Santi: plain, Japan	39	f iii
Kanturk: Irish Rep	13	C4
Kanwa: Nigeria	67	C1
Kanye: Botswana	72	D3
Kanyu: China	36	C3
Kaochow: China	37	A4
Kaohsiung: Taiwan	37	D5
Kaohsiunghsien: Taiwan		
Kaolan see Lanchow		
Kaoping: China	36	B2
Kaouar: & l., China	36	C2
Kaposvár: Hungary	20	C3
Kapuskasing: r., Can	59	D2
Kapuskasing: & r., Canada	59	D2
Kara: Bogaz-Gol: gulf, U.S.S.R	28	G5
Karabük: Turkey	28	C5
Karachi: Pakistan	32	A4
Karaganda: U.S.S.R.	29	L4
Karakoram Pass: China/India	32	C1
Kara Kum: des., U.S.S.R.	29	H6
Karapiro: N.Z.	41	C2
Karasburg: Namibia	72	B3
Kara-Tau: U.S.S.R.	26	J3
Karasu: r., U.S.S.R.	29	K5
Karaul: U.S.S.R.	27	L3
Karbala: Iraq	30	D4
Kardla: U.S.S.R.	17	D4
Kargil: India	32	C2
Karhula: Finland	17	E3
Kari: Nigeria	67	C1
Kariba Lake: & dam & gorge, Zambia/Zimb.	72	D2
Kariba-yama: mtn., Japan	39	a ii
Karibib: Namibia	72	B3
Karkar I.: Namibia	72	
Karlovac: Yugoslavia	21	C3
Karlovy Vary: Czech	20	B2
Karlshamn: Sweden	17	B4
Karlskoga: Sweden	17	B4
Karlskrona: Sweden	17	C4
Karlsruhe: Ger. F.R	24	B2
Karlstad: Sweden	17	B4
Karlstad: U.S.A.	61	F3
Karnaphuli Reservoir: Bangladesh	38	A2
Karnataka: State, India	32	C6
Kárpathos: i., Greece	21	E5
Karpenision: Greece	21	D5
Kars: Turkey	28	E5
Kartaly: U.S.S.R.	29	J3
Kärün: r., Iran	30	E4
Karvina: Poland	20	C3
Karwar: India	32	B6
Kasai: r., Zaire	71	C9
Kasai: Japan	39	a ii
Kasaoka: Japan	39	B3
Kasba Lake: Canada	46	P4
Kasempa: Zambia	72	D1
Kasese: Uganda	70	F7
Kashan: Iran	30	F4
Kashgar see Sufu	31	L3
Kashihara: Japan	39	g iv
Kashima: Japan	39	g iv
Kashima-nada: bay, Japan	39	f iv
Kashiwa: Japan	39	f iv
Kashiwazaki: Japan	39	C2
Kashmar: Iran	30	G4
Kashmor: Pakistan	32	A3
Kasi: U.S.S.R.	29	J2
Kaslo: Canada	62	C1
Kásos: i., Greece	21	E5
Kassala: Sudan	69	N5
Kassel: Ger. F.R	24	B1

Name	Page	
Kasugai: Japan	39	
Kasukabe: Japan	39	
Kasumigaura: lake, Japan	39	
Katahdin, Mount: U.S.A.	59	
Katanning: Australia	42	
Katerini: Greece	21	
Katha: Burma	38	
Katherine: Australia	40	
Kathiawar: State, India	32	
Kathiraveli: Sri Lanka	32	
KATMANDU: Nepal	32	
Katoomba: Austl	43	
Katowice: Poland	20	
Katrine: l., Scot	11	
Katrineholm: Sweden	17	
Katsina: Nigeria	67	
Katsina: r., Nigeria	67	
Katsina Ala: Nigeria	67	
Katsunuma: Japan	39	
Kanagawa: Pref., Japan	39	
Katsuura: Japan	39	
Kattegat: str., Denmark/Norway	17	
Kauai: i., Hawaiian Is	45	
Kaufbeuren: Ger. F.R.	25	
Kaufman: U.S.A.	58	
Kaukauna: U.S.A.	58	
Kaunas: U.S.S.R.	17	
Kaura Namoda: Nig	67	
Kavacha: U.S.S.R.	27	
Kavaje: Albania	21	
Kavála: Greece	21	
Kavieng: Pap. N.G	40	
Kawachi-nagano: Japan	39	
Kawagama Lake: Can	56	
Kawagoe: Japan	39	
Kawaguchi: Japan	39	
Kawartha Lake: Can	56	
Kawasaki: Japan	39	
Kawerau: N.Z.	41	
Kawkareik: State, Burma	38	
Kayes: Mali	68	
Kayseri: Turkey	28	
Kazach'ye: U.S.S.R.	27	
Kazakh: S.S.R.	28/9	
Kazakh Uplands: U.S.S.R.		
Kazalinsk: U.S.S.R.	29	
Kazan: U.S.S.R.	28	
Kazanlak: Bulg.	21	
Kazatin: U.S.S.R.	20	
Kaziranga: India	33	
Kazo: Japan	39	
Kazusa: Japan	39	
Kéa: i., Greece	21	
Keady: N. Ireland	13	
Keal, Loch: Scot	10	
Keansburg: U.S.A.	55	
Kearney: U.S.A.	53	
Kearny: U.S.A.	63	
Kebbi: r., Cameroun	67	
Kebock Head: c., Scot	10	
Kecskemét: Hungary	20	
Keele: England	14	
Keeling Is: see Cocos Is		
Keen: Mt., Scotland	10	
Keene: U.S.A.	55	
Keeper Hill: Irish Republic	13	
Keeseville: U.S.A.	57	
Keetley: U.S.A.	63	
Keetmanshoop: Namibia	72	
Keewatin: Canada	61	
Keffi: Nigeria	67	
Keffin Hausa: Nig	67	
Keflavik: Iceland	16	
Kehsi Mansam: Burma	38	
Keighley: England	12	
Keihoku: Japan	39	
Keith: Scotland	10	
Kelang: Malaysia	38	
Kelheim: Ger. F.R	24	
Kellerberrin: Austl	42	
Kelleys Island: U.S.A.	54	
Kelliher: Canada	61	
Kellogg: U.S.A.	62	
Kells: Irish Republic	13	
Kelowna: Canada	62	
Kelsey Hd.: Eng	14	
Kelso: Scotland	11	
Keluang: Malaysia	38	
Kelvington: Canada	61	
Kemerovo: U.S.S.R.	29	
Kemi: Finland	16	
Kemi: & r., Fin	16	
Kemijärvi: Finland	16	
Kempsey: Austl	43	
Kempston: England	15	
Kempt, Lac: Can	57	
Kempten: Ger. F.R	25	
Kemptville: Can	57	
Kenabeek: Can.	56	
Kenai Peninsula: U.S.A.	46	
Kendal: England	12	
Kendari: Indon.	35	
Kenhardt: S. Afr	72	
Kenilworth: Eng	15	
Kenitra: Morocco	68	
Ken Loch: Scotland	11	
Kenmare: & r., Irish Republic	13	
Kenmore: N. Dak., U.S.A.	53	
Kennebec: r., U.S.A.	55	
Kennebunkport: U.S.A.	55	
Kennedy: Canada	61	
Kennett: U.S.A.	50	
Kennett: r., Eng	15	
Kennewick: U.S.A.	62	
Kennicott: U.S.A.	46	
Kennisis Lake: Can	56	
Kenogami: & r., Can	58	
Kenogamissi Falls: & l., Canada	56	
Kenora: Canada	61	
Kenosha: U.S.A.	58	
Kent: Co., England	15	
Kent: U.S.A.	54	
Kent, Vale of: England	15	
Kentucky: State & r., U.S.A.	58/9	
Kentucky Lake: U.S.A.	51	
Kentucky Turnpike: hwy., U.S.A.	58	
KENYA:		
Kenya, Mt.: Kenya	71	
Keokuk: U.S.A.	58	
Keppel Bay: Austl	42	
Kerala: State, India	32	
Kerang: Australia	43	

84 Lanzhou/Lushai Hills

Page ref.
Lanzhou see Lanchow 34 C3
Laoag Philippines 35 G7
Lao Cai Vietnam 38 C2
Laois Co., Irish Rep. 13 D4
Laon France 22 B2
LAOS 38 –
Lapalisse France 23 B2
La Paloma Uruguay 66 D3
La Paz Argentina 66 C3
La Paz Bolivia 64 E7
La Paz Mexico 48 D5
Lapeer U.S.A. 56 B6
La Pelada Arg. 66 B3
La Perade Canada 57 N3
la Petite Pierre Fr. 22 C2
La Plata Arg. 66 C3
La Pocatière Canada 57 Q2
Lappeenranta Fin. 16 E3
Laprairie Canada 57 M4
La Providence Can. 57 N4
Laptev Sea U.S.S.R. 27 P2
Laptev Strait U.S.S.R. 27 R3
Lapua Finland 16 D3
La Puerta Arg. 66 A2
La Punta Arg. 66 B2
L'Aquila Italy 21 B4
Larache Morocco 19 A5
Laramie U.S.A. 53 D2
Laranjeiras do Sul Brazil 66 D2
Laranjinha r., Brazil 66 D1
Larche Basse-Alpes, France 23 C3
Larche Lot et Garonne, France 23 B2
Larder Lake sett., Canada 56 F1
Laredo U.S.A. 50 C4
Largs Scotland 11 D4
La Rioja Prov., Arg. 66 A3
Lárisa Greece 21 D5
Larive, Lac Can. 56 H2
Lark r., England 15 G2
la Rochelle France 23 A2
la Roche-sur-Yon Fr. 23 A2
La Romana Dom. Rep. 49 N6
La Ronge & lake Canada 61 D1
Larsen Ice Shelf Antarctica 65 F17
Larus, Lake Canada 61 G2
Larvik Norway 17 A4
Lasalle France 23 B3
Las Cruces U.S.A. 52 D4
la Seyne-sur-mer France 23 C3
La Serena Chile 65 D9
Lashburn Canada 60 D2
Lashio Burma 38 B2
Las Lajitas Arg. 66 B1
Las Lomitas Arg. 66 B1
Las Palmas Canary Is. 68 B3
Las Peñas Arg. 66 B3
La Spezia Italy 25 B3
Las Piedras Uruguay 66 C3
Lassen Peak mtn., U.S.A. 63 B3
Lassen Volcanic Nat. Park U.S.A. 63 B3
L'Assomption Canada 57 M4
L'Assomption r., Can. 57 M3
Las Termas Arg. 66 B2
Lastoursville Gabon 71 B8
Last Mountain, Lake Canada 61 E2
Las Varillas Arg. 66 B3
Las Vegas Nev., U.S.A. 63 C4
Las Vegas N. Mex., U.S.A. 53 D3
Latakia Syria 28 D6
Latchford Canada 56 F2
Latina Italy 21 B4
La Toma Arg. 66 A3
la Tour-du-Pin Fr. 23 C2
La Turque Canada 57 N2
Latvian Soviet Socialist Republic U.S.S.R. 17 D4
Lau Nigeria 67 C2
Lauder Scotland 11 F4
Launceston Austl. 40 b i
Launceston England 14 B4
Laurel Md., U.S.A. 54 D5
Laurel Miss., U.S.A. 51 E3
Laurel Mont., U.S.A. 62 E2
Laureldale U.S.A. 54 E4
Laurencekirk Scot. 10 F3
Laurentides, Parc des Canada 57 O2
Lausanne Switzerland 25 B2
Laut i., Indonesia 35 F11
Lauzon Canada 57 O3
Lava Beds Nat. Monument U.S.A. 63 B3
Lavaisse Arg. 66 A3
Laval France 22 A2
Lavalle Catamarea, Argentina 66 A2
Lavalle Corrientes, Argentina 66 C2
Lavenham England 15 G2
Laverton Australia 42 c i
Lavielle, Lac Canada 56 G4
Lawgi Australia 42 D2
Lawrence U.S.A. 55 J2
Lawrence Kans., U.S.A. 58 A4
Lawton U.S.A. 50 C3
Laxford, Loch Scot. 10 C1
Lea r., England 15 F3
Leach r., England 15 E3
Lead U.S.A. 53 E2
Leader Canada 60 D2
Leadon r., England 14 D3
Leamington Canada 56 C7
Leandro N. Alem Argentina 66 C2
Leane, Lough Irish Republic 13 B4
Leatherhead England 15 F3
Leavenworth U.S.A. 58 B4
LEBANON 28 D7
Lebanon N.H., U.S.A. 57 N6
Lebanon Oreg., U.S.A. 62 B3
Lebanon Pa., U.S.A. 54 D4
Lebanon Tenn., U.S.A. 51 E2
le Blanc France 23 B2
Lebork Poland 20 C2
le Cateau France 22 B1
Lecce Italy 21 C4
Lecco Italy 25 B2
Lech r., Ger. F.R. 25 C2
le Chambon Feugerolles Fr. 23 B2
Lechiguanas, Isla de las Argentina 66 C3
Lechlade England 15 E3
Lechtal valley, Aus. 25 C2
le Conquet France 22 a i
le Creusot France 23 B2
le Croisic France 22 a i
Lectoure France 23 B3
Ledbury England 14 D2
Leduc Canada 60 C2
Lee r., Irish Rep. 13 B5
Lee U.S.A. 55 G2
Leeds Co., Canada 57 J5
Leeds England 12 E3
Leeds N. Dak., U.S.A. 53 F1
Leeds U.S.A. 57 P5
Leek England 14 D1
Leer Ger. F.R. 24 B1
Leesburg U.S.A. 54 C5
Leeton Australia 43 C4
Leeuwarden Neth. 24 B1
Leeuwin, Cape Austl. 42 b ii
Leeward Is. West Indies 49 O6
Lefroy, Lake Austl. 42 c ii
Legaspi Phil. 35 G8
Leghorn (Livorno) Italy 25 C3
Legnano Italy 25 B2
Legnica Poland 20 C2
Leh India 32 C2
le Havre France 22 B2
Lehighton U.S.A. 54 E4
Lehrte Ger. F.R. 24 B1
Leicester England 15 E2
Leicestershire Co., England 15 F2
Leichhardt Range Australia 42 C2
Leiden Neth. 24 A1
Leigh England 12 D3
Leigh Creek Austl. 43 A4
Leighton Buzzard England 15 F3
Leinster, Mt. Irish Republic 13 E4
Leipzig Ger. D.R. 24 C1
Leiria Portugal 19 A5
Leiston England 15 H2
Leith Scotland 11 E4
Leitrim Co., Irish Republic 13 C2
Leixlip Irish Rep. 13 E3
Leiyang China 37 B4
Lek r., Neth. 24 B1
Lekki Lagoon Nig. 67 A2
Léman, Lac see Geneva, Lake of 22 B2
le Mans France 22 B2
Leme Brazil 66 a i
Lemgo Ger. F.R. 24 B1
Lemmenjoen Nat. Park Finland 16 E2
le Monastier France 23 B3
le Mont Dore mtn., France 23 B2
Lena r., U.S.S.R. 27 P5
Lene, Lough Irish Republic 13 D3
Leninabad U.S.S.R. 29 L5
Leninakan U.S.S.R. 28 E5
Leningrad U.S.S.R. 17 F4
Leninogorsk U.S.S.R. 29 N3
Lenin Peak mtn., U.S.S.R. 29 L6
Leninsk-Kuznetskiy U.S.S.R. 29 O3
Lennox and Addington Co., Canada 56 H5
Lennoxville Canada 57 O4
Lenore, Lake Can. 61 E2
Lenox U.S.A. 55 G2
Lens France 22 B2
Lenuf Libya 69 J2
Leoben Austria 20 C3
Leominster England 14 D2
Leominster U.S.A. 55 J2
León Mexico 48 F5
Léon Spain 19 A4
Leon r., U.S.A. 50 C3
Leonora Austl. 42 c i
Leoville Canada 60 D2
Lepel U.S.S.R. 20 E2
L'Epiphanie Can. 57 M4
Lepontine Alps mtns., Italy/Switz 25 B2
le Puy France 23 B2
Léré Chad 67 C2
Lerida Spain 19 C4
Lerma, Valle de Arg. 66 A2
Le Roy U.S.A. 54 C2
Lerwick Shet. Is. 10 b i
les Bains du-Mont-Dore France 23 B2
Les Baux France 23 B3
Lesbos i., Greece 21 E5
Les Cayes Haiti 49 M6
Les Ecréhou is. Channel Islands 14 a ii
les Eyzies France 23 B3
Leskovac Yugo. 21 D4
Les Landes reg., Fr. 23 A3
Leslie Scotland 11 E3
Les Monts Faucilles mtns., France 22 C2
LESOTHO 72 D4
Les Sables-d'Olonne France 23 A2
Les Saintes is., Lesser Antilles 49 O6
les Sept Îles Fr. 22 a i
Lesser Antilles is. West Indies 49 O6
Lesser Slave Lake Canada 60 B1
Les Saintes Maries France 23 B3
Lesueur, Mt. Austl. 42 b ii
Leszno Poland 20 C2
Letchworth England 15 F3
Letchworth State Park U.S.A. 54 C2
Lethbridge Canada 62 D2
Leticia Colombia 64 D4
le Touquet France 22 B1
Letpadan Burma 38 B3
le Tréport France 22 B1
Letterkenny Irish Rep. 13 D2
Leuven Belgium 22 B1
Levack Canada 56 D3
Levádheia Greece 21 D5
Levange Norway 16 B3
Leveque, Cape Austl. 40 C4
Leven Scotland 11 F3
Leven, Loch Scot. 11 E3
Leven r., Scot. 10 D3
le Verdon France 23 A2
Leverkusen Ger. F.R. 24 B1
le Vigan France 23 B3
Lévis & Co., Can. 57 O3
Levittown U.S.A. 54 F4
Levkás i., Greece 21 D5
Lewes England 15 G4
Lewis i., Scot. 10 B1
Lewis r., U.S.A. 62 B2
Lewisburg U.S.A. 54 D4
Lewis Pass N.Z. 41 B3
Lewiston Maine, U.S.A. 57 P5
Lewiston Idaho, U.S.A. 62 C2
Lewiston N.Y., U.S.A. 54 A1
Lewistown Mont., U.S.A. 62 E2
Lewistown Pa., U.S.A. 54 C4
Lexington Ky., U.S.A. 58 D4
Lexington Mass., U.S.A. 55 J2
Leyburn England 12 E2
Leydsdorp S. Africa 72 E3
Leyland England 12 D3
Leyre r., France 23 A3
Leyte i., Phil. 35 G8
Lhasa China 33 F3
Lhokseumawe Indon. 38 B5
l'Hospitalet France 23 B3
Li r., China 37 A5
Liaocheng China 36 C2
Liaoning Prov., China 36 D1
Liaotung Bay China 36 D1
Liaotung Penin. China 36 D2
Liaoyang China 36 D1
Liard r., Canada 46 L4
Liberec Czech. 20 C2
Libby U.S.A. 62 C2
Liberal U.S.A. 50 B2
LIBERIA 68 D7
Liberty N.Y., U.S.A. 54 F3
Liberty Pa., U.S.A. 54 C3
Libourne France 23 A3
LIBREVILLE Gabon 70 A7
LIBYA 68/9 J3
Libyan Desert Africa 69 K3
Libyan Plateau Egypt 69 L2
Licheng China 36 B2
Lichfield England 15 E2
Lichinga Mozambique 71 G10
Lichtenburg S. Afr. 72 D4
Lichwan Hupeh, China 37 A3
Lichwan Kiangsi, China 37 C4
Licking r., U.S.A. 58 D4
Lida U.S.S.R. 20 E2
Liddel Water r., Scotland 11 F4
Lidköping Sweden 17 B4
Lido Italy 25 C2
LIECHTENSTEIN 25 B2
Liège Belgium 22 C1
Liencheng China 37 C4
Lienchiang Fuchow, China 37 C4
Lienchiang Kwangtung, China 37 B5
Lienhua Shan mtns., China 37 C5
Lienshui China 36 C3
Lien Shui r., China 37 B4
Lienyunkang China 36 C3
Lienz Austria 25 C2
Liepāja U.S.S.R. 17 D4
Lier Belgium 22 B1
Liestal Switzerland 25 B2
Leitrim Co., Irish Rep. 13 C2
Liévin France 22 B1
Lièvre, du r., Can. 57 K4
Lièvres, Îles aux Can. 57 Q2
Liffey r., Irish Republic 13 E3
Lifford Irish Rep. 13 D2
Ligny hist., Belg. 22 B1
Liguria reg., Italy 25 B3
Ligurian Alps mtns., Italy 25 B3
Ligurian Apennines mtns., Italy 25 B3
Lihsien China 37 B4
Lijo r., Finland 16 E2
Likasi Zaire 71 E10
Likiang China 38 C1
Liling China 37 B4
Lilla Bælt str., Denmark 17 A4
Lille France 22 B1
Lillehammer Norway 17 B3
Lillestrøm Norway 17 B4
Lillooet Canada 62 B1
Lilly U.S.A. 54 B4
Lilongwe Malawi 72 E1
LIMA Peru 64 C6
Lima N.Y., U.S.A. 54 C2
Lima Ohio, U.S.A. 58 D3
Limagne r., France 23 B2
Limavady N. Irel. 13 E1
Limburg Ger. F.R. 24 B1
Limburg reg., Neth. 24 B1
Limchow see Hoppo 37 A5
Lime U.S.A. 62 C3
Limeira Brazil 66 a i
Limerick & Co., Irish Republic 13 C4
Limfjorden fd., Denmark 17 A4
Limko China 38 D3
Límnos i., Greece 21 D5
Limoges France 23 B2
Limon U.S.A. 53 E3
Limousin Old Prov., France 23 B2
Limpopo r., Africa 72 E3
Lin'an China 37 C3
Linares Mexico 50 C5
Linares Spain 19 B5
Linchu China 36 C2
Lincoln Argentina 66 B3
Lincoln Canada 56 F6
Lincoln England 15 F1
Lincoln Ill., U.S.A. 58 C3
Lincoln Nebr., U.S.A. 58 A3
Lincoln N.H., U.S.A. 57 O5
Lincolnshire Co., England 15 F1
Lincoln Wolds hills, England 12 F3
Lindau Ger. F.R. 25 B2
Linden U.S.A. 55 F4
Lindesay, Mt. Austl. 42 b ii
Lindos Rhodes 21 E5
Lindsay Canada 56 G5
Line Is. Pacific O. 44/5 K7
Linesville U.S.A. 56 E8
Linfen China 36 B2
Ling r., Scotland 10 C2
Lingchiu China 36 B2
Lingchuan China 36 B2
Lingchwan China 37 B4
Lingen Ger. F.R. 24 B1
Lingga i., Indon. 35 C11
Linghsien Hunan, China 37 B4
Linghsien Shantung, China 36 C2
Lingling China 37 B4
Lingman Lake Canada 61 G2
Lingshan China 37 A5
Lingshih China 36 B2
Lingshou China 36 B2
Lingshui China 38 E3
Linguère Senegal 68 B5
Lingwu China 36 A2
Lingyuan China 36 C1
Lingyun China 38 D2
Linhai China 37 D4
Linhsien Kwangtung, China 37 B5
Linhsien Shansi, China 36 B2
Linhuanchi China 36 C3
Lini China 36 C2
Linju China 36 B3
Linköping Sweden 17 C4
Linli China 37 B4
Linlithgow Scot. 11 E4
Linnhe, Loch Scot. 10 C3
Linping China 37 B5
Linslade England 15 F3
Linton Canada 57 N2
Linton U.S.A. 53 E1
Lintsang China 38 C2
Lintsing China 36 C2
Lintung China 36 A3
Linwood U.S.A. 54 F5
Linwu China 37 B4
Linyi China 36 C2
Linz Austria 25 C2
Lions, Gulf of Fr. 23 B3
Lipari Is. Italy 21 B5
Lipetsk U.S.S.R. 28 D3
Liphook England 15 F3
Liping China 37 A4
Lipo China 37 A4
Lippstadt Ger. F.R. 24 B1
Lipton Canada 61 E2
Lipu China 37 B5
Lisbellaw N. Irel. 13 D2
LISBON Portugal 19 A5
Lisbon U.S.A. 57 O5
Lisburn N. Irel. 13 E2
Lisburne, Cape U.S.A. 46 B3
Liscannor Bay Irish Republic 13 B4
Lisdoonvarna Irish Republic 13 B3
Lishih China 36 B2
Lishui Chekiang, China 37 D4
Lishui Kiangsu, China 37 C3
Lisianski i., Hawaiian Islands 44 H4
Lisieux France 22 B2
Liskeard England 14 B4
L'Islet Co., Can. 57 P2
Lismore Australia 43 D3
Lismore Irish Rep. 13 D4
Lismore I. Scot. 10 C3
Lisnaskea N. Irel. 13 D2
Listowel Canada 56 E6
Listowel Irish Rep. 13 B4
Litang China 37 A5
Litchfield U.S.A. 55 G3
Lithgow Australia 43 D4
Lithuanian S.S.R. U.S.S.R. 17 D4
Lititz U.S.A. 54 D4
Little Andaman i., Indian Ocean 38 A4
Little Bahama Bank The Bahamas 51 G4
Little Bitter Lake Egypt 69 Ins.
Little Black r., U.S.A. 57 Q2
Little Colorado r., U.S.A. 63 E5
Little Current r., Can. 58 C1
Little Current sett., Canada 56 D4
Little Dart r., Eng. 14 C4
Little Falls town, N.Y., U.S.A. 54 F1
Little Falls town, Minn., U.S.A. 58 B2
Littlefield U.S.A. 50 B3
Little Goose Dam U.S.A. 62 C2
Little Grand Rapids Canada 61 F2
Littlehampton Eng. 15 F4
Little Kanawha r., U.S.A. 59 D4
Little Karroo plat., South Africa 72 C5
Little Longlac Can. 58 C2
Little Minch channel, Scotland 10 B2
Little Missinaibi Lake Canada 56 B1
Little Ouse r., Eng. 15 G2
Littleport England 15 G2
Little Rock U.S.A. 50 D3
Little St. Bernard Pass Italy/France 25 B2
Little Sioux r., U.S.A. 58 A3
Little Smoky r., Can. 60 B2
Little Snake r., U.S.A. 52 D2
Littlestown U.S.A. 54 C5
Littleton U.S.A. 57 O5
Little Valley town, U.S.A. 54 B2
Little Vermilion, Lake Canada 61 G2
Liuan China 37 C3
Liuchow China 37 A5
Liuyang China 37 B4
Lively Canada 56 D3
Livermore, Mt. U.S.A. 50 B3
Livermore Falls sett., U.S.A. 57 P5
Liverpool England 12 D3
Liverpool U.S.A. 54 D1
Liverpool Bay Eng. 12 C3
Liverpool Range Australia 43 D4
Livingston Scotland 11 E4
Livingston Mont., U.S.A. 62 D2
Livingston N.J., U.S.A. 55 F4
Livingston Tenn., U.S.A. 51 E2
Livingstone Falls Zaire 71 B9
Livingstonia Malawi 71 F10
Livo r., Finland 16 E2
Livorno see Leghorn
Livradois, Massif du mtns., France 23 B2
Liyang China 37 C3
Lizard England 14 A5
Lizard Pt. England 14 A5
Ljubljana Yugoslavia 20 B3
Ljungan r., Sweden 16 C3
Ljungby Sweden 17 B4
Ljusdal Sweden 16 C3
Ljusnan r., Sweden 16 C3
Llandeilo Wales 14 B3
Llandovery Wales 14 C3
Llandrindod Wells Wales 14 C2
Llandudno Wales 14 C1
Llanelli Wales 14 B3
Llanfairfechan Wales 14 C1
Llanfyllin Wales 14 C2
Llangefni Wales 14 B1
Llangollen Wales 14 C2
Llanidloes Wales 14 C2
Llano U.S.A. 50 C3
Llano Estacado plat., U.S.A. 53 E4
Llanos de Guarayos plain, Bolivia 64 F7
Llanos de La Rioja plain, Argentina 66 A2
Llanos, Sierra de los ra., Argentina 66 A3
Llanos de Guarayo plain, Bolivia 64 F7
Llanrwst Wales 14 C1
Llantrisant Wales 14 C3
Llanwern Wales 14 D3
Llanwrtyd Wells Wales 14 C2
Lleyn Peninsula Wales 14 B2
Lloret de Mar Spain 19 C4
Lloyd Lake Canada 60 D1
Lloydminster Can. 60 D2
Llyn Clywedog Reservoir Wales 14 C2
Lo r., China 36 A2
Loanhead Scotland 11 E4
Lobatse Botswana 72 D4
Lobito Angola 71 B10
Lobos Argentina 66 C4
Locarno Switz. 25 B2
Lochaline Scot. 10 C3
Lochalsh, Kyle of penin., Scotland 10 C2
Lochboisdale Scot. 10 A2
Lochcarron Scot. 10 C2
Lochgelly Scot. 11 E3
Lochgilphead Scot. 11 C3
Loching China 37 D4
Lochinver Scot. 10 C1
Lochmaben Scot. 11 E4
Lochmaddy Scot. 10 A2
Lochnagar mtn., Scotland 10 E3
Loc Ninh Vietnam 38 D4
Lochy, Loch Scot. 10 D3
Lock Barrage Can. 57 K1
Lockerbie Scot. 11 E4
Lock Haven U.S.A. 54 C3
Lockport U.S.A. 54 B1
Lodi Italy 25 B2
Lodi U.S.A. 63 B4
Łódź Poland 20 C2
Loei Thailand 38 C3
Lofoten Islands Norway 16 B2
Loftus England 12 F2
Lofty Range Austl. 43 A4
Logan W. Va., U.S.A. 59 D4
Logan Utah, U.S.A. 63 D3
Logan r., Austl. 42 C2
Logan, Mt. Can. 46 H4
Logan, Mull of cape, Scotland 11 C5
Logansport U.S.A. 58 C3
Logroño Spain 19 B4
Loho China 36 B3
Loire r., France 23 A2
Loja Ecuador 64 C4
Loja Spain 19 B5
Lokan Reservoir Finland 16 E2
Lokchang China 37 B4
Lokka Finland 16 E2
Løkken Norway 16 A3
Loko Nigeria 67 B2
Lokoja Nigeria 67 B2
Loling China 36 C2
Lolland i., Denmark 17 B5
Lomas de Vallejos Argentina 66 C2
Lomas de Zamora Argentina 66 C3
Lombardy reg., Italy 25 B2
Lombardy, Plain of Italy 25 B2
Lomblen i., Indon. 35 G12
Lombok i. & str., Indonesia 35 F12
Lomé Togo 68 F7
Lommel Belgium 22 C1
Lomond, Loch Scot. 11 D3
Lonan China 36 A3
London Canada 56 D6
LONDON & Met. Co., United Kingdom 15 F3
Londonderry & Co., N. Ireland 13 D2
Londonderry U.S.A. 55 H1
Londrina Brazil 66 D1
Lonely Island Can. 56 D4
Long, Loch Scot. 11 D3
Long Bay U.S.A. 51 G3
Long Beach city, U.S.A. 63 C5
Longbenton England 12 E1
Long Branch U.S.A. 55 F4
Long Crendon Eng. 15 E3
Long Eaton Eng. 15 E2
Longford & C., Irish Republic 13 D3
Long I. Australia 42 C2
Long Island Bahamas 49 L5
Long Island U.S.A. 55 H4
Long Island Sound U.S.A. 55 H3
Longlac Canada 58 C2
Long Lake Mich., U.S.A. 56 B4
Long Lake N.Y., U.S.A. 57 L6
Long Mountain Wales 14 C2
Longmont U.S.A. 53 D2
Long Mynd hill, England 14 D2
Long Point Man., Canada 61 F2
Long Point & bay, Ont., Canada 56 E7
Longridge England 12 D3
Long Sault Rapids Canada 56 F3
Long Sutton Eng. 15 G2
Longton England 14 D2
Longuyon France 22 C2
Longview Tex., U.S.A. 50 D3
Longview Wash., U.S.A. 62 B2
Longwy France 22 C2
Long Xuyen Vietnam 38 D4
Loning China 36 B3
Lons le Saunier Fr. 23 C2
Looe England 14 B4
Lookout, Cape U.S.A. 51 G3
Loon Lake town, Canada 60 D2
Loop Head cape, Irish Republic 13 B4
Lopez, Cape Gabon 71 A8
Loping China 37 C4
Lorain U.S.A. 59 D3
Lorca Spain 19 B5
Lord Howe Rise Pacific Ocean 44 F9
Lorena Brazil 66 a i
Loretteville Canada 57 O3
Lorient France 22 a i
L'Orignal Canada 57 L4
Lorn, Firth of est., Scotland 10 C3
Lorne Australia 43 B5
Lörrach Ger. F.R. 25 B2
Lorraine Old Prov., France 22 C2
Lorrainville Can. 56 F2
Los Alamos U.S.A. 52 D3
Los Andes Chile 65 D10
Los Angeles U.S.A. 63 C5
Los Gigantes mtn., Argentina 66 B3
Loshan China 36
Lossiemouth Scot. 10
Lost r., U.S.A. 54
Los Telares Arg. 66
Lostwithiel England 14
Lot r., France 23
Lota r., Finland/U.S.S.R. 16
Lotbinière & Co., Canada 57
Lothian Reg., Scot. 11 E
Loting Hopeh, China 36
Loting Kwangtung, China 37
Louboma Congo 71
Loue r., France 23
Loughborough Eng. 15
Lough Conn Irish Rep. 13
Loughrea Irish Rep. 13
Loughton Eng. 15
Louisburgh Irish Rep. 13
Louisiana State, U.S.A. 50
Louisiana town, Mo., U.S.A. 58
Louis Trichardt South Africa 72
Louisville Ky., U.S.A. 58
Louisville Nebr., U.S.A. 58
Loum-Chantiers Cameroun 67
Loup r., Nebr., U.S.A. 53
Loup City U.S.A. 53
Loup, du r., Canada 57
Lourdes France 23
Louth England 12
Louth Co., Irish Rep. 13
Lovelock U.S.A. 63
Lowell U.S.A. 55
Lowelltown U.S.A. 57
Lower California State, Mexico 48
Lower Foster Lake Canada 61
Lower Granite Dam U.S.A. 62
Lower Lough Erne Northern Ireland 13
Lower Monumental Dam U.S.A. 62
Lower Red Lake U.S.A. 58
Lower Tunguska r., U.S.S.R. 27
Lowestoft England 15
Lowther Hills Scot. 11
Lowville U.S.A. 57
Loxton Australia 43
Loyalsock Creek U.S.A. 54
Loyang China 36
Loyuan China 37
Lu r., see Salween 34
Lualaba r., Zaire 71
Luan r., China 36
Luanda Angola 71
Luang Prabang Laos 38
Luangwa Nat. Park Zambia 71
Luanshya Zambia 72
Lubango Angola 72
Lubbock U.S.A. 50
Lübeck & bay, German F.R. 24
Lubéron, Montagne du France 23
Lubicon Lake Canada 60
Lublin Poland 20
Lubok Sikiping Indon. 38
Lubumbashi Zaire 71
Lucan Canada 56
Lucan Irish Rep. 13
Lucas r., Argentina 66
Lucas Channel Can. 56
Lucca Italy 25
Luce Bay Scotland 11
Lucerne Canada 60
Lucerne see Luzern 25
Luchai China 37
Luchiang Taiwan 37
Lucin U.S.A. 63
Luckenwalde Ger. D.R. 24
Lucknow Canada 56
Lucknow India 32
Lüdenscheid Ger. F.R. 24
Lüderitz Namibia 72
Ludhiana India 32
Ludington U.S.A. 58
Ludlow England 14
Ludlow Calif., U.S.A. 63
Ludlow Pa., U.S.A. 56
Ludlow Vt., U.S.A. 55
Ludlowville U.S.A. 54
Ludvika Sweden 17
Ludwigsburg Ger. F.R. 24
Ludwigshafen German F.R. 24
Ludwigslust Ger. D.R. 24
Lufeng China 37
Lufkin U.S.A. 50
Luga & r., U.S.S.R. 17
Lugano Switz. 25
Lugg r., U.K. 14
Lugo Spain 19
Lugoj Romania 20
Lugnaquillia mtn., Irish Republic 13
Luho China 36
Luichart, Loch Scot. 10
Luing i., Scot. 11
Lujan Argentina 66
Lule r., Sweden 16
Luleå Sweden 16
Luleburgaz Turkey 21
Lulung China 36
Lumberton U.S.A. 51
Lumby Canada 62
Lumsden Canada 61
Lumsden N.Z. 41
Luna, Lago de Arg. 66
Lund Sweden 17
Lundar Canada 61
Lundy i., England 14
Lune r., England 12
Lüneburg & Heath, German F.R. 24
Lunéville France 22
Lungchuan Chekiang, China 37
Lungchuan Kwangtung, China 37
Lunghui China 37
Lunghsien China 36
Lunghwa China 36
Lungkiang see Tsitsihar 34
Lungnan China 37
Lungshan China 37
Lungsheng China 37
Lungyen China 37
Lupeni Romania 21
Lure France 22
Lurgan N. Ireland 13
LUSAKA Zambia 72
Lusambo Zaire 71
Luseland Canada 60
Lushai Hills India 33

Lushan/Metagama 85

Page ref.
nan, China 36 B3
hih, China 36 B3
nun, China 36 D2
sac-les-Châteaux,
rance 23 B2
, China 36 D2
en, China 38 C1
on, England 15 F3
sk, U.S.S.R. 20 E2
erworth, England 15 E2
KEMBOURG 22 C2
EMBOURG,
uxembourg 22 C2
or, Egypt 69 M3
ern (Lucerne),
ity & l., Switz. 25 B2
on, i., Phil. 35 G7
y, France 23 B2
v, U.S.S.R. 20 D3
anhsien, China 36 C2
anping, China 36 C1
khoy Islands,
S.S.R. 27 R3
l, Mt., Canada 60 C2
ster, Scotland 10 E1
sele, Sweden 16 C3
sele Lappmark,
eog. reg., Sweden 16 C2
d, England 15 G4
enburg, S. Africa 72 E4
ney, England 14 D3
sa Lake, U.S.S.R. 16 F3
ens, U.S.A. 54 D4
e Bay, England 14 D4
e Regis, England 14 C4
ington, England 15 E4
m, England 12 D3
chburg, U.S.A. 59 E4
dhurst, England 15 E4
donville, N.Y.,
S.A. 54 B1
donville, Vt., U.S.A. 57 N5
ner, r., England 14 B4
mouth, England 14 C3
n, U.S.A. 55 K2
ne, U.S.A. 57 J6
n Lake, sett., Can. 61 E1
on, England 14 C3
r., Scotland 10 D3
, Loch, Scot. 10 D3
n Mountain,
sett., U.S.A. 57 M5
nnais, Old Prov.,
rance 23 B2
ns (Lyon), Fr. 23 B2
ns, U.S.A. 54 C1
France 22 B1
er Station, Can. 57 O3
va, U.S.S.R. 29 H2
am St. Anne's,
ngland 12 C3
elton, N.Z. 41 B3
on, Canada 62 B1
án, Jordan 30 C4
nselkä, hills,
nland 16 E2
anshan, China 36 C3
arianhamina, Fin. 17 D3
as (Meuse), r.,
etherlands 24 B1
astricht, Neth. 24 B1
blethorpe, Eng. 15 G1
doo, U.S.A. 54 D4
Alester, U.S.A. 50 C3
Allen, U.S.A. 50 C4
cao, Port. overseas
rov., China 37 B5
capa, Brazil 64 H3
Arthur's Head,
ape, Scotland 11 C4
cclesfield, Eng. 14 D1
Clintock, Canada 61 G1
Clintock Channel,
anada 46 P1
Clure Strait, Can. 46 L1
Comb, U.S.A. 50 D3
Connellsburg,
S.A. 54 B5
Cook, U.S.A. 53 E2
Dermitt, U.S.A. 63 C3
cdonnell Ranges,
ustralia 40 E5
Dowell Lake, Can. 61 G2
cduff, Scotland 10 F2
ceió, Brazil 64 L5
cequece, Moz. 72 E2
cerata, Italy 21 B4
Farlane, r., Can. 60 D1
Gehee, U.S.A. 50 D3
Gill, U.S.A. 63 D4
cgillycuddy's Reeks,
ins., Irish Rep. 13 B4
Grath, U.S.A. 46 D1
Graw, U.S.A. 54 D2
Gregor, Can. 60 F3
chadodorp, S. Afr. 72 E4
chars, The, dist.,
cotland 11 D5
chattie, Lake, Austl. 42 A3
cheng, China 37 C3
chida, Japan 39 f iv
chrihanish, & bay,
cotland 11 C4
chu Picchu, Peru 64 D6
chynlleth, Wales 14 C2
cias Nguema
iyogo, i., Equatorial
uinea 68 G8
nnes Lake, Can. 61 G2
ntosh, U.S.A. 53 E1
cintyre, r., Austl. 43 D3
ckay, Australia 42 C2
ckay, Lake, Austl. 40 D5
Keansburg, U.S.A. 54 D4
ckenzie, r., Austl. 42 C2
ckenzie, r., Can. 46 J3
ckenzie, Guyana 49 P8
ckenzie Bay, Can. 46 H3
Kenzie Island,
anada 61 G2
ckinac, Straits of,
S.A. 58 D2
ckinac Island,
S.A. 56 A4
Kinley, Mt., U.S.A. 46 E4
Kinney, U.S.A. 50 C3
cklin, Canada 60 D2
clear, r., Austl. 43 D4
Lennan, Canada 60 B1
Minnville, U.S.A. 62 B2
cnean Lower,
ough, N. Ireland 13 D2
cnean Upper,
ough, Irish Rep. 13 C2
comb, U.S.A. 58 B3
con, France 23 B2
con, U.S.A. 51 F3
coun Lake, Can. 61 E1
cquarie I., Southern
cean 44 E12
Rae, U.S.A. 51 F3
croom, Irish Rep. 13 C5
Tier, Canada 56 F4
da, r., Nigeria 67 B2

Page ref.
Madagali, Nigeria 67 C1
Madagascar, see Malagasy Rep. 71 –
Madagascar Basin, Indian Ocean 33 d vii
Madagascar Ridge, Indian Ocean 33 c viii
Madang, Pap.-N.G. 40 H2
Madaoua, Niger 67 B1
Madawaska, & r., Canada 56 H4
Madaya, Burma 38 B2
Maddalena Pass, Italy/France 25 B3
Madeira, i., Atlantic O. 68 B2
Madeira, r., Brazil 64 F5
Madeleine, Îles-de-la-, is., Canada 47 X7
Madera, U.S.A. 63 B4
Madesimo, Italy 25 B2
Madhya Pradesh, State, India 32 C4
Madison, Conn., U.S.A. 55 H3
Madison, Fla., U.S.A. 51 F3
Madison, Ind., U.S.A. 58 C4
Madison, Maine, U.S.A. 57 Q5
Madison, S. Dak., U.S.A. 58 A3
Madison, Wis., U.S.A. 58 C3
Madison, r., U.S.A. 62 D2
Madisonville, U.S.A. 58 C4
Madiun, Indonesia 35 E12
Madoc, Canada 56 H5
Madras, India 32 D6
MADRID, Spain 19 B4
Madrid, U.S.A. 57 K5
Madsen, Canada 61 G2
Madura, i., Indon. 35 E12
Maebashi, Japan 39 C2
Maesteg, Wales 14 C3
Mafeking, S. Africa 72 D4
Mafra, Brazil 66 E2
Magadan, U.S.S.R. 27 S6
Magallanes, see Punta Arenas 65 D14
Magami, Nigeria 67 B1
Magaria, Niger 67 B1
Magdalena, Arg. 66 C4
Magdalena, r., Col. 64 D2
Magdeburg, Ger. D.R. 24 C1
Magee I., N. Ireland 13 F2
Magellan, Strait of, Chile 65 E14
Magenta, Italy 25 B2
Maggiore, Lake, Italy 25 B2
Maghera, N. Ireland 13 E2
Magherafelt, N. Irel. 13 E2
Magnet, Canada 61 F2
Magnetawan, Can. 56 F4
Magnitogorsk, U.S.S.R. 29 H3
Magnolia, U.S.A. 50 D3
Magog, Canada 57 N4
Magpie, r., Canada 58 D2
Magrath, Canada 60 C3
Magude, Moz. 72 E4
Magumeri, Nigeria 67 C1
Magwe, & Divis., Burma 38 B2
Mahanadi, r., India 32 D4
Mahanoy City, U.S.A. 54 D4
Maharashtra, State, India 32 C5
Maha Sarakham, Thailand 38 C3
Mahia Peninsula, N.Z. 41 C2
Mahón, Menorca 19 C5
Mahwah, U.S.A. 55 F3
Maidenhead, Eng. 15 F3
Maidstone, Canada 60 D2
Maidstone, England 15 G3
Maiduguri, Nigeria 67 C1
Maigue, r., Irish Republic 13 C4
Maimana, Afghanistan 29 J6
Main, r., Ger. F.R. 24 B2
Main, r., N. Irel. 13 E2
Main Barrier Range, Australia 43 B4
Mai-Ndombe Lake, Zaire 71 C8
Maine, Old Prov., Fr. 22 A2
Maine, r., Irish Republic 13 B4
Maine, State, U.S.A. 59 G2
Mainé-Soroa, Niger 67 C1
Mainland, i., Ork. Is. 10 d iv
Mainland, i., Shet. Is. 10 b i
Maiskhal, Bangl. 33 F4
Maitland, Australia 43 D4
Maitland, r., Canada 56 D6
Maizuru, Japan 39 C2
Majorca, i., see Mallorca 19 C5
Majunga, Malagasy Republic 71 I11
Makabe, Japan 39 g iii
Makarikari Salt Pan, Botswana 72 D3
Makassar, Strait of, Indonesia 35 F11
Makat, U.S.S.R. 28 G4
Makeni, Sierra Leone 68 C7
Makeyevka, U.S.S.R. 28 D4
Makhachkala, U.S.S.R. 28 F5
Makó, Hungary 20 D3
Makobe Lake, Can. 56 E2
Makran, geog. reg., Iran/Pakistan 30 H5
Makurazaki, Japan 39 B3
Makurdi, Nigeria 67 B2
Makushino, U.S.S.R. 29 K2
Malabar Coast, India 32 B6
Malacca, Strait of, Indonesia/Malaysia 38 C6
Maladetta, France 23 B3
Maladetta Massif, France/Spain 23 B3
Málaga, Spain 19 B5
Malaga, U.S.A. 54 E5
MALAGASY REPUBLIC (Madagascar) 71 –
Malahide, Irish Rep. 13 E3
Malaita, Solomon Is. 40 L2
Malakal, Sudan 69 M7
Malakand, Pakistan 32 B2
Malang, Indonesia 35 E12
Malanje, Angola 71 C9
Malar, Lake, Sweden 17 C4
Malartic, Canada 56 G1
Malatya, Turkey 28 D6
MALAWI 71 F10
Malaya, penin., Asia 38 C6
Malawi (Nyasa), Lake, E. Africa 71 F10
MALAYSIA 35 –
Malbaie, r., Canada 57 P2
Mal Bay, Irish Rep. 13 B4
Malbork, Poland 20 C2
Malden I., Pacific O. 45 K7
MALDIVES (Maldive Is.) 31 K9
Maldonado, Uruguay 66 C3
Maléa, Cape, Greece 21 D5

Page ref.
Malekula, i., New Hebrides 40 M4
Malesherbes, France 22 B2
Malheur, r. & Lake, U.S.A. 62 C3
MALI 68 E5
Malindi, Kenya 71 H8
Malin Head, cape, Irish Republic 13 D1
Maliwun, Burma 38 B4
Mallaig, Scotland 10 C3
Mallorca (Majorca), i., Balearic Islands 19 C5
Mallow, Irish Rep. 13 C4
Malmberget, Sweden 16 D2
Malmédy, Belgium 22 C1
Malmesbury, England 14 D3
Malmesbury, S. Africa 72 B5
Malmö, Sweden 17 B4
Maloja Pass, Switz. 25 B2
Malone, U.S.A. 57 L5
Malonga, Zaire 71 D10
Måløy, Norway 16 A3
Malplaquet, hist., France 22 B1
Malpelo Island, Colom. 64 B3
MALTA 21 B5
Malta, U.S.A. 62 E2
Maltby, England 12 E3
Maltion Nature Park, Finland 16 E2
Malton, England 12 F2
Maluku, is., see Moluccas 35 H10
Malvan, India 32 B5
Malvern, U.S.A. 54 E4
Malvern Hills, Eng. 14 D2
Mamaia, Romania 21 E4
Mamainse Hill, Can. 56 A2
Mamba, Japan 39 e iii
Mamfe, Cameroun 67 B2
Mamry, Lake, Poland 20 D2
Man, Isle of, U.K. 12 B2
Manaar, Sri Lanka 32 a ii
Manaar, Gulf of, India/Sri Lanka 32 C7
Manacle Point, Eng. 14 A4
Manado, Indonesia 35 G10
MANAGUA, Nicaragua 49 J7
MANAMA, Bahrain 30 F5
Mana Pass, China 32 C2
Manapouri, Lake, N.Z. 41 A4
Manasquan, U.S.A. 55 F4
Manaus, Brazil 64 F4
Manazuru, Japan 39 f iv
Manchester, England 12 D3
Manchester, Conn., U.S.A. 55 H3
Manchester, Mass., U.S.A. 55 K2
Manchester, Mich., U.S.A. 56 A7
Manchester, N.H., U.S.A. 55 J2
Manchester, N.Y., U.S.A. 54 C2
Manchester, Pa., U.S.A. 54 D4
Manchuria, reg., China 34 H2
Mandal, Norway 17 A4
Mandalay, & Divis., Burma 38 B2
Mandan, U.S.A. 53 E1
Mandara Mtns., Nigeria/Cameroun 67 C1
Mandasor, India 32 C4
Mando, Nigeria 67 B1
Mandurah, Australia 42 b ii
Manfredonia, Italy 21 C4
Mangache, Malawi 72 F1
Mangalia, Romania 21 E4
Mangalore, India 32 B6
Mangotsfield, Eng. 14 D3
Mangueira, Lagoa, Brazil 66 D3
Mangum, U.S.A. 50 C3
Mangyshlak Peninsula, U.S.S.R. 28 G5
Manhattan, U.S.A. 50 C2
Manheim, U.S.A. 54 D4
Manica, Moz. 72 E2
Manicouagan Penin., Canada 59 G2
Manifold, Cape, Australia 42 A2
Manigotagan Lake, Canada 61 F2
Manila, r., Irish Republic 13 B3
MANILA, Philippines 35 G8
Manipur, State, India 33 F4
Manisa, Turkey 21 E5
Manistee, & r., U.S.A. 58 C3
Manistique, U.S.A. 58 C2
Manitoba, prov., Canada 61 F2
Manitoba, Lake, Can. 61 F2
Manito Lake, Canada 60 D2
Manitou, Canada 61 F3
Manitou Island, U.S.A. 58 C2
Manitou Lake, Can. 56 B2
Manitoulin, Co., Can. 56 D4
Manitoulin Island, Canada 56 C4
Manitouwadge, Canada 58 C2
Manitowaning, & bay, Canada 56 D4
Manitowik Lake, Can. 56 A1
Manitowoc, U.S.A. 58 C3
Maniwaki, Canada 57 K3
Manizales, Colombia 64 C2
Manjimup, Austl. 42 b ii
Manjra, r., India 32 C5
Mankato, U.S.A. 58 B3
Mankoya, Zambia 72 C1
Mankulam, Sri Lanka 32 b ii
Manlius, U.S.A. 54 E1
Mannheim, Ger. F.R. 24 B2
Manning, Canada 60 B1
Mannville, Canada 60 C2
Manokwari, Indon. 35 J11
Manorhamilton, Irish Republic 13 C2
Manouane, Lac, Can. 57 L2
Manouanis, Lake, Can. 59 F1
Manresa, Spain 19 C4
Manseau, Canada 57 N3
Mansfeld, Ger. D.R. 24 C1
Mansfield, Australia 43 C5
Mansfield, England 15 E1
Mansfield, Mass., U.S.A. 55 J2
Mansfield, Ohio, U.S.A. 59 D3
Mansfield, Pa., U.S.A. 54 C3
Mansfield, Mount, U.S.A. 57 N5
Mansfield Woodhouse, England 15 E1
Manta, Ecuador 64 B4
Mantes-Gassicourt, Fr. 22 B2
Mantua (Mantova), Italy 25 C2
Manus, i., Pap.-N.G. 40 H1

Page ref.
Manville, U.S.A. 54 F4
Manzala, Lake, Egypt 69 Ins.
Manzanillo, Mexico 48 F6
Maple Creek, town, Canada 60 D3
Maple Shade, U.S.A. 54 F5
MAPUTO, Moz. 72 E4
Maputo Elephant Reserve, Moz. 72 E4
Maracaibo, & lake, Venezuela 49 M7
Maracay, Venezuela 49 N7
Maradi, Niger 67 B1
Maradi, r., Niger/Nig. 67 B1
Marajó, I. of, Brazil 64 J4
Maramba (Livingstone), Zambia 72 D2
Marambaia, Ilha da, Brazil 66 b i
Maranoa, r., Austl. 42 C3
Marañon, r., Peru 64 C4
Marapa, r., Argentina 66 A2
Maraş, Turkey 28 D6
Marathon, Canada 58 C2
Marathón, Greece 21 D5
Marazion, England 14 A4
Marble Bar, Austl. 40 B5
Marburg, Ger. F.R. 24 B1
Marcelino Escalada, Argentina 66 B3
Marcelino Ramos, Braz. 66 D2
Marcellus, U.S.A. 54 D2
March, England 15 G2
Marche, Old Prov., Fr. 23 B2
Marches, The, reg., Italy 25 C3
Marchienne, Belgium 22 B1
Mar Chiquita, Laguna, Argentina 66 B3
Marcos Juárez, Arg. 66 B3
Marcos Paz, Arg. 66 C3
Marcus I., Pacific O. 44 E4
Marcus Necker Rise, Pacific Ocean 44 G5
Marcy, Mount, U.S.A. 57 M3
Mar del Plata, Arg. 65 G11
Mardin, Turkey 28 E6
Maree, Loch, Scot. 10 C2
Marfa, U.S.A. 50 B3
Margam, Wales 14 C3
Marganets, U.S.S.R. 29 K4
Margaret Lake, Can. 60 B1
Margarita Island, Venezuela 49 O7
Margate, England 15 H3
Margate, S. Africa 72 E5
Margeride, Monts de la, France 23 B3
Mariana Is., Pacific O. 44 D5
Mariana Trench, Pac. O. 44 D5
Marianske Lazne, Czechoslovakia 20 B3
Marias, r., U.S.A. 62 D2
María Teresa, Arg. 66 B3
Maria Van Diemen, Cape, N.Z. 41 B1
Maribor, Yugoslavia 20 C3
Marie-Galante, i., Leeward Islands 49 O6
Mariental, Namibia 72 B3
Mariestad, Sweden 17 B4
Marietta, U.S.A. 54 D4
Marieville, Canada 57 M4
Mariga, Nigeria 67 B1
Mariinsk, Achinsk, U.S.S.R. 29 O2
Marine City, U.S.A. 56 C7
Marinette, U.S.A. 58 C2
Maringa, Brazil 66 D1
Marinheiros, Ilha dos, i., Brazil 66 D3
Marion, Ind., U.S.A. 58 C3
Marion, Iowa, U.S.A. 58 B3
Marion, Mass., U.S.A. 55 K3
Marion, N.Y., U.S.A. 54 C1
Marion, Ohio, U.S.A. 58 D3
Marion, Lake, U.S.A. 51 F3
Marion Reef, Austl. 42 D1
Maritime Alps, France 23 C3
Maritsa, r., Greece 21 E4
Markdale, Canada 56 E5
Market Deeping, Eng. 15 F2
Market Drayton, Eng. 14 D2
Market Harborough, England 15 F2
Market Rasen, Eng. 12 F3
Market Weighton, Eng. 12 F3
Markham, Canada 56 F6
Markinch, Scotland 11 E3
Markovo, U.S.S.R. 27 U5
Marlboro, Mass., U.S.A. 55 J2
Marlboro, N.H., U.S.A. 55 H2
Marlboro, N.Y., U.S.A. 55 G3
Marlborough, Australia 42 C2
Marlborough, England 15 E3
Marles, France 22 B1
Marlin, U.S.A. 50 C3
Marlow, England 15 F3
Marmande, France 23 B3
Marmara, Sea of, Tur. 21 E4
Marmora, Canada 56 H5
Marne, r., France 22 B2
Maroua, Cameroun 67 C1
Marple, England 12 D3
Marquesas Is., Pac. O. 45 M7
Marquette, U.S.A. 58 C2
Marrakesh, Morocco 68 D2
Marra Mts., Sudan 69 K6
Marree, Australia 43 A3
Marsabit Nat. Reserve, Kenya 70 G7
Marsala, Sicily 21 B5
Marseilles, France 23 C2
Marshall, U.S.A. 50 D3
Marshall Is., Pac. O. 44 F6
Marshalltown, U.S.A. 58 B3
Marshfield, U.S.A. 58 B3
Martha's Vineyard, i., U.S.A. 55 K3
Martigny, Switz. 25 B2
Martigues, France 23 C3
Martin, Czech. 20 C3
Martinique, i., Windward Islands 49 O7
Martinsburg, Pa., U.S.A. 54 B4
Martinsburg, W. Va., U.S.A. 54 C5
Martinsville, U.S.A. 51 G2
Martin Vaz, i., Atl. O. 8 H10
Marton, N.Z. 41 C3
Mary (Merv), U.S.S.R. 29 J6
Maryborough, Queens., Australia 42 D3

Page ref.
Maryborough, Vict., Australia 43 B5
Maryfield, Canada 61 E3
Maryland, State, U.S.A. 59 E4
Maryport, England 12 C2
Marysville, U.S.A. 54 D4
Maryville, U.S.A. 51 F2
Masai Mara Game Reserve, Kenya 71 G8
Masaka, Uganda 70 F8
Mascarene Basin, Indian Ocean 33 d vi
MASERU, Lesotho 72 D4
Masham, England 12 E2
Mashan, China 37 A5
Mashhad, Iran 29 H6
Mashkel, r., Pakistan 32 c iv
Masira, i., Oman 30 G6
Mask, Lough, Irish Republic 13 B3
Maskinongé, & r., Canada 57 N3
Maskinongé, Co., Can. 57 L2
Mason, Lake, Austl. 42 b i
Mason City, U.S.A. 58 B3
Massabesic Lake, U.S.A. 55 J2
Massachusetts, State, U.S.A. 55 H2
Massachusetts Bay, U.S.A. 55 K2
Massachusetts Turnpike, hwy., U.S.A. 55 G2
Massaguet, Chad 67 D1
Massakori, Chad 67 D1
Massawa, Ethiopia 69 N5
Massawippi, Lac, Canada 57 N4
Massena, U.S.A. 57 L5
Massey, Canada 56 C3
Massif Central, mtns., France 23 B3
Massillon, U.S.A. 59 D3
Masson, Canada 57 K4
Masterton, N.Z. 41 C3
Mastic Beach, town, U.S.A. 55 H4
Mastigouche, Parc, Canada 57 M3
Mastung, Pakistan 32 A3
Masu, Nigeria 67 C1
Masuda, Japan 39 B3
Matachewan, Canada 56 E2
Matadi, Zaire 71 B9
Matagalpa, Nicaragua 49 J7
Matagami, & lake, Canada 59 E2
Matagorda Bay, U.S.A. 50 C4
Matagorda I., U.S.A. 50 C4
Matale, Sri Lanka 32 b ii
Matameye, Niger 67 B1
Matamoros, Mexico 50 C4
Matane, Canada 59 G2
Matanzas, Cuba 49 K5
Matapan, Cape, Greece 21 D5
Matara, Sri Lanka 32 b iii
Matarîya, Egypt 69 Ins.
Matatiele, S. Africa 72 D5
Mataura, r., N.Z. 41 A4
Matawan, U.S.A. 55 F4
Mateka Falls, Zaire 71 B8
Matera, Italy 21 C4
Matheson, Canada 56 E1
Mathura, India 32 C3
Matinenda Lake, Can. 56 C3
Matlock, England 15 E1
Mato Grosso, Plateau of, Brazil 64 H7
Matopo Hills, Zimb. 72 D3
Matsudo, Japan 39 f iv
Matsue, Japan 39 B2
Matsumoto, Japan 39 C2
Matsusaka, Japan 39 c ii
Matsuyama, Japan 39 B3
Mattagami, r., Can. 59 D2
Mattawa, Canada 56 G3
Mattawin, r., Can. 57 M3
Matterhorn, mtn., Switzerland 25 B2
Mattituck, U.S.A. 55 H4
Mattoon, U.S.A. 58 C4
Maturin, Venezuela 49 O8
Maubeuge, France 22 B1
Maughold Head, cape, I. of Man 12 B2
Maui, i., Hawaiian Is. 45 K4
Maumee, & r., U.S.A. 56 B8
Maumere, Indonesia 35 G12
Maun, Botswana 72 C2
Maurice, Parc National de la, Canada 57 N3
MAURITANIA 68 –
MAURITIUS 33 d vii
Mawkmai, Burma 38 B2
Maxville, Canada 57 L4
May, i., Scotland 11 F3
May, Cape, U.S.A. 59 F4
Mayaguez, Puerto Rico 49 N6
Maybole, Scotland 11 D4
Mayenne, town & r., France 22 A2
Mayerthorpe, Canada 60 B2
Mayfield, U.S.A. 58 C4
Maykop, U.S.S.R. 28 D5
Maymyo, Burma 38 B2
Maynard, U.S.A. 55 J2
Maynooth, Canada 56 H4
Maynooth, Irish Rep. 13 E3
Mayo, Canada 46 H4
Mayo, Co., Irish Rep. 13 B3
Mayoumba, Gabon 71 B8
Mayson Lake, Canada 60 D1
Mayville, U.S.A. 56 F7
Mazar-i-Sharif, Afg. 29 K6
Mazatlán, Mexico 48 E5
Mazhabong Lake, Canada 56 C3
Mazoe, Zimbabwe 72 E2
MBABANE, Swaziland 72 E4
M'Bakaou Reservoir, Cameroun 67 C2
Mbala, Tanzania 71 F9
Mbandaka, Zaire 71 C8
Mbarara, Uganda 71 F8
Mbéré, r., Cameroun/Chad 67 D2
Mbonge, Cameroun 67 B3
Mburucuyá, Arg. 66 C2
Mead, U.S.A. 62 C2
Mead, Lake, U.S.A. 63 D4
Meadow Lake, town, Canada 60 D2
Meadow Lake Provincial Park, Canada 60 D2
Meadville, U.S.A. 56 E8
Meaford, Canada 56 E5
Meander River, town, Canada 60 B1
Meath, Co., Irish Rep. 13 E3
Meaux, France 22 B2
Mecca, Saudi Arabia 30 C6

Page ref.
Mechanic Falls, sett., U.S.A. 57 P5
Mechanicsburg, U.S.A. 54 C4
Mechelen, Belgium 22 B1
Mecklenburg, Old State, German D.R. 24 C1
Medan, Indonesia 38 B6
Médéa, Algeria 19 C5
Medellín, Colombia 64 C2
Medfield, U.S.A. 55 J2
Medford, N.J., U.S.A. 54 F5
Medford, Okla., U.S.A. 50 C2
Medford, Oreg., U.S.A. 62 B3
Medford Station, U.S.A. 55 G4
Medgidia, Romania 21 E4
Medias, Romania 20 D3
Medicine Hat, Can. 60 C2
Medina, U.S.A. 54 B1
Medina, Lago, Arg. 66 C2
Medinat-ash-Sha'b, Yemen P.D.R. 30 D8
Mediterranean Sea 68/9 –
Mednogorsk, U.S.S.R. 29 H3
Médoc, reg., France 23 A2
Medway, r., England 15 G3
Medway, U.S.A. 55 J2
Meerut, India 32 C3
Mega, Ethiopia 69 N8
Mégantic, Co., Can. 57 O3
Mégantic, Lac, Can. 57 P4
Mégara, Greece 21 D5
Meghalaya, State, India 33 F3
Megiscane, Canada 56 H1
Megiscane, r., Can. 57 J1
Meig, r., Scotland 10 D2
Meihsien, China 37 C5
Meikle Says Law, mtn., Scotland 11 F4
Meiktila, Burma 38 B2
Meiningen, Ger. D.R. 24 C1
Meissen, Ger. D.R. 24 C1
Meitan, China 37 A4
Mekambo, Gabon 70 B7
Mekinac, Lac, Can. 57 N2
Meknes, Morocco 68 D2
Mekọ, Nigeria 67 A2
Mekong, r., S.E. Asia 35 D7
Mekong Delta, Vietnam 38 D5
Mel, Ilha do, i., Braz. 66 E2
Melaka, Malaysia 38 C6
Melanesia, geog. reg., Pacific Ocean 44 E7
Melbourn, England 15 G2
Melbourne, Australia 43 C5
Melbourne, England 15 E2
Melbourne, U.S.A. 51 F4
Melfort, Canada 61 E2
Melincué, Argentina 66 B3
Melita, Canada 61 E3
Melksham, England 14 D3
Melo, Uruguay 66 D3
Melrose, Scotland 11 F4
Melrose, U.S.A. 62 D2
Melrose, U.S.A. 62 E2
Melton Mowbray, Eng. 15 F2
Melun, France 22 B2
Melville, Canada 61 E2
Melville Bay, Grnld. 47 X1
Melville I., Austl. 40 E3
Melville Island, Can. 46 N1
Melvin, Lough, Irish Republic 13 C2
Memmingen, Ger. F.R. 25 C2
Memphis, hist., Egypt 69 M3
Memphis, U.S.A. 51 E2
Memphrémagog, Lac, Canada 57 N4
Menai Bridge, Wales 14 B1
Menai Straits, Wales 14 B1
Mendham, U.S.A. 54 F4
Mendip Hills, Eng. 14 D3
Mendocino, Cape, U.S.A. 48 B1
Mendoza, Argentina 65 E10
Mêne, Congo 70 C7
Mengcheng, China 36 C3
Mengshan, China 37 B5
Mengtsz, China 38 C2
Mengyin, China 36 C2
Menindee, & lake, Austl. 43 B4
Meningie, Australia 43 A5
Menominee, U.S.A. 58 C2
Menomonee Falls, town, U.S.A. 58 C3
Menorca, i., Balearic Is. 19 C5
Mentawai Is., Indon. 35 B11
Mentekab, Malaysia 38 C6
Menton, France 23 C3
Meon, r., England 15 E4
Meppel, Neth. 24 B1
Meramec, r., U.S.A. 50 D4
Merano, Italy 25 C2
Mercara, India 32 C6
Merced, U.S.A. 63 B4
Mercedes, Corrientes, Argentina 66 C2
Mercedes, San Luis, Argentina 66 A3
Mercedes, Uruguay 66 C3
Mercersburg, U.S.A. 54 C5
Mercier Barrage, dam, Canada 57 K3
Mere, England 14 D3
Meredith, U.S.A. 57 O6
Mergui, & arch., Burma 38 B4
Mérida, Mexico 48 J5
Mérida, Spain 19 A5
Meriden, U.S.A. 55 H3
Meridian, U.S.A. 51 E3
Meroe, Sudan 69 M5
Merredin, Australia 42 b ii
Merrickville, Canada 57 K5
Merrimack, r., U.S.A. 55 J1
Mersea I., England 15 G3
Merseburg, Ger. D.R. 24 C1
Mersey, r., England 12 D3
Merseyside, Met. Co., England 12 C3
Mersin, Turkey 28 C6
Mersing, Malaysia 38 C6
Merthyr Tydfil, Wales 14 C3
Merton, England 15 F3
Merv, see Mary 29 J6
Mesa, U.S.A. 63 D5
Mesabi Range, U.S.A. 58 B2
Mesa Verde Nat. Park, U.S.A. 52 D3
Meseta Meridional, mtns., Spain 19 B5
Meseta Septentrional, mtns., Spain 19 B4
Messen Nat. Park, Australia 43 A5
Mesopotamia, geog. reg., Iraq 30 E4
Messina, S. Africa 72 E3
Messina, Sicily 21 C5
Messina, Strait of, It. 21 C5
Messini, Greece 21 D5
Mestre, Italy 25 C2
Metagama, Canada 56 D2

Name	Page	ref
Metaline: U.S.A.	62	C2
Methil: Scotland	11	E3
Methuen: U.S.A.	55	J2
Methwold: England	15	G2
Methy Lake: Canada	60	D1
Mettur: India	32	C6
Metz: France	22	C2
Meulaboh: Indon.	38	B6
Meuse (Maas) r., Belgium/France	22	B1
Mevagissey: England	14	B4
Mew I.: N. Irel.	13	F2
Mexborough: England	12	E3
Mexicali: Mexico	63	C5
Mexican Hat: U.S.A.	63	E4
Mexican Plateau: Mex.	48	F5
MEXICO	48	–
Mexico: Maine, U.S.A.	57	P5
Mexico: Mo., U.S.A.	58	B4
Mexico: N.Y., U.S.A.	54	D1
Mexico, Gulf of:	48/9	
MEXICO CITY: Mex.	48	G6
Mézières: France	22	B2
Mi: r., China	36	C2
Miami: Ariz., U.S.A.	63	D5
Miami: Fla., U.S.A.	51	F4
Miami: r., Ohio, U.S.A.	58	D4
Miami Beach: city, U.S.A.	51	F4
Miāneh: Iran	28	F6
Miaoli: Taiwan	37	D5
Mica Creek: Canada	62	C1
Michael Point: Canada	56	C4
Micheh: China	36	B2
Michel: Canada	60	C3
Michigan: State, U.S.A.	58	–
Michigan, Lake: U.S.A.	58	C3
Michigan City: U.S.A.	58	C3
Michipicoton: Canada	56	A2
Mickle Fell: England	12	D2
Micronesia: geog. reg.: Pacific Ocean	44	F6
Midale: Canada	61	E3
Mid-Atlantic Ridge: Atlantic Ocean	8	A1
Middelburg: Neth.	24	A1
Middelburg: S. Afr.	72	D4
Middleburg: N.Y., U.S.A.	55	F2
Middleburg: Pa., U.S.A.	54	C4
Middleburgh: U.S.A.	57	M5
Middle Granville: U.S.A.	55	G1
Middle Island: Can.	56	C8
Middleport: U.S.A.	54	B1
Middlesboro: U.S.A.	51	F2
Middlesbrough: Eng.	12	E2
Middlesex: Co.	56	D6
Middle Swabian Jura Nature Park: German F.R.	25	B2
Middle Swan: Austl.	42	b ii
Middleton: England	12	D3
Middleton-in-Teesdale: England	12	D2
Middletown: Conn., U.S.A.	55	H3
Middletown: Del., U.S.A.	54	E5
Middletown: N.Y., U.S.A.	55	F3
Middletown: Ohio, U.S.A.	58	D4
Middletown: Pa., U.S.A.	54	D4
Middlewich: England	14	D1
Mid Glamorgan: Co., Wales	14	C3
Midhurst: England	15	F4
Mid-Indian Basin: Indian Ocean	33	f v
Mid-Indian Ridge: Indian Ocean	33	e vii
Midland: Canada	56	B2
Midland: Mich., U.S.A.	56	A6
Midland: Tex., U.S.A.	50	B3
Midleton: Irish Rep.	13	C5
Midnapore: India	32	E4
Midsomer Norton: England	14	D3
Midway: Canada	62	C2
Midway Is.: Hawaiian Islands	44	H4
Midwest: U.S.A.	52	F2
Mie: Pref. Japan	39	c ii
Mielec: Poland	20	D2
Mienchih: China	36	A3
Mienhsien: China	36	A3
Mienyang: China	37	B3
Mieres: Spain	19	A3
Mifflinburg: U.S.A.	54	C4
Mihara: Japan	39	B3
Mihsien: China	36	B3
Mijares: r., Spain	19	B3
Mikasa: Japan	39	D1
Miki: Japan	39	a ii
Mikka: r., Canada	60	C1
Mikkeli: Finland	16	E3
Mikonos: i., Greece	21	E5
Mikura-jima: i., Japan	39	D3
Milagro: Argentina	66	A3
Milan (Milano): Italy	25	B2
Milan: U.S.A.	58	B7
Milano see Milan	25	B2
Milbank: U.S.A.	58	A2
Mildenhall: England	15	G2
Mildmay: Canada	56	D5
Mildura: Australia	43	B4
Miles: Australia	42	D3
Miles City: U.S.A.	53	D1
Milestone: Canada	61	E3
Miletus: Turkey	21	E5
Milford: England	15	F3
Milford: Irish Rep.	13	D1
Milford: Conn., U.S.A.	55	G3
Milford: Mass., U.S.A.	55	J2
Milford Haven: Wales	14	A3
Milford Sound: N.Z.	41	A3
Miling: Australia	42	b ii
Milk: r., Canada/U.S.A.	60	D3
Milk River: town, Canada	60	C3
Millau: France	23	B3
Millbrook: Canada	56	G5
Millbury: U.S.A.	55	J2
Mill City: Nev., U.S.A.	62	B3
Mill City: Oreg., U.S.A.	62	B3
Mill Creek: U.S.A.	58	C6
Milledgeville: U.S.A.	51	F3
Mille Lacs, Lake: U.S.A.	58	B2
Millers Falls: town, U.S.A.	55	H2
Millersville: U.S.A.	54	D4
Millerton: U.S.A.	55	G3
Millet: Canada	60	C2
Mill Point: Scot.	11	C4
Mill Hall: U.S.A.	54	C4
Millicent: Australia	43	B5
Millinocket: U.S.A.	59	G2
Millmerran: Austl.	42	D3
Millom: England	12	C2
Millstreet: Irish Rep.	13	B4
Millville: U.S.A.	54	E5
Milngavie: Scotland	11	D4
Milos: i., Greece	21	D5
Milparinka: Australia	43	B3
Milroy: U.S.A.	54	C4
Milton: Canada	56	F6
Milton: Pa., U.S.A.	54	D3
Milton: Vt., U.S.A.	57	M5
Milton-Freewater: U.S.A.	62	C2
Milton Keynes: Eng.	15	F2
Milton Ness: pt., Scot.	10	F3
Miltown Malbay: Irish Republic	13	B4
Milverton: Canada	56	C6
Milverton: England	14	C3
Milwaukee: U.S.A.	58	C3
Mimizan: France	23	A3
Min: r., China	37	C4
Minaki: Canada	61	G3
Minahouch: Japan	39	c iii
Minamata: Japan	39	B3
Minami-alps-kokuritsu-kōen: nat. park, Japan	39	C2
Minamiboso-kokuritsu-kōen: nat. park, Japan	39	f iv
Minas: Uruguay	66	C3
Minas Gerais: State, Brazil	66	a i
Minbu: Burma	38	A2
Minch: channel, Scotland	10	B2
Minchuan: China	36	A4
Mindanao: i., Phil.	35	H9
Minden: Ger. F.R.	24	B1
Minden: U.S.A.	50	D3
Mindoro: i., Phil.	35	G8
Mine Centre: Canada	58	B2
Minehead: England	14	C3
Mine Head: cape, Irish Republic	13	D5
Mineral Wells: town, U.S.A.	50	C3
Minersville: U.S.A.	54	D4
Minet: Canada	56	E3
Mingulay: i., Scot.	10	A3
Minitonas: Canada	61	E2
Minna: Nigeria	67	F4
Minneapolis: U.S.A.	58	B3
Minnedosa: Canada	61	E2
Minnesota: r., U.S.A.	58	A3
Minnesota: State, U.S.A.	58	–
Mino-mikawa-kogen: mtns., Japan	39	d i
Minot: U.S.A.	53	E1
Minsk: U.S.S.R.	20	E2
Mintsing: China	37	C4
Minusinsk: U.S.S.R.	29	P3
Mio: r., U.S.A.	56	A5
Mir: Niger	67	G3
Miraflores Locks: Panama	49	Ins.
Miram Shah: Pakistan	32	B2
Miranda de Ebro: Spain	19	B4
Mirande: France	23	B3
Mirecourt: France	22	C2
Mirim, Lagoa: Brazil/Uruguay	66	D3
Mirim, Lagoa do: Brazil	66	C2
Mirnhay: r., Argentina	66	C2
Mirtoon Sea: Greece	21	D5
Mirzapur: India	32	D3
Misawa: Japan	39	D1
Mishiba: Japan	39	e iv
Misiones: Prov., Arg.	66	D2
Misiones: Sierra de: ra., Argentina	66	D2
Miskolc: Hungary	20	D3
Misool: i., Indonesia	35	J11
Missinaibi: r., Canada	59	D1
Missinaibi Lake: Can.	56	B1
Monfalcone: Italy	25	C2
Mississagi: r., Canada	56	B3
Mississagi Provincial Forest: Canada	56	B2
Mississauga: Canada	56	F6
Mississippi: State & r., U.S.A.	50	D3
Mississippi Strait: Can.	56	B4
Mississippi Sound: U.S.A.	51	E3
Missoula: U.S.A.	53	D2
Missouri: r., U.S.A.	53	G3
Missouri: State, U.S.A.	50	B4
Missouri Coteau: U.S.A.	60	D3
Mistassibi: r., Can.	59	D1
Mistassini, Lac: Can.	47	V6
Mistassini Park: Can.	59	F2
Mistley: England	15	H3
Misurata: Libya	68	H2
Mitaka: Japan	39	f iv
Mitcheldean: Eng.	14	D3
Mitchell: Austl.	42	C3
Mitchell: r., Austl.	40	G4
Mitchell: Canada	56	D6
Mitchell: U.S.A.	53	F2
Mitchelstown: Irish Republic	13	C4
Mitchimamekus: r., Can.	57	L2
Mitilíni: Greece	21	E5
Mito: Japan	39	D2
Mitsang Shan: mtns., China	36	A3
Mitsukedo: Japan	39	f iii
Mittelland Canal: Germany F.R.	24	B1
Mitú: Colombia	64	D3
Miura: Japan	39	f iv
Miya: r., Japan	39	c ii
Miyake-jima: i., Japan	39	D3
Miyako: Japan	39	D2
Miyakonojo: Japan	39	B3
Miyazaki: Japan	39	B3
Miyun: China	36	C1
Mizen Head: cape, Cork, Irish Rep.	13	B5
Mizen Head: cape, Wicklow, Irish Rep.	13	E4
Mizoram: Union Territ.: India	33	F4
Mizunami: Japan	39	d i
Mjölby: Sweden	17	C4
Mjøsa: lake, Norway	17	B3
Mladá Boleslav: Czechoslovakia	20	C3
Mława: Poland	20	D2
Moab: U.S.A.	63	E3
Moak Lake: Canada	61	F2
Moar Lake: Canada	61	G2
Moascar: Egypt	69	Ins.
Moate: Irish Rep.	13	D3
Mobara: Japan	39	g iv
Mobaye: Cen. Afr. Emp.	69	K8
Moberly: U.S.A.	58	B4
Mobile: U.S.A.	51	E3
Mobridge: U.S.A.	53	E1
Moçâmedes: Angola	72	A2
Mocuba: Moz.	72	F2
Moda: Nigeria	67	C1
Modane: France	23	C2
Modder River: town, South Africa	72	C4
Modena: Italy	25	C3
Modesto: U.S.A.	63	B4
Moe: Australia	43	C5
Moel Ferna: mtn., Wales	14	B2
Moelfre: mtn., Dyfed, Wales	14	B3
Moelfre: mtn., Powys, Wales	14	B2
Moengo: Surinam	64	H2
Moffat: Scotland	11	E4
MOGADISCIO: Somali Republic	69	P8
Mogaung: Burma	38	B1
Mogi das Cruzes: Braz.	66	a i
Mogi-Guaçu: r., Brazil	66	a i
Mogil'ev: U.S.S.R.	20	F2
Mogil'ev Podol'skiy: U.S.S.R.	20	E3
Mogi-Mirim: Brazil	66	a i
Mogocha: U.S.S.R.	27	O7
Mogok: Burma	38	B2
Mogollon Plateau: U.S.A.	63	D5
Mohammadia: Algeria	19	C5
Mohammedia: Mor.	68	D2
Mohawk: r., U.S.A.	54	F2
Mohill: Irish Rep.	13	D3
Möhne Strausee: lake, German F.R.	24	B1
Monty: U.S.A.	29	L4
Moira: r., Canada	56	H5
Moira: U.S.A.	57	L5
Mo i Rana: Norway	16	C2
Mojave: des. & r., U.S.A.	63	C5
Mold: Wales	14	C1
Moldau: r., see Vltava	24	C2
Moldavian S.S.R.: U.S.S.R.	20	E3
Mole: r., England	15	F3
Molepolole: Botswana	72	C3
Molières: France	23	B3
Mollendo: Peru	64	D7
Molles: Uruguay	66	C3
Molodechno: U.S.S.R.	20	E2
Molopo: r., Bots./South Africa	72	C4
Molson: Canada	61	F2
Molson Lake: Canada	61	F2
Moluccas (Maluku): is., Indonesia	35	H10
Molucca Sea: Indon.	35	H11
Molveno: Italy	25	C2
Mombasa: Kenya	71	G8
MONACO	23	C3
Monadhliath Mts.: Scotland	10	D2
Monaghan & Co.: Irish Republic	13	E2
Mona Passage: str., W. Indies	49	N6
Monar, Loch: Scot.	10	C2
Monarch Sound: Canada	60	A2
Monasterevin: Irish Republic	13	D3
Monavullagh Mts.: Irish Republic	13	D4
Monchegorsk: U.S.S.R.	16	F2
Mönchen-Gladbach: German F.R.	24	B1
Moncton: Canada	47	X7
Monday: r., Par.	66	D2
Mondo: Chad	67	D1
Mondovi: Italy	25	B3
Monet: Canada	57	K1
Money Head: cape, Scotland	11	C5
Moneymore: N. Irel.	13	E2
Monfalcone: Italy	25	C2
Mong Cai: Vietnam	38	C2
Monger, Lake: Austl	42	b ii
Mong Hang: Burma	38	B2
Mong Mit: Burma	38	B2
MONGOLIA	35	–
Mongu: Zambia	72	C2
Moniaive: Scotland	11	E4
Monifieth: Scotland	10	F3
Monkoto: Zaire	72	C1
Monmouth: Ill., U.S.A.	58	B3
Monmouth: Maine, U.S.A.	57	P5
Monmouth: Wales	14	D3
Monnow: r., England	14	D3
Monocacy: r., U.S.A.	54	C5
Monroe: La., U.S.A.	50	D3
Monroe: Mich., U.S.A.	56	B6
Monroe: N.Y., U.S.A.	55	F3
Monroeville: U.S.A.	51	E3
Mons: Belgium	22	B1
Montagu I.: U.S.A.	46	F5
Montague: France	23	A2
Montana: State.: U.S.A.	52	–
Montargis: France	23	B3
Montauban: France	23	B3
Montauk & pt., U.S.A.	55	H3
Montbéliard: France	23	C2
Montcalm: Co., Can.	57	L4
Montceau-les-Mines: France	23	B2
Mont Cenis Pass: Fr.	23	C2
Mont Clare: U.S.A.	54	E4
Mont-de-Marsan: town, France	23	A3
Montebello: Canada	57	L4
Monte Bello Is.: Australia	40	A5
Monte Carlo: Monaco	23	C3
Monte Caseros: Arg.	66	C3
Montego Bay: town, Jamaica	49	L6
Montélimar: France	23	B3
Monte Lindo: r., Par.	66	C1
Monte Lindo Grande: r., Argentina	66	C2
Montemorelos: Mexico	50	C4
Montenegro: Brazil	66	B2
Monte Quemado: Arg.	66	B2
Monterey: & bay, U.S.A.	63	B4
Monteros: Argentina	66	A2
Monterrey: Mexico	48	F6
Montes Claros: Brazil	64	K7
MONTEVIDEO: Uruguay	66	C3
Montgomery: Ala., U.S.A.	51	E3
Montgomery: N.Y., U.S.A.	55	F3
Montgomery: Pa., U.S.A.	54	D3
Montgomery: Wales	14	C2
Monticello: U.S.A.	54	F3
Monti del Gennargentu: mtn., Sardinia	19	a i
Montigny, Lac: Can.	56	H1
Montijo: Portugal	19	A5
Mont Joli: town, Can.	59	G2
Mont Laurier: town, Canada	57	K3
Montluçon: France	23	B2
Montmagny: & Co., Canada	57	P3
Montmartre: Canada	61	E2
Montmédy: France	22	C2
Montmirail: France	22	B2
Montmorency: Canada	57	O3
Montmorency: r., Canada	57	O2
Monto: Australia	42	D2
Montour Falls: town, U.S.A.	54	D2
Montpelier: France	23	B3
Montpelier: Idaho, U.S.A.	62	D3
Montpelier: Vt., U.S.A.	57	N5
Montréal: Canada	57	M4
Montréal: r., Ont., Canada	56	A2
Montreal: r. & lake, Sask. Canada	61	D2
Montreal Lake: town, Canada	61	D2
Montreuil: France	22	B1
Montreuil-Bellay: Fr.	23	A2
Montreux: Switz.	23	C2
Montrose: Scotland	10	F3
Montrose: Colo., U.S.A.	52	D3
Montrose: Pa., U.S.A.	54	E3
Mont St. Michel: i., France	22	a i
Montserrat: i., Leeward Islands	49	O6
Mont-Tremblant, Parc Provincial: Can.	57	L3
Montvalheur: Pa. de, mtn., France	23	B3
Monywa: Burma	38	B2
Monza: Italy	25	B2
Monze: Zambia	72	C2
Moodus: U.S.A.	55	H3
Moonta: Australia	43	A4
Moora: Australia	42	b ii
Moore, Lake: Australia	42	b i
Moorfoot Hills: Scot.	11	E4
Moorhead: U.S.A.	53	F1
Mooreesburg: S. Afr.	72	B5
Moose: r., Canada	59	D1
Moose Jaw: Canada	61	D2
Moose Lake & sett.: Canada	61	E2
Mooselookmeguntic Lake: U.S.A.	57	P5
Moose Mountain Park: Canada	61	E2
Moosilauke, Mt.: U.S.A.	57	O5
Moosomin: Canada	61	E2
Moosonee: Canada	47	T6
Moosup: U.S.A.	55	J3
Mora: Sweden	17	B3
Moradabad: India	32	C3
Morar, Loch: Scot.	10	C3
Moratuwa: Sri Lanka	32	a ii
Morava: r., Czech.	20	C3
Moravia: U.S.A.	54	D2
Morawa: Australia	42	b i
Morbihan: Old Prov., France	22	a i
Morden: Canada	61	F3
More, Loch: Scot.	10	D1
Moreau: r., U.S.A.	53	E1
Morecambe: & bay, England	12	D2
Moree: Australia	42	C3
Morehead City: U.S.A.	51	G3
Morelia: Mexico	48	F6
Morena, Sierra: mtns., Spain	19	A3
Moresby I.: U.S.A.	54	E5
Moretonhampstead: England	14	C4
Moreton-in-Marsh: England	15	E2
Morgan City: U.S.A.	50	D4
Morgantown: U.S.A.	59	E4
Mori: Japan	39	D1
Moriki: Nigeria	67	D1
Morioka: Japan	39	D2
Moriston: r., Scot.	10	D2
Moriyama: Japan	39	c i
Morlaix: France	22	a i
Morley: England	12	E3
Mornington I., Austl.	42	A2
Moro: r., N. Ireland	13	D2
Moron: Argentina	66	c ii
Morondava: Malagasy Republic	71	H12
Morotai: i., Indon.	35	H10
Morpeth: England	12	E1
Morris: Canada	61	F3
Morrisburg: Canada	57	K5
Morrison: U.S.A.	58	B3
Morristown: N.J., U.S.A.	54	F3
Morristown: N.Y., U.S.A.	57	K5
Morristown: Tenn.: U.S.A.	51	F2
Morrisville: N.J., U.S.A.	54	F2
Morrisville: N.Y., U.S.A.	54	J3
Morrisville: Vt., U.S.A.	57	N5
Morro da Igreja: mtn., Brazil	66	B2
Morro do Capão Doce: mtn., Brazil	66	B2
Mors: i., Denmark	17	A4
Morse: Canada	60	D2
Morshansk: U.S.S.R.	28	E3
Mortara: Italy	25	B2
Morte Point: Eng.	14	B3
Moruya: Australia	43	D5
Morvan: reg., France	23	B2
Morven: mtn., Scot.	10	E1
Morwell: Australia	43	C5
Mosbach: Ger. F.R.	24	B1
Moscow: Idaho, U.S.A.	62	C2
Moscow: Pa., U.S.A.	54	E3
Moscow: U.S.S.R.	28	D2
Mosel (Moselle): r., Ger F.R./France	24	B1
Moses Lake: town, U.S.A.	62	C2
Moshannon: U.S.A.	54	C3
Moshi: Nig.	67	B3
Moshi: Tanzania	71	G8
Mosjøen: Norway	16	B2
Moss: Norway	17	B4
Mossâka: S. Afr.	72	C1
Mossbank: Canada	60	D2
Mossel Bay: town, S. Africa	72	C5
Mossendjo: Congo	72	B1
Mossley: England	12	D3
Mossoró: Brazil	64	M5
Mostaganem: Algeria	19	C5
Mostar: Yugoslavia	21	C4
Mostoos Hills: Canada	60	D1
Mosul: Iraq	30	D3
Motala: Sweden	17	C4
Motherwell: Scot.	11	E4
Motril: Spain	19	B5
Motueka: N.Z.	41	B3
Moulins: France	23	B2
Moulmein: Burma	38	B3
Moultrie: U.S.A.	51	F3
Moundsville: U.S.A.	59	D4
Mountain Ash: Wales	14	C3
Mountain Home: U.S.A.	62	C3
Mountain Sheep Dam: U.S.A.	62	C2
Mountaintop: U.S.A.	54	C3
Mount Airy: town, U.S.A.	54	C5
Mt. Assiniboine Prov. Park: Canada	62	C1
Mount Barker: town, Australia	42	b ii
Mount Carmel: town, U.S.A.	54	D4
Mount Clemens: town, U.S.A.	56	C7
Mt. Desert Island: U.S.A.	59	G3
Mount Etna: sett., Australia	40	F7
Mt. Egmont Nat. Park: N.Z.	41	B2
Mount Forest: town, Canada	56	E6
Mount Gambier: town, Australia	43	B5
Mount Holly: town, U.S.A.	54	F5
Mt. Holly Springs: sett., U.S.A.	54	C4
Mount Isa: sett., Australia	40	F5
Mount Jewett: sett., U.S.A.	54	B3
Mount Kisco: town, U.S.A.	55	G3
Mount Lavinia: town, Sri Lanka	32	a ii
Mount Lyall: sett., Australia	40	b i
Mount Magnet: sett., Australia	42	b i
Mountmellick: Irish Republic	13	D3
Mount Morgan: town, Australia	42	D2
Mount Morris: town, U.S.A.	54	C2
Mount Pleasant: town, U.S.A.	58	D3
Mount Rainier Nat. Park: U.S.A.	62	B2
Mountrath: Irish Republic	13	D3
Mount Revelstoke Nat. Park: Canada	62	C1
Mount Robson Prov. Park: Canada	60	B2
Mount Savage: sett., U.S.A.	54	B5
Mount's Bay: Eng.	14	A4
Mountsorrel: Eng.	15	F2
Mount Union: town, U.S.A.	54	C4
Mount Vernon: town, Ill., U.S.A.	58	C4
Mount Vernon: town, Ind., U.S.A.	58	C4
Mount Vernon: town, N.Y., U.S.A.	55	G3
Mount Vernon: town, Wash., U.S.A.	62	B1
Mourne Mts.: N. Irel.	13	E2
Mousehole: England	14	A4
Moville: Irish Rep.	13	D1
Mowping: China	36	D2
Moy: r., Ireland	13	B2
Moy: r., Irish Rep.	13	C2
Moyale: Kenya	70	G7
Moyen-Atlas: mtns., Morocco	68	D2
Mozambique: Moz.	72	F1
MOZAMBIQUE	72	–
Mozambique Basin: Indian Ocean	33	b viii
Mozambique Channel: Indian Ocean	72	F2
Mozyr': U.S.S.R.	20	E2
Mpanda: Tanzania	71	F10
Mtwara: Tanzania	71	H10
Muang Khon Kaen: Thailand	38	C3
Muang Lampang: Thailand	38	B3
Muang Nan: Thailand	38	C3
Muang Phitsanulok: Thailand	38	C3
Muang Phrae: Thai.	38	C3
Muar: Malaysia	38	C6
Muar: r., Malaysia	38	C6
Mubi: Nigeria	67	C1
Muchinga Mts.: Zambia	71	F10
Much Wenlock: Eng.	14	D2
Muck: i., Scotland	10	B3
Muckle Roe: i., Shetland Islands	10	b i
Muckno Lough: Irish Republic	13	E2
Muçum: Brazil	66	B2
Muddus Nat. Park: Sweden	16	D2
Mudgee: Australia	43	C4
Mudjatik: r., Can.	60	D1
Muerto: r., Arg.	66	B1
Mufu Shan: mtns., China	37	B4
Mühlhausen: Ger. D.R.	24	C1
Mukachevo: U.S.S.R.	20	D3
Mukalla: Yemen P.D.R.	30	E8
Mukden (Shenyang): China	36	D1
Mukinbudin: Austl.	42	b ii
Muko: Japan	39	b ii
Mukutawa: r., Can.	61	F2
Mülheim: Ger. F.R.	24	B1
Mulhouse: France	22	C2
Mull: i. & sound, Scotland	10	C3
Mullaghareirk Mts.: Irish Republic	13	B4
Mullaghcarn: mtn., Northern Ireland	13	D2
Mullaghmore: mtn., Northern Ireland	13	E2
Mullaittivu: Sri Lanka	32	b ii
Müller Mts.: Indon.	35	E10
Mull Head: cape, Orkney Islands	10	e iii
Mullewa: Australia	42	b i
Mullet, The: pen., Irish Republic	13	A2
Mullinger: Irish Rep.	13	D3
Multan: Pakistan	32	B2
Mumbles, The: Wales	14	C3
Mumbles Head: cape, Wales	14	C3
Mun: r., Thailand	38	C3
Muna: i., Indon.	35	G12
Mun-Aya: r., Cameroun	67	
München see Munich	25	
Muncie: U.S.A.	58	
Muncy: U.S.A.	54	
Mundare: Canada	60	
Mundo: r., Spain	19	
Mungallala: r., Australia	42	
Mungbere: Zaire	70	
Mungo: r., Cam.	67	
Munich (München): German F.R.	25	
Münster: Ger. F.R.	24	
Munuscong Lake:	56	
Muong Phalane: Laos	38	
Muong Sen: Vietnam	38	
Muong Sing: Laos	38	
Muonio: Finland	16	
Muonio: r., Finland/Sweden	16	
Mur: r., Austria	25	
Mur: France	22	
Murchison: r., Austl.,	40	
Murcia: Spain	19	
Mureşul: r., Rom.	20	
Muret: France	23	
Murfreesboro: U.S.A.	51	
Murgon: Australia	42	
Murmansk: U.S.S.R.	16	
Murom: U.S.S.R.	28	
Muroran: Japan	39	
Muroto-zaki: cape, Japan	39	
Murphy Creek: sett., Canada	62	
Murray: r., Austl	43	
Murray: U.S.A.	63	
Murray Bridge: Austl	43	
Murrumbidgee: r., Australia	43	
Murupara: N.Z.	41	
Murwillumbah: Austl.	42	
Muş: Turkey	30	
Musashino: Japan	39	
Muscat: Oman	30	
Muscatine: U.S.A.	58	
Musin: Nigeria	67	
Muskegon: & r., U.S.A.	56	
Muskoka, Lake: Can.	56	
Muskogee: U.S.A.	50	
Musselburgh: Scot.	11	
Musselshell: r., U.S.A.	62	
Mussoorie: India	32	
Mustafakemalpasa: Turkey	21	
Mustang Island: U.S.A.	50	
Muswellbrook: Australia	43	
Mutano: Angola	72	
Mutsu: Japan	39	
Mutsu-wan: bay, Japan	39	
Mutton I: Irish Republic	13	
Mutubé: Nigeria	67	
Muyun-Kum: des., U.S.S.R.	29	
Muzaffarpur: India	32	
Mwanza: Tanzania	71	
Mweru, Lake: Zaire	71	
Myakka River Nat. Park: U.S.A.	51	
Mycenae: Greece	21	
Myerstown: U.S.A.	54	
Myingan: Burma	38	
Myitkyina: Burma	38	
Mymensingh: Bangl.	33	
Mynydd Bach: Wales	14	
Mynydd Du hills: Wales	14	
Mynydd Eppynt: hills, Wales	14	
Myrdalsjökull: ice-cap, Iceland	16	
Mysore: India	32	
Mystery Lake: Canada	61	
Mystic: U.S.A.	55	
My Tho: Vietnam	38	
Naas: Irish Republic	13	
Nachingwea: Tan	71	
Nacogdoches: U.S.A.	50	
Nacunday: & r., Par.	66	
Nador: Morocco	19	
Naestved: Denmark	17	
Nafud: des., Saudi Arabia	30	
Nagahama: Japan	39	
Naga Hills: India/Burma	33	
Nagaland: State, India	33	
Nagano: Japan	39	
Nagaoka: Kyoto, Japan	39	
Nagaoka: Japan	39	
Nagapattinam: India	32	
Nagara: r., Japan	39	
Nagarjuna: India	32	
Nagasaki: Japan	39	
Nagashima: Japan	39	
Nagato: Japan	39	
Nagles Mts.: Irish Republic	13	
Nagoya: Japan	39	
Nagpur: India	32	
Nagykanizsa: Hung.	20	
Naha: Ryukyu Is.	34	
Nahanni Nat. Park: Canada	46	
Nahuel Mapá: Arg	66	
Naicam: Canada	61	
Nailsworth: Eng	14	
Nain: Canada	47	
Naini Tal: India	32	
Nairn: & r., Scot.	10	
NAIROBI: Kenya	71	
Najd: geog. reg., Saudi Arabia	30	
Naka: Japan	39	
Nakaminato: Japan	39	
Nakatsu: Japan	39	
Nakhichevan: U.S.S.R.	28	
Nakhodka: U.S.S.R.	34	
Nakhon Phanom: Thailand	38	
Nakhon Ratchasima: Thailand	38	
Nakhon Sawan: Thai.	38	
Nakhon Si Thammarat: Thai.	38	
Nakina: Canada	56	
Naknek: U.S.A.	46	
Nakuru: Kenya	71	
Nakusp: Canada	62	
Nal: r., Pakistan	32	
Namangan: U.S.S.R.	28	
Nambour: Australia	42	
Nam Dinh: Vietnam	38	

Name	Page	ref
nib Desert:		
amibia	72	A3
MIBIA		
outh-West Africa):		
noi: r., Austl	43	C4
npa: U.S.A.	62	C3
npula: Moz	72	F2
ces: Norway	16	B3
ntu: Burma	38	B2
tu: Canada	62	A1
r.: Belgium	22	B1
: r., Thailand	38	C3
aimo: Canada	62	B2
'an: China	37	C5
o: Japan	39	C2
chang: Hupeh, china	36	B3
chang: Kiangsi, china	37	C4
cheng: China	37	C4
chwan: China	37	A4
Clár: I., Scot.	10	D1
cy: France	22	C2
dia Devi: mtn., dia	32	C2
dan: Japan	39	a ii
feng: China	37	C4
ga Eboko: Cam	67	C3
ga Parbat: mtn., dia	32	B1
gapinon: Indon.		
gchen Japo: China	34	A4
tein: China	36	C4
hsiung: China	37	B4
jing see Nanking	36	C3
kang: China	37	B4
kiang: China	36	A3
rina (Nanjing): china	36	C3
kung: China	37	C4
ng: mtns., China	37	B4
ing: China	37	A5
ping: China	37	C4
sei: see rukyu Islands	34	H5
Shan: ra., China	34	B3
so: Japan	39	C2
ntasket Beach: wn.	55	K2
tes: France	23	A4
ticoke: U.S.A.	54	C2
to: Japan	39	c ii
ton: Canada	60	C2
tow: Taiwan	37	D5
tucket: & i., A.	55	K3
tucket Sound: S.A.	55	K3
tung: China	36	D3
twich: England	14	D1
ty-môch servoir: Wales	14	C2
umea : i., Tuvalu		
vang: China	36	B3
vang, Lake: China	36	B3
yuki: Kenya	70	G7
Cabo de: Spain	19	C5
itsu: Japan	39	C2
a: U.S.A.	63	B4
anee: Canada	57	J5
er: N.Z.	41	C2
erville: Canada	57	M4
es: Italy	21	B4
es: U.S.A.	54	C2
a: England	15	G2
& Pref.: Japan	39	b ii
coorte: Austl.	43	B5
ada: r., India	32	C2
dham: Australia	43	C4
erth: Wales	14	B3
onne: France	23	B4
la: Japan	39	g iv
ta: Australia	43	C4
abri: Australia	43	C4
agansett a: U.S.A.	55	J3
an: r., Austl	43	C4
andera: Austl	43	C4
agin: Australia	42	b ii
omine: Austl.	43	C4
pan	39	g iv
to: Shikoku, pan	39	B3
k: Norway	16	C2
yan-Mar: U.S.S.R.	26	H4
a Ridge: Pac.O	45	R9
aby: England	15	E2
hua: U.S.A.	55	J2
ville: U.S.A.	51	E2
: India	32	B5
Lake: Finland	16	D3
rawa: Nigeria	67	B2
au: The Bahamas	51	G4
au Mts.: Indon.	40	F1
au, Lake: Egypt	69	M4
jö: Sweden	17	B4
i: Indonesia	38	B6
l: Prov., S. Afr	72	E4
anal Reactor sting Station: S.A.	62	D3
itoches: U.S.A.	50	D3
ss: U.S.A.	55	J2
pan: Indon.	38	D6
raliste: Cape: stralia	42	b ii
atuck: U.S.A.	55	D3
ghton: Canada	56	D3
RU:	44	F7
r.: Irish Rep.	13	E3
rin: Cape: S.S.R.	27	U5
sota: r., U.S.A	50	C3
r.: Scotland	10	D1
Loch: Scot.	10	D1
aktos: Greece	21	D5
lion: Greece	21	D5
s: i., Greece	21	E5
ro: Japan	39	C1
.: Peru	64	D7
the: pt., Eng.	11	H3
Turkey	21	E5
nimeki: Cam	67	C1
AMENA: Chad	67	D1
a: Zambia	71	E2
.: Irel.	13	E2
holis: Greece	21	D5
ne: r., Australia	42	C3
-Dag: U.S.S.R.	28	G4
aska: State. S.A.	53	E2
aska City: U.S.A.	58	A3
es: France	23	B4
r.: U.S.A.	61	B4
r.: Ger F.R	24	B2
tham Market: Eng	15	H2
les, The: cape, gland	1	

Name	Page	ref
Neenah: U.S.A.	58	C3
Neepawa: Canada	61	F2
Nefyn: Wales	14	B2
Negra, Laguna: Uru.	66	D3
Negomba: Sri Lanka	32	a ii
Negro: r., Arg	65	F12
Negro: r., Brazil	66	E2
Negro: r., Brazil	64	F4
Negro: r., Paraguay	66	C1
Negro: r., Uruguay	66	C3
Negros: i., Phil.	35	G9
Nehbandar: Iran	30	H4
Neichu: China	36	B2
Neimenggu: Aut. Reg., see Inner Mongolia		
Neisiang: China	36	B3
Neisse (Nysa): r., Ger. D.R./Poland	24	C1
Neiva: Colombia	64	C3
Nejamilm Lake: Canada	61	F1
Nellore: India	32	C6
Nelson: Canada	62	C2
Nelson: England	12	D3
Nelson: N.Z.	41	B3
Nelson: r., Canada	61	G3
Nelson, Cape: Austl.	43	B5
Nelson House: Can.	61	F1
Nelson Lakes Nat. Park: N.Z.	41	B3
Nema: Mauritania	68	D5
Neman: r., U.S.S.R.	17	D4
Neman: r., U.S.S.R.	20	E2
Nembe: Nigeria	67	B3
Nemegos: Canada	56	B2
Nemegosenda: r., Canada	56	C1
Nemiskam Park: Can.	56	C1
Nemuro: Japan	34	L2
Nemours: France	22	C2
Nenagh: Irish Rep.	13	C4
Nenana: U.S.A.	46	F4
Nene: r., England	15	F2
Neosho: r., U.S.A.	58	A4
NEPAL:	32	D3
Nepewassi Lake: Canada	56	C1
Nephin: U.S.A.	63	D4
Nephin: mtn., Irish Republic	13	
Nephin Beg Range: mtns., Irish Rep.	13	B2
Nerchinsk: U.S.S.R.	27	O7
Neretva: r., Yugo.	21	C4
Neskaupstadhur: Ice.	16	c i
Nesquehoning: U.S.A.	54	E4
Nesss, Loch: Scot.	10	D2
Neston: England	14	C1
Netherdale: Austl.	42	C2
NETHERLANDS:	24	B1
Neubrandenburg: Ger. D.R.	24	C1
Neuchâtel: &l., Switzerland	25	B2
Neudorf: Canada	60	E5
Neufchâtel: Belg	22	C2
Neufchâteau: France	22	C2
Neumünster: Ger F.R	24	B1
Neunkirchen: Ger F.R	24	B2
Neuquén: Argentina	65	E11
Neuquén: r., Arg	66	C1
Neuruppin: Ger. D.R	24	C1
Neuse: r., U.S.A	51	E2
Neusiedler, Lake: Austria	20	C3
Neuss: German F.R	24	B1
Neustadt: Canada	56	E5
Neustadt: Ger. F.R	24	B2
Neustrelitz: Ger. D.R	24	C1
Neuves-Maisons: Fr.	22	C2
Nevada: State, U.S.A	63	C4
Nevada, Sierra: mtns., Spain	19	B5
Nevada, Sierra: ra., U.S.A.	63	C4
Nevada City: U.S.A.	63	B4
Never: U.S.S.R.	27	P7
Nevers: France	23	B2
Neversink Reservoir: U.S.A.	54	F3
Nevis: Canada	62	D1
Nevis: i., Leeward Islands	49	O6
Nevis, Loch: Scot.	10	C3
Newtown: Wales	14	C2
New Amsterdam: Indian Ocean	33	f viii
Newark: Del., U.S.A.	54	E5
Newark: England	15	E2
Newark: N.Y. U.S.A	54	C1
Newark: Ohio, U.S.A.	59	D3
Newark-on-Trent: Eng.	15	F1
Newark Valley: town. U.C.A.	54	E2
New Baltimore: Mich., U.S.A.	56	C7
New Baltimore: N.Y. U.S.A.	54	F2
New Bedford: U.S.A.	55	K3
New Berlin: U.S.A.	54	E2
New Bern: U.S.A.	51	G2
Newberry: U.S.A.	58	C2
Newbiggin-by-the-Sea: England	12	E1
New Boston: U.S.A.	55	G2
New Braunfels: U.S.A	50	C4
New Britain: U.S.A.	55	H3
New Britain: i., Papua-New Guinea	40	J2
New Brunswick: U.S.A	54	F5
New Brunswick: Prov., Canada	47	W7
Newburgh: Canada	57	J5
Newburgh: Scotland	10	E3
Newburgh: U.S.A.	55	F3
Newburn: England	12	E1
Newbury: England	15	E3
Newburyport: U.S.A	55	K2
New Bussa: Nigeria	67	A2
New Caledonia: i., Pacific Ocean	40	L5
New Caledonian Basin: Pacific Ocean	44	G8
New Canaan: U.S.A	55	G3
Newcastle: Austl	43	D4
Newcastle: Canada	57	W7
Newcastle: N. Irel.	13	F2
Newcastle: S. Afr.	72	E4
Newcastle: Del., U.S.A.	54	E5
New Castle: Pa., U.S.A	59	D3
Newcastle: Wyo., U.S.A.	53	E2
Newcastle Emlyn: Wales	14	B2
Newcastle-under-Lyme: England	14	D1
Newcastle-upon-Tyne: England	12	E1
Newcastle West: Irish Republic	13	B4
Newdegate: Austl	42	b ii
NEW DELHI: State, India	32	C3
Newell Lake: Canada	60	C2

Name	Page	ref
Newenharn, Cape: U.S.A.	46	C5
Newent: England	14	D2
Newfane: U.S.A.	54	B1
Newfield: U.S.A.	54	E5
New Forest: reg., England	15	E4
Newfoundland: Prov., Canada	47	Y6
Newfoundland Basin: N. Atlantic Ocean	8	F3
New Freedom: U.S.A.	54	D5
New Galloway: Scot.	11	D4
New Georgia: i., Solomon Islands	40	K2
New Glasgow: Can.	47	X7
New Guinea: i., Indon./Pap.-N.G.	40	—
New Hamburg: Can.	56	E6
New Hampshire: State, U.S.A.	57	O6
New Hartford: Conn., U.S.A.	55	H3
New Hartford: N.Y., U.S.A.	54	F1
Newhaven: England	15	G4
New Haven: U.S.A.	55	H3
New Hebrides: arch., Pacific Ocean	40	M4
New Holland: U.S.A.	54	D4
New Iberia: U.S.A.	50	D3
New Ipswich: U.S.A.	55	J2
New Ireland: i., Papua-New Guinea	40	J1
New Jersey: State, U.S.A.	55	F5
New Liskeard: Can.	56	F2
New London: Conn., U.S.A.	55	H3
New London: N.H., U.S.A.	55	J1
New Milford: U.S.A.	55	G3
New Mills: England	12	E3
Newnan: U.S.A.	51	F3
Newnham: England	14	D3
New Orleans: U.S.A.	50	D4
New Oxford: U.S.A.	54	C5
New Paltz: U.S.A.	55	F3
New Plymouth: N.Z.	41	B2
Newport: I. of Wight, England	14	E4
Newport: Salop, Eng.	14	D2
Newport: Ky., U.S.A.	58	D4
Newport: N.H., U.S.A.	55	H1
Newport: Oreg. U.S.A.	62	B3
Newport: R.I., U.S.A.	55	J3
Newport: Vt., U.S.A.	57	N3
Newport: Wales	14	C3
Newport News: U.S.A.	59	E4
Newport-on-Tay: Scotland	10	E3
Newport Pagnell: England	15	F2
New Preston: U.S.A.	55	G3
New Providence: i., The Bahamas	51	G4
Newquay: England	14	A4
New Quay: Wales	14	B2
New Romney: Eng.	15	G3
New Ross: Irish Rep.	13	E4
Newry: N. Ireland	13	E2
New South Wales: State, Australia	43	C4
Newton: Iowa, U.S.A.	58	B3
Newton: Kans., U.S.A.	50	C2
Newton: N.J., U.S.A.	54	F3
Newton: N.C., U.S.A.	57	K5
Newton Abbot: Eng.	14	C4
Newton le Willows: England	12	D3
Newton Stewart: Scotland	11	D5
Newtown: Wales	14	C2
Newtownabbey: N. Irel.	13	F2
Newtownards: N. Irel.	13	F2
New Hamilton: N. Ireland	13	D2
Newtownstewart: N. Ireland	13	D2
New Ulm: U.S.A.	58	B3
Newville: U.S.A.	54	C4
New Westminster: Canada	62	B2
NEW YORK: U.S.A.	55	G3
New York State Barge Canal: U.S.A.	54	E1
New York State Thruway: hwy., U.S.A.	54	C1
NEW ZEALAND:	41	—
Neyagawa: Japan	39	b ii
Neyland: Wales	14	B3
Nez de Jobourg: pt., France	14	b i
Nez Perce Dam: U.S.A.	62	C2
Ngadda: r., Nigeria	65	C1
Ngambe: Cameroon	67	C3
Ngami, Lake: Bots.	72	C3
N'Gaoundéré: Cam.	67	C2
Ngauruhoe: mtn., New Zealand	41	C2
Ngorongoro Conservation Area: Tanzania	71	F8
Nguru: Nigeria	67	C1
Nha Trang: Vietnam	38	D3
Niagara: & Co., Can.	56	F6
Niagara Escarpment: hills, Canada	56	E6
Niagara Falls: city, U.S.A.	56	F6
Niagara Falls: U.S.A	54	A1
Niagara-on-the-Lake: Canada	56	F6
NIAMEY: Niger	68	F6
Niantic: U.S.A.	55	H3
Nias: i., Indon.	38	B6
NICARAGUA:	49	—
Nicaragua, Lake: Nic.	49	J7
Nice: France	23	C4
Niceville: U.S.A.	59	D3
Nicholas: r., U.S.A.	58	B2
Nicholson: U.S.A.	54	E3
Nicholson Dam: Can.	56	A2
Nicobar Is.: Indian O.	38	A5
Nicolet: &r. & Co., Canada	57	N3
Nicosia: See NICOSIA		
Niebere Tauern: mtns., Austria	25	C2
Nieuport: Belgium	22	B1
Nieuw Singkil: Indon.	38	B6
NIGER:		
Niger: r., W. Africa	68	G7

Name	Page	ref
Niger: State.	67	B2
NIGERIA:	67	—
Night Hawk Lake: Canada	56	E1
Nihoa: i., Hawaiian Islands	44	J4
Niigata: Japan	39	C2
Niihama: Japan	39	B3
Niihau: i., Hawaiian Islands	44	J4
Nii-shima: i., Japan	39	C3
Nijmegen: Neth.	24	B1
Nikolayev: U.S.S.R.	28	C4
Nikolayevsk: U.S.S.R.	28	F4
Nikko-kokuritsu-kōen: nat. park, Japan	39	C2
Nikopol': U.S.S.R.	28	C4
Niksic: Yugoslavia	21	C4
Nil Biru: Prov., Sudan	69	M6
Nile: r., Africa	69	M4
Niles: U.S.A.	58	C3
Nilgiri Hills: India	32	C6
Nîmes: France	23	B3
Nimrud: Iraq	28	E6
Nimule: Sudan	69	M8
9 de Julio: Argentina	66	C3
Ninety Mile Beach: Australia	43	C5
Nineveh: Iraq	28	E6
Ningcheng: China	36	C1
Ninghai: China	37	D4
Ninghsia Hu (Ningxia): Prov., China	36	A2
Ninghua: China	37	C4
Ningi: Nigeria	67	B1
Ningkuo: China	37	C4
Ningshen: China	36	A3
Ningsiang: China	37	B4
Ningte: China	37	C4
Ningtu: China	37	C4
Ningwu: China	36	B2
Ningxia see Ninghsia Hu	36	A2
Ningyuan: China	37	B4
Niobara: r., U.S.A	53	F2
Niort: France	23	A2
Nipawin: Canada	61	E2
Nipawin Provincial Park: Canada	61	E2
Nipigon &l. : Can.	58	C2
Nipissing: Co. & l.: Canada	56	F3
Nipissing Game Preserve: Canada	57	F3
Niš: Yugoslavia	21	D4
Nishinomiya: Japan	39	b ii
Nishiwaki: Japan	39	a ii
Nith: r., Canada	56	E6
Nith: r., Scotland	11	D4
Nithdale: val., Scotland	11	F4
Nitra: Czechoslovakia	20	C3
Niuchuang Haicheng: China	36	D1
Nivelles: Belgium	22	B1
Nivernais: Old Prov., France	23	B2
Niverville: Canada	61	F3
Nizhniy-Tagil: U.S.S.R.	29	J2
Nkakago: Nigeria	67	B3
Nkongsamba: Cam	67	B3
Noank: U.S.A.	55	H3
Nobel: Canada	56	E4
Nobeoka: Japan	39	B3
Noboribetsu: Japan	39	f iv
Noda: Japan	39	f v
Nodaway: r., U.S.A	58	A3
Noelville: Canada	56	E3
Nogales: Mexico	48	B1
Nogales: U.S.A.	63	D5
Nogaysk: U.S.S.R.	28	D4
Nogent-sur-Seine: France	22	C2
Nogoyá: &r., Arg	66	C3
Noire: r., Canada	57	J2
Noirmoutier: Jersey	14	a ii
Noirmoutier, Île de: France	22	a i
Nojima-zaki: cape, Japan	39	f v
Nokia: Finland	16	D3
Nokomis: &l., Can.	61	E2
Nome: U.S.A.	46	B4
Nominingue: Canada	57	K3
Nonacho Lake: Can.	60	O4
Nong Khai: Thailand	38	C3
Noordoostpolder: polder, Netherlands	24	B1
Noranda: Canada	56	G1
Nord: r., Canada	57	K3
Norden: Ger. F.R	24	B1
Nordenham: Ger. F.R	24	B1
Norderney: i., Ger. F.R	24	B1
Nordfjordeid: Nor.	16	A3
Nordhausen: Ger. D.R	24	C1
Nordhorn: Ger. F.R	24	B1
Nördlingen: Ger. F.R	24	C2
Nordvik: U.S.S.R.	27	O3
Nore: r., Kilkenny, Irish Republic	13	D4
Nore: r., Laois, Irish Republic	13	D4
Norfolk: Nebr., U.S.A.	53	F2
Norfolk: N.Y., U.S.A.	57	L5
Norfolk: Va., U.S.A.	59	E4
Norfolk: Co.:Eng.	15	G2
Norfolk, I.:		
Norfolk Broads: reg., England	15	H2
Norfolk Island: Pac. O.	44	F9
Noril'sk: U.S.S.R.	27	L4
Norman: r., Austl.	40	G2
Normandy: Old Prov., France	22	A2
Normanton: Austl.	43	C3
Norman Wells: Can.	46	K3
North Sound: U.S.A.	55	G3
Norridgewock: U.S.A.	57	P5
Norristown: U.S.A.	54	E4
Norrköping: Sweden	17	C4
Norrtälje: Sweden	17	D4
Norseman: Austl.	42	c ii
Norte, Sierra del: ra., Argentina	66	B3
North Adams: U.S.A.	55	H2
Northallerton: England	12	E2
Northam: Australia	42	b ii
Northampton: U.S.A.	55	H2
Northampton: Eng.	15	F2
Northamptonshire: Co., England	15	F2
North Anson: U.S.A	57	P5
North Attleboro: U.S.A.	55	J3
North Battleford: Can	60	D2

Name	Page	ref
North Bay: town, Canada	56	F3
North Bend: Ore., U.S.A.	62	B3
North Bend: Pa. U.S.A	54	C3
North Bennington: U.S.A.	55	G2
North Berwick: Scot.	11	F3
North Berwick: U.S.A.	55	K1
North Billerica: U.S.A.	55	J3
North Brookfield: U.S.A.	55	H2
North Canadian: r., U.S.A.	53	E3
North Cape: N.Z.	41	B1
North Cape: Norway	16	E1
North Cape: Canada	56	B8
North Carolina: State. U.S.A.	51	F2
North Cascades Nat. Park: U.S.A.	62	B2
North Channel: British Isles	13	F1
North Chelmsford: U.S.A.	55	J2
Northcliffe: Austl.	42	b ii
North Collins: U.S.A.	54	B2
North Dakota: State. U.S.A.	53	E1
North Dorset Downs: England	14	D4
North Downs: hills. England	15	G3
North Dvina: r., U.S.S.R.	28	F1
North Easton: U.S.A.	55	J2
Northeast Providence Channel: The Bahamas	51	G4
North Eifel Nature Park: Ger. F.R.	24	B1
Northern Indian. Lake: Canada	61	F1
Northern Ireland: admin. reg., U.K	13	E2
Northern Territory: Territ., Australia	40	—
Northern Sporades: is., Greece	21	D5
North Esk: r., Scot.	10	F3
Northfield: N.H. U.S.A	55	H2
Northfield: Minn. U.S.A.	58	B3
Northfield: Vt., U.S.A.	57	N5
North Fiji Basin: Pacific Ocean	44	G8
Northfleet: England	15	G3
North Foreland: pt., England	15	H3
North Grosvenor Dale: U.S.A.	55	J3
North Haven: U.S.A.	55	H3
North Hinksey: England	15	E3
North Kent: I. & r., Canada	61	F1
NORTH KOREA:	36	—
Northland: dist., N.Z.	41	B1
North Little Rock: U.S.A.	50	B3
North Oxford: U.S.A.	55	J2
North Pacific Ocean:	44/5	—
North Platte: & r., U.S.A.	53	E2
North Point: U.S.A.	56	B4
Northport: U.S.A.	55	G4
North Ronaldsay: i., Orkney Islands	10	e iii
North Saskatchewan: r., Canada	60	D2
North Sea: Europe	12	G2
North Seal: r., Can.	61	E1
North Sos'va: r., U.S.S.R.	26	J5
North Sound: Irish Republic	13	B3
North Sound, The: bay, Orkney Islands	10	e iii
North Syracuse: U.S.A	54	D1
North Tees: r., Canada	56	D6
North Tonawanda: U.S.A.	56	G6
North Tyne: r., England	12	D1
North Uist: i., Scot.	10	—
Northumberland: U.S.A.	54	D4
Northumberland: Co., Canada	56	H5
Northumberland: Co.: England	12	D1
Northumberland Is.: Australia	42	D2
Northumberland Nat. Park: England	12	D1
Northville: U.S.A.	55	F1
North Wabasca Lake: Canada	60	C1
North Walsham: Eng	15	H2
Northwest Highlands: mtns. Scotland	10	—
Northwest Pac. Basin: Pacific Ocean	44	E3
Northwest Providence Channel: The Bahamas	51	G4
Northwest Territories: Territ., Canada	46/7	–4
North York Moors: Nat. Park. England	14	D1
North Yorkshire: Co., England	12	E2
Norquay: Canada	61	D2
Norton: U.S.A.	59	D4
Norton Sound: U.S.A.	46	B4
Norwalk: U.S.A.	55	G3
NORWAY:	16/17	—
Norway: r., U.S.A	57	P5
Norway House: Can	61	F2
Norwich: Canada	56	E7
Norwich: England	15	H2
Norwich: Conn., U.S.A.	55	H3
Norwich: N.Y., U.S.A.	54	E2
Norwood: Canada	56	H5
Norwood: Mass., U.S.A.	55	J3
Norwood: N.Y. U.S.A	57	L5
Noshiro: Japan	39	C1
Noss Hd.: Scotland	10	E1
Noss Bé: Malagasy Republic	71	I10
Nossob: r.Bots./Namibia	72	C4
Noteć: r., Poland	20	C2
Notogawa: Japan	39	c i

Name	Page	ref
Noto-Hanto: penin., Japan	39	C2
Notre Dame du Laus: Canada	57	K3
Notre-Dame-du-Nord: Canada	56	F2
Notre Dame Mts.: Canada	59	G2
Nottawasaga Bay: Can.	56	E5
Nottingham: England	15	E1
Nottinghamshire: Co., England	15	E1
Nouadhitou: Mauritania	68	B4
NOUAKCHOTT: Mauritania	68	B5
NOUMÉA: New Caledonia	40	M5
Nova Iguaçu: Brazil	66	b i
Novar: Canada	56	F4
Novara: Italy	25	B2
Nova Scotia: Prov., Canada	47	X7
Nova Scotia Basin: N. Atlantic Ocean	8	F4
Nova Sofala: Moz	72	E3
Novaya Zemlya: is., U.S.S.R.	26	H3
Novgorod: U.S.S.R.	28	C3
Novi Ligure: Italy	25	B3
Novi Pazar: Yugo.	21	D4
Novocherkassk: U.S.S.R.	28	E4
Novograd Volynskiy: U.S.S.R.	20	E2
Novo Hamburgo: Brazil	66	D2
Novo-kuznetsk: U.S.S.R.	29	O3
Novomoskovsk: U.S.S.R.	28	D3
Novonazvayevka: U.S.S.R.	28	E2
Novopolotsk: U.S.S.R.	20	E1
Novosibirsk: U.S.S.R.	29	N3
Novosibirskoye Ostrova: is., U.S.S.R.	27	R2
Novorossiysk: U.S.S.R.	28	D5
Novozensk: U.S.S.R.	28	F4
Nowa Sól: Poland	20	C2
Nowy Port: U.S.S.R.	26	K4
Nowra: Australia	43	D4
Nowy Sącz: Poland	20	D3
Noxon Rapids Dam: U.S.A.	62	C2
Nsukka: Nigeria	67	B2
Nubian Desert: Sudan	69	M4
Nueces: r., U.S.A.	50	C4
Nueva Galia: Arg	66	C3
Nueva Palmira: Uru	66	C3
Nuevo Laredo: Mex	50	C4
Nuits-St. Georges: France	23	B2
Nullarbor Plain: Austl	42	D7
Numan: Nigeria	67	C2
Numazu: Japan	39	e iv
Nunda: U.S.A.	54	C2
Nunde: U.S.A.	56	H7
Nuneaton: England	15	E2
Nungesser, Lake: Can.	61	G2
Nunivak: i., Bering Sea	46	B4
Nunkiang: China	34	H1
Nuoro: Sardinia	19	a i
Nuremberg (Nürnberg): German F.R	24	C2
Nurmes: Finland	16	E3
Nürnberg see Nuremberg	24	C2
Nuri: Mt. Australia	43	C4
Nushki: Pakistan	32	A3
Nut Mountain & sett.: Canada	61	E2
Nuwara Eliya: Sri Lanka	32	b ii
Nuweveld Range: South Africa	72	C5
Nyahururu: Kenya	70	G7
Nyala: Sudan	69	K6
Nyasa (Malawi): Lake: E. Africa	71	F10
Nybro: Sweden	17	C4
Nye: U.S.A.	62	C2
Nyenchen Tangliha: ra., China	32/3	P4
Nyiregyháza: Hungary	20	D3
Nykøbing: Denmark	17	B5
Nykøbing: Denmark	17	C4
Nyköping: Sweden	17	C4
Nynäshamn: Sweden	17	C4
Nyiranï: Austria	25	B2
Nyon: Switz.	25	B2
Nysa: Poland	20	C2
Nysa: r., see Neisse		
Nyssa: U.S.A.	62	C3
Oa: penin., Scotland	11	B4
Oa, Mull of: channel, Scotland	11	B4
Oadby: England	15	E2
Oahe Reservoir: U.S.A.	53	E1
Oahu: i., Hawaiian Islands	45	K3
Oak Bluffs: U.S.A.	55	K3
Oakdale: U.S.A.	55	G4
Oakengates: England	14	D2
Oakes: U.S.A.	53	F1
Oakfield: U.S.A.	54	F4
Oakham: England	15	F2
Oakharbor: U.S.A.	55	B8
Oak Island: Canada	61	E1
Oakland: Calif. U.S.A.	63	B4
Oakland: Maine. U.S.A.	57	Q5
Oak Ridge: U.S.A.	51	F4
Oakville: Canada	56	F6
Oakville: U.S.A.	55	G3
Oamaru: N.Z.	41	B4
Oamishirasato: Japan	39	g iv
Oaxaca: Mex.	48	G6
Ob: r., U.S.S.R.	26	J4
Ob, Gulf of: U.S.S.R.	26/7	K4
Oba: Canada	56	D2
Oba: Nigeria	67	B2
Oban: Nigeria	67	B2
Oban: Scotland	10	C3
Obal's Hills: Nigeria	67	C2
Obama: Japan	39	c ii
Obbia: Somali Rep	69	P7
Oberammergau: German F.R	25	C2
Oberhausen: Ger. F.R	24	B1
Obihiro: Japan	39	f iv
Obidos: Brazil	64	F4
Obi Is.: Indonesia	35	H11
Obu: Japan	39	c i
Ocala: U.S.A.	51	F4
Ocean Falls: town. Canada	62	A1
Ocean Island: Pac. O	44	F7

Name	Page	ref
Oceanlake U.S.A	62	B3
Oceanport U.S.A	55	F4
Oceanside U.S.A	63	C5
Ochil Hills Scotland	10	E3
Ocmulgee r. U.S.A	51	F3
Oconee r. U.S.A	51	F3
Oda Japan	39	B2
Odate Japan	39	D1
Odawara Japan	39	f iv
Odda Norway	17	A3
Ödemis Turkey	21	E5
Odense Denmark	17	B4
Odenton U.S.A	54	D5
Odenwald mts. German F R	24	B2
Oder (Odra) r. Ger D R /Poland	24	C1
Odessa U.S.A	50	B3
Odessa U.S.S.R	28	C4
O Donnell Point Canada	56	E4
Odra r. see Oder	24	C1
Oeno Island Pac O.	45	N9
Ofa Nigeria	67	A2
Offaly Co. Irish Rep	13	D3
Offenburg Ger F R	24	B2
Ofunato Japan	39	D2
Oga Japan	39	C2
Ogaden reg. Ethiopia	69	O7
Oga-Hanto penin. Japan	39	C2
Ogaki Japan	39	c i
Ogallala U.S.A	53	E2
Ogano Japan: Saitama. Japan	39	f iii
Ogawa Baraki. Japan	39	g iii
Ogbomosho Nigeria	67	A2
Ogden U.S.A	63	D3
Ogdensburg U.S.A	57	K5
Oglesby U.S.A	58	C3
Oglio r. Italy	25	C2
Ogoja Nigeria	67	B2
Ogoki r. Canada	58	C1
Oguma Nigeria	67	B2
Ogun r & State. Nigeria	67	A2
Ogunquit U.S.A	55	K1
Oguta Nigeria	67	B2
Ogwashi Uku Nig	67	B2
Ohai N.Z	41	A4
Ohakune N.Z	41	C2
Ohara Japan	39	g iv
Ohara Japan	39	D1
Ohio State U.S.A	59	D4
Ohio r. U.S.A	58	C4
Ohito Japan	39	e iv
Ohre (Eger) r. Czechoslovakia	24	C1
Ohrid Lake Albania/ Yugoslavia	21	D4
Oi r. Japan	39	b i
Oich Loch Scotland	10	D2
Oil City U.S.A	59	F8
Oise r. France	22	B2
Oiso Japan	39	f iv
Oita Japan	39	B3
Ojika-Hanto penin. Japan	39	D2
Ojos del Salado mtn. Argentina	64	E9
Oka Nigeria	67	B2
Oka r. U.S.S.R	28	E2
Okanagan Lake Can	62	C2
Okanogan r. Canada/ U.S.A	62	C2
Okaya Japan	39	C2
Okayama Japan	39	B3
Okazaki Japan	39	d ii
Okeechobee, Lake U.S.A	51	F4
Okehampton England	14	B4
Oke-Iho Nigeria	67	A2
Okene Nigeria	67	B2
Okha India	32	A4
Okhotsk U.S.S.R	27	R6
Okhotsk Sea of U.S.S.R	27	—
Okigwi Nigeria	67	B2
Oki-gunto i. Japan	39	B2
Okinawa i. Ryukyu Islands	34	H5
Okitipupa Nigeria	67	A2
Oklahoma State. U.S.A	50	C2
Oklahoma City U.S.A	50	C2
Oklawaha r. U.S.A	51	F4
Okmulgee U.S.A	50	C2
Okor r. Nig/Cam	67	B2
Okotoks Canada	60	C2
Okovango r. Angola/ Namibia	72	C2
Okovango Basin marsh. Botswana	72	C2
Okpara r. Nigeria/ Benin	67	A2
Okposi Nigeria	67	B2
Okrika Nigeria	67	B2
Okt'abr'sk U.S.S.R	29	H4
Okushiri-shima i. Japan	39	C1
Okuta Nigeria	67	A2
Okutama Japan	39	f iv
Olancha U.S.A	63	C3
Öland i. Sweden	17	D4
Olbia Sardinia	19	a ii
Old Bridge U.S.A	55	F4
Oldenburg Ger F R	24	B1
Oldenzaal Neth	24	B1
Old Fletton England	15	F2
Old Forge U.S.A	54	E3
Old Fort U.S.A	54	C4
Oldham England	12	D3
Oldman r. Can	62	D2
Oldmeldrum Scot	10	F2
Old Name r. Eng	15	F2
Olds Canada	62	D1
Old Sarum hist. England	15	E3
Old Saybrook U.S.A	55	H3
Old Speckle Mt U.S.A	57	P5
Olduvai Gorge Tanzania	71	G8
Old Wives Lake Canada	61	D2
Olean U.S.A	54	B2
Olekminsk U.S.S.R	27	P5
Olenegorsk U.S.S.R	16	F2
Olenek r. U.S.S.R	27	P3
Olhão Portugal	19	A5
Olimar Grande r. Uruguay	66	D3
Olimpo Brazil	66	D3
Oliva Argentina	66	C2
Olivenza Spain	62	C2
Olney England	15	F2
Olomouc Czech	20	C3
Olonzac France	23	B3
Oloron-Ste-Marie France	23	A3
Olpe German F R	24	B1
Olsztyn Poland	20	D2
Olten Switzerland	25	B2
Oltul r. Romania	21	D4
Olympia Greece	21	D5
Olympia U.S.A	62	B2
Olympic Nat. Park U.S.A	62	B2
Olympus mtn. Greece	21	D5
Omagh N. Ireland	13	D2
Omaha U.S.A	58	A3
OMAN	30	G6
Oman, Gulf of Arabian Sea	30	G6
Omaruru Namibia	72	B3
Ome Japan	39	f iv
Omdurman Sudan	69	M5
Omemee Canada	56	G5
Omigawa Japan	39	g iv
Om-hachiman Japan	39	c i
Omiya Japan	39	f iv
Omo Nigeria	67	B2
Omoko r. Nigeria	67	B2
Omsk U.S.S.R	29	L2
Omu-Aran r. Nig	67	A2
Omuo Nigeria	67	A2
Omuta Japan	39	B3
Omutinskoye U.S.S.R	29	K2
Onaping r. Canada	56	D3
Onaping Lake Canada	56	D2
Onaway U.S.A	56	A4
Ondo St. State. Nigeria	67	A2
Onega, Lake U.S.S.R	28	D1
Oneida r. U.S.A	54	E1
O Neill U.S.A	53	F2
Onekotan r. U.S.S.R	27	S8
Oneonta U.S.A	54	E1
Onishi Japan	39	f iii
Onitsha Nigeria	67	B2
Ono Japan	39	a ii
Onslow Bay r. U.S.A	51	G3
Onstwedde Neth	24	B1
Ontario r. Canada	56	F5
Ontario Prov. Canada	47	S6
Ontario, Lake Canada/ U.S.A	56/7	
Ontario U.S.A	62	C3
Oodnadatta Austl	40	F6
O'okiep S. Africa	72	B4
Ooldea Australia	40	E7
Oologah Reservoir U.S.A	58	A4
Oostelijk Flevoland polder. Neth	24	B1
Oosterhesselen Neth	24	B1
Oosterhout Neth	24	B2
Ootacamund India	32	C6
Opanake Sri Lanka	32	b ii
Opasatica, Lake Can	56	F1
Opasquia Canada	61	G2
Opatija Yugoslavia	20	C3
Opava Czech	20	C3
Opelika U.S.A	51	E3
Opelousas U.S.A	50	D3
Opeongo Lake Can	56	G4
Ophir U.S.A	62	B2
Opi Nigeria	67	B2
Opobo Nigeria	67	B3
Opochka U.S.S.R	17	E4
Opole Poland	20	C2
Oporto Portugal	19	A4
Oppdal Norway	17	B3
Opunaki N.Z	41	C2
Oradea Romania	20	D3
Oraison France	23	D3
Orange Australia	43	C4
Orange France	23	B3
Orange r. Namibia/S. Africa	72	B4
Orange Mass. U.S.A	55	H2
Orange Tex. U.S.A	50	D3
Orangeburg U.S.A	51	F3
Orange Free State Prov. S. Africa	72	D4
Orangeville Canada	56	E6
Oranienburg Ger D R	24	C1
Orbigo r. Spain	19	C4
Orbost Australia	43	C5
Orchard Beach U.S.A	54	D5
Orchy r. Scotland	10	D3
Ord r. Australia	40	D4
Ordale Canada	60	D2
Orduña r. Belgium	22	C1
Ordos Plateau China	36	A2
Ordzhonikidze U.S.S.R	28	E5
Örebro Sweden	17	C4
Oregon State. U.S.A	62	B3
Oregon City U.S.A	62	B2
Orekhovo-Zuyevo U.S.S.R	28	D2
Orel U.S.S.R	28	D3
Orem U.S.A	63	D3
Orenburg U.S.S.R	28	H3
Orense Spain	19	A4
Orford England	15	H2
Orford Ness penin. England	15	H2
Organ Pipe Cactus Nat. Park U.S.A	63	D5
Orgeyev U.S.S.R	20	E3
On Lake Finland	16	F3
Orillia Canada	56	F5
Orinoco r. Ven	64	F2
Oriskany U.S.A	54	E1
Orissa State. India	32	D4
Oristano Sardinia	19	a ii
Orizaba & mtn. Mex	48	G6
Orkanger Norway	16	A3
Orkney Is. Scotland	9	C1
Orlando U.S.A	51	F4
Orléans Old Prov. France	22	B2
Orléans France	22	B2
Orleans Mass. U.S.A	55	K3
Orleans U.S.A	57	N5
Orleans, Île d' r. Canada	57	P3
Orléans, Forêt d' Fr	22	B2
Orme r. France	22	B2
Ormskirk England	12	D3
Ormstown Canada	57	L4
Ornain r. France	22	C2
Örnsköldsvik Sweden	16	D3
Orofino U.S.A	62	C2
Oron Nigeria	67	B3
Oronsay r. Scotland	11	B3
Oroshaza Hungary	20	D3
Orrin r. Scotland	10	D2
Orsha U.S.S.R	28	D3
Orsk U.S.S.R	29	H3
Orthe, Forêt d' France	22	B2
Orther r. France	23	A3
Ortigueira Spain	19	A4
Ortler mtn. Italy	25	C2
Oruro Bolivia	64	D3
Orvieto Italy	21	B4
Orwell r. England	15	G2
Osage r. & State. U.S.A	58	B2
Osaka & Pref. Japan	39	b ii
Osaka-wan bay. Japan	39	b ii
Osawa Canada	56	G6
O-shima r. Japan	39	C3
Oshkosh U.S.A	58	C3
Oshogbo Nigeria	68	F7
Osijek Yugoslavia	21	C3
Oskaloosa U.S.A	58	B3
Oskarshamn Sweden	17	C4
Oskelaneo Canada	57	K1
Oslo Norway	17	B4
Oslofjorden fd. Nor	17	B4
Osmanabad India	32	C5
Osnabruck Ger F R	24	B1
Osogbo Nigeria	67	A2
Osorno Brazil	66	D2
Osse r. Nigeria	67	B2
Ossining U.S.A	55	G3
Ostend Belgium	22	B2
Osterdal r. Sweden	17	B3
Ostersund Sweden	16	B3
Ostiglia Italy	25	C2
Ostrava Czech	20	C3
Ostrov U.S.S.R	17	E4
Ostrovnoye U.S.S.R	27	T4
Ostrowiec Swietokrzyski Pol.	20	D2
Ostrow Wielkopolski Poland	20	C2
Osumi Is. Japan	34	J4
Osun r. Nigeria	67	A2
Oswaldtwistle r. U.S.A	57	K5
Oswego & r. U.S.A	54	D1
Oswestry England	14	C4
Otaciilo Costa. Brazil	66	E2
Otago dist. N.Z	41	A4
Otago Peninsula N.Z	41	B4
Otaki Japan	39	g iv
Otaru Japan	39	D1
Otira Tunnel N Z	41	B3
Otley England	12	E3
Otra r. Norway	17	A4
Otranto, Str. of Mediterranean Sea	21	C5
Otsego Lake U.S.A	54	F2
Otsu Japan	39	b i
Otta Norway	16	A3
Ottawa Canada	57	K4
Ottawa Ill. U.S.A	58	C3
Ottawa Kans. U.S.A	58	A4
Ottawa r. Canada	56	G3
Ottawa-Carleton Co. Canada	57	K4
Otter Lake Canada	61	E1
Ottery St. Mary England	14	C4
Öttingen Ger. F R	24	B2
Ottumwa U.S.A	58	B3
Otukpa Nigeria	67	B2
Otukpo Nigeria	67	B2
Otway, Cape Austl	43	B5
Ouachita r. U.S.A	50	D3
Ouachita Mts. U.S.A	50	D3
OUAGADOUGOU Upper Volta	68	E6
Ouargla Algeria	68	B1
Oubangui r. Africa	69	K8
Oudenaarde Belgium	22	B1
Oudtshoorn S. Africa	72	C5
Ouessant, Île d' (Ushant) France	22	a i
Ouezzane Morocco	68	D2
Oughter, Lough Irish Republic	13	D2
Oujda Morocco	68	E2
Oulangan Nat. Park Finland	16	F4
Oulu Finland	16	F4
Oulu Lake Finland	16	E3
Ounas r. Finland	16	F4
Oundle England	15	F2
Oureau r. Canada	57	M3
Ourthe r. Belgium	22	C1
Ou-Sammaku mts. Japan	39	D2
Ouse r. E Sussex. England	15	G4
Ouse r. N Yorks. England	12	F3
Oust r. France	22	a i
Outardes, aux r. Canada	59	G1
Outer Hebrides is. Scotland	10	A2
Outer Skerries is. Shetland Islands	10	c i
Outjo Namibia	72	B3
Outlook Canada	60	D2
Outokumpu Finland	16	F3
Ouyen Australia	43	B5
Ovalle Chile	66	B2
Oversee Ger. F R	18	D2
Overton Wales	14	D2
Övertorneå Sweden	16	D2
Oviedo Spain	19	B4
Ovindoli Italy	19	B5
Owando Congo	71	C8
Owasco Lake U.S.A	54	E1
Owatonna U.S.A	58	B3
Owel, L. Irish Rep	13	D3
Owen Mt. N.Z	41	B3
Owen Falls Uganda	70	F7
Owensboro U.S.A	58	C4
Owens Lake U.S.A	63	C4
Owen Sound & town Canada	56	E5
Owen Stanley Range. Papua-New Guinea	40	H2
Owerri Nigeria	67	B2
Owen r. Nigeria	67	B2
Owl r. Canada	61	G1
Owo Nigeria	67	B2
Owosso U.S.A	56	A6
Owyhee Reservoir U.S.A	62	C3
Oxbow Canada	61	F2
Oxbow Dam U.S.A	62	C2
Oxelösund Sweden	17	D4
Oxford England	15	F2
Oxford Mich. U.S.A	56	B6
Oxford N.Y. U.S.A	54	E1
Oxford Co. Canada	56	E6
Oxford Lake Canada	61	F2
Oxford House Can.	61	F2
Oxfordshire Co. England	15	F2
Oxnard U.S.A	63	C5
Oxus r. Amu Dar ya	29	J6
Oyem Cameroon	71	B7
Oykel r. Scotland	10	D2
Oyo & State. Nig	67	A2
Oyodo Japan	39	b ii
Oyonnax France	23	C2
Oyster Haven Irish Republic	13	C5
Ozark Plateau U.S.A	58	B4
Ozarks, Lake of the U.S.A	58	B4
Özd Hungary	20	D3
Ozu Japan	39	B3
Paan see Batang	34	B5
Paarl S. Africa	72	B5
Pabbay r. Scotland	10	A2
Pachacamac Peru	64	C6
Pachung China	36	A3
Pacific City U.S.A	62	B2
Pacific Grove U.S.A	63	B4
Pacific Ocean	44/5	—
Padang Indonesia	35	C11
Padangsidimpuan Indonesia	38	B6
Paddle Prairie town. Canada	60	B1
Paddockwood Can	61	E1
Paderborn Ger. F R	24	B1
Padova see Padua	25	C2
Padre Island U.S.A	50	C4
Padstow England	14	B4
Padua (Padova) Italy	25	C2
Paducah U.S.A	58	C4
Paeroa N.Z	41	C2
Pafuri Mozambique	72	E3
Pagan Burma	38	B2
Page U.S.A	63	D4
Pagwa River town. Canada	56	C1
Pahsien China	36	C1
Pai r. Nigeria	67	C2
Paide U.S.S.R	17	E4
Paignton England	14	C4
Paiho China	36	B3
Pahokow China	36	B3
Paijänne r. Finland	16	E3
Paimboeuf France	22	a i
Paimpol France	22	a i
Painesville U.S.A	56	D3
Painswick England	14	D3
Paintsville U.S.A	56	C4
Paisley Canada	56	D5
Paisley Scotland	11	D3
Paiyunopo China	36	A1
Pajakumbuh Indon.	38	C7
Paka Nigeria	67	C1
Pakanbaru Indon.	38	C6
Paki Nigeria	67	B1
PAKISTAN	32	—
Pak Lay Laos	38	C3
Pakokku Burma	38	B2
Pakowki Lake Can.	60	C3
Pakse Laos	38	D3
Pakwach Uganda	70	F7
Pakwash, Lake Can.	61	G2
Pala Chad	67	C2
Palapye Botswana	72	D3
Palatka U.S.A	51	F4
Palau Is. Caroline Is.	35	J9
Palauk Burma	38	B4
Palaw Burma	38	B4
Palawan r. Phil.	35	F9
Palembang Indon.	35	C11
Palencia Spain	19	B4
Palermo Sicily	21	B5
Palestine U.S.A	50	C3
Palghat India	32	C6
Palime Togo	68	F7
Palisade U.S.A	63	D4
Palisades Dam U.S.A	62	D3
Palk Strait India/ Sri Lanka	32	a ii
Pallas-Ounastunturin Nat. Park Finland	16	E2
Palliser, Cape N.Z	41	C3
Palma de Mallorca Mallorca	19	C5
Palmares do Sul Brazil	66	D2
Palmas, Cape Liberia	68	D8
Palmeira Brazil	66	D2
Palmer U.S.A	55	H2
Palmerland penin. Antarctica	85	E17
Palmerston Canada	56	E6
Palmerston North New Zealand	41	C3
Palmerton U.S.A	54	E4
Palmyra Syria	24	D7
Palmyra Pa. U.S.A	54	D4
Palmyra r. Argentina	66	B2
Palmyra Island Pacific Ocean	45	J6
Paloh Indonesia	38	D6
Palomar U.S.A	62	C1
Palos, Cabo de Spain	19	B5
Palouse Hills U.S.A	62	C2
Palo Verde U.S.A	63	D5
Palpalá Argentina	66	A1
Pamiers France	23	A1
Pamirs mtns. Pakistan	29	L6
Pamlico Sound U.S.A	51	G2
Pampa geog reg. Argentina	65	F11
Pampa de Patria Par	50	B2
Pampas Hills Canada	61	C2
Pampa de las Salinas salt lake. Argentina	66	A3
Pampa de las Guanacos sett. Arg	66	A3
Pampa Húmeda geog reg. Argentina	66	
Pampa seca geog reg. Argentina	66	
Pamplona Spain	19	B4
Panache, Lake Can	56	D4
PANAMA	49	L8
Panama Panama	49	Ins.
Panama Canal Pan	49	Ins.
Panama City U.S.A	51	E3
Panama, Gulf of Panama	64	C2
Panama Canal Panama	49	Ins.
Pancevo Yugoslavia	21	D4
Pando Uruguay	66	D3
Panevezys U.S.S.R	17	E3
Pangbourne England	15	F3
Pangnirtung Canada	47	W3
Pangong Range China	32	D5
Panguitch U.S.A	63	D4
Panjim India	32	B5
Pankshin Nigeria	67	B2
Panshan China	36	C1
Pant r. England	15	G3
Pantar r. Indonesia	35	G12
Pantelleria r. Sicily	21	B5
Panther Mt. U.S.A	54	D5
Panyu China	37	B5
Paoan China	36	C1
Paochang China	36	B1
Paoki China	36	A3
Paoshan China	36	A4
Paoteh China	36	B1
Paoteng China	36	B1
Paoting (Chingyuan) China	36	C2
Paotow (Baotou) China	36	A1
Paotsing China	37	A4
Paoying China	36	C3
Papakura N.Z	41	B2
Papa Stour r. Shetland Islands	10	b i
Papa Westray r. Orkney Islands	10	e iii
Papenburg Ger. F R	24	B1
Papineau Co. Can	57	K4
Papineau, Lac. Can	57	L4
Papineau-Labelle Parc. Canada	57	K3
Paps, The mtn. Irish Republic	13	B4
PAPUA-NEW GUINEA	40	—
Papua i. Dist. Pap N G	40	G2
Papua, Gulf of Papua-New Guinea	40	G2
Pará r. Brazil	64	H4
Paracas Peru	64	C6
Paracel (Xisha) Is. China	38	E3
Paradis Canada	57	J1
Paradise U.S.A	58	C4
Paraguari Paraguay	66	C2
PARAGUAY	64	—
Paraiba do Sul r. Brazil	66	b i
Paraibuna & r. Brazil	66	a i
Paraitinga r. Brazil	66	a i
Parakou Benin	68	F7
PARAMARIBO Surinam	64	G2
Paramushir i. U.S.S.R	27	S7
Paraná r. Argentina	66	B3
Paraná State. Brazil	66	D1
Paraná r. Argentina	66	C2
Paraná de las Palmas r. Arg	66	C3
Paranaguá Brazil	66	E2
Paraná Guazú r. Argentina	66	C3
Paraná Ibicuy r. Argentina	66	C3
Paranapanema r. Brazil	66	a ii
Parbati r. India	32	C4
Parbhani India	32	C5
Parchim Ger. D R	24	C1
Pardo r. Parana. Brazil	66	E2
Pardo r. Rio Grande do Sul. Brazil	66	D2
Pardubice Czech	20	C3
Parent, Lac Canada	56	H1
Parentis France	23	A3
Parepare Indonesia	35	F11
Paris Canada	56	E6
PARIS France	22	B2
Paris U.S.A	50	C3
Park City U.S.A	63	D3
Parkersburg U.S.A	56	D3
Parkesburg U.S.A	54	E5
Parkes Australia	43	D5
Park Hill town. Canada	56	D6
Park Range mtns. U.S.A	63	E3
Park Rapids town. U.S.A	58	A2
Parksville Canada	62	B2
Parma Italy	25	C3
Parma U.S.A	59	D3
Parnaiba Brazil	64	K4
Parnassos mtn. Greece	24	D5
Parnu U.S.S.R	17	E4
Paroo r. Austl	43	B3
Parramatta Australia	43	D4
Parry Is. Canada	46	D1
Parry Sound Co. Canada	56	E5
Parry SSound Co. Canada	56	E4
Parsons U.S.A	58	A4
Partenen Austria	25	C2
Partenkirchen German F R	25	C2
Parthenay France	23	A2
Partizansk U.S.S.R	27	Q9
Partry Mts Irish Republic	13	B3
Pasadena U.S.A	63	C5
Pasaje r. Argentina	66	B3
Pascagoula & r. U.S.A	51	E3
Pascani Romania	20	E3
Pasco U.S.A	62	C2
Pas de Calais see Straits of Dover	22	B1
Pasfield Lake Can	61	D1
Pasir Mas Malaysia	38	C5
Pasni Pakistan	32	c iv
Paso de los Libres Argentina	66	C2
Paso de los Toros Uruguay	66	C3
Paso de Patria Par	66	C2
Pasqua Canada	61	E2
Pasquia Hills Canada	61	E1
Passage de la Déroute Channel Is./France	14	a ii
Passage West town. Irish Republic	13	C5
Passau Ger. F R	25	C2
Passchendaele Belg	22	B1
Passero, Cape Sicily	21	C5
Passo Fundo Brazil	66	D2
Passos Brazil	66	D2
Passumpsic r. U.S.A	57	N5
Pasto Colombia	64	C3
Patagonia geog reg. Argentina	65	D13
Patapsco Reservoir U.S.A	54	D5
Patay France	22	B2
Patchewollock Australia	43	B5
Patchogue U.S.A	55	G4
Patchway England	14	D3
Pategi Nigeria	67	B2
Paterson U.S.A	55	F4
Pathankot India	32	C7
Pathfinder Reservoir U.S.A	62	E3
Patiala India	32	C7
Pátmos r. Greece	21	E5
Patna India	32	E4
Patos, Lagoa dos Brazil	66	D3
Patos Brazil	64	K5
Patras Greece	21	D5
Patrai r. Greece	21	D5
Pattani Thailand	38	C5
Pattaya Thailand	38	C3
Patton U.S.A	54	C4
Patung China	37	A3
Pau France	23	A3
Pauillac France	23	A3
Paulista Brazil	66	a i
Paulistana Brazil	64	K5

Name	Page
Paulo Afonso Falls Brazil	64
Paulsboro U.S.A	54
Pavia Italy	25
Pavlodar U.S.S.R	29
Pawling U.S.A	55
Pawtucket U.S.A	55
Payette r. U.S.A	62
Paysandú Uruguay	66
Pays d'Albret geog reg. France	23
Pays de Caux geog reg. France	22
Peace r. Canada	60
Peacehaven England	15
Peace River town. Canada	60
Peak District Nat. Park England	15
Peake Deep N. Atl O	2
Peale, Mt. U.S.A	63
Pearl r. U.S.A	51
Pearl River town. U.S.A	55
Pearsall U.S.A	50
Peary Channel Canada	47
Pease r. U.S.A	50
Peć Yugoslavia	21
Pechenga U.S.S.R	16
Pechora r. U.S.S.R	29
Peckville U.S.A	54
Pecos r. U.S.A	50
Pécs Hungary	20
Pedras Altas Brazil	66
Pedro Miguel Locks Panama	49
Pedro, Point Sri Lanka	32
Pedro H. Fernández Argentina	66
Peebinga Australia	43
Peebles Scotland	11
Pee Dee r. U.S.A	51
Peekskill U.S.A	55
Peel Co. Canada	56
Peel I. of Man	12
Peel Fell mtn. Scot	11
Peerless Lake Can	60
Pegasus Bay N.Z	41
Pegu (r Divis. Burma	38
Peh r. China	37
Pehchen China	36
Pehpei China	36
Pei-an China	37
Peichiang Taiwan	37
Peihai China	37
Peiliu China	37
Peipus, Lake U.S.S.R	17
Peixe, Lagoa do Brazil	66
Peixe Rio do r. Brazil	66
Pexing (Beijing) China	36
Peking Shih (Beijing Shi) Municipality. China	36
Pelee, pt. & passage. Canada	56
Pelee Island i. & sett. Canada	56
Pelican Bay Canada	61
Pelican Lake Canada	61
Pelican Mts. Canada	60
Pelican Narrows Can	61
Pelican Point Namibia	72
Peljekaise Nat. Park Sweden	16
Peloponnese penin. Greece	21
Pelotas Brazil	66
Pelotas r. Brazil	66
Pelusium, Bay of Egypt	69
Pelvoux, Mont France	23
Pematang Siantar Indonesia	35
Pemba Mozambique	71
Pemba r. Zambia	71
Pemba i. Tanzania	71
Pemberton Austl	42
Pembina r. Alberta Canada	60
Pembina U.S.A	58
Pembina r. Canada/ U.S.A	58
Pembroke Canada	56
Pembroke Wales	14
Pembroke Dock Wales	14
Pembrokeshire Coast Nat Park Wales	14
Pemigwasset r. U.S.A	57
Peña Colorado mtn. U.S.A	55
Penacook U.S.A	55
Peñarroya Spain	19
Penarth Wales	14
Penasco r. U.S.A	53
Pencarrow Mynydd mtn. Wales	14
Pendembu Sierra Leone	68
Pendleton U.S.A	62
Pend Oreille Lake U.S.A	62
Penetanguishene Can	56
Penfield U.S.A	54
Penganga r. India	32
Pengaluru China	36
P'enghu China	37
P'engshui China	37
Pengtse China	37
Penhold Canada	62
Penicuik Scotland	11
Penicuik r. U.S.A	54
Penmaenmawr Wales	14
Penmarch, Pte. de France	22
Pennan r. India	32
Pennine Alps mtns. Switzerland	25
Pennines, The mtns. England	12
Pennington U.S.A	54
Pennsburg U.S.A	54
Pennsville U.S.A	54
Pennsylvania State. U.S.A	59
Pennsylvania Turnpike U.S.A	54
Pennsylvania Turnpike N.E. Extension hwy. U.S.A	54
Penn Yan U.S.A	54
Penobscot r. U.S.A	57
Penobscot Bay U.S.A	59
Penrith Australia	43

	Page	ref.
ith: England	12	D2
yn: England	14	A4
acola: U.S.A.	51	E3
acola Dam: U.S.A.	58	B4
icton: Canada	62	C2
ire Pt.: England	14	B4
land Firth: str., cotland	9	C1
land Hills: Scot.	11	E4
y-Ghent: mtn., igland	12	D2
a: U.S.S.R.	28	F3
ance: England	14	A4
ance: r., Canada	61	D2
ia: U.S.A.	58	C3
cton Reservoir: S.A.	54	F2
y Is.: Australia	42	D2
ue: Canada	60	D2
njon: Australia	42	b i
amino: Argentina	66	B3
onca: r., Can.	59	F2
jeux: France	23	B2
jord: dist., Fr.	23	B2
asie: U.S.A.	54	E4
: U.S.S.R.	28	H2
ik: Bulgaria	21	D4
nne: France	22	B2
ignan: France	23	B3
ault, Lake: Can.	61	G2
y: r., England	14	D2
hore: England	14	D2
ian Gulf see ulf, The	30	F5
: Australia	42	b ii
: Canada	57	J5
: Scotland	10	E3
: Co., Canada	56	D6
Amboy: U.S.A.	55	F4
U:	64	–
Basin: Pacific O.	45	Q8
-Chile Trench: acific Ocean	45	S9
gia: Italy	21	B4
gorria: Argentina	66	C2
iro: Italy	25	C3
cadores: is., iwan	37	C5
ara: Italy	21	B4
hiera: Italy	25	C2
awar: Pakistan	32	B2
ac: France	23	A3
luma: U.S.A.	63	B4
nge: Luxembourg	22	C2
wawa: Canada	56	H4
rborough: Austl.	43	A4
rborough: & Co., anada	56	G5
rborough: Eng.	15	F2
rborough: U.S.A.	55	J2
rhead: Scotland	10	G2
r I.: Southern O.	65	A17
rlee: England	12	E2
r Pond Lake: anada	60	D1
rsburg: Mich., S.A.	56	B8
rsburg: Va., S.A.	59	E4
rsfield: England	15	F3
ne: N.Z.	41	B3
skey: U.S.A.	58	D2
fied Forest Nat. rk: U.S.A.	63	E4
la: Romania	21	D3
olia: Canada	56	C7
opavlovsk: S.S.R.	29	K3
opavlovsk-amchatskiy: S.S.R.	27	S7
ópolis: Brazil	66	b i
oseni: Romania	21	D3
ozavodsk: U.S.S.R.	28	C1
khovo: U.S.S.R.	29	K2
eulak: Indonesia	38	B6
ensey: England	15	G4
sey, Vale of: Eng.	15	E3
ano: Argentina	66	B3
er Bergland: plat., erman F.R.	24	B2
er Wald: mtns., erman F.R.	24	B2
zheim: Ger. F.R.	24	B2
ngna: Thailand	38	B5
om Dongrak tns., Thailand	38	C4
Rang: Vietnam	38	D4
n Thiet: Vietnam	38	D4
thalung: Thailand	38	C5
ps: U.S.A.	54	C2
nix City: U.S.A.	51	E3
Buri: Thailand	38	C4
adelphia: N.Y., S.A.	57	K5
adelphia: Pa., S.A.	54	E5
IPPINES, THE	35	–
ppine Sea: Pac. O.	44	C5
ppine Trench: acific Ocean	44	B6
psburg: Mont., S.A.	62	D2
psburg: Pa., S.A.	54	B4
ip I.: Australia	43	C5
psburg: Kans., S.A.	50	C2
psburg: Pa., S.A.	54	E4
mont: U.S.A.	55	G2
OM PENH: ampuchea	38	D4
enix: Ariz., U.S.A.	63	D5
enix: N.Y., U.S.A.	54	D1
onix I.: Pac. O.	44	H7
enix Is.: Pac. O.	44	H7
enixville: U.S.A.	54	E4
ng Saly: Laos	38	C2
Cuong: Vietnam	38	D4
ket: Thailand	38	B5
m Troun: Kam.	38	D4
cenza: Italy	25	B2
ra-Neamt: Rom.	20	E3
ve: r., Italy	25	C2
ardy: Old Prov., Fr.	22	B2
nanal: Argentina	66	B1
kering: England	12	F2
kering, Vale of: ngland	12	F2
on: Canada	56	H5
on: N.Z.	41	B3
ure Butte: sett., anada	60	C3
dmont: reg., Italy	25	B3
dra Sola: Uruguay	66	C3
dras Negras: exico	50	B4
ksämäki: Finland	16	E3
inen: l., Finland	16	E3
re: U.S.A.	53	E2
reville: Canada	57	N3
arsaari: Finland	16	D3
ermaritzburg: outh Africa	72	E4

	Page	ref.
Pietersburg: S. Africa	72	D3
Piet Retief: S. Africa	72	E4
Pigeon: U.S.A.	56	B6
Pigeon: r., Canada/U.S.A.	58	B2
Pigeon Bay: Man., Canada	61	F2
Pigeon Bay: Ont., Canada	56	C8
Pigeon Lake: Canada	60	C2
Piggott: U.S.A.	50	D2
Pihlaja Lake: Finland	16	E3
Pihtipudas: Finland	16	E3
Pihu: China	37	C4
Pikangikum, Lake: Can.	61	G2
Pikeville: U.S.A.	59	D4
Pikwitonei: Canada	61	F1
Pila: Italy	25	B2
Pila: Poland	20	C2
Pilaga: r., Argentina	66	C2
Pilar: Paraguay	66	C2
Pilcomayo, Parque Nacional: Argentina	66	C2
Pilot Mound: Canada	61	F3
Pima: U.S.A.	63	E5
Pinar del Rio: Cuba	49	K5
Pinawa: Canada	61	F2
Pincher Creek: town, Canada	62	D2
Pinconning: U.S.A.	56	B6
Pindamonhangaba: Brazil	66	a i
Pindus Mts.: Greece	21	D5
Pine: cr., U.S.A.	54	C3
Pine Bluff: sett., U.S.A.	50	D3
Pine Camp: U.S.A.	57	K5
Pine Creek: U.S.A.	56	H8
Pine Falls: sett., Canada	61	F2
Pine Grove: U.S.A.	54	D4
Pine Islands: U.S.A.	51	F5
Pine Island Sound: U.S.A.	51	F4
Pine Plains: sett., U.S.A.	55	G3
Pine Point: sett., Canada	46	N4
Pinerolo: Italy	25	B3
Pine Valley: town, Canada	60	A1
Ping: r., Thailand	38	B3
Pingchang: China	37	A3
Pingchuan: China	36	C1
Pingelly: Australia	42	b ii
Pinghu: China	37	D3
Pingi: China	36	C2
Pingkiang: China	37	B4
Pingku: China	36	C1
Pingkuo: China	37	A5
Pingli: China	36	A3
Pingliang: China	36	A2
Pinglo: Kwangsi Chuang: China	37	B5
Pinglo: Ninghsia Hui, China	36	A2
Pingnam: China	37	B5
Pingnan: China	37	C4
Pingsiang: China	37	B4
Pingtan: China	37	C4
Pingtang: China	37	A4
Pingtingshan: China	36	B3
Pingtu: China	36	C2
Pingtung: Taiwan	37	D5
Pingyang: China	37	D4
Pingyao: China	36	B2
Pingyin: China	36	C2
Pingyuan: China	36	C2
Pinhai (Tungkan): China	36	C3
Pinhal: Brazil	66	a i
Pinhsien: Shantung, China	36	C2
Pinhsien: Shensi, China	36	A2
Pinjarra: Australia	42	b ii
Pinkiang see Harbin	34	H1
Pinnaroo: Australia	43	B5
Pins, Pointe aux: Canada	56	D7
Pinsk: U.S.S.R.	20	E2
Pinto: Argentina	66	B2
Pinto: U.S.A.	54	B5
Pinto Butte: mtn., Canada	60	D3
Pinyang: China	37	A5
Pioche: U.S.A.	63	D4
Piombino: Italy	21	B4
Pipmuacan Lake: Canada	59	F2
Piquiri: r., Brazil	66	D1
Piracicaba: & r., Brazil	66	a i
Piraí do Sul: Brazil	66	E1
Piraieus: Greece	21	D5
Piraju: Brazil	66	E1
Pirané: Argentina	66	C2
Pirapó: r., Paraguay	66	C2
Pirapó: r., Paraguay	66	C2
Pirarajá: Uruguay	66	D3
Piratini: r., Brazil	66	C2
Piratini: r., Brazil	66	D3
Pirgos: Greece	21	D5
Pirmasens: Ger. F.R.	24	B2
Pirna: Ger. D.R.	24	C1
Pisa: Italy	25	C3
Piscatosine, Lac: Canada	57	K3
Pisek: Czech.	24	C2
Pistoia: Italy	25	C3
Pit: r., U.S.A.	63	B3
Pitcairn Island: Pac. O.	45	M9
Pite: r., Sweden	16	D2
Piteå: Sweden	16	D2
Pitești: Romania	21	D4
Pitlochry: Scotland	10	E3
Pitman: U.S.A.	54	E5
Pittsburg: Kans., U.S.A.	58	B4
Pittsburg: Tex., U.S.A.	50	D3
Pittsburgh: U.S.A.	59	E3
Pittsfield: Mass., U.S.A.	55	G2
Pittsfield: N.H., U.S.A.	55	J1
Pittsford: U.S.A.	54	C1
Pittston: U.S.A.	54	E3
Piyang: China	36	B3
Placentia Bay: Can.	47	Z7
Plácido Rosas: Uru.	66	D3
Plainfield: Conn., U.S.A.	55	J3
Plainfield: N.J., U.S.A.	54	F4
Plainview: U.S.A.	50	B3
Plainville: U.S.A.	55	H3
Plantaurel, Montagnes du: France	23	B3
Plata, Río de la: est., Arg./Uruguay	66	C4
Plateau: State, Nigeria	67	B2
Plateau des Minquiers: is. Channel Islands	22	a i
Platte: r., U.S.A.	53	E2
Plattling: Ger. F.R.	25	C2
Plattsburg: U.S.A.	57	M5
Plattsmouth: U.S.A.	58	A3
Plauen: Ger. D.R.	24	C1

	Page	ref.
Playgreen, Lake: Can.	61	F2
Pleasant Gap: U.S.A.	54	C4
Pleasanton: U.S.A.	50	C4
Pleasantville: N.J., U.S.A.	54	F5
Pleasantville: N.Y., U.S.A.	55	G3
Plenty, Bay of: N.Z.	41	C2
Plentywood: U.S.A.	53	E1
Plessisville: Canada	57	O3
Pleven: Bulgaria	21	D4
Płock: Poland	20	C2
Ploești: Romania	21	E4
Plomb du Cantal: mtn., France	23	B2
Plombières: France	22	C2
Plön: German F.R.	24	C1
Plonge, Lac la: Can.	60	D1
Plougasnou: France	22	a i
Plovdiv: Bulgaria		
Plum Coulee: Canada	61	F3
Plumtree: Zimbabwe	72	D3
Plunge: U.S.S.R.	17	D4
Plym: r., England	14	B4
Plymouth: England	14	B4
Plymouth: Mass., U.S.A.	55	K3
Plymouth: Mich., U.S.A.	56	B7
Plymouth: N.H., U.S.A.	57	O6
Plympton: England	14	B4
Plynlimon: mtn., Wales	14	C2
Plyussa: r., U.S.S.R.	17	E4
Piura: Peru	64	B5
Plzen: Czech.	20	B3
Po: r., Italy	25	C2
Poai: China	36	B2
Poblado Celeste: Uru.	66	C3
Pocatello: U.S.A.	62	D3
Pocklington: England	12	F3
Poções: Brazil	64	K6
Pocomoke City: U.S.A.	59	E4
P'ohang: S. Korea	39	A2
Pohsien: China	36	C3
Poiana Brașov: Rom.	20	E3
Pointe Noire: town, Congo	71	B8
Point Pleasant: U.S.A.	55	F4
Point Reyes Nat. Seashore: U.S.A.	63	B4
Poisson Blanc, Lac: Canada	57	K4
Poissy: France	22	B2
Poitiers: France	23	B2
Poitou: Old Prov., Fr.	23	A2
Poix: France	22	B2
Pokaran: India	32	B3
Pokhara: Nepal	32	D3
Pola see Pula	21	B4
POLAND	20	C2
Polegate: England	15	G4
Poli: Cameroun	67	C2
Pollensa: Mallorca	19	C5
Polotsk: U.S.S.R.	20	E1
Poltava: U.S.S.R.	28	C4
Polunochnoye: U.S.S.R.	29	J1
Polyarnyy: U.S.S.R.	16	F2
Pomeroy: U.S.A.	59	D4
Pomona: Namibia	72	B4
Ponape: i., Caroline Islands	44	E6
Ponca City: U.S.A.	50	C2
Ponce: Puerto Rico	49	N6
Pondicherry: India	32	C6
Pond Inlet: sett., Canada	47	U2
Ponferrada: Spain	19	A4
Ponoka: Canada	62	D1
Ponta Grossa: Brazil	66	D2
Pont-à-Mousson: Fr.	22	C2
Ponta Porã: Brazil	64	G8
Pontardulais: Wales	14	B3
Pontarlier: France	23	C2
Pontchartrain, Lake: U.S.A.	50	D3
Ponte Alta do Norte: Brazil	66	D2
Pontefract: England	12	E3
Ponteix: Canada	60	D3
Ponteland: England	12	E1
Pontevedra: Spain	19	A4
Pontiac: U.S.A.	58	D3
Pontiac: Co., Can.	56/7	J3
Pontianak: Indonesia	38	D7
Pontic Mts.: Turkey	28	C5
Pontivy: France	22	a i
Pontoise: France	22	B2
Pontremoli: Italy	25	B3
Pontresina: Switz.	25	B2
Pont Rouge: sett., Canada	57	O3
Pontypool: Wales	14	C3
Ponza: i., Italy	21	B4
Poolewe: Scotland	10	C2
Pool Malebo: Zaire	71	C8
Poona see Pune	32	B5
Poopo, Lake: Bolivia	64	E7
Popai: China	37	A5
Poplar: r., Canada	61	F2
Pontypridd: Wales	14	C3
Poole: England	15	E4
Poole Bay: England	15	E4
Poperinghe: Belg.	22	B1
Poplar Bluff: U.S.A.	58	B4
Poplar Hill: sett., Canada	61	G2
Popocatepetl: volc., Mexico	48	G6
Porbandar: India	32	A4
Porcupine: Canada	56	D1
Porcupine Hills: Can.	61	E2
Porcupine Plain: sett., Canada	61	E2
Pordenone: Italy	25	C2
Poreč: Yugoslavia	25	C2
Pori: Finland	16	D3
Pornic: France	22	a i
Poros: Greece	21	D5
Porsangen: fd., Nor.	16	E1
Porsgrunn: Norway	17	A4
Port Adelaide: Austl.	43	A4
Portadown: N. Ireland	13	E2
Portaferry: N. Ireland	13	F2
Portage: U.S.A.	54	B4
Portage: r., U.S.A.	56	B8
Portage Bay: Canada	61	F2
Portage la Prairie: town, Canada	61	F3
Portal: U.S.A.	61	E3
Port Alberni: Canada	62	B2
Port Albert: Austl.	43	C5
Portalegre: Portugal	19	A5
Port Alfred: Canada	57	P1
Port Alfred: S. Africa	72	D5
Port Alice: Canada	62	A1
Port Allegany: U.S.A.	54	B3
Port Angeles: U.S.A.	62	B2
Portarlington: Irish Republic	13	D3
Port Arthur: U.S.A.	50	D4
Port Arthur see Thunder Bay	58	C2
Port Askaig: Scotland	11	B4
Port Augusta: Austl.	43	A4

	Page	ref.
PORT-AU-PRINCE: Haiti	49	M6
Port Austin: U.S.A.	56	B5
Port Barcarès: Fr.	23	B3
Port Blair: Andaman Is.	38	A4
Port Bou: Spain	19	C4
Port Burwell: Canada	56	E7
Port Byron: U.S.A.	54	D1
Port Cartier: Canada	59	G1
Port Cartier Sept Îles Park: Canada	59	G1
Port Chalmers: N.Z.	41	B4
Port Clinton: U.S.A.	56	C8
Port Colborne: Can.	56	F7
Port Credit: Canada	56	F6
Port de Bouc: France	23	B3
Port Deposit: U.S.A.	54	D5
Port Dickson: Mal.	38	C6
Port Dover: Canada	56	E7
Port Edward: Canada	56	C6
Port Elgin: Canada	56	D5
Port Elizabeth: S. Afr.	72	D5
Port Ellen: Scot.	11	B4
Porteño: r., Arg.	66	C1
Porter: U.S.A.	57	P6
Port Erin: I. of Man	12	B2
Porter Lake: Can.	60	D1
Port Fuad: Egypt	69	Ins.
Port Gentil: Gabon	71	A8
Port Glasgow: Scot.	11	D4
Portglenone: N. Irel.	13	E2
Port Harcourt: Nig.	67	B3
Port Hardy: Canada	62	A1
Port Hawkesbury: Canada	47	X7
Porthcawl: Wales	14	C3
Port Hedland: Austl.	40	B5
Port Henry: U.S.A.	57	M5
Porthmadog: Wales	14	B2
Port Hope: Canada	56	G6
Port Huron: U.S.A.	58	D3
Portimão: Portugal	19	A5
Port Isaac: England	14	B4
Portishead: England	14	D3
Port Jefferson: U.S.A.	55	G4
Port Jervis: U.S.A.	54	F3
Portland: Australia	43	B5
Portland: Conn., U.S.A.	55	H3
Portland: Maine, U.S.A.	57	P6
Portland: Oreg., U.S.A.	62	B2
Portland, Isle of: England	14	D4
Portlaoise: Irish Rep.	13	D3
Port Lincoln: Austl.	40	F7
Port Loring: Canada	56	F4
Port Macquarie: Australia	43	D4
Port Moller: U.S.A.	46	C5
Port Monmouth: U.S.A.	55	F4
PORT MORESBY: Papua-New Guinea	40	H2
Portnahaven: Scotland	11	B4
Port Nelson: Canada	61	G1
Portneuf: Canada	57	O3
Portneuf: Co., Can.	57	N3
Port Nolloth: South Africa	72	B4
Port Norris: U.S.A.	54	E5
Pôrto Alegre: Brazil	66	D3
Pôrto Alexandre: Angola	72	A2
Pôrto Belo, Ponta do: pt., Brazil	66	E2
Portobello: Panama	49	L8
Pôrto Camargo: Braz.	66	D1
Pôrto Feliz: Brazil	66	a i
Portofino: Italy	25	B3
Port of Ness: Scot.	10	B1
PORT OF SPAIN: Trinidad & Tobago	49	O7
Portogruaro: Italy	25	C2
PORTO NOVO: Benin	68	F7
Pôrto Torres: Sardinia	19	a i
Pôrto União: Brazil	66	D2
Porto Vecchio: Corsica	19	a i
Pôrto Velho: Brazil	64	F5
Port Perry: Canada	56	G5
Port Phillip Bay: Australia	43	B5
Port Pirie: Australia	43	A4
Portree: Scotland	10	B2
Port Rowan: Canada	56	E7
Portrush: N. Irel.	13	E1
Port Safaga: Egypt	69	M3
Port Said: Egypt	69	M2
Port St. Joe: U.S.A.	51	E4
Port Shepstone: S. Afr.	72	E5
Portsmouth: England	15	E4
Portsmouth: N.H., U.S.A.	55	K1
Portsmouth: Ohio, U.S.A.	58	D4
Portsmouth: Va., U.S.A.	59	E4
Portsoy: Scotland	10	F2
Port Stanley: Canada	56	D7
Portstewart: N. Irel.	13	E1
Port Sudan: Sudan	69	N5
Port Sulphur: U.S.A.	51	E4
Port Talbot: Wales	14	C3
Port Taufiq: Egypt	69	Ins.
Porttipahta: l., Fin.	16	E2
Port Townsend: U.S.A.	62	B2
PORTUGAL	19	A5
Portumna: Irish Rep.	13	C3
Port Vendres: France	23	B3
Portville: U.S.A.	54	B2
Port Weld: Malaysia	38	C6
Port Weller: Canada	56	F6
Porvoo: Finland	17	E3
Posadas: Argentina	66	C2
Poshan: China	36	C2
Postmasburg: S. Africa	72	C4
Potchefstroom: S. Afr.	72	D4
Poteet: U.S.A.	50	C4
Potenza: Italy	21	C4
Potgietersrus: S. Afr.	72	D3
Poti: U.S.S.R.	28	E5
Potiskum: Nigeria	67	C1
Potosí: Bolivia	64	E7
Potow: China	36	C2
Potrerillos: Chile	64	E9
Potsdam: Ger. D.R.	24	C1
Potsdam: U.S.A.	57	L5
Potters Bar: England	15	F3
Potton: England	15	F2
Pottstown: U.S.A.	54	E4
Pottsville: U.S.A.	54	D4
Pouce Coupé: Can.	60	A1
Poughkeepsie: U.S.A.	55	G3
Poultney: U.S.A.	57	M6
Pouso Alegre: Brazil	66	a i
Poussé: Cameroun	67	C1
Poverty Bay: N.Z.	41	C2
Powassan: Canada	56	F3
Powder: r., U.S.A.	53	D1
Powderview: Can.	61	F2
Powell: U.S.A.	62	E3
Powell, Lake: U.S.A.	63	D4
Powell River: town, Canada	62	B2
Powys: Co., Wales	14	C2

	Page	ref.
Poyang: China	37	C4
Poyang, Lake: China	37	C4
Poznań: Poland	20	C2
Pozo Hondo: Arg.	66	B2
Prachuap Khiri Khan: Thailand	38	B4
Prades: France	23	B3
PRAGUE: Czech.	20	B3
Praia da Rocha: Port.	19	A5
Prato: Italy	25	C3
Prawle Pt.: England	14	C4
Preeceville: Canada	61	E2
Preesall: England	12	D3
Preissac, Lake: Can.	56	G1
Prelate: Canada	60	D2
Přerov: Czech.	20	C3
Prescott: Canada	57	K5
Prescott: Co., Can.	57	L4
Prescott: U.S.A.	63	D5
Preseli, Mynydd: hills., Wales	14	B3
Presidencia de la Plaza: Argentina	66	C2
Presidencia Roque Sáenz Peña: Arg.	66	B2
Prešov: Czech.	20	D3
Prespa, Lake: Europe	21	D4
Presque Isle: town, U.S.A.	59	G2
Press: Canada	57	J1
Prestatyn: Wales	14	C1
Presteigne: Wales	14	C2
Preston: England	12	D3
Preston: Idaho, U.S.A.	62	D3
Prestonpans: Scot.	11	F4
Prestwick: Scotland	11	D4
Prêto: r., Brazil	66	b i
PRETORIA: S. Africa	72	D4
Prettyboy Reservoir: U.S.A.	54	D5
Préveza: Greece	21	D5
Příbram: Czech.	20	B3
Price: Utah, U.S.A.	63	D4
Prichard: U.S.A.	51	E3
Prieska: S. Afr.	72	C4
Priest Lake: U.S.A.	60	B2
Prilep: Yugoslavia	21	D4
Primero: r., Arg.	66	B3
Primrose Lake: Can.	60	D2
Prince Albert: Can.	61	D2
Prince Albert Nat. Park: Canada	60	D2
Prince Edward: Co., Canada	56	H5
Prince Edward Bay: Canada	57	J6
Prince Edward I.: Prov., Canada	47	X7
Prince Edward Islands: Ind. O.	33	b ix
Prince George: Can.	46	L6
Prince of Wales I.: Canada	47	Q2
Prince of Wales I.: U.S.A.	46	J5
Prince Patrick I.: Canada	46	L1
Prince Rupert: Can.	46	J6
Princes Risborough: England	15	F3
Princeton: Canada	62	B2
Princeton: U.S.A.	54	F4
Princeville: Canada	57	O3
Principe: i., Gulf of Guinea	70	A7
Prineville: U.S.A.	62	B3
Pripet: r., U.S.S.R.	20	E2
Pripet Marshes: U.S.S.R.	28	B3
Priština: Yugoslavia	21	D4
Privas: France	23	B3
Prizren: Yugoslavia	21	D4
Procter: Canada	62	C2
Progreso: Mexico	48	J5
Prokop'yevsk: U.S.S.R.	29	O3
Prome: Burma	38	B3
Propriano: Corsica	19	a i
Proserpine: Australia	42	C2
Prosser: U.S.A.	62	C2
Provence: Old Prov., France	23	C3
Provence Alps: mtns., France	23	C3
Providence: U.S.A.	55	J3
Providence, Cape: New Zealand	41	A4
Provincetown: U.S.A.	55	K2
Provo: U.S.A.	63	D3
Provost: Canada	62	D1
Prudhoe: England	12	E2
Prudhoe Bay: sett., U.S.A.	46	F2
Pruszków: Poland	20	D2
Prut: r., Romania/U.S.S.R.	20	E3
Przemyśl: Poland	20	D3
Pskov: & l., U.S.S.R.	17	E4
Pucheng: Fukien, China	37	C4
Pucheng: Shensi, China	36	A3
Puchi: China	37	B4
Pudasjärvi: Finland	16	E2
Pudsey: England	12	E3
Puebla: Mexico	48	G6
Pueblo: U.S.A.	53	E3
Puerco: r., U.S.A.	63	E4
Puerh: China	38	C2
Puerto Adela: Par.	66	D1
Puerto Aisén: Chile	65	D13
Puerto Ayacucho: Venezuela	64	E2
Puerto Barrios: Guat.	48	J6
Puerto Cabello: Ven.	49	N7
Puerto Constanza: Argentina	66	C3
Puerto Cooper: Par.	66	C1
Puerto Deseado: Arg.	65	E13
Puerto Ibicuy: Arg.	66	C3
Puerto Limón: Costa Rica	49	K8
Puertollano: Spain	19	B5
Puerto Montt: Chile	65	D12
Puerto Naranjito: Arg.	66	C2
Puerto Piracuacito: Argentina	66	C2
PUERTO RICO	49	N6
Puerto Rico Trench: N. Atlantic Ocean	8	D5
Puerto Tirol: Arg.	66	C2
Puerto Velaz: Arg.	66	C2
Puerto Victoria: Arg.	66	D2
Puerto Ybapobó: Paraguay	66	C1
Puffin I.: Irish Rep.	13	A5
Puhsien: China	36	D2
Pukaskwa Nat. Park: Canada	58	C2
Pukatawagan: Canada	61	E1
Pukeashun, Mt.: Can.	60	B2
Pukekohe: N.Z.	41	B2
Pukow: China	36	C3
Pula (Pola): Yugo.	21	B4
Pulantien: China	36	D2

	Page	ref.
Pulaski: U.S.A.	59	D4
Pulborough: England	15	F4
Puli: Taiwan	37	D5
Pullman: U.S.A.	62	C2
Punakha: Bhutan	33	E3
Pune (Poona): India	32	B5
Punjab: State, India	32	C2
Punkaharju: Finland	16	E3
Puno: Peru	64	D7
Punta Arenas (Magallanes): Chile	65	D14
Punta del Este: Uruguay	66	D3
Punta Gallinas: pt., Colombia	49	M7
Punta Piedras: pt., Argentina	66	C4
Puntarenas: Costa Rica	49	K8
Punxsutawney: U.S.A.	54	B4
Pur: r., U.S.S.R.	27	K4
Purbeck, Isle of: geog. reg., Eng.	14	D4
Purcellville: U.S.A.	54	C5
Puri: India	32	E5
Purnea: India	32	E3
Pursat: Kampuchea	38	C4
Purús: r., Brazil	64	F5
Pusan: S. Korea	34	H3
Pushkin: U.S.S.R.	17	F4
Putien: China	37	C4
Putoran Mts.: U.S.S.R.	27	M4
Puttalam: Sri Lanka	32	a ii
Putumayo: r., South America	64	D4
Puula Lake: Finland	16	E3
Puyang: China	36	B2
Puy de Sancy: mtn., France	23	B2
Pwllheli: Wales	14	B2
Pyärnu: r., U.S.S.R.	17	E4
Pyatigorsk: U.S.S.R.	28	E5
Pyavozero, Lake: U.S.S.R.	16	F2
Pyhä Lake: town, Finland	16	E3
Pyhä Lake: Finland	17	D3
Pyhäselkä: l., Finland	16	E3
Pyinmana: Burma	38	B3
Pymatuning Reservoir: U.S.A.	56	E8
PYONGYANG: N. Korea	34	H3
Pyramid: hist., Egypt	69	M3
Pyramid Lake: U.S.A.	63	C4
Pyrenees: mtns., France/Spain	23	B3
Pyrenees Occidentales: reg., France	23	B3
Qasr Farafra: Egypt	69	L3
QATAR	30	F5
Qattara Depression: Egypt	69	L3
Qila Saifullah: Pak.	32	A2
Qazvin: Iran	28	G6
Qingdao see Tsingtao	36	D2
Qinlingshan: mtns., see Tsinling Shan	36	A3
Qomul see Hami	34	A2
Quabbin Reservoir: U.S.A.	55	H2
Quadros, Lagoa dos: Brazil	66	E2
Quakertown: U.S.A.	54	E4
Quan Long: Vietnam	38	D5
Quang Ngai: Vietnam	38	D3
Quang Tri: Vietnam	38	D3
Quang Yen: Vietnam	38	D2
Quantocks: hills, England	14	C3
Qu'Appelle: r., Can.	61	E2
Qu'Appelle Arm Dam: Canada	60	D2
Quaraí: & r., Brazil	66	C3
Quarryville: U.S.A.	54	D5
Quarzazate: Morocco	68	D2
Queanbeyan: Austl.	43	C5
Québec: Canada	57	O3
Québec: Co., Can.	57	N2
Québec: Prov., Can.	47	W6
Quedlinburg: Ger. D.R.	24	C1
Queen Adelaide Arch.: Chile	65	D14
Queen Charlotte Is.: Canada	46	J6
Queen Charlotte Sound: Canada	46	K6
Queen Charlotte Strait: Canada	62	A1
Queen Elizabeth Forest Park: Scot.	11	D3
Queen Elizabeth Is.: Canada	46	O1
Queensferry: Scot.	11	E4
Queensland: State, Australia	40	G5
Queenstown: N.Z.	41	A3
Queenstown: U.S.A.	54	D5
Queguay Chico: r., Uruguay	66	C3
Queguay Grande: r., Uruguay	66	C3
Quelimane: Moz.	72	F2
Quelpart I. see Cheju I.	34	H4
Quemoy: China	37	C5
Que Que: Zimbabwe	72	D2
Quesnel: Canada	46	L6
Quesnel Lake: Can.	62	B1
Quetico Provincial Park: Canada	58	B2
Quetta: Pakistan	32	A2
Quezon City: Phil.	35	G8
Quiberon: France	22	a i
Quiberon, Baie d': France	22	a i
Quiindy: Paraguay	66	C2
Quill Lake: town, Canada	61	E2
Quill Lakes: Canada	61	E2
Quilmes: Argentina	66	C3
Quilpie: Australia	42	B3
Quimili: Argentina	66	B2
Quimper: France	22	a i
Quimperlé: France	22	a i
Quinag: mtn., Scot.	10	C1
Quincy: Ill., U.S.A.	58	B4
Quincy: Mass., U.S.A.	55	J2
Quinebaug: r., U.S.A.	55	J3
Quines: Argentina	66	A3
Qui Nhon: Vietnam	38	D4
Quinta: Brazil	66	D3
Quinze, Lac des: Canada	56	F2
Quirke Lake: Can.	56	C3
QUITO: Ecuador	64	C4
Quibala: Angola	71	B9
Qum: Iran	30	F4
Qunfidha: Sau. Arab.	30	D7
Quoich, Loch: Scot.	10	C2
Quorn: Australia	43	A4
Quorn: Canada	58	B2
Quyou: Canada	57	J4

90 Raahe/Ste. Anne de Beaupré

Place	Page	ref.
Raahe: Finland	16	D3
Raasay: *i.* & Sound Scotland	10	B2
RABAT: Morocco	68	D2
Rabaul: Papua-New Guinea	40	J1
Raccoon: *r.*, U.S.A.	58	B3
Race, Cape: Canada	47	Z7
Rach Gia: Vietnam	38	D5
Racibórz: Poland	20	C2
Racine: U.S.A.	58	C3
Radenthein: Australia	25	C2
Radisson: Canada	62	E1
Radium Hill: Austl.	43	B4
Radnor Forest: Wales	14	C2
Radom: Poland	20	D2
Radomsko: Poland	20	C2
Radstadt: Austria	20	B3
Radstock: England	14	D3
Radville: Canada	61	E3
Rae: Canada	46	M4
Raeside, Lake: Austl.	42	c i
Rafaela: Argentina	66	B3
Ragusa: Sicily	21	B5
Rahama: Nigeria	67	B1
Raichur: India	32	C5
Rainbow Lake: *town*, Canada	60	B1
Rainier, Mount: U.S.A.	62	B2
Rainy: *r.*, Canada/U.S.A.	58	B2
Rainy Lake: Canada/U.S.A.	58	B2
Rainy River: Canada	61	G3
Raipur: India	32	D4
Raisen: *r.*, U.S.A.	56	B8
Raisio: Finland	17	D3
Rajahmundry: India	32	D5
Rajasthan: *State*, India	32	B3
Rajkot: India	32	B4
Rajshahi: Bangladesh	32	E4
Rakaia: *r.*, N.Z.	41	B3
Rakvere: U.S.S.R.	17	E4
Raleigh: U.S.A.	51	G2
Raleigh Bay: U.S.A.	51	G3
Ralston: Canada	60	C2
Ramādi: Iraq	30	D4
Rambouillet: France	22	B2
Rame Head: *c.*, Eng.	14	B4
Ramillies: *hist.*, Belgium	22	B1
Ramor, Lough: Irish Republic	13	D3
Ramore: Canada	56	E1
Rampur: India	32	C3
Ramree: *i.*, Burma	38	A3
Ramsey: England	15	F2
Ramsey: I. of Man	12	B2
Ramsey: U.S.A.	55	F3
Ramsey I.: Wales	14	A3
Ramsgate: England	15	H3
Rancagua: Chile	65	D10
Ranchi: India	32	E4
Randalstown: N. Ireland	13	E2
Randers: Denmark	17	A4
Randolph: Mass., U.S.A.	55	J2
Randolph: N.Y., U.S.A.	56	G7
Randolph: Utah, U.S.A.	63	D3
Randolph: Vt., U.S.A.	57	N6
Rangeley: U.S.A.	57	P5
Rangeley Lake: U.S.A.	57	P4
Ranger Lake: Can.	56	B3
Rangia: India	38	A1
Rangitaiki: *r.*, N.Z.	41	C2
RANGOON: Burma	38	B3
Rangpur: Bangl.	32	E3
Raniganj: India	32	E4
Rankin Inlet: Can.	47	R4
Rankin's Springs: *town*, Australia	43	C4
Rannoch, Loch: Scot.	10	D3
Rannoch Moor: Scot.	10	D3
Rann of Kutch: *geog. reg.*, India	32	A4
Ranong: Thailand	38	B5
Rantauprapat: Indon.	38	B6
Rapallo: Italy	25	B3
Rapid City: U.S.A.	53	E2
Rapides-des-Joachimes: *sett.*, Canada	56	H3
Rapperswil: Switz.	25	B2
Raquette Lake: U.S.A.	57	L6
Ras: Libya	69	J2
Ras al Hadd: *cape*, Oman	30	G6
Ras Dashan: *mtn.*, Ethiopia	69	N6
Rasht: Iran	28	F6
Rat: *r.*, Canada	61	F1
Rathdowney: Irish Republic	13	D4
Rathdrum: Irish Republic	13	E4
Rathenow: Ger. D.R.	24	C1
Rathfriland: N. Irel.	13	E2
Rathkeale: Irish Republic	13	C4
Rathlin I.: N. Ireland	13	E1
Rath Luirc: Irish Republic	13	C4
Ratlam: India	32	C4
Ratnagiri: India	32	B5
Ratnapura: Sri Lanka	32	b ii
Raton: U.S.A.	53	E3
Rattray: Scotland	10	E3
Raukumara Range: New Zealand	41	C2
Rauma: Finland	17	D3
Raunds: England	15	F2
Ravena: U.S.A.	55	G2
Ravenglass: England	12	C2
Ravenna: Italy	25	C3
Raven Point, The: Irish Republic	13	E4
Ravensburg: Ger. F.R.	25	B2
Ravensthorpe: Austl.	42	c ii
Ravenswood: Austl.	42	C1
Ravi: *r.*, Pakistan	32	B2
Rawalpindi: Pakistan	32	B2
Rawdon: Canada	57	M3
Rawlins: U.S.A.	52	D2
Rawmarsh: England	12	E3
Rawson: Buenos Aires, Argentina	66	B3
Rawson: Chubut, Argentina	65	E12
Rawtenstall: Eng.	12	D3
Ray: U.S.A.	63	D5
Rayleigh: England	15	G3
Raymond: Canada	62	D2
Raymond: U.S.A.	62	B2
Raymondville: U.S.A.	50	C4
Raystown Branch: *r.*, U.S.A.	54	B4
Ré, Île de: France	23	A2
Rea: *r.*, England	14	D2
Rea, Lake: Irish Republic	13	C3
Reading: England	15	E3
Reading: Mass., U.S.A.	55	J2
Reading: Pa., U.S.A.	54	E4
Realicó: Argentina	66	B4
Rebecca, Lake: Australia	42	c ii
Recherche, Archipelago of the: Australia	42	c ii
Rechitsa: U.S.S.R.	20	F2
Recife: Brazil	64	L5
Recklinghausen: German F.R.	24	B1
Reconquista: Arg.	66	C2
Recreo: Argentina	66	A2
Red: *r.*, Canada	61	F3
Red: *r.*, U.S.A.	50	D3
Red Bank: U.S.A.	55	F4
Redberry Lake: Can.	60	D2
Red Bluff: *town*, U.S.A.	63	B3
Redbridge: England	15	G3
Redcar: England	12	E2
Red Cedar Lake: Canada	56	F3
Redcliff: Canada	60	C2
Redcliffe: Australia	42	D3
Red Cliffs: *town*, Australia	43	B4
Red Deer: & *r.*, Alta., Canada	60	C2
Red Deer: *r.*, Sask., Canada	61	E2
Red Deer Lake: Can.	61	E2
Redding: U.S.A.	63	B3
Redditch: England	15	E2
Rede: *r.*, England	12	D1
Redfield: U.S.A.	53	F2
Reditt: Canada	61	G3
Red Lake: Canada	61	G2
Red Lake: *r.*, U.S.A.	58	A2
Red Lion: U.S.A.	54	D5
Red Mesa: *town*, U.S.A.	63	E4
Redmond: Ore., U.S.A.	62	B3
Redmond: Utah, U.S.A.	63	D4
Redon: France	22	a i
Red River of the North: *r.*, Can./U.S.A.	58	A2
Redruth: England	14	A4
Red Sea	30	C6/7
Red Sea Hills: Egypt	69	M3
Red Sucker, Lake: Canada	61	G2
Redvers: Canada	61	E3
Redwater: Canada	60	C2
Red Wing: U.S.A.	58	B3
Redwood Falls: *town*, U.S.A.	58	A3
Ree, Lough: Irish Republic	13	C3
Reeds Gap: U.S.A.	54	C4
Reefton: N.Z.	41	B3
Reepham: England	15	H2
Regensburg: Ger. F.R.	24	C2
Reggio di Calabria: Italy	21	C5
Reggio nell' Emilia: Italy	25	C3
Regina: Canada	61	E2
Rei: *r.*, Cameroun	67	C2
Reï-Bouba: Cameroun	67	C2
Reidsville: U.S.A.	51	G2
Reigate: England	15	F3
Reindeer: *r.*, Canada	61	E1
Reindeer Island: *i.*, Canada	61	F2
Reindeer, Lake: Canada	61	E1
Reisterstown: U.S.A.	54	D5
Remoulins: France	23	B3
Remscheid: Ger. F.R.	24	B1
Renfrew: Canada	57	J4
Renfrew: Scotland	11	D4
Refrew: *Co.*, Can.	57	J4
Rengat: Indonesia	38	C7
Renish Pt.: *c.*, Scot.	10	B2
Renkum: Netherlands	24	B1
Renmark: Australia	43	B4
Rennes: France	22	a i
Reno: U.S.A.	63	C4
Renovo: U.S.A.	54	C3
Rensselaer: U.S.A.	55	G2
Repetigny: Canada	57	M4
Republic: U.S.A.	62	C2
Republican: *r.*, U.S.A.	50	C2
REPUBLIC OF SOUTH AFRICA:	72	–
Repulse Bay: Austl.	42	C2
Reša: Yugoslavia	21	B3
Resistencia: Arg.	66	C2
Reşiţa: Romania	21	D3
Resolute: Canada	47	Q2
Resolution I.: Can.	47	W4
Reston: Canada	61	E3
Réthimnon: Crete	21	D5
Retsof: U.S.A.	54	C2
Réunion: *i.*, Ind. O.	33	d vii
Reus: Spain	19	C4
Reuse: *r.*, Switz.	25	B2
Reutlingen: Ger. F.R.	25	B2
Revelstoke: Canada	62	C1
Revermont: *hills*, France	23	C2
Revilla Gigedo Is.: Pacific Ocean	45	O5
Rewari: India	32	C3
Rexburg: U.S.A.	62	D3
Reykjanes Ridge: N. Atlantic Ocean	8	G2
REYKJAVÍK: Iceland	16	a ii
Reynaldo Cullen: Argentina	66	B3
Reynaud: Canada	61	D2
Reynolds Point: U.S.A.	56	B3
Reynoldsville: U.S.A.	54	B3
Reynosa: Mexico	50	C4
Rēzekne: U.S.S.R.	17	E4
Rhaetian Alps: *mtns.*, Switzerland	25	B2
Rhayader: Wales	14	C2
Rheden: Netherlands	24	B1
Rheidol: *r.*, Wales	14	B2
Rheims (Reims): Fr.	22	B2
Rheine: Ger. F.R.	24	B1
Rheinfelden: Switz.	25	B2
Rheydt: Ger. F.R.	24	B1
Rhine: *r.*, Europe	24	B1
Rhinebeck: U.S.A.	55	G3
Rhinelander: U.S.A.	58	C2
Rhinns Pt: *c.*, Scot.	11	B4
Rhins, The: *geog. reg.*, Scotland	11	C5
Rhinog Fawr: *pk.*, Wales	14	C2
Rhiw: *r.*, Wales	14	C2
Rhondda: Wales	14	C3
Rhode Island: *State*, U.S.A.	55	J3
Rhodes: *i.*, Greece	21	E5
Rhodesia *now* ZIMBABWE–RHODESIA	72	–
Rhodes Nyanga Nat. Park: Zimbabwe	72	E2
Rhodope Mts.: Bulgaria/Greece	21	D4
Rhône: *r.*, France	23	B3
Rhuddlan: Wales	14	C1
Rhum: *i.* & *sd.*, Scotland	10	B3
Rhyddhywel: *pk.*, Wales	14	C2
Rhyl: Wales	14	C1
Rhymney: Wales	14	C3
Riau Archipelago: Indonesia	35	C10
Ribadavia: Spain	19	A4
Ribadeo: Spain	19	A4
Ribble: *r.*, England	12	D3
Ribeira de Iguape: *r.*, Brazil	66	E1
Ribeirão Prêto: Brazil	64	J8
Ribérac: France	23	B2
Riberalta: Bolivia	64	E6
Riccarton: N.Z.	41	B3
Riccione: Italy	25	C3
Rice Lake: Canada	56	G5
Rich, Cape: Canada	56	E5
Richardson: *r.*, Can.	60	C1
Richardson Lake: U.S.A.	57	P5
Richelieu: *r.*, Can.	57	M4
Richfield: U.S.A.	63	D4
Richfield Springs: U.S.A.	54	E2
Richford: U.S.A.	57	N5
Richland: U.S.A.	62	C2
Richlands: U.S.A.	59	D4
Richmond: Ont., Canada	57	K4
Richmond: & Co., Qué., Canada	57	N4
Richmond: England	12	E2
Richmond: Ind., U.S.A.	58	D4
Richmond: Ky., U.S.A.	58	D4
Richmond: Maine, U.S.A.	57	Q5
Richmond: Mich., U.S.A.	56	C7
Richmond: Va., U.S.A.	59	E4
Richmond Hill: *sett.*, Canada	56	F6
Richwood: U.S.A.	59	D4
Riddle: U.S.A.	62	B3
Rideau: *r.*, Canada	57	K4
Rideau Lake: Can.	57	J5
Ridgecrest: U.S.A.	63	C4
Ridgefield: U.S.A.	55	G3
Ridgely: U.S.A.	54	E6
Ridgetown: Canada	56	D7
Ridgway: U.S.A.	54	B3
Riding Mt.: *mtn.*, Canada	62	E2
Riding Mountain National Park: Can.	61	E2
Riesa: Ger. D.R.	24	C1
Rieti: Italy	21	B4
Rifle: U.S.A.	52	D3
Rifle: *r.*, U.S.A.	56	B5
Riga: U.S.S.R.	17	D4
Riga, Gulf of: U.S.S.R.	17	D4
Rigaud: Canada	57	L4
Rihand Reservoir: India	32	D4
Riihimäki: Finland	17	D3
Rijau: Nigeria	67	B1
Rijeka: Yugoslavia	21	B3
Rijswijk: Neth.	24	A1
Rillito: U.S.A.	63	D5
Rima: *r.*, Nigeria	67	B1
Rimbey: Canada	62	D1
Ringim: Nigeria	67	B1
Rimini: Italy	25	C3
Rimouski: Canada	59	G2
Rimutaka Tunnel: New Zealand	41	C3
Rincão: Brazil	66	E2
Ringkøbing: Denmark	17	A4
Ringkøbing Fjord: Denmark	17	A4
Ringvass: *i.*, Norway	16	C2
Ringwood: England	15	E4
Rinn Lough: Irish Republic	13	D3
Riobamba: Ecuador	64	C4
Rio Branco: *town*, Brazil	64	E5
Río Cuarto: *town*, Argentina	66	B3
Rio de Janeiro: *city* & *State*, Braz.	66	b i
Rio-del-Rey: *town*, Cameroun	67	B3
Rio do Sul: *sett.*, Brazil	66	E2
Río Gallegos: *town*, Argentina	65	E14
Rio Grande: *town*, Brazil	66	D3
Rio Grande: *r.*, Mexico/U.S.A.	48	F4
Rio Grande Rise: S. Atlantic Ocean	8	G11
Rio Grande do Sul: *State*, Brazil	66	D2
Riom: France	23	B2
Riondel: Canada	62	C2
Rio Negro: *sett.* & *r.*, Parana Brazil	66	E2
Rio Pardo: *sett.*, Brazil	66	D2
Río Tercero: *sett.*, Argentina	66	B3
Riou Lake: Canada	60	D1
Ripley: England	15	E1
Ripley: U.S.A.	56	F7
Ripon: England	12	E2
Risca: Wales	14	C3
Ritter, Mt.: U.S.A.	63	C4
Riva: Italy	25	C2
Rivadavia: Buenos Aires, Argentina	66	B4
Rivadavia: Salta, Argentina	66	B1
Rive-de-Gier: France	23	B2
Rivera: Uruguay	66	C3
Riverdale: U.S.A.	55	F4
Riverhead: U.S.A.	55	H4
Riverhurst: Canada	62	E1
Riverina: *geog. reg.*, Australia	43	C5
Rivers: Canada	61	E2
Rivers: *State*, Nig.	67	B3
Rivers, Lake of the: Canada	61	D3
Riverside: U.S.A.	63	C5
Rivers Inlet: *town*, Canada	62	A1
Riverton: Canada	61	F2
Riverton: U.S.A.	62	E3
River Valley: *sett.*, Canada	56	E3
Riviera di Levante: *coast*, Italy	25	B3
Riviera di Ponente: *coast*, Italy	25	B3
Rivière à Pierre: *sett.*, Canada	57	N3
Rivière du Loup: *town*, Canada	57	Q2
Rivière-Du-Moulin: *sett.*, Canada	57	O1
RIYADH: Saudi Arabia	30	E6
Roanne: France	23	B2
Roanoke: U.S.A.	59	E4
Roanoke: *r.*, U.S.A.	51	G2
Roanoke Rapids: *town*, U.S.A.	51	G2
Roaring Spring: U.S.A.	54	B4
Roaringwater Bay: Irish Republic	13	B5
Robbinsville: U.S.A.	54	F4
Robe, Mt.: Austl.	43	B4
Robert, Cape: Can.	56	C4
Roberval: Canada	57	N1
Robesonia: U.S.A.	54	D4
Robin Hood's Bay: England	12	F2
Robinson Gorge Nat. Park: Australia	42	C3
Robinvale: Australia	43	B4
Roblin: Canada	61	E2
Robson, Mt.: Canada	60	B2
Robstown: U.S.A.	50	C4
Rocamadour: France	23	B3
Rocas Island: Brazil	8	G8
Roccaroso: Italy	21	B4
Rocha: Uruguay	66	D3
Rochdale: England	12	D3
Rochdale: U.S.A.	55	J2
Rochechouart: Fr.	23	B2
Rochefort-sur-Mer: France	23	A2
Rochester: England	15	G3
Rochester: N.H., U.S.A.	55	K1
Rochester: Minn., U.S.A.	58	B3
Rochester: Mich., U.S.A.	56	B7
Rochester: N.Y., U.S.A.	54	C1
Rock: *r.*, U.S.A.	58	C3
Rockall Plateau: N. Atlantic Ocean	8	J2
Rockford: U.S.A.	58	C3
Rockglen: Canada	61	D3
Rockhampton: Austl.	42	D2
Rock Hill: *town*, U.S.A.	51	F3
Rock Island: *sett.*, Canada	57	N4
Rock Island: *city*, U.S.A.	58	B3
Rock Lake: U.S.A.	61	F3
Rockland: Canada	57	K4
Rockland: U.S.A.	55	K2
Rocklands Reservoir: Australia	43	B5
Rockport: U.S.A.	55	K2
Rock Springs: *town*, U.S.A.	63	E3
Rockville: Conn., U.S.A.	55	H3
Rockville: Md., U.S.A.	54	C5
Rockwood: U.S.A.	57	Q4
Rocky Ford: *town*, U.S.A.	53	E3
Rocky Island Lake: Canada	56	B3
Rocky Mount: *town*, U.S.A.	51	G2
Rocky Mountain House: Canada	62	D1
Rocky Mountains: Canada/U.S.A.	46/8	–
Rocky Mtns. Nat. Park: U.S.A.	53	D2
Rocky Point: *town*, U.S.A.	55	H4
Rocky Saugeen: *r.*, Canada	56	E5
Rocroi: France	22	B2
Roden: *r.*, England	14	D2
Rodez: France	23	B3
Rodney: Canada	56	D7
Rodos: Rhodes	21	E5
Roebling: U.S.A.	54	F4
Roermond: Neth.	24	B1
Roeselare: Belgium	22	B1
Roger, Lac: Canada	56	G2
Rogers, Mt.: U.S.A.	51	F2
Rogers City: U.S.A.	58	D2
Rojas: Argentina	66	B3
Rolândia: Brazil	66	D1
Rolla: U.S.A.	58	B4
Roma: Australia	42	C3
Romain, Cape: U.S.A.	51	G3
Roman: Romania	20	E3
ROMANIA:	20	D3
Romano, Cape: U.S.A.	51	F4
Romans: France	23	C2
ROME: Italy	21	B4
Rome: Ala., U.S.A.	51	E3
Rome: N.Y., U.S.A.	54	E1
Romeo: U.S.A.	56	B7
Romilly-sur-Seine: France	22	B2
Romney: U.S.A.	54	B5
Romney Marsh: Eng.	15	G3
Romsey: England	15	E4
Rona: *i.*, Scotland	10	C2
Ronay: *i.*, Scotland	10	A2
Ronda: Spain	19	A5
Rondout Reservoir: U.S.A.	55	F3
Ronkonkoma: U.S.A.	55	G4
Rønne: Bornholm, Denmark	17	B4
Roosendaal: Neth.	24	A1
Roosevelt: U.S.A.	61	F3
Roosevelt Dam: U.S.A.	63	D5
Root Portage: Canada	58	B1
Ropp: Nigeria	67	B2
Roquebrune: France	23	C3
Roquefort: France	23	A3
Roquefort: France	23	B3
Roraima: *mtn.*, S. America	64	F2
Rorketon: Canada	61	F2
Røros: Norway	16	B3
Rorschach: Switzerland	25	B2
Rørvik: Norway	16	B3
Rosa, Monte: Italy/Switzerland	25	B2
Rosario: Argentina	66	B3
Rosario: *r.*, Arg.	66	A1
Rosario de la Frontera: Arg.	66	B2
Rosario de Lerma: Argentina	66	A1
Rosario del Tala: Argentina	66	C3
Rosário do Sul: Brazil	66	D3
Roscoff: France	22	a i
Roscommon: & Co., Irish Republic	13	C3
Roscrea: Irish Rep.	13	D4
Roseau: *r.*, U.S.A./Canada	58	A2
Roseburg: U.S.A.	62	B3
Rosehearty: Scotland	10	F2
Roseires: Sudan	69	M6
Rosendaël: France	22	B1
Rosenheim: Ger. F.R.	25	C2
Rosetown: Canada	62	E1
Rosetta: Egypt	69	M2
Rosetta: *r.*, Austl.	42	C2
Rose Valley: *town*, Canada	61	E2
Roseville: U.S.A.	63	B4
Rosevear: Canada	60	B2
Roslavl': U.S.S.R.	28	C3
Rossan Pt.: Irish Republic	13	C2
Ross Barnett Reservoir: U.S.A.	50	D3
Rosseau, Lake: Can.	56	F4
Ross Island: *i.*, Can.	61	F2
Rossiter: U.S.A.	54	B4
Rossland: Canada	62	C2
Rosslare Harbour: Irish Republic	13	E4
Rosslare Pt.: Irish Republic	13	E4
Ross of Mull: *penin.*, Scotland	10	B3
Ross-on-Wye: Eng.	14	D3
Rosthern: Canada	60	D2
Rostock: Ger. D.R.	24	C1
Rostov: U.S.S.R.	28	D4
Roswell: U.S.A.	53	E4
Roth: Ger. F.R.	24	C2
Rothbury: England	12	E1
Rothenburg: Ger. F.R.	24	C2
Rother: *r.*, Eng.	15	G4
Rotherham: England	12	E3
Rothes: Scotland	10	E2
Rothesay: Scotland	11	C4
Rothwell: Northants., England	15	F2
Rothwell: W. Yorks., England	12	E3
Roti: *i.*, Indonesia	35	G13
Roto: Australia	43	C4
Rotorua: N.Z.	41	C2
Rotterdam: Neth.	24	A1
Rottweil: Ger. F.R.	25	B2
Roubaix: France	22	B1
Rouen: France	22	B2
Rouffach: France	22	C2
Roughty: *r.*, Irish Republic	13	B5
Rouleau: Canada	61	E2
Roulette: U.S.A.	56	G8
Round Lake: Canada	56	H4
Roundup: U.S.A.	62	E2
Rourkela: India	32	E4
Rousay: *i.*, Ork. Is.	10	d iii
Roussillon: *Old Prov.*, France	23	B3
Rouyn: Canada	56	F1
Rovaniemi: Finland	16	E2
Rovereto: Italy	25	C2
Rovigo: Italy	25	C2
Rovinj: Yugoslavia	25	C2
Rovno: U.S.S.R.	20	E2
Roxburgh: N.Z.	41	A4
Roxbury: U.S.A.	54	F2
Royal Leamington Spa: England	15	E2
Royal Oak: U.S.A.	56	B7
Royal Tunbridge Wells: England	15	G3
Royan: France	23	A2
Royersford: U.S.A.	54	E4
Royston: England	15	F2
Ruaha Nat. Park: Tanzania	71	F9
Ruahine Range: N.Z.	41	C3
Ruapehu: *mtn.*, N.Z.	41	C2
Rub'al Khali: *geog. reg.*, Saudi Arabia	30	E7
Rubha a' Geadna: *pt.*, Scotland	11	B3
Rubha a' Mhail: *pt.*, Scotland	11	B4
Rubha Ardvule: *pt.*, Scotland	10	A2
Rubha Cóigeach: *pt.*, Scotland	10	C1
Rubha Dubh: *pt.*, Scotland	10	B3
Rubha Hunish: *pt.*, Scotland	10	B2
Rubha Réidh: *pt.*, Scotland	10	C2
Rubtsovsk: U.S.S.R.	29	N3
Rudnichnyy: U.S.S.R.	28	G2
Rudok: China	32	C2
Ruffec: France	23	B2
Rufino: Argentina	66	B3
Rugby: England	15	E2
Rugeley: England	15	E2
Ruhr: *district*, German F.R.	24	B1
Rukwa, Lake: Tan.	71	F9
Rum: *r.*, U.S.A.	58	B2
Rumford: U.S.A.	57	P5
Rumoi: Japan	39	D1
Rump Mountain: U.S.A.	57	O4
Rumson: U.S.A.	55	F4
Rumi Punco: Arg.	66	A2
Rum Jungle: *town*, Australia	40	E3
Runcorn: England	14	D1
Rupert: U.S.A.	62	D3
Ruse: Bulgaria	21	E4
Rush: Irish Republic	13	E3
Rushden: England	15	F2
Rushville: U.S.A.	54	C2
Russell: Canada	61	E2
Russell: N.Z.	41	B2
Russell: *Co.*, Canada	57	K4
Russellville: U.S.A.	50	D2
Russian Mission: U.S.A.	46	C4
Russian Soviet Federated Socialist Republic: U.S.S.R.	26/7	–
Ruth: U.S.A.	63	D4
Rutherglen: Scotland	11	D4
Ruthin: Wales	14	C1
Rutland: U.S.A.	57	N6
Ruvuma: *r.*, Moz./Tan.	71	G10
Ruwenzori, Mt.: Ug.	70	F7
RUWANDA:	71	E8
Ryan, Loch: Scotland	11	C5
Ryazan': U.S.S.R.	28	D3
Rybachiy Peninsula: U.S.S.R.	16	F2
Rybach'ye: U.S.S.R.	29	M5
Rybinsk: & *res.*, U.S.S.R.	28	D2
Rybnik: Poland	20	C2
Ryohaku-Sanchi: *mtns.*, Japan	39	
Ryde: England	15	
Rye: England	15	
Ryhope: England	12	
Ryugasaki: Japan	39	
Ryukyu (Nánsei) Is.: Pacific Ocean	34	
Ryukyu Trench: Pac. O.	44	
Rzeszów: Poland	20	
Rzhev: U.S.S.R.	28	
Saa: Cameroun	67	
Saale: *r.*, Ger. D.R.	24	
Saalfeld: Ger. D.R.	24	
Saar: *r.* & *State*, German F.R.	24	
Saarbrucken: German F.R.	24	
Saaremaa: *i.*, U.S.S.R.	17	
Saariselka: *hills*, Finland/U.S.S.R.	16	
Saarlouis: Ger. F.R.	24	
Šabac: Yugoslavia	21	
Sabah: *State*, Mal.	35	
Sabadell: Spain	19	
Sabourin, Lac: Can.	56	
Sable, Cape: Canada	47	
Sable, Cape: U.S.A.	51	
Sabon Birni: Nigeria	67	
Sacandaga: *r.* & *res.*, U.S.A.	57	
Sachigo, Lake: Can.	61	
Sackets Harbor: U.S.A.	57	
Saco: & *r.*, U.S.A.	57	
Saco de Tapes: *bay*, Brazil	66	
Sacramento: & *r.*, U.S.A.	63	
Sacramento Mts.: U.S.A.	53	
Saddleback: *mtn.*, England	12	
Sado: *i.*, Japan	39	
Sado-Kaikyo: *str.*, Japan	39	
Saeki: Japan	39	
Säffle: Sweden	17	
Safford: U.S.A.	63	
Saffron Walden: Eng.	15	
Safi: Morocco	68	
Saga: Japan	39	
Sagaing: & *Divis.*, Burma	38	
Sagami-nada: *gulf*, Japan	39	
Sagamihara: Japan	39	
Sagamore: U.S.A.	55	
Sagamu: Nigeria	67	
Sage: U.S.A.	63	
Sag Harbor: *town*, U.S.A.	55	
Saginaw: & *bay*, U.S.A.	58	
Saguaro National Monument: U.S.A.	63	
Saguenay: *r.*, Canada	57	
Sagunto: Spain	19	
Sahara Desert: N. Afr.	68/9	
Saharan Atlas: *ra.*, Algeria	68	
Saharanpur: India	32	
Sai: *r.*, India	32	
Saigon *now* Ho Chi Minh City	38	
Saimaa: *lake*, Finland	16	
Sain Shanda: Mong.	34	
St. Abb's Head: Scot.	11	
St. Affrique: France	23	
St. Agapit: Canada	57	
St. Agnes: England	14	
St. Agnes: *i.*, Scilly Isles	14	
St. Agnes Head: *c.*, England	14	
St. Albans: England	15	
St. Albans: Vt., U.S.A.	57	
St. Albans: W. Va., U.S.A.	59	
St. Alban's Head: England	14	
St.-Alexandre: Can.	57	
St. Alexis des Monts: Canada	57	
St. Amand: France	22	
St. Amand Mont-Rond: France	23	
St. Andrews: & *Bay*, Scotland	10	
St. André, Plaine de: France	22	
St. Ann's Head: Wales	14	
St. Anselme: Canada	57	
St. Anthony: U.S.A.	62	
St. Anton: Australia	25	
Saint Arnaud: Austl.	43	
St. Aubin: Jersey	14	
St. Augustine: U.S.A.	51	
St. Austell: England	14	
St. Austell Bay: Eng.	14	
St. Basile: Canada	57	
St. Bees: England	12	
St. Bees Head: Eng.	12	
St. Brides Bay: Wales	14	
St. Brieuc: France	22	
St. Catharines: Can.	56	
St. Catherine's Pt.: England	15	
St. Césaire: Canada	57	
St. Chamond: France	23	
St. Charles: Canada	57	
St. Charles: U.S.A.	56	
St. Christophers (St. Kitts): *i.*, Leeward Islands	49	
St. Clair: & *r.*, Mich., U.S.A.	56	
St. Clair: Pa., U.S.A.	54	
St. Clair, L.: Canada/U.S.A.	56	
St. Claude: France	23	
St. Cloud: U.S.A.	58	
St. Columb Major: England	14	
St. Croix: *r.*, Minn., U.S.A.	58	
St. Croix: *i.*, W. Indies	49	
St. David's: Wales	14	
St. David's Head: Wales	14	
St. Denis: Canada	57	
St. Denis: France	22	
St. Dié: France	22	
St. Dizier: France	22	
St. Donat: Canada	57	
Ste. Agathe: Canada	57	
Ste. Angèle de Laval: Canada	57	
Ste. Anne: Canada	61	
Ste. Anne: *r.*, Can.	57	
Ste. Anne de Beaupré: Canada	57	

Name	Page	ref
Anne de Bellevue:		
,anada	57	M4
, Camille: Canada	57	P3
, Emélie: Canada	57	M3
, Famille: Canada	57	P2
, Foy: Canada	57	O3
, Elias, Mt.: Can.	46	G4
, Elias Mts.: Can.	46	H4
, Julienne: Canada	57	M4
, Marie: Canada	57	P3
, Marguerite: r.	57	P3
Malagasy Republic	71	I13
, Menehould: Fr.	22	C2
, Rose du Lac: Canada	61	J2
, Rose du Nord: Canada	57	P1
, Savine: France	22	B2
,ntes: France	23	A2
, Therese: Canada	57	M4
, Etienne: France	23	B2
, Eustache: Canada	57	M4
, Félicien: Canada	59	F2
Félix de Valois: Canada	57	M3
, Finan's Bay: Irish Republic	13	A5
, Flour: France	23	B2
, Francis, Cape: South Africa	72	C5
, Francis, Lake: Canada	57	L4
, Francis: r., U.S.A.	57	L4
, François: r. Can.	57	N4
, François, Lac: ,anada	57	O4
, Gabriel: Canada	57	M3
, Gallen: Switz.	25	B2
, Gaudens: France	23	C3
, Gédéon: Canada	57	P4
, George: Australia	42	C3
, George: U.S.A.	63	D4
, George, Cape: George: Canada	51	F4
, Georges: Canada	57	P3
, George's Channel: Irish Rep./Wales	13	F5
, Gérard: Canada	57	O4
, Germain: France	22	B2
, Gotthard Pass: Switzerland	25	B2
, Govan's Head: Wales	14	A3
, Guillaume: Canada	57	N4
, Hedwidge: Canada	59	E2
, Helena: r. South Atlantic Ocean	8	K9
, Helena Bay: S. Afr.	72	B5
, Helena Sound: U.S.A.	51	F3
, Helens: U.S.A.	62	D3
, Helens: U.S.A.	62	B2
, Helier: Jersey	14	a ii
, Henri: Canada	57	O3
, Hilaire: Canada	57	M4
, Hubert: Canada	57	M4
, Hyacinthe: Canada	57	N4
, Ignace, Isle: Can.	58	C2
, Ingbert: Ger. F.R.	24	B2
, Invite: Canada	57	L3
, Ives: Cambs.: Eng.	15	F2
, Ives, Corn.: Eng.	14	A4
, Jacques: Can.	57	M4
, Jean: Canada	57	M4
, Jean, Lac: Can.	57	O1
, Jean-de-Luz: France	23	A3
, Jean de Matha: Canada	57	M3
, Jean, Maurienne: France	23	C2
, Jean-Pied-de-Port: France	23	A3
, Jean Port Joli: Canada	57	P2
, Jérôme: Qué.: Canada	57	O1
, Jérôme: Qué.: Canada	57	L4
, Joachim: Can.	57	L4
,nt John: Canada	47	W7
, John: U.S.A.	61	F3
, John, Lac: Can.	57	P3
,nt John: r. Canada/U.S.A.	59	G2
, John's: Canada	47	Z7
, Johns: r., U.S.A.	51	F4
, Johnsbury: U.S.A.	57	N5
, John's Pt.: N. Irel.	13	F2
, Johneville: France	54	F1
, Joseph: Canada	57	P3
, Joseph, & r.: Mich., U.S.A.	58	C3
, Joseph, Mo.: U.S.A.	58	B4
, Joseph Island: Canada	56	B3
, Joseph, Lake: Canada	58	B1
, Julien: France	23	B2
, Junien: France	23	B2
, Just: England	14	A4
, Kitts: i., see Christophers: est.	49	O6
, Lawrence: r.: Canada	57	Q2
, Lawrence, Gulf of: Canada	47	X7
, Lawrence: r.: Bering Sea	46	B4
, Léonard: Canada	57	N3
, Lin: Canada	57	M4
, Lô: France	22	A2
, Louis, Lac: Can.	57	M4
, Louis: U.S.A.	58	B4
, Louis: Senegal	68	B5
, LUCIA:	49	O7
, Magnus Bay: Shetland Islands	10	b i
, Malachie: Canada	57	P3
, Malo: Canada	57	F3
, Malo: France	22	a i
, Malo, Gulf of: Fr.	22	a i
, Marc: des-Carrières: Canada	57	N3
, Leeward Islands	49	O6
, Martin: i., see Martin: Can.	61	F2
, Martin's: i.. Scilly Isles	14	c iv
, Mary: i., Canada	60	C3
, Mary: i.: U.S.A.	61	C3
, Mary Peak: mtn., Australia	43	A4
, Marys: Australia	40	b i
, Marys: Canada	56	D6
, Marys: U.S.A.	54	B3
, Mary's: i., Scilly Isles	14	c iv
, Marys: r.: Marys: U.S.A.	51	F3
, Mary's: r., U.S.A.	14	A3
, Mawes: Eng.	14	A4
, Bering Sea	46	A4

Name	Page	ref
St. Maurice: Switz.	25	B2
St.-Maurice, Parc du: Canada	57	M2
St.-Maurice: r., Can.	57	N2
St. Maxime: France	23	C3
St. Michel des Saints: Canada	57	M3
St. Montz: Switz.	25	B2
St. Nation: r., Can.	57	K4
St. Nazaire: France	22	a i
St. Neots: England	15	F2
St. Omer: France	22	B1
Saintonge: reg., Fr	22	A2
St. Pacôme: Canada	57	Q2
St. Pamphile: Can.	57	Q2
St. Pascal: Canada	60	C2
St. Paul: Canada	58	B2
St. Paul: i., Ind. O.	33	f viii
St. Paul, Cape: Ghana	68	F7
St. Paul l'Ermite: Can.	57	M4
St. Paul Rocks: N. Atlantic Ocean	8	H7
St. Peter: U.S.A.	58	B3
St. Peter Port: Guernsey	14	a ii
St. Pete's: Jersey	14	a ii
St. Petersburg: U.S.A.	51	F4
St. Philippe de Néri: Canada	57	Q2
St. Pie: Canada	57	N4
St. Pierre: Canada	57	F3
St. Pierre, Co.: Canada	57	N3
St. Pierre & Miquelon: is., Atl.O.	47	Y7
St.-Pierre-Quilbignon: France	22	a i
St. Pol: France	22	B1
St. Pölten: Austria	20	C3
St. Pons: France	23	B3
St. Prosper: Canada	57	P3
St. Quentin: France	22	B2
St. Raphael: Canada	57	P3
St. Raphaël: France	23	C3
St. Raymond: Can.	57	O3
St. Regis: r., U.S.A.	57	M5
St. Rémi: Canada	57	M4
St. Romuald: Canada	57	O3
St. Servan: France	22	a i
St. Timothée: Canada	57	L4
St. Tite: Canada	57	N3
St. Theresa Point: Canada	61	G2
St. Thomas: Canada	56	D7
St. Thomas: i.. W. Indies	49	O6
St. Tropez: France	23	C3
St. Valéry-en-Caux: France	22	B2
St. Vallier: Canada	57	P3
St. Vincent: i.. Windward Islands	49	O7
St. Walburg: Canada	60	D2
Saipan: i., Pacific O.	44	D5
Saitama: Pref., Japan	39	f iii
Saiwûn: Yemen P.D.R.	30	E7
Sakai: Japan	39	b ii
Sakai-minato: Japan	39	A3
Sakakawea, Lake: U.S.A.	53	E1
Sakata: Japan	39	C2
Sakatawi Lake: Can.	56	C2
Sakété: Benin	67	A2
Sakhalin: i., U.S.S.R.	27	R7
Sakhalin Bay: U.S.S.R.	27	R7
Saki: Nigeria	67	A2
Sakishima Group: is.. Ryukyu Islands	39	G6
Sakura: Japan	39	b ii
Sakurai: Japan	39	B1
Salachi: China	36	B1
Saladillo: r.. Santa Fe, Arg	66	B3
Saladillo: r.. Sant.: Argentina	66	B2
Salado: r., Mexico	50	C4
Salala: Oman	30	F7
Salamanca: Spain	19	A4
Salamanca: U.S.A.	54	B2
Salavina: Argentina	66	B2
Sala y Gómez: i.. Pacific Ocean	45	P9
Salcombe: England	14	C4
Sale: England	12	D3
Salekhard: U.S.S.R.	26	H3
Salem: India	32	C6
Salem: Mass., U.S.A.		K2
Salem: N.J., U.S.A.	54	E5
Salem: N.Y., U.S.A.	55	G1
Salem: Oreg., U.S.A.	62	B2
Salem: Scotland	10	C3
Salerno: Italy	21	B4
Salford: England	12	D3
Salgótarján: Hung.	20	C3
Salí: r., Argentina	66	B2
Salida: U.S.A.	53	D3
Saliers: France	23	B3
Salihli: Turkey	21	E5
Salima: Malawi	71	E1
Salina: Kans., U.S.A.	50	C2
Salina: Mo., U.S.A.	50	C2
Salina La Antigua: salt lake, Argentina	66	A2
Salinas: Calif., U.S.A.	62	B3
Saline: r., U.S.A.	50	D3
Salisbury: Australia	43	A4
Salisbury: England	15	F3
Salisbury: Conn., U.S.A.	55	G2
Salisbury: Md., U.S.A.	59	E4
Salisbury: Zimbabwe	72	E2
Salisbury Plain: Eng.	15	F3
Salitre-Cué: Par.	66	C2
Sally Gap: Irish Rep.	13	C3
Salmo: Canada	62	C2
Salmon: r.. U.S.A.	62	D2
Salmon: r., Canada	62	O4
Salmon Arm: Canada	62	C1
Salmon Falls: r.. U.S.A.	57	O6
Salmon Reservoir: U.S.A.	57	K6
Salmon River Mts.: U.S.A.	62	C2
Salo: Finland	17	D3
Salon de Provence: France	23	C3
Salop: Co., England	14	D2
Salpausselka: geog reg., Finland	17	D3
Salsacate: Argentina	66	B2
Sal'sk: U.S.S.R.	28	E4
Salt: r., Ariz., U.S.A.	63	D5
Salt: r., Mo., U.S.A.	58	B4
Salta: & prov., Arg.	66	A1
Saltash: England	14	B4
Saltcoats: Canada	61	E2

Name	Page	ref
Saltcoats: Scotland	11	D4
Saltee Is.: Irish Rep.	13	E4
Salt Fork: r.. Okla./Tex., U.S.A.	53	E3
Salt Fork: r.. Tex., U.S.A.	53	E4
Saltillo: Mexico	48	D4
Salt Lake City: U.S.A.	62	C4
Salto: Brazil	66	a i
Salto: Uruguay	66	C3
Salton Sea: l., U.S.A.	63	C5
Salt Range: Pak.	32	B2
Saluzzo: Italy	25	B2
Salvador (Bahia): Braz.	64	L6
Salvator Rossa Nat. Park: Australia	42	C2
Salween (Lu): r.. Asia	34	B7
Salzach: r., Austria	25	C2
Salzburg: & prov.. Austria	25	C2
Salzgitter: Ger. F.R.	24	C1
Sama de Langreo: Spain	19	A4
Samah: China	38	D3
Samar: i., Phil.	35	H8
Samara: r., U.S.S.R.	28	F3
Samarai: Indon.	35	F11
Samarkand: U.S.S.R.	29	K6
Sämarrä: Iraq	30	D4
Sambalpur: India	32	D4
Sambolabo: Cameroon	67	C2
Sambre: r., Belgium/France	22	B1
Samburu Game Reserve: Kenya	70	G2
Sam Neua: Laos	38	B4
Samoa Is.: Pac. O.	44	H8
Samoëns: France	23	C2
Samos: i., Greece	21	E5
Samothrace: i.. Greece	21	E4
Sampacho: Argentina	66	B3
Sam Rayburn Reservoir: U.S.A.	50	D3
Samsun: Turkey	28	D5
Samut Songkhram: Thailand	38	C4
San'a: Yemen, A.R.	30	D7
Sanaga: r., Cam.	67	C3
San Ángelo: U.S.A.	50	B3
San Antonio: & r.. U.S.A.	50	C4
San Antonio: Ibiza	19	C4
San Benito Is.: Mex.	48	C4
San Bernardino: U.S.A.	63	C5
San Blas, Cape: U.S.A.	51	E4
Sanborville: U.S.A.	57	O6
San Carlos: Uruguay	66	D3
Sancerre: France	23	B2
San Clemente: r.. U.S.A.	63	C5
San Cosme: Arg	66	B3
San Cristóbal: Arg.	66	B3
San Cristóbal: Venez.	64	C2
San Cristóbal: i.. Solomon Islands	40	L3
Sand, Lake: Canada	61	G3
Sanda: Japan	39	b ii
Sanda I.: Scotland	11	C4
Sandakan: Malaysia	35	G5
Sanday: i. & sd.. Orkney Islands	10	e iii
Sandbach: England	12	D1
Sandefjord: Norway	17	B4
Sandgate: England	15	F3
Sandhurst: Austl.	42	D3
San Diego: U.S.A.	63	C5
Sand Lake Station: Canada	56	A2
Sandnes: Norway	17	A4
Sandomierz: Poland	20	D2
Sandoval: U.S.A.	58	C4
Sandown: Burma	38	A2
Sandown: England	15	E4
Sandpoint: U.S.A.	62	C1
Sandray: i., Scotland	10	A3
Sandstone: Australia	42	b i
Sandusky: r.. U.S.A.	56	C8
Sandvika: Norway	17	B4
Sandviken: Sweden	17	C3
Sandwich: England	15	H3
Sandy: England	15	F2
Sandy: U.S.A.	63	D3
Sandy: r., U.S.A.	57	P5
Sandy Bay: Canada	61	E1
Sandy Cape: Austl.	42	D2
Sandy Lake: i. & sett.: Canada	61	G2
San Felíu de Guixols: Spain	19	C4
San Félix: i., Chile	65	B9
San Fernando: Chile	65	D10
San Fernando: Phil.	35	G7
San Fernando: Spain	19	A5
San Fernando: Trin. & Tobago	49	O7
San Fernando de Apure: Venezuela	64	E2
Sanfjället Nat. Park: Sweden	16	B3
San Francisco: U.S.A.	63	B4
San Francisco: r.. Argentina	66	B1
San Francisco: r.. U.S.A.	52	D4
San Francisco del Chañar: Arg	66	B2
San Francisco del Monte de Oro: Arg.	66	B2
Sanford: Fla., U.S.A.	51	F4
Sanford: Maine. U.S.A.	55	K1
Sanford: N.C., U.S.A.	51	F3
Sangamon: r., U.S.A.	58	C4
Sangar: U.S.S.R.	27	P5
San Genaro: Arg.	66	B3
Sangar: China	36	D3
Sangkan: r., China	36	C1
Sangre de Cristo Range: U.S.A.	53	D3
San Gregorio: Uru.	66	C3
Sanho: China	36	C1
San Ignacio: Uruguay	66	C3
San Jacinto: Uruguay	66	C3
San Javier: r., Arg.	66	B2
San Javier: Arg.	66	C3
Sanjo: Japan	39	C2
San Joaquin: Paraguay	66	C1
San Joaquin: r.. U.S.A.	63	B4
San Jorge: Argentina	66	B3
SAN JOSÉ: Costa Rica	49	K7
San José: Paraguay	66	C1
San José: U.S.A.	62	B4

Name	Page	ref
San Jose: r.. N.M., U.S.A.	52	D4
San José de Feliciano: Argentina	66	C3
San José de Mayo: Uruguay	66	C3
San Juan: Argentina	65	E10
San Juan: r., Mexico	63	D4
San Juan: Puerto Rico	49	N6
San Juan: U.S.A.	63	D4
San Juan Bautista: Paraguay	66	C2
San Juan Mts.: U.S.A.	52	D3
San Justo: Buenos Aires, Argentina	66	C3
San Justo: Santa Fe, Argentina	66	B3
Sankang: China	37	A4
Sankt Veit: Austria	25	C2
San Lorenzo: Ec.	64	C3
San Lorenzo: r.. Argentina	66	B1
Sanlúcar de Barremeda: Spain	19	A5
San Luis: & prov.. Argentina	66	B3
San Luis: Mexico	63	D5
San Luis, Sierra de: r., Argentina	66	A3
San Luis Obispo: & bay, U.S.A.	63	B4
San Luis Potosí: Mexico	48	F5
San Manuel: U.S.A.	63	D5
San Marcos: U.S.A.	50	C4
SAN MARINO: & town	25	C3
San Martín: Argentina	66	A2
San Miguel: U.S.A.	63	B5
San Miguel del Monte: Argentina	66	C4
San Miguel de Tucumán: Argentina	66	b i
Sannan: Japan	39	b i
San Nicolás: Arg.	66	B3
San Nicolas: i., U.S.A.	63	C5
San Pedro: Buenos Aires, Argentina	66	C3
San Pedro: Jujuy. Argentina	66	B1
San Pedro: Misiones. Argentina	66	D2
San Pedro: Paraguay	66	C2
San Pedro: U.S.A.	63	D5
San Rafael: Arg.	65	E10
San Ramón: Uru.	66	C3
San Ramón de la Nueva Orán: Arg.	66	B1
San Remo: Italy	25	B3
San Salvador: i.. Bahamas	49	M5
San Sebastian: Spain	19	B4
San Severo: Italy	21	B4
Sansha: China	37	D4
Sanshui: China	37	C4
Santa Ana: U.S.A.	63	C5
Santa Barbara: U.S.A.	63	C5
Santa Barbara Channel: U.S.A.	63	C5
Santa Bárbara do Sul: Brazil	66	D2
Santa Catalina: i. & gulf, U.S.A.	63	C5
Santa Catarina: State. Brazil	66	D2
Santa Catarina, Ilha de: i., Brazil	66	E2
Santa Clara: Cuba	49	L5
Santa Cruz: Bolivia	64	F7
Santa Cruz: i., U.S.A.	63	B4
Santa Cruz: r., U.S.A.	63	C5
Santa Cruz do Sul: Brazil	66	D2
Santa Cruz Is.: Solomon Islands	40	M3
Santa Fe: & prov.. Argentina	66	B3
Santa Fe: r., Arg.	66	B3
Santa Isabel: i.. Solomon Islands	40	K2
Santa Lucia: & r.. Uruguay	66	D3
Santa Lucia: r., Arg.	66	C3
Santana do Livramento: Brazil	66	C3
Sta. Margherita di Pula: Sardinia	19	a ii
Santa Maria: Brazil	66	D2
Santa Maria: r.,U.S.A.	63	D5
Santa Maria: i., Braz.	66	A2
Santa Maria di Leuca, Cape: Italy	21	C5
Santa Marta: Colom.	64	M7
Santander: Spain	19	B4
Santa Paula: U.S.A.	63	C5
Santarém: Brazil	64	H4
Santarém: Portugal	19	A5
Santa Rita de Catuna: Argentina	66	A3
Santa Rosa: Arg.	65	F11
Santa Rosa: Brazil	66	C2
Santa Rosa: Paraguay	66	C2
Santa Rosa: Calif., U.S.A.	63	B4
Santa Rosa: N.M., U.S.A.	53	E4
Santa Rosa: i., U.S.A.	63	B5
Santa Vitória do Palmer: Braz.	66	D3
Santiago: Chile	65	D10
Santiago: Dom. Rep.	49	M6
Santiago: Mexico	48	F5
Santiago de Cuba: Cuba	49	L5
Santiago de Compostela: Spain	19	A4
Santiago del Estero: & prov., Argentina	66	B2
Santo Ángelo: Brazil	66	D2
Santo António: Mato Grosso, Braz.	64	F5
Santo António: Rio Grande do Sul, Brazil	66	D2
SANTO DOMINGO: Dominican Republic	49	N6
Santos: Brazil	66	a i

Name	Page	ref
Santo Tomé: Corrientes, Argentina	66	C2
Santo Tomé: Santa Fe, Argentina	66	B3
Sanvic: France	22	B2
Sanyati: r., Zimbabwe	72	D2
Sanyuan: Fukien, China	37	C4
Sanyuan: Shensi, China	36	A3
Sarajevo: Yugo.	21	C4
Saranac Lake: town. U.S.A.	57	L5
Saranac Lakes: U.S.A.	57	L5
Saranac: r., U.S.A.	57	M5
Sarandi Grande: Uru.	66	C3
Sarandí del Yi: Uru.	66	C3
Saransk: U.S.S.R.	28	F3
Sarapul: U.S.S.R.	28	G2
Sarasota: U.S.A.	51	F4
Saratoga Springs: town, U.S.A.	55	G1
Saratov: U.S.S.R.	28	F3
Saravane: Laos	38	D3
Sarawak: State. Malaysia	35	E10
Sardinia: i., Med. Sea	19	a i
Sareks Nat. Park: Sweden	16	C2
Sargasso Sea: N. Atlantic Ocean	8	D5
Sarh: Chad	69	J7
Sark: i., Channel Islands	14	a ii
Sarlat: France	23	B3
Sarles: U.S.A.	61	F3
Sarnia: Canada	56	C7
Sarny: U.S.S.R.	20	E2
Sarpsborg: Norway	17	B4
Sarrebourg: France	22	C2
Sarreguemines: Fr.	22	C2
Sartène: Corsica	19	a i
Sarthe: r., France	22	a i
Sapele: Nigeria	67	B2
Sapporo: Japan	39	D1
São André: Brazil	66	a i
São Bernado do Campo: Brazil	66	a i
São Borja: Brazil	66	C2
São Caetano do Sul: Brazil	66	a i
São Carlos: Brazil	66	D2
São Francisco: r.. Brazil	64	K6
São Francisco: r.. de: i., Brazil	66	E2
São Francisco de Paula: Brazil	66	D2
São Francisco do Sul: Brazil	66	E2
São Gabriel: Brazil	66	D3
São Jerónimo: Brazil	66	D3
São Joâoda Boa Vista: Brazil	66	a i
São Joaquim: Braz.	66	E2
São José: Brazil	66	E2
São José do Campos: Brazil	66	a i
São Leopoldo: Braz	66	D2
São Lourenço do Sul: Brazil	66	D3
São Luis: Brazil	66	K4
São Luis Gonzaga: Brazil	66	D2
São Paulo: Brazil	66	a i
Saon: Japan	39	c i
São Roque, Cabo de: Brazil	64	L5
São Sebastião, Ilha de: i., Brazil	66	a i
São Vicente: Brazil	66	a i
São Vicente, C. de: Portugal	19	A5
Sasayama: Japan	39	b i
Sasebo: Japan	39	A3
Sasaginnigak, Lake: Canada	61	F2
Saskatchewan: Prov. & r., Canada	60	D2
Saskatoon: Canada	62	E1
Sassari: Sardinia	19	a i
Satara: India	32	B5
Satara Range: India	32	C4
Satte: Japan	39	f iii
Satu-Mare: Romania	20	D3
Satun: Thailand	38	C5
Sauce: Argentina	66	C3
SAUDI ARABIA	30	E6
Saueriand: geog reg.: German F.R.	24	B1
Saugeen: r., Canada	56	C7
Saugerties: U.S.A.	55	G2
Sauk Centre: U.S.A.	58	B2
Sault Ste. Marie: Canada	56	D2
Sault Ste. Marie: U.S.A.	58	D2
Saumur: France	23	A2
Saûternes: France	23	A3
Sauze d'Oulx: Italy	25	B2
Sava: r., Yugoslavia	21	C4
Savage: U.S.A.	53	D5
Savannah: Ga., U.S.A.	51	F3
Savannah: Tenn., U.S.A.	51	E3
Savannah: r., U.S.A.	51	F3
Savannakhet: Thai.	38	C4
Saverne: France	22	C2
Savigliano: Italy	25	B2
Savona: Italy	25	B3
Savonlinna: Finland	16	E3
Savoy: Old Prov.: Fr.	23	C2
Savoy Alps: mtns..	23	C2
Saw: Burma	38	A2
Sawankhalok: Thailand	38	B3
Sawara: Japan	39	g iv
Sawel: mtn. N. Irel.	13	D3
Sawu Sea: Indonesia	35	G12
Saxmundham: England	15	H2
Saxonville: U.S.A.	55	J2
Saxton: U.S.A.	54	B4
Sayabourly: Laos	38	B4
Sayama: Japan	39	f iv
Sayre: U.S.A.	54	D3
Sayreville: U.S.A.	55	H4
Sca Fell: mtn.. England	12	C2
Scalasaig: Scotland	11	B3
Scalloway: Shetland Islands	10	b i
Scalpay: i., Scotland	10	B3
Scapa Flow: anch.. Orkney Islands	10	d iv
Scarba: i., Scotland	11	C3
Scarborough: England	12	F2
Scariff I.: Irish Rep.	13	A5
Scarp I.: Scotland	10	A2
Scavaig Loch: Scot.	10	B3
Sceaux: France	22	B1
Schaffhausen: Ger. F.R.	25	B2
Scheffervville: Canada	47	W6
Scheldt: r., Neth.	24	A1

Name	Page	ref
Schenectady: U.S.A.	55	G2
Schiedam: Neth.	24	A1
Schiehallion: mtn.. Scotland	10	D3
Schio: Italy	25	C2
Schmalkalden: German D.R.	24	C1
Schorhane: & cr.. U.S.A.	55	F2
Schoonebeek: Neth.	24	B1
Schouwen Duiveland: i., Netherlands	24	A1
Schumacher: Canada	56	E1
Schuyler: U.S.A.	58	A3
Schuylkill Haven: U.S.A.	54	D4
Schwäbisch-Gmünd: German F.R.	25	B2
Schwandorf: Ger. F.R.	24	C2
Schwärbisch Hall: German F.R.	24	B2
Schweinfurt: Ger. F.R.	24	B2
Schweiningen: German F.R.	25	B2
Schwerin: Ger. D.R.	24	C1
Schwyz: Switzerland	25	B2
Scilly, Isles of: U.K.	14	c iii
Scituate: U.S.A.	55	K2
Scituate Reservoir: U.S.A.	55	J3
Scoresby Sound: Greenland	47	FF2
Scotia Sea: S. Atl. O.	8	G13
Scott I.: Southern O	44	G13
Scott Lake: Canada	60	D1
Scottsbluff: U.S.A.	53	E2
Scottsville: U.S.A.	54	C4
Scottstown: Canada	57	O4
Scoune: Scotland	10	C1
Scrabster: Scotland	10	C1
Scranton: U.S.A.	54	E3
Scridain, Loch: Scot.	11	B3
Scudder: Canada	56	C8
Scugog, Lake: Can.	56	G5
Scunthorpe: England	12	F3
Seabrook: U.S.A.	54	E5
Seaford: England	15	G4
Seaforth: Canada	56	D6
Seaforth, Loch: Scot.	10	B2
Sea Girt: U.S.A.	55	F4
Seaham: England	12	F2
Seal: r., Canada	61	F1
Seal, Cape: S. Africa	72	C5
Searchmont: Canada	56	A3
Searsport: U.S.A.	59	G3
Seascale: England	12	C2
Seaside: U.S.A.	62	B2
Seaside Heights: U.S.A.	55	F5
Seaton: England	14	C4
Seattle: U.S.A.	62	B2
Sebago Lake: U.S.A.	57	P6
Sebakwe: r., Zimb.	72	E2
Sebewaing: U.S.A.	56	B6
Sebha Oasis: Libya	68	H3
Sechura Desert: Peru	64	B5
Seco: r., Argentina	66	B2
Sedalia: U.S.A.	58	B4
Sedan: France	22	B2
Sedbergh: England	12	D2
Seefel: Austria	25	C2
Seeheim: Namibia	72	B4
Segamat: Malaysia	38	C5
Segovia: r., Hond./Nicaragua	49	K7
Segovia: Spain	19	B4
Ségre: r., Spain	19	C4
Segunda Punta: Arg.	66	C3
Segundo: r., Arg.	66	B3
Segura: r., Spain	19	B5
Seidan: Japan	39	a ii
Seil: i., Scotland	11	C3
Seinäjoki: Finland	16	D3
Seine: r., France	22	B2
Sekondi-Takoradi: Ghana	68	E7
Selby: England	12	E3
Selden: U.S.A.	55	G4
Selenga: r., Mong	34	C2
Sélestat: France	22	C2
Selety-Tengiz, Lake: U.S.S.R.	29	L3
Selinsgrove: U.S.A.	54	D4
Selkirk: Canada	61	F2
Selkirk: Scotland	11	F4
Selkirk Mts.: Canada	62	C1
Sellersville: U.S.A.	54	E4
Sellwood: Canada	56	E1
Selma: U.S.A.	51	E3
Selsey Bill: hd., Eng.	15	F4
Selukwe: Zimbabwe	72	E2
Selva: Argentina	66	B2
Selvas: geog. reg.: Brazil	64	F5
Semarang: Indon.	35	E12
Seminoe Reservoir: U.S.A.	53	D2
Semiozernoye: U.S.S.R.	29	J3
Semipalatinsk: U.S.S.R.	29	N3
Semnän: r., Iran	30	G6
Senanga: Zambia	72	C1
Sendai: Honshu. Japan	39	D2
Sendai: Kyushu. Japan	39	B3
Seneca Falls: town. U.S.A.	54	D3
Seneca Lake: U.S.A.	54	D3
SENEGAL	68	B6
Senegal: r., Maur./Senegal	68	C5
Senja: i., Norway	16	C2
Senlis: France	22	B1
Sennar Dam: Sudan	69	M6
Sennetere: Canada	56	H1
Sens: France	22	B2
SEOUL (Kyongsong): S. Korea	36	H3
Sept Iles: town. Canada	47	W6
Sequoia Nat. Park: U.S.A.	63	C4
Serang: Indonesia	35	D12
Seremban: Malaysia	38	C6
Serengeti Nat. Park: Tanzania	71	F8
Séres: Brunei	35	E10
Sermo: Italy	29	C3
Serov: U.S.S.R.	28	H3
Serowe: Botswana	72	D3
Serpa Pinto: Angola	72	B1
Serra da Apucarana: ra., Brazil	66	D1
Serra da Fartura: r..	66	D2
Serra da Mantiqueira: ra., Brazil	66	a i

Name	Page	ref
Serra da Pitanga: ra. Brazil	66	D1
Serra de Maracaju: ra. Brazil	66	C1
Serra do Cangucu: ra. Brazil	66	D3
Serro do Espinhilo: ra. Brazil	66	C2
Serra do Lagarto: ra. Brazil	66	D1
Serra do Mar: ra. Rio de Janeiro, Brazil	66	b i
Serra do Mar: ra. Santa Catarina, Braz	66	E2
Serra do Paranapiacaba: ra. Brazil	66	E1
Serra dos Parecis: ra. Brazil	64	F6
Serra dos Dourados: ra. Brazil	66	D1
Serra Geral: ra. Braz	66	D2
Serrai: Greece	21	D4
Serra Vermelha: ra. Brazil	66	D1
Serrezuela: Argentina	66	A3
Serro das Encantadas: ra. Brazil	66	D3
Serro do Navio: Braz	64	H3
Sestriere: Italy	25	B2
Sète: France	23	B3
Sétif: Algeria	19	D5
Seto-naikai (Inland Sea): Japan	39	B3
Seto-naikai- kokuritsu-köen nat. park. Japan	39	a ii
Seto-naikai- kokuritsu-köen nat. park. Japan	39	a ii
Settle: England	12	D2
Setúbal: Portugal	19	A5
Seul. Lac: Canada	58	B1
Sevan. Lake: U.S.S.R	28	F5
Sevastopol': U.S.S.R	28	C5
Seven Heads: hd. Irish Republic	13	C5
Sevenoaks: England	15	G3
Severn: r. Canada	61	G2
Severn: r. England	14	D3
Severnaya Zemlya: is. U.S.S.R.	27	M2
Severomorsk: U.S.S.R	16	F2
Severoural'sk: U.S.S.R	29	J1
Sevier: r. & lake. U.S.A.	63	D4
Seville: Spain	19	A5
Sèvre Nantaise: r. France	23	A2
Sèvre Niortaise: r. France	23	A2
Sèvres: France	22	B2
Seward: U.S.A.	46	F4
Seward Peninsula: U.S.A.	46	C3
Sexsmith: Canada	60	B1
SEYCHELLES	33	d v
Seychelles-Mauritius Plateau: Ind. Ocean	33	e vi
Seydhisfjördhur: Ice.	16	c i
Seymour: Conn. U.S.A.	55	G3
Seymour: Tex. U.S.A	50	G5
Sézanne: France	22	B2
Sfax: Tunisia	68	H2
's Gravenhage see The Hague		
Sgurr Mor: mtn. Scotland	10	D2
Sgurr na Ciche: mtn. Scotland	10	C3
Sha Alam: Malaysia	38	C6
Shaftesbury: England	14	D3
Shagan: Nigeria	67	A1
Shah Faisalabad: Pak	32	B2
Shahjahanpur: India	32	C3
Shaho: China	36	B2
Shahrüd: Iran	28	H6
Shahsien: China	37	C4
Shalym: U.S.S.R	28	E4
Shamattawa: Canada	61	G1
Shamokin: U.S.A.	54	D4
Shamrock: U.S.A.	50	B2
Shamva: Zimbabwe	72	E2
Shandong see Shantung		
Shangani: Zimbabwe	72	D2
Shangcheng: China	36	C3
Shangchow: China	36	A3
Shanghai: China	37	D3
Shanghai Shih: Prov. China	37	D3
Shanghang: China	37	C4
Shangho: China	36	C3
Shanghsien: China	36	A3
Shangjao: China	37	C4
Shangkao: China	37	C3
Shangkiu: China	36	C3
Shanglin: China	37	A5
Shangshui: China	36	B3
Shangse: China	37	A5
Shangtu: China	36	B1
Shangyu: China	37	B4
Shanhaikuan: China	36	C2
Shanhsien: China	36	B3
Shanklin: England	15	E4
Shannon: r. Irish Republic	13	C4
Shannon Airport: Irish Republic	13	B4
Shannon Airport: Irish Republic	13	B4
Shannon, Mouth of the: Irish Republic	13	B4
Shansi (Shänxi): Prov. China	36	B2
Shan States: Burma	38	B2
Shantung (Shandong): Prov. China	36	C2
Shantung Penin.: China	36	D2
Shänxi: Prov. see Shansi		
Shensi	36	B2
Shanyin: China	36	A2
Shaohing: China	37	D3
Shaokuan: China	37	C4
Shaowu: China	37	C4
Shaoyang: China	37	B4
Shap: England	12	D2
Shapinsay: i. Orkney Islands	10	e iii
Sharbot Lake: Can.	57	J5
Sharjah: U.A.E.	30	G5
Sharon: Conn. U.S.A.	55	G3
Sharon: Mass. U.S.A	55	J2
Sharon: Pa. U.S.A	59	D3
Sharpnose Pts.: England	14	B4
Shasi: China	37	B3
Shasta, Mount: U.S.A.	63	B3
Shasta Lake: U.S.A.	63	B3

Name	Page	ref
Shatsky Rise: Pac. O.	44	F3
Shatt al Arab: r. Iraq/Iran	30	E4
Shattuck: U.S.A.	50	C2
Shaunavon: Canada	60	D3
Shawnee: Ill. U.S.A.	58	C4
Shawnee: Okla. U.S.A.	50	C2
Shayang, Lake: China	36	C3
Sheboygan: U.S.A	58	C3
Sheefry Hills: Irish Republic	13	B3
Sheelin, Lough: Irish Republic	13	D3
Sheep Haven: bay. Irish Republic	13	D1
Sheerness: England	15	G3
Sheffield: England	15	E1
Sheffield: Ala. U.S.A.	51	E3
Sheffield: Mass. U.S.A.	55	G2
Sheffield: Pa. U.S.A.	56	F8
Sheffield Junction: U.S.A.	56	G8
Shefford: Co. Can	57	N4
Shefford: England	15	F2
Shehun: Nigeria	67	C1
Shekki: China	37	B5
Sheklung: China	37	B5
Shelburne: Canada	56	E5
Shelby: U.S.A	62	D2
Shelbyville: U.S.A.	51	E3
Sheldon Springs: sett. U.S.A.	57	N5
Shelekov Bay: U.S.S.R	27	S5
Shellbrook: Canada	60	D2
Shelley: U.S.A	62	D3
Shellharbour: Austl.	43	D4
Shelton: Conn. U.S.A.	55	G3
Shelton: Wash. U.S.A.	62	B3
Shemankar: r. Nig.	67	B2
Shenandoah: r. U.S.A.	59	E4
Shenandoah Nat. Park: U.S.A.	59	E4
Shenchih: China	36	B2
Shendam: Nigeria	67	B2
Shendi: Sudan	69	M5
Shenkiu: China	36	C3
Shenmu: China	36	B2
Shensi (Shänxi): Prov. China	36	A2
Shenyang see Mukden	36	D1
Shepetovka: U.S.S.R	20	E2
Shepherdston: U.S.A.	54	C5
Sheppaerton: Austl.	43	C5
Sheppey, Isle of: England	15	G3
Shepshed: England	15	E2
Shepton Mallet: England	14	D3
Sherbrooke: & Co. Canada	57	O4
Sherborne: England	14	D4
Sherburne: U.S.A	54	E2
Shere Hill: Nigeria	67	B2
Sheridan: U.S.A.	52	D2
Sheringham: England	15	H2
Sherkin I.: Irish Rep.	13	B5
Sherlovaya Gora: U.S.S.R.	27	O7
Sherman: Canada	50	C2
Sherridon: Canada	61	E1
Sherrill: U.S.A.	54	E1
's-Hertogenbosch: Netherlands	24	B1
Sherwood: U.S.A	61	E3
Shetland Islands: Scot.	10	Ins.
Shetucket: r. U.S.A.	55	H3
Shevchenko: U.S.S.R	28	G5
Sheyenne: r. U.S.A	52	F1
Shiant Is.: Scotland	10	B3
Shiant Sound: Scot.	10	B3
Shibeli: r. Som. Rep.	69	D1
Shibetsu: Japan	39	D1
Shiel, Loch: Scotland	10	C3
Shiel: r. Scotland	10	C2
Shieldaig: Scotland	10	C2
Shifnal: England	14	D2
Shiga: & Pref. Japan	39	b i
Shigaraki: Japan	39	c ii
Shigatse: China	32	E3
Shihchan: China	27	P7
Shihchu: China	37	A3
Shihchuan: China	36	A3
Shihkiachwang: China	36	B2
Shihlung: China	37	A5
Shihmen: China	37	B4
Shihping: China	37	A4
Shihtao: China	36	D2
Shijiazhuang see Shihkiachwang	36	B2
Shikoku: i. Japan	39	B3
Shikotsu-toya- kokuritsu-köen: nat. park. Japan	39	D1
Shillong: India	32	F3
Shima: Japan	39	c ii
Shima-Hanto: penin. Japan	39	c ii
Shimizu: Japan	39	C2
Shimoga: India	32	C6
Shimonota: Japan	39	e iii
Shimonoseki: Japan	39	A2
Shimotsuma: Japan	39	f iii
Shin, Loch: Scotland	10	D1
Shinglehouse: U.S.A	54	B1
Shingu: Japan	39	C3
Shinjo: Japan	39	D2
Shiogama: Japan	39	D2
Shiono-zaki: cape. Japan	39	C3
Ship Bottom: U.S.A.	55	F5
Shipki Pass: China/India	32	C2
Shipley: England	12	E3
Shippensburg: U.S.A	54	C4
Shipshaw: Canada	59	F2
Shipston on Stour: England	15	E2
Shirakawa: Japan	39	D2
Shiraoi: Japan	39	D1
Shiräz: Iran	30	F5
Shire: r. Malawi/Mozambique	72	E2
Shitoumiao: China	36	A1
Shizunai: Japan	39	D1
Shizuoka: Japan	39	C3
Shkodër: Albania	21	C4
Shoal Lake: sett. Canada	61	E2
Shoal Lake: Canada	61	E2
Shoal. Lakes: Canada	61	E2
Shoalwater Bay: Austl.	42	D3
Shoebury Ness: penin. England	15	G3
Shoemakersville: U.S.A.	54	E4

Name	Page	ref
Shohsien: China	36	B2
Sholapur: India	32	C5
Shoreham-by-Sea: England	15	F4
Shortland Is.: Solomon Islands	40	K2
Shouhsien: China	36	C3
Showyang: China	36	B2
Shreveport: U.S.A	50	D3
Shrewsbury: England	14	D2
Shrewsbury: U.S.A	55	J2
Shrub Oak: U.S.A.	55	G3
Shu: r. China	37	B4
Shuangfeng: China	37	B4
Shucheng: China	37	C3
Shuichi: China	37	C4
Shulu: China	36	C3
Shunan: China	37	C4
Shunchang: China	37	C4
Shuni: Nigeria	67	B1
Shuntak: China	37	B5
Shuswap Lake: Canada	62	C1
Shuyang: China	36	C3
Shuzenji: Japan	39	e v
Shwangkiao: China	34	d2
Shwebo: Burma	38	B2
Si: r. China	37	B5
Sialkot: Pakistan	32	B2
Sian, Gulf of: Mal./Thailand	38	C4
Sian (Xi'an): China	36	A3
Siang: r. Hunan, China	37	B4
Siang: r. Kwangsi Chuang, China	37	A5
Siangfan: China	36	B3
Siangsiang: China	37	B4
Siangtan: China	37	B4
Siangyang: China	36	B3
Siaokan: China	37	B3
Siaotsing: r. China	36	C2
Siapu: China	37	C4
Siauliai: U.S.S.R	17	C4
Sibenik: Yugoslavia	21	C4
Sibi: Pakistan	32	A3
Sibiu: Romania	20	D3
Sibley: U.S.A	58	A3
Sibolga: Indonesia	38	A6
Sibsagar: India	38	A1
Sibu: Sarawak, Mal.	38	E6
Siccus: r. Australia	43	A4
Sichuan: Prov. see Szechwan	37	A4
Sichwan: China	36	B3
Sicilian Channel: Sicily	21	B5
Sicily: i. Italy	21	B5
Sidi-bel-Abbès: Alg	19	B5
Sidlaw Hills: Scotland	10	E3
Sidmouth: England	14	C4
Sidney: N.Y. U.S.A	54	E2
Sidney: N. Dak. U.S.A.	53	E1
Sidney Lanier, Lake: U.S.A.	51	J3
Skies: Norway	17	C2
Skipton: England	12	D2
Sidra: & gulf. Libya	69	J2
Siedlce: Poland	20	D2
Sieg: r. Ger. F.R	24	B1
Siegburg: Ger. F.R.	24	B1
Siegen: Ger. F.R.	24	B1
Siem Reap: Kampuchea	38	C4
Siena: Italy	21	B4
Sienfeng: China	37	A4
Sienku: China	37	D4
Sienning: China	37	B4
Sienyang: China	36	A3
Siero: Spain	19	A4
Siete Puntas: r. Par.	66	D5
Sifton: Canada	61	E2
Sighet Marmatiei: Romania	20	D3
Sigiriya: Sri Lanka	32	b ii
Siglufjördhur: Iceland	16	B1
Sigüenza: Spain	19	B4
Sihsien: China	37	C4
Sihwa: China	36	B3
Siirt: Turkey	28	E6
Sikhote Alin' Range: U.S.S.R.	27	Q8
Sikkim: State. India	32	E3
Silchar: India	33	F4
Silistra: Bulgaria	21	E4
Siljan: lake. Sweden	17	C3
Silkeston: U.S.A.	58	C4
Sillamäe: U.S.S.R	17	E4
Silloth: England	12	C2
Silsden: England	12	D2
Silver Bay: town. U.S.A.	58	B2
Silver Bell: U.S.A.	63	D5
Silver City: U.S.A	52	D4
Silver Creek: sett. U.S.A.	56	F7
Silvermine Mts.: Irish Republic	13	C4
Silver Peak: town. U.S.A.	63	C4
Silver Spring: town. U.S.A.	54	C5
Silverstone: England	15	E2
Silverton: Colo. U.S.A	52	D3
Silverton: Ore. U.S.A	62	B3
Simanggang: Sarawak, Malaysia	38	E6
Simcoe: Canada	56	E6
Simcoe. Co.: Canada	56	E5
Simcoe, Lake: Can.	56	F5
Simeulue: i. Indon.	38	A6
Simferopol': U.S.S.R	28	C5
Simla: India	32	C2
Simon, Lac: Canada	57	K2
Simonstown: S. Africa	72	B5
Simoom Sound: town. Canada	60	A1
Simplon Pass: Switz	25	B2
Simpson Desert: Australia	41	F5
Simpson Island: Can.	58	C2
Simsbury: U.S.A.	55	H3
Sinabang: Indonesia	38	A6
Sinai: mt. Egypt	30	B5
Sinaia: Romania	21	D3
Sincheng: China	37	D4
Sincheng: China	34	A5
Sinclair, Mt.: Canada	56	F8
Sinclair's Bay: Scot.	10	E1
Sind: Prov. Pakistan	32	A3
Sinfeng: China	37	B4
Singan see Sian	38	C6
SINGAPORE	38	C6
Singaradja: Indonesia	35	F12
Sing Buri: Thailand	38	B4
Singen: Ger. F.R.	25	B2
Singida Hkamti: Burma	38	B2
Singkawang: Indon.	38	D6
Singkep: i. Indonesia	38	C11
Singleton: Australia	43	D4
Singtai: China	36	B2
Singtze: China	37	B4
Sinhwa: China	37	B4
Sining: China	34	C3

Name	Page	ref
Sinkiang: China	36	B2
Sinkiang-Uighur Aut. Reg.: China	31	M2
Sinnady, Lake: Pol.	20	D2
Sinop: Turkey	28	D5
Sintai: China	36	C2
Sintang: Indonesia	38	E7
Sintien: China	37	B4
Sintu: China	37	B5
Sinuiju: N. Korea	34	G3
Sinyang: China	36	B3
Sinyeh: China	36	B3
Sion: Switzerland	25	B2
Sion Mills: N. Ireland	13	D2
Sioux City: U.S.A	58	A3
Sioux Falls: city. U.S.A.	58	A3
Sioux Lookout: Can	58	B1
Siping: China	36	B3
Sipiwesk: & lake. Can	61	F1
Siqueira Campos: Brazil	66	E1
Sira: r. Norway	17	A4
Sirahama: Japan	39	f v
Siretul: r. Romania	20	E3
Sirte: Libya	68	J2
Sir Wilfrid Laurier, Mt.: Canada	60	B2
Sisak: Yugoslavia	21	C3
Sishen: South Africa	72	C4
Sisiang: China	36	A3
Sisophon: Kampuchea	38	C4
Sisseton: U.S.A	58	A2
Sistan: geog. reg. Iran	30	H4
Sistema Ibérico: mtns. Spain	19	B4
Sisteron: France	23	C3
Sitapur: India	32	D3
Sitges: Spain	19	C4
Sittang: r. Burma	38	B3
Sittingbourne: Eng	15	G3
Siuan: China	37	B4
Siushui: China	37	B4
Sivas: Turkey	28	D6
Siverskiy: U.S.S.R	17	F4
Siwa: Egypt	69	L3
Skagerrak: str. Denmark/Norway	17	A4
Skagway: U.S.A	46	H5
Skanderborg: Denmark	17	A4
Skåne: geog. reg. Sweden	17	C4
Skaneateles: & lake. U.S.A.	54	D2
Skeena: r. Canada	46	K6
Skegness: England	12	G2
Skelleftee: r. Sweden	16	C2
Skellefteå: Sweden	16	D2
Skelmersdale: Eng	12	D2
Skernes: Irish Rep	13	E3
Ski: Norway	17	B4
Skibbereen: Irish Republic	13	B5
Skiddaw: mtn. Eng	12	C2
Skien: Norway	17	A4
Skipton: England	12	D2
Skiros: r. Greece	21	D5
Skive: Denmark	17	A4
Skokholm I.: Wales	14	A3
Skomer I.: Wales	14	A3
Skopje: Yugoslavia	21	D4
Skovde: Sweden	17	C4
Skowhegan: U.S.A	57	Q5
Skownan: Canada	61	F2
Skye: i. Scotland	10	B2
Slagelse: Denmark	17	A4
Slaney: r. Irish Rep	13	E4
Slantsy: U.S.S.R	17	E4
Slate Islands: Canada	58	C2
Slatington: U.S.A	54	E4
Slave: r. Canada		
Slave Lake: town. Canada	60	C1
Slavonski Brod: Yugoslavia	21	C3
Sleaford: England	13	F2
Slea Hd.: Irish Rep	13	A4
Sleat, Pt. of: Scot	10	C2
Sleat, Sound of: Scotland	10	C2
Sleetmute: U.S.A	46	D4
Slieve Anierin: mtn. Irish Republic	13	D2
Slieve Aughty Mts.: Irish Republic	13	C3
Slieve Beagh: N. Irel	13	D2
Slieve Bloom: mtns. Irish Republic	13	D3
Slieve Car: mtn. Irish Republic	13	B2
Slieve Donard: mtn. N. Ireland	13	F1
Slieve Elva: mtn. Irish Republic	13	B3
Slievefelim Mts.: Irish Republic	13	C4
Slieve Gallion: mtn. N. Ireland	13	E1
Slieve Gamph: mtn. Irish Republic	13	C2
Slieve Golden: mtn. N. Ireland	13	E2
Slieve Mish Mts.: Irish Republic	13	B4
Slievenamon: mtn. Irish Republic	13	D4
Slieve Rushen: mtn. N. Ireland	13	D2
Slieve Snaght: mtn. Irish Republic	13	D1
Sligo & Co.: Irish Rep	13	C2
Sligo Bay: Irish Republic	13	C2
Slioch: mtn. Scot.	10	C2
Sliven: Bulgaria	21	E4
Slocan: Canada	62	D1
Slough: England	15	F3
Slutsk: U.S.S.R	20	E2
Slyne Head: Irish Republic	13	A3
Smederevo: Yugoslavia	21	D4
Smith: r. U.S.A	62	D1
Smith, Cape: Canada	61	L3
Smithfield: U.S.A	63	D3
Smith Mountain Reservoir: U.S.A.	59	E4
Smiths Falls: town. Canada	57	J5
Smoky: r. Canada	60	B1
Smoky: r. U.S.A	50	C2
Smoky Falls: town. Canada	59	D1
Smoky Hill: r. U.S.A	53	E3
Smoky Lake: Canada	60	C2
Smøla: i. Norway	16	B2
Smolensk: U.S.S.R	28	C3
Smyrna: U.S.A	54	E4
Snag: Canada	46	H4
Snake: r. U.S.A	62	C3
Snake Lake: Canada	60	D1

Name	Page	ref
Snaefell: mtn. Isle of Man	12	B2
Sniadwy, Lake: Pol.	20	D2
Snizort, Loch: Scot	10	B2
Snowdon: mtn. Wales	14	B1
Snowdonia Nat. Park: Wales	14	C2
Snow Lake: sett. Canada	61	E2
Snow Mountain: U.S.A.	57	P4
Snowy: r. Australia	43	C5
Snowy Mts.: Austl	43	C5
Snuol: Kampuchea	38	D4
Snyder: U.S.A.	50	B3
Soar: r. England	15	E2
Soay Sound: Scotland	10	B2
Soba: Nigeria	67	B1
Sobat: r. Sudan/Ethiopia	69	M7
Sobue: Japan	39	c i
Soche (Yarkand): China	31	L3
Sochi: U.S.S.R.	28	D5
Society Is.: Pac. O.	45	K8
Socotra: i. Arabian Sea	30	F8
Socorro: U.S.A	52	D4
Soda Mts.: Libya	68	H3
Sodankylä: Finland	16	E2
Soda Springs: town. U.S.A.	62	D3
Söderhamn: Sweden	17	C3
Södertälje: Sweden	17	C4
Soest: Ger. F.R	24	B1
Soest: Netherlands	24	B1
Sofala (Beira): Moz.	72	E2
SOFIYA: Bulgaria	21	D4
Sognafjorden: fd. Norway	17	A3
Sogndal: Norway	16	A3
Soham: England	15	G2
Soissons: France	22	B2
Söke: Turkey	21	E5
Sokol: U.S.S.R	28	E2
Sokoto: & State. Nigeria	67	B1
Sokoto: r. Nigeria	67	B1
Soledade: Brazil	66	D2
Solent, The: channel. England	15	E4
Soligorsk: U.S.S.R	20	E2
Solihull: England	15	E2
Solikamsk: U.S.S.R	28	H2
Sol'-iletsk: U.S.S.R	28	H3
Solimões: r. see Amazon	64	E4
Solingen: Ger. F.R	24	B1
Sollefteå: Sweden	16	C3
Sologne: geog. reg. France	22	B2
Solomon: r. U.S.A	50	C2
SOLOMON ISLANDS	40	K/L2
Solomon Rise: Pac. O.	44	K8
Solon: U.S.A	56	D8
Solothurn: Switzerland	25	B2
Solway Firth: est. England	12	C2
Somali Basin: Indian Ocean	33	d iv
SOMALI REPUBLIC	69	P8
Sombor: Yugoslavia	20	C3
Sombrero: i. & passage. W. Indies	49	O6
Sombrio: Brazil	66	E2
Sombrio, Lagoa do: Brazil	66	E2
Somerset: Canada	61	F3
Somerset: Ky. U.S.A.	58	D4
Somerset: Mass. U.S.A.	55	J3
Somerset: Co. Eng.	14	C3
Somerset East: S. Afr.	72	D5
Somerset I.: Canada	47	R2
Somerset Reservoir: U.S.A.	55	H1
Somers Point: town. U.S.A.	54	F5
Somersworth: U.S.A	55	K1
Somerton: England	14	D3
Somerville: U.S.A	55	H3
Someşul: r. Rom.	20	D3
Somme: r. France	22	B2
Sommières: France	23	B3
Son: r. India	32	D4
Sønderborg: Denmark	17	A5
Søndre Strømfjord: Greenland	47	Z3
Sondrio: Italy	25	B2
Songea: Tanzania	71	G10
Songkhla: Thailand	38	C5
Son La: Vietnam	38	C2
Sonobe: Japan	39	b i
Sonora: Mexico	63	D5
Sonwald: mtn. Ger. F.R	24	B2
Sopot: Poland	20	C2
Sopron: Hungary	20	C3
Sorel: Canada	57	M3
Soria: Spain	19	B4
Soriano: Uruguay	66	C3
Sorocaba: Brazil	66	a ii
Soroki: U.S.S.R	20	E3
Sørøya: i. Norway	16	D1
Sorrento: Italy	21	B4
Sorsele: Sweden	16	C2
Sortavala: U.S.S.R	17	F3
Sos'va: U.S.S.R	29	J2
Souderton: U.S.A	54	E4
Souk Ahras: Algeria	19	D5
Sounding Lake: Canada	60	C2
South: r. Canada	56	F7
Southam: England	15	E2
Southampton: Canada	56	E5
Southampton: England	15	E4
Southampton: U.S.A	55	H4
Southampton I.: Can	47	T4
South Atlantic Ocean	78	—
South Australia: state. Australia	40	E/F 6
South Australian Basin: Pac. O	44	B10
South Baymouth: Canada	56	C4
South Bend: U.S.A	58	C3
South Benfleet: Eng	15	G3
South Berwick: U.S.A.	55	K1
Southborough: Eng	15	G3
South Boston: U.S.A	51	L2
South Branch Mtn.: U.S.A.	54	B5
South Branch Potomac: r. U.S.A	59	E4
Southbridge: U.S.A	55	H2
South Carolina: State. U.S.A.	51	K3
South Cave: Eng	12	F2
South China Sea	35	E8
South Dakota: State. U.S.A.	53	E2
South Dayton: U.S.A	56	F7

Name	Page
South Deerfield: U.S.A.	55
South Dorset Downs: hills. England	14
South Downs: hills. England	15
South Fork: U.S.A	54
Southeast Indian Basin: Ind. O	33 j
Southeast Indian Ridge: Ind. O	33 h
Southeast Pacific Basin: Pac. O	44 0
South East Point: Australia	43
Southend: Canada	61
Southend-on-Sea	
Southern Alps: N.Z	41
Southern Cross: Austl	42
Southern Indian Lake: sett. & I.: Canada	61
Southern Ocean	33
Southern Sierra: Mex	48 L
Southern Uplands: Scotland	11
Southey: Canada	60
South Fiji Basin: Pacific Ocean	44
South Foreland: hd. England	15
South Georgia: i. Atlantic Ocean	65 L
S. Glamorgan: Co. Wales	14
South Hadley: U.S.A	55
South Indian Basin	33
South Island: N.Z	41
South Knife: r. Can	61
SOUTH KOREA	34
Southland: Dist. N.Z	41
South Lyon: U.S.A	56
South Molton: Eng	14
Southold: U.S.A	55
South Orkney Is.: Southern Ocean	65 J
South Pacific Ocean	44/5
South Paris: U.S.A	57
South Platte: r. U.S.A.	53
South Pearl: r. China	37
South Point: U.S.A	56
South Porcupine: Can	59
Southport: Australia	42
Southport: England	12
South Portland: U.S.A	57
South Ridge: U.S.A	57
South River: sett. Canada	56
South River: town. U.S.A	54
South Ronaldsay: i. Orkney Islands	10
South Sandwich Is.: Southern Ocean	65 N
South Sandwich Trench: S. Atl. O	8 H
South Saskatchewan: r. Canada	60
South Seal: r. Canada	61
South Shetland Is.: Southern Ocean	65 G
South Shields: Eng	12
South Sioux City: U.S.A	58
South Sound: Irish Republic	13
S. Tyne: r. England	12
South Uist: i. Scot.	10
Southwark: England	15
Southwell: England	15
South-West Africa now NAMIBIA	72
Southwest Cape: N.Z	41
Southwest Indian Ridge: Ind. O	33 c
Southwest Pacific Basin: Pac. O	45 K
South Windham: U.S.A.	57
Southwold: England	15
South Yorkshire: Co. England	12
Sovetsk: U.S.S.R	17
Soviet Harbour: U.S.S.R	27
Sowerby Bridge: Eng	12
SPAIN	19
Spalding: England	15
Spandau: Ger. F.R	24
Spangler: U.S.A	54
Spanish: Canada	56
Spanish: r. Canada	56
Spanish Head: I. of Man	12
Spanish Town: Jamaica	49
Sparks: U.S.A	63
Sparrows Point: town. U.S.A.	54
Spartanburg: U.S.A	51
Spärti: Greece	21
Spartivento, Cape: Italy	21
Spartivento, C.: Sard	19
Spasskoye: U.S.S.R	39
Speed: U.S.A	58
Speedwell, Cape: U.S.S.R.	
Speers: Canada	60
Spencer: Iowa, U.S.A.	58
Spencer Gulf: Austl	40
Spencer: Mountains: New Zealand	41
Spenser Mountains: New Zealand	
Sperrin Mts.: N. Irel	13
Sounds, The: N.Z	41
Soundview: U.S.A	55
Sousa: r. Canada/U.S.A.	
Sousse: Tunisia	68
Spessart: r. Ger. F.R	24
Spey: r. Scotland	10
Speyer: German F.R	24
Spiekeroog: i. German F.R	24
Spilsby: England	15
Spirit River: town. Canada	
Spitsbergen (Svalbard): is. Arctic Ocean	26
Spittal: Austria	25
Split: Yugoslavia	21
Split Lake: sett. & I.: Canada	61
Splügen Pass: Italy/Switzerland	25
Spokane: U.S.A	62
Spoleto: Italy	21
Spragge: Canada	56
Spree: r. Ger. D.R	24

Spring/Texoma, Lake 93

	Page	ref
ng r, U S A	58	B4
ngbok S Africa	72	B4
ngdale Ark, S A	58	B4
nger U S A	53	E3
ngfield Colo, S A	53	E3
ngfield Ill, U S A	58	C4
ngfield Mass, S A	55	H2
ngfield Mo, S A	58	B4
ngfield Ohio, S A	58	D4
ngfield Oreg, S A	62	B3
ngfield Vt, U S A	55	H1
ngsure Australia	42	C2
ng Valley town, S A	55	F3
ngville N Y, S A	54	B2
ngville Utah, S A	63	D3
ice Woods rovincial Park Can	61	F3
ngabera Moz	72	E3
rn Head England	12	G3
amish Canada	62	B2
am Lake U S A	57	O6
aw Rapids Hydro am Canada	61	E2
LANKA	32	–
ensk U S S R	27	O7
hsien China	36	C3
shui China	36	C2
tzuwang Chi nina	36	B1
k, Loch Scotland	10	D1
kpool Canada	56	D2
ks Mts Irish Rep	13	B4
le German F R	24	B1
ford England	14	D2
fordshire Co, ngland	14	D2
ford Springs town, S A	55	H3
nes England	15	F3
bridge England	14	D4
worthy Cape anada	47	R0
nford England	15	F2
nford Conn, S A	55	G3
nford N Y, S A	54	F2
nford Bridge Eng	12	F2
nbridge Station anada	57	M4
ndish U S A	56	B6
nhope England	12	D2
hope U S A	54	F4
ke Dimitrov ulgaria	21	D4
nley England	12	E2
NLEY Falkland lands	65	G14
nstead Co, Can	57	N4
nsted England	15	G3
nthorpe Australia	43	D3
achowice Poland	20	D2
a Zagora Bulgaria	21	E4
City Canada	61	E2
gard Szczeciński oland	20	C2
nberg Ger F R	25	C2
ogard Gdański Pol	20	C2
t Bay England	14	C4
t Point England	14	C4
t Point Orkney lands, Scotland	9	C1
ssfurt Ger D R	24	C1
e College U S A	54	C4
esboro U S A	51	F3
esville U S A	51	F2
unton U S A	59	E4
vanger Norway	17	A4
veley England	15	E1
velot Belgium	22	C1
vropol' U S S R	28	E4
well Australia	43	B5
vner Canada	56	E5
bbins U S A	46	C4
elton U S A	54	D4
gerwald hills, erman F R	24	C2
nbach Canada	61	F3
nkjer Norway	16	B3
llenbosch S Afr	72	B5
vio Nat Park aly	25	C2
vio Pass Italy	25	C2
ndal Ger D R	24	C1
phens City U S A	54	B5
ppes geog reg, S S R	29	
ling U S A	53	E2
ling Ill, U S A	58	C3
litamak U S S R	28	H3
tler Canada	62	D1
ubenville U S A	59	D3
venage England	15	F3
vens Point town, I S A	58	C3
venston Scotland	11	D4
wart Island N Z	41	A4
wart Is olomon Islands	40	L2
warton Scotland	11	D4
wartstown N Irel	13	E2
wartstown U S A	54	D5
yr Austria	25	C2
water N Y, U S A	55	G2
water Okla, S A	50	C2
water Creek Can	60	D3
on England	15	F2
char r, Scotland	11	D4
Yugoslavia	21	D4
ing Alta, Canada	62	D2
ing Ont, Canada	56	H5
ing Scotland	11	E3
ing, Mt Austl	42	b ii
ing Range Austl	42	b ii
ing Ranges Nat ark Australia	42	b ii
ckbridge England	15	E3
ckbridge U S A	55	G2
CKHOLM Sweden	17	C4
ckport England	12	D3
cksbridge England	12	E3
cks Reservoir Eng	12	D3
ckton Calif, U S A	63	B4
ckton Utah, U S A	63	D3
ckton-on-Tees ngland	12	E2
kton Plateau S A	50	B3
er hd, Scotland	10	C1
kenchurch England	15	F3
ke-on-Trent Eng	14	D2
kesley England	12	E2
e England	14	D2
necliffe Canada	56	H3
ne Harbor U S A	54	F5
nehaven Scot	10	F3
Stonehenge hist, England	15	E3
Stonehouse England	14	D3
Stonewall Canada	61	F2
Stonington U S A	55	J3
Stony Brook U S A	55	G4
Stony Creek town, U S A	55	H3
Stony, Lake Man, Canada	61	F1
Stony Lake Ont Can	56	G5
Stony Mountain Can	61	F2
Stony Plain town, Canada	60	C2
Stony Point town, U S A	55	G3
Stony Rapids town, Canada	61	D1
Stony Tunguska r, U S S R	27	M5
Stora Lule Lake Sweden	16	C2
Størdalshalsen Nor	16	B3
Store Bælt str, Denmark	17	B4
Stor Lake Sweden	16	B3
Stormont Co, Canada	57	L4
Stornoway Scotland	10	B1
Storr mtn, Scotland	10	B2
Storuman & lake, Sweden	16	C2
Stouffville Canada	56	F6
Stoughton Canada	61	E3
Stoughton U S A	55	J2
Stour r, Dorset, England	14	D4
Stour r, Essex, England	15	H3
Stourbridge Eng	14	D2
Stourport-on-Severn England	14	D2
Stout, Lake Canada	61	G2
Stowmarket England	15	H2
Stow-on-the-Wold England	15	E3
Strabane N Ireland	13	D2
Stradbally Irish Republic	13	D3
Strafford U S A	55	J1
Straits of Dover (Pays de Calais) England/France	15	H3
Strangford Lough N Ireland	13	F2
Stranorlar Irish Rep	13	D2
Stranraer Scotland	11	C5
Strasbourg France	22	C2
Strasbourg Canada	61	E2
Strasburg Pa, U S A	54	D5
Strasburg Va, U S A	54	B6
Stratford Canada	56	E6
Stratford N Z	41	B2
Stratford U S A	55	G3
Stratford-upon-Avon England	15	E2
Strathaven Scotland	11	D4
Strathclyde Reg, Scotland	11/12	B3
Strathcona Provincial Park Canada	62	A2
Strathmore Canada	62	D1
Strathmore val, Scotland	10	F3
Strathroy Canada	56	D7
Strath Tay r, Scot	10	E3
Strathy r, Scotland	10	D1
Strathy Point Scot	10	E1
Stratton England	14	B4
Straubing Ger F R	24	C2
Strawberry Mt U S A	62	C3
Street England	14	D3
Stresa Italy	25	B2
Strobl Austria	25	C2
Strokestown Irish Republic	13	C3
Stroma i, Scotland	10	E1
Stromboli volc, Italy	21	C5
Stromeferry Scotland	10	C2–3
Stromness Ork Is, Scotland	9	C1
Strömsund Sweden	16	C3
Stronsay i & firth, Orkney Islands	10	e iii
Stroud England	14	D3
Stroudsburg U S A	54	E3
Strumble Head Wales	14	A2
Stryy U S S R	20	D3
Stuart Highway Austl	40	E4/5
Stung Treng Kampuchea	38	D4
Sturgeon r, Ont, Canada	56	E2
Sturgeon r, Sask, Canada	60	D2
Sturgeon Bay Canada	61	F2
Sturgeon Falls town, Canada	56	F3
Sturgeon Lake Canada	60	B1
Sturgeon Landing Can	61	E2
Sturgis Canada	61	E2
Sturt Desert Australia	43	B3
Sturt, Mt Australia	43	B3
Stuttgart Ger F R	25	B2
Stuttgart U S A	50	D3
Stykkishólmur Iceland	16	a i
Styria Prov, Austria	25	C2
Suakin Sudan	69	N5
Suancheng China	37	C3
Subotica Yugoslavia	20	C3
Suceava Romania	20	E3
Suchan U S S R	34	J2
Suchiate Mexico	48	H7
Suchow (Suzhou) China	37	D3
Suchow (Tungshan) China	36	C3
Suck r, Irish Rep	13	C3
Sucre Bolivia	64	E7
SUDAN	69	L6
Sudbury Canada	56	E3
Sudbury Co, Canada	56	C2
Sudbury England	15	G2
Sudd swamp, Sudan	69	M7
Sudeten Mts Czech/Poland	20	C2
Sue Peaks mtn, U S A	50	B4
Suez Egypt	69	Ins.
Suez Canal Egypt	69	Ins.
Suez, Gulf of Egypt	69	M3
Suffern U S A	55	F3
Suffield U S A	55	H3
Suffolk Co, England	15	H2
Suffolk Va, U S A	59	E4
Sufu (Kashgar) China	31	L3
Sugar Creek town, U S A	58	B4
Sugarloaf Mt U S A	57	P4
Sugarloaf Point Australia	43	D4
Sugito Japan	39	f iii
Suhsien China	36	C3
Sui Pakistan	32	A3
Suichong China	36	D1
Suichwan China	37	B4
Suigo-tsukuba-kokuritsu-kōen nat park, Japan	39	g iii
Suihsien Anwhei, China	36	C3
Suihsien Hupeh, China	37	B3
Suining China	36	C3
Suiping China	36	B3
Suir r, Irish Republic	13	D4
Suita Japan	39	b ii
Suiteh China	36	B2
Suiyang China	37	A4
Sukagawa Japan	39	D2
Sukhona r, U S S R	28	E1
Sukhumi U S S R	28	E5
Sukkur Pakistan	32	A3
Sula Is Indonesia	35	H11
Sulaiman Range Pak	32	A2
Sulawesi i, see Celebes	35	G11
Sulgrave England	15	E2
Sullivan Lake Canada	62	D1
Sullom Voe sd, Shetland Islands	10	b i
Sulphur r, U S A	50	C3
Sulphur Springs town, U S A	50	C3
Sultan Canada	56	C2
Sulu Sea Indonesia	35	F9
Sulzbach-Rosenberg German F R	24	C2
Sumatra (Sumatera) i, Indonesia	35	C11
Sumba i, Indonesia	35	F12
Sumbawa i, Indon	35	F12
Sumburgh Head Shetland Islands	10	b ii
Sumen Bulgaria	21	E4
Sumgait U S S R	28	F5
Summerland Canada	62	C2
Summit U S A	46	F4
Summit Hill U S A	54	E4
Sumoto Japan	39	a ii
Sumprabaum Burma	38	B1
Sumter U S A	51	F3
Sumy U S S R	28	C3
Sunagawa Japan	39	D1
Sunapee Lake U S A	55	H1
Sunart, Loch Scot	10	C3
Sunburst U S A	61	C3
Sunbury England	15	F3
Sunbury U S A	54	D4
Suncho Corral Arg	66	B2
Suncook U S A	55	J1
Sundarbans geog reg, Bangl	32/3	E4
Sunda Strait Indon	35	D12
Sunderland England	12	E2
Sundre Canada	62	D1
Sundridge Canada	56	F4
Sundsvall Sweden	16	C3
Sungai Petani Mal	40	C5
Sungari r, China	34	H1
Sungari Reservoir China	34	H2
Sungchi China	37	C4
Sunghsien China	36	B3
Sungkan China	37	A4
Sungkiang China	37	D3
Sungtao China	37	B4
Sungyang China	37	C4
Sunndalsøra Norway	16	A3
Sunnyside U S A	62	B2
Sun Valley town, U S A	62	D3
Sunyi China	37	B5
Suo-nada sea, Japan	39	B3
Suonenjoki Finland	16	E3
Superior Ariz, U S A	63	D5
Superior Wis, U S A	58	B2
Superior, Lake Canada/U S A	58	C2
Suphan Buri Thailand	38	C4
Supu China	37	B4
Surabaja Indonesia	35	E12
Surakarta Indonesia	35	E12
Surat India	32	B4
Surat Thani Thailand	38	B5
Surgut U S S R	29	L1
SURINAM	64	G3
Surrey Co, England	15	F3
Surtsey i, Ice	16	a ii
Susa Italy	25	B2
Susanville U S A	63	B3
Susquehanna r, U S A	54	D5
Sussex U S A	54	F3
Sussex, Vale of England	15	F4
Susuman U S S R	27	R5
Susung China	37	C3
Sutherland Canada	60	D2
Sutlej r, Pakistan	32	B2
Sutsien China	36	C3
Sutton Ont, Canada	56	F5
Sutton Qué, Canada	57	N4
Sutton Coldfield Eng	15	E2
Sutton in Ashfield England	15	E1
Suttor r, Australia	42	C2
Suwa Japan	39	C2
Suwannee r, U S A	51	F4
Suzak U S S R	29	K5
Suzhou see Suchow	37	D3
Suzuka & r, Japan	39	c ii
Suzuka-Sammyaku mts, Japan	39	c i
Suzu-misaki cape, Japan	39	C2
Svendborg Denmark	17	B4
Sventa r, U S S R	17	D4
Sverdlovsk U S S R	29	J2
Sverdrup Is Canada	46	P1
Svetozarevo Yugo	21	D4
Svir' r, U S S R	28	C1
Swabian Jura hills, German F R	25	B2
Swadlincote England	15	E2
Swaffham England	15	G2
Swain Post Canada	61	G2
Swain Reefs Austl	42	D2
Swainsboro U S A	51	F3
Swakopmund Namibia	72	A3
Swale, The est, England	15	G3
Swale r, England	12	E2
Swaledale val, Eng	12	E2
Swalinbar Irish Rep	13	D2
Swan r, Australia	42	b ii
Swan, Lake Canada	61	E2
Swanage England	15	E4
Swan Hill town, Austl	43	B5
Swan Hills town, Canada	60	B2
Swan Hills Canada	60	B2
Swan Lake sett, Can	61	E2
Swansea Bay Wales	14	C3
Swanton U S A	57	M5
Swastika Canada	56	E1
Swatow China	37	C5
SWAZILAND	72	E4
Swedeland U S A	54	E4
SWEDEN	16/17	–
Swedesboro U S A	54	E5
Sweetgrass Canada	60	C3
Sweet Home U S A	62	B3
Sweetwater U S A	50	B3
Sweetwater Canal Egypt	69	Ins.
Swellendam S Africa	72	C5
Swift Current town, Canada	62	E1
Swilly, Lough Irish Republic	13	D1
Swindon England	15	E3
Swinford Irish Rep	13	C3
Świnoujście Poland	20	B2
SWITZERLAND	25	B2
Swords Irish Rep	13	E3
Sybil Head Irish Rep	13	A4
Sydenham r, Can	56	D7
Sydney Australia	43	D4
Sydney Canada	47	X7
Sydney, Lake Canada	61	G2
Sykesville U S A	54	B3
Syktyvkar U S S R	28	G1
Sylacauga U S A	51	E3
Sylhet Bangladesh	33	F4
Sylvan Lake town, Canada	60	C2
Syracuse Sicily	21	C5
Syracuse U S A	54	D1
Syr Dar'ya (Jaxartes) r, U S S R	29	K5
Syston England	15	E2
Syzran' U S S R	28	F3
Szczecin Poland	20	B2
Szczecinek Poland	20	C2
Szczytno Poland	20	D3
Szechwan (Sichuan) Prov, China	37	A3
Szechwan, Red Basin of China	37	A3
Szeged Hungary	20	D3
Székesfehérvár Hung	20	C3
Szenan China	37	A4
Szewui China	37	B5
Szolnok Hungary	20	D3
Szombathely Hungary	20	C3
Tabacal Argentina	66	B1
Tabara r, Nigeria	67	C2
Taber Canada	62	D2
Table Rock Reservoir U S A	58	B4
Tabor Czechoslovakia	20	B3
Tabora Tanzania	71	F8
Tabou Ivory Coast	68	D8
Tabrīz Iran	28	F6
Tabuk Saudi Arabia	30	C5
Ta Chi r, China	37	C4
Tachikawa Japan	39	f iv
Tachu China	37	A3
Tacloban Philippines	35	G8
Tacna Peru	64	D7
Tacoma U S A	62	B2
Taconite Harbor U S A	58	B2
Taco Pozo Argentina	66	B2
Tacuarembo Uruguay	66	C3
Tacuarembó Chico r, Uruguay	66	C3
Tacuari r, Uruguay	66	D3
Tadcaster England	12	E3
Tadoule, Lake Canada	61	F1
Tadoussac Canada	57	Q1
Tadzhik S S R U S S R	29	L6
Taegu S Korea	34	H3
Taejon S Korea	34	H3
Taerh-hanmaoming-anlienhochi China	36	B1
Taf r, Wales	14	B3
Tafang Kweichow, China	38	D1
Tafeng Kiangsu, China	36	D3
Tafilalet Oasis Morocco	68	E2
Tafi Viejo Argentina	66	A2
Taganrog U S S R	28	D4
Tagliamento r, Italy	25	C2
Tagus (Tajo) r, Portugal/Spain	19	A5
Tagwai r, Nigeria	67	B1
Tahan mtn & nat park, Malaysia	38	C6
Tahiti i, Society Is	45	L8
Tahoe, Lake U S A	63	C4
Tahsien China	37	A3
Tahsin China	37	A5
Tahsis Canada	62	A2
Tai, Lake China	37	D3
Taian China	36	C2
Taichow China	36	C3
Taichung Taiwan	37	D5
Taihape N Z	41	C2
Taiho Anhwei, China	36	C3
Taiho Kiangsi, China	37	B4
Taihsien China	36	B2
Taihsing China	36	D3
Taihu China	37	C3
Taikang China	36	B3
Taiku China	36	B2
Taim Brazil	66	D3
Tain Scotland	10	D2
Tainan Taiwan	37	D5
Taining China	37	C4
Taipai Shan mtn, China	36	A3
TAIPEI Taiwan	37	D4
Taipeihsien Taiwan	37	D5
Taiping China	37	C3
Taiping Malaysia	38	C6
Taishun China	37	C4
Taitao Peninsula Chile	65	C13
Taitung Taiwan	37	D5
TAIWAN	37	D5
Taiyuan China	36	B2
Taiyun Shan mtns, China	37	C4
Ta'iz Yemen	30	D8
Tajimi Japan	39	d i
Tajo r, see Tagus	19	B4
Tak Thailand	38	B3
Takada Japan	39	C2
Takaishi Japan	39	b ii
Takaka N Z	41	B3
Takamatsu Japan	39	B3
Takaoka Japan	39	C2
Takasago Japan	39	a ii
Takashima Japan	39	c i
Takatsuki Japan	39	b ii
Takhing China	37	B5
Takikawa Japan	39	D1
Takingeun Indonesia	38	B6
Taku China	36	C2
Takua Pa Thailand	38	B5
Takum Nigeria	67	B2
Takla Makan des, China	31	M3
Talara Peru	64	B4
Talata Mafara Nig	67	B1
Talaud Is Indonesia	35	H10
Talavera, Isla i, Par	66	C2
Talavera de la Reina Spain	19	B5
Talbot, Cape Austl	40	D3
Talca Chile	65	D11
Talcottville U S A	55	H3
Tali Shensi, China	36	A3
Tali Yunnan China	38	C1
Tali r, China	36	A2
Talladega U S A	51	E3
Tallaght Irish Rep	13	E3
Tallahassee U S A	51	F3
Tallinn U S S R	17	D4
Tallow Irish Rep	13	C4
Tama r, Japan	39	f iv
Tamale Ghana	68	E7
Tamaqua U S A	54	E4
Tamar r, England	14	B4
Tamatave Malagasy Republic	71	J11
Tambov U S S R	28	E3
Tamiaoshan China	37	A4
Tamil Nadu State, India	32	C6
Taming China	36	B2
Tămovo Bulgaria	21	E4
Tampa & bay U S A	51	F4
Tampere Finland	16	D3
Tampico Mexico	48	G5
Tamtsak Bulak Mong	34	F1
Tamworth Australia	43	D4
Tamworth England	15	E2
Tana fd, Norway	16	E1
Tana r, Finland/Norway	16	E2
Tana, Lake Ethiopia	69	N6
Tanabe Japan	39	C3
Tanah Rata Malaysia	38	C6
Tanana U S A	46	E3
TANANARIVE Malagasy Republic	72	J11
Tanat r, Wales	14	C2
Tancheng China	36	C3
Tandil Argentina	65	G11
Tandou Lake Austl	43	B4
Tandragee N Irel	13	E2
Taneytown U S A	54	C5
Tanezrouft geog reg, Algeria	68	E4
Tanfeng China	36	B3
Tanga Tanzania	71	G9
Tanganyika, L Tanzania	68	E8
Tangaza Nigeria	67	A1
Tangho China	36	B3
Tangku China	36	C2
Tangshan Anhwei, China	36	C3
Tangshan Hopeh, China	36	C2
Tangtu China	37	C3
Tangyang China	37	B3
Tanimbar Is Indon	35	J12
Tanjongbalai Indon	38	B6
Tanshui Taiwan	37	D4
Tanyang China	36	C3
TANZANIA	71	F9
Taohsien China	37	B4
Taormina Sicily	21	C5
Taoyuan China	37	B4
Tapajos r, Brazil	64	G5
Tapani, Lac Canada	57	K3
Tapa Shan mtns, China	36	A3
Tapenaga r, Arg	66	C2
Tapieh Shan mtns, China	37	C3
Tappi-zaki cape, Japan	39	D1
Tapti r, India	32	C4
Tapu China	37	C5
Tapuaenuku mtn, New Zealand	41	B3
Taquara Brazil	66	D2
Taquari r, Minas Gerais, Brazil	66	E1
Taquari r, Rio Grande do Sul, Braz	66	D2
Tara U S S R	29	L2
TARABULUS (Tripoli) Libya	68	H2
Tarakan Indonesia	35	F10
Taranaki dist, N Z	41	B2
Taransay i, Scotland	10	A2
Taranto & g, Italy	21	C4
Tarare France	23	B2
Tararua Range N Z	41	C3
Tarascon France	23	B3
Tarawa i, Gilbert Islands	44	G6
Tarazona de Aragon Spain	19	B4
Tarbat Ness pt, Scotland	10	E2
Tarbert Strathclyde Scotland	11	C4
Tarbert Western Isles, Scotland	10	B2
Tarbes France	23	B3
Tardenois geog reg, France	22	B2
Taree Australia	43	D4
Tarim r, China	31	M2
Tarko-Sale U S S R	27	K5
Tarn r, France	23	B3
Tarnów Poland	20	D3
Taroom Australia	42	C3
Tarpeniya Bay U S S R	27	R8
Tarragona Spain	19	C4
Tarratine U S A	57	Q4
Tarrytown U S A	55	G3
Tartary, Gulf of U S S R	27	R8
Tartu U S S R	17	E4
Tarutung Indonesia	38	B6
Tarviso Italy	25	C2
Tas r, England	15	H2
Tashkent U S S R	29	K5
Tasman, Mt N Z	41	B3
Tasman Bay N Z	41	B3
Tasmania State & i, Australia	40	b i
Tasman Mts N Z	41	B3
Tasman Nat Park New Zealand	41	B3
Tassili n Ajjer plat, Algeria	68	G3
Tata Morocco	68	D3
Tatabánya Hungary	20	C3
Tatarsk U S S R	29	M2
Tatebayashi Japan	39	f iii
Tateyama Japan	39	f v
Tatien China	37	C4
Tatry mtns, Czech	20	C3
Tatui Brazil	66	a i
Tatung China	36	B1
Taubaté Brazil	66	a i
Taumarunui N Z	41	C2
Taungdwingyi Burma	38	B2
Taunggyi Burma	38	B2
Taunton England	14	C3
Taunton U S A	55	J3
Taunus mtns, German F R	24	B1
Taupo & l, N Z	41	C2
Tauranga N Z	41	C2
Taureau Réservoir Canada	57	M3
Taurus Mts Turkey	28	C6
Tavai Paraguay	66	C2
Tavares Brazil	66	D3
Tavda U S S R	29	K2
Tavda r, U S S R	29	J2
Tavira Portugal	19	A5
Tavistock Canada	56	E6
Tavistock England	14	B4
Tavoy Burma	38	B4
Taw r, England	14	C4
Tawas City U S A	56	B5
Tawas Island U S A	56	B5
Tawas Point U S A	58	D3
Tawitawi i, Phil	35	G9
Tawu Taiwan	37	D5
Tay r, Scotland	10	E3
Tay, Firth of est, Scotland	10	E3
Tay, Lake Australia	42	c ii
Tay, Loch Scotland	10	D3
Taylor Canada	60	A1
Taymyr, Lake U S S R	27	N3
Taymyr Peninsula U S S R	27	N2
Tay Ninh Vietnam	38	D4
Tayshet U S S R	29	Q2
Tayside Reg, Scot	10	E3
Tayu China	37	B4
Tayung China	37	B4
Taz r, U S S R	27	L4
Tazin Lake Canada	60	D1
Tbilisi U S S R	28	E5
Tchina r, Cameroun	67	C2
Tczew Poland	20	C2
Teague U S A	50	C3
Tean China	37	C4
Te Anau, Lake N Z	41	A4
Te Awamutu N Z	41	C2
Tebicuary r, Paraguay	66	C2
Tebicuary-Mi r, Par	66	C2
Tebingtinggi Indon	38	B6
Tecuci Romania	20	E3
Tecumseh Canada	56	C7
Tecumseh U S A	56	B7
Teedale val, Eng	12	D2
Tees r, England	12	E2
Teesside Co, Eng	12	E2
Teeswater sett, Can	56	D5
Tegina Nigeria	67	B1
TEGUCIGALPA Hond	49	J7
Tehchow China	36	C2
TEHRĀN Iran	28	G6
Tehua China	37	C4
Tehuantepec g & isthmus, Mexico	48	H6
Teifi r, Wales	14	B2
Teignmouth Eng	14	C4
Tekely U S S R	29	M5
Tekirdağ Turkey	21	E4
Te Kuiti N Z	41	C2
Tel Aviv-Jaffa Israel	30	B4
Telč Czechoslovakia	20	C3
Telford England	14	D2
Tell el Kebir Egypt	69	Ins.
Telok Anson Mal	38	C6
Telukbetung Indon	35	D12
Temagami Canada	56	F2
Temagami, Lake Can	56	E3
Temagami Provincial Forest Canada	56	E2
Teme r, England	14	D2
Temir-Tau U S S R	29	L3
Temiscaming & Co, Canada	56	F3
Témiscamingue, Lac Canada	56	F2
Temora Australia	43	C4
Tempio Pausania Sardinia	19	a i
Temple Pa, U S A	54	E4
Temple Tex, U S A	50	C3
Templemore Irish Republic	13	D4
Temuco Chile	65	D11
Tenasserim & divis, Burma	38	B4
Tenbury Wells Eng	14	D2
Tenby Wales	14	B3
Tenda Pass France/Italy	25	B3
Tende France	23	C3
Tenerife i, Canary Islands	68	B3
Ténès Algeria	19	C5
Tengchung China	38	B2
Tenghsien Honan, China	36	B3
Tenghsien Hopeh, China	36	C2
Tengiz, Lake U S S R	29	K3
Tengkow China	36	A1
Tengyun China	37	B5
Tenkiller Ferry Reservoir U S A	50	D2
Tennant Creek town, Australia	40	E4
Tennessee State & r, U S A	51	E2
Tenterden England	15	G3
Tenterfield Australia	43	D3
Ten Thousand Islands U S A	51	F4
Ter r, Spain	19	C4
Teramo Italy	21	B4
Tercero r, Argentina	66	B3
Teresina Brazil	64	K5
Terme di Valdieri Italy	25	B3
Termez U S S R	29	K6
Termoli Italy	21	B4
Tern r, England	14	D2
Ternate i, Indon	35	H10
Terneuzen Neth	24	A1
Terni Italy	21	B4
Ternopol' U S S R	20	E3
Terrace Canada	46	K6
Terracina Italy	21	B4
Terrebonne & Co, Canada	57	M4
Terre Haute U S A	58	C4
Terry U S A	53	D1
Terschelling i, Neth	24	B1
Teruel Spain	19	B4
Tepic Mexico	48	F5
Teplice Czechoslovakia	20	B2
Tessaoua Niger	67	B1
Tessenei Ethiopia	69	N5
Test r, England	15	E3
Tetbury England	14	D3
Tete Mozambique	72	E2
Teterow Ger D R	24	B1
Tetovo Yugoslavia	21	D4
Tetu, Lake Canada	61	G2
Teuco r, Argentina	66	B1
Teulon Canada	61	F2
Teutoburger Wald mtns, Ger F R	24	B1
Teviot r, Scotland	11	F4
Teviotdale val, Scot	11	F4
Tewkesbury England	14	D3
Texarkana U S A	50	D3
Texas State, U S A	50	–
Texas City U S A	50	D4
Texel i, Netherlands	24	A1
Texoma, Lake U S A	50	C3

Name	Page	ref
Tezpur: India	33	F3
Thabazimbi: S. Africa	72	D3
THAILAND:	38	–
Thakhek: Laos	38	C3
Thal: desert, Pakistan	32	B2
Thalwil: Switzerland	25	B2
Thame: & r, England	15	F3
Thames: N.Z.	41	C2
Thames: r, England	15	F3
Thames: r, Canada	56	D7
Thames Estuary: Eng.	15	H3
Thamesford: Canada	56	E6
Thamesville: Canada	56	D7
Thanh Hoa: Vietnam	38	D3
Thanjavur: India	32	C6
Thar Desert: India/Pakistan	32	B3
Thargomindah: Austl	42	B3
Tharon: Burma	38	B3
Thaungdut: Burma	38	B2
Thayetmyo: Burma	38	B3
Thebes: hist. Egypt	69	M3
The Dalles: U.S.A.	62	B2
Thedford: Canada	56	D6
The Forks: sett. U.S.A.	57	Q4
Theodore: Australia	42	D2
Theodore Roosevelt Nat. Memorial. U.S.A.	53	E1
Theresa: U.S.A.	57	K5
Thermopolis: U.S.A.	62	E3
Thessalon: Canada	56	B3
Thessalonica: Greece	21	D4
Thetford: England	15	G2
Thetford Mines: Can.	57	G2
The Wash: bay, Eng.	15	G2
Thicket Portage: Can.	61	F1
Thief, Lake: U.S.A.	61	F3
Thief River Falls: town, U.S.A.	58	A2
Thiérache: France	22	B2
Thiers: France	23	B2
Thionville: France	22	C2
Thira: i. Greece	21	E5
Thirsk: England	12	E2
Thirty Thousand Islands: arch., Can.	56	D4
Thisted: Denmark	17	A4
Thivai: Greece	21	D5
Thjorsá: r., Iceland	16	b ii
Thomaston: U.S.A.	55	G3
Thomaston: Irish Rep.	13	D4
Thomasville: Ala., U.S.A.	51	E3
Thomasville: Ga., U.S.A.	51	F3
Thompson: Canada	61	F1
Thompson: r. Canada	60	B1
Thompson: U.S.A.	54	E3
Thompson: Ga., U.S.A.	51	F3
Thompsonville: U.S.A.	55	H3
Thonon: France	23	C2
Thore: r, France	23	B3
Thorhild: Canada	60	C2
Thornbury: Canada	56	E5
Thornbury: England	14	D3
Thornaby-on-Tees: England	12	E2
Thorne: England	12	F3
Thornhill: Scotland	11	E4
Thornhurst: U.S.A.	54	E3
Thornton: England	12	C3
Thornton: U.S.A.	55	J3
Thorold: Canada	56	F6
Thorsby: Canada	60	C2
Thouars: France	23	A2
Thrapston: England	15	F2
Three Hills: town, Can.	60	C2
Three Kings Is.: N.Z.	41	B1
Three Points, Cape: Ghana	69	M3
Three Rivers: U.S.A.	55	H2
Three Springs: town, Australia	42	b i
Thrushnel: r. England	14	B4
Thule: Greenland	47	W1
Thun: r. Switzerland	25	B2
Thunder Bay (Fort William, Port Arthur): city & b. Canada	58	C2
Thunder Bay: r. U.S.A.	56	B5
Thung Song: Thailand	38	B5
Thurgau: Co.	25	B2
Thüringer Wald: mtns. German D.R.	24	C1
Thuringia: old state. German D.R.	24	C1
Thurles: Irish Republic	13	D4
Thurmaston: England	15	F2
Thurmont: U.S.A.	54	C5
Thursday I.: Australia	40	G3
Thurso: Canada	57	K4
Thurso: & r. Scotland	10	E5
Tiahuanaco: Bolivia	64	E7
Tianjin see Tientsin	36	C2
Tiaret: Algeria	19	C5
Tibagi: & r. Brazil	66	D1
Tibati: Cameroun	67	C2
Tiber: r. Italy	21	B4
Tiber Dam: U.S.A.	62	D2
Tibesti: highlands, Chad	69	K4
Tibet: Prov. China	32	E2
Tiblemont, Lake: Can.	56	H1
Ticino: r. Switzerland	25	B2
Ticonderoga: U.S.A.	57	M6
Tidioute: U.S.A.	56	F8
Tienchang: China	36	B1
Tienchen: China	36	B1
Tienkiang: China	37	A3
Tienpao: China	37	D2
Tientai: China	37	D4
Tientsin (Tianjin): & municipality China	36	C2
Tientung: China	37	A5
Tien-yen: Vietnam	37	A5
Tierra del Fuego: i. Argentina/Chile	65	E14
Tietar: r. Spain	19	A5
Tieté: r. Brazil	66	a i
Tiffin: U.S.A.	56	D8
Tignes Reservoir: Fr.	23	C2
Tigris: r. Iraq	30	D4
Tijirebon: Indonesia	35	D12
Tijuana: Mexico	63	C5
Tijucas: & r. Brazil	66	E2
Tiko: Cameroun	67	B3
Tiksi: U.S.S.R.	27	P3
Tikura: Japan	39	f v
Tilburg: Netherlands	24	B1
Tilbury: Canada	56	C7
Tilcara: Argentina	66	B1
Tillabéry: Niger	68	F6
Tillamook: U.S.A.	62	B2
Tillicoultry: Scotland	11	E4
Tilsonburg: Canada	56	E6
Tilt: r. Scotland	10	E3
Tilton: U.S.A.	55	J1
Timaru: New Zealand	41	B3
Timbákion: Crete	21	D5
Timbuktu see Tombouctou	68	E5
Timişoara: Romania	20	D3
Timiskaming: Co. Can.	56	E2
Timmins: Canada	56	D1
Timor: Indonesia	35	H12
Timor Sea: Australia/Indonesia	40	B/C3
Timote: Argentina	66	B4
TIMPHU: Bhutan	32	E3
Timsah, Lake: Egypt	29	Ins
Tinghing: China	36	C2
Tinghir: Morocco	68	D2
Tinghsien: China	36	B2
Tingnan: China	37	B5
Tingpien: China	36	A2
Tingtao: China	36	C2
Tinogasta: Argentina	66	B2
Tinos: i. Greece	21	E5
Tintagel: England	14	B4
Tintagel Head: England	14	B4
Tinto: Argentina	66	B2
Tinto: Cameroun	67	B2
Tionaga: Canada	56	C1
Tionesta: U.S.A.	54	F8
Tioga: r. U.S.A.	54	C2
Tioughnioga: r. U.S.A.	54	D2
Tipperary: North Riding sub-Co. Irish Rep.	13	D4
Tipperary: South Riding sub-Co. Irish Rep.	13	D4
Tipperary: & Co. Irish Republic	13	C4
TIRANE: Albania	21	C4
Tiraspol: U.S.S.R.	20	E3
Tire: Turkey	21	E4
Tiree: i. Scotland	10	B3
Tirgoviste: Romania	20	D3
Tirgu-Jiu: Romania	21	D4
Tirgu Mureş: Romania	20	D3
Tirso: r. Sardinia	19	a ii
Tiruchirapalli: India	32	C6
Tirunelveli: India	32	C7
Tisdale: Canada	61	F2
Tissamaharama: Sri Lanka	32	b ii
Tississat Falls: Eth.	69	N6
Tista: r. Bang./India	32	E3
Titicaca, Lake: Bolivia/Peru	64	E7
Titograd: Yugoslavia	21	C4
Titovo Užice: Yugo.	21	C4
Titov Veles: Yugoslavia	21	C4
Tittabawassee: r. U.S.A.	56	A7
Titusville: U.S.A.	56	F8
Tiverton: England	14	C4
Tiverton: U.S.A.	55	J3
Tivoli: Italy	21	B4
Tiumpan Hd: Scotland	10	B1
Tizi-Ouzou: Algeria	19	C5
Tlemcen: Algeria	19	B5
Toba: Japan	39	c ii
Toba, Lake: Indonesia	35	B6
Tobago: r. Trin. & Tob.	49	O7
Tobermore: N. Ireland	13	E2
Tobermory: Canada	56	D4
Tobermory: Scotland	10	B3
Tobin, Lake: Canada	61	E2
Tobol: r. U.S.S.R.	29	K2
Tobol'sk: U.S.S.R.	29	K2
Tobruk: Libya	69	K2
Tocantins: r. Brazil	64	J4
Toccoa: U.S.A.	51	F3
Tocumwal: Australia	43	C5
Todmorden: England	12	D3
Toe Head: Irish Rep.	13	B5
Toe Head: Scotland	10	A3
Tofield: Canada	60	C2
Tofino: Canada	60	A2
Togane: Japan	39	g iv
TOGO:	67	F7
Toi: Japan	39	e v
Tokaanu: New Zealand	41	C2
Tokelau Is.: Pacific Ocean	44	H7
Toki: Japan	39	d i
Tokoname: Japan	39	c ii
Tokorozawa: Japan	39	f iv
Tokoto: China	36	B1
Tokushima: Japan	39	B1
Tokuyama: Japan	39	B1
Tokyo: & Pref. Japan	39	f iv
Tokyo-wan: bay. Japan	39	f iv
Tolbukhin: Bulgaria	21	E4
Toledo: Spain	19	B5
Toledo: Ohio, U.S.A.	56	C8
Toledo: Ore. U.S.A.	58	B3
Toledo, Montes de: mtns. Spain	19	B5
Toledo Bend Reservoir: U.S.A.	50	D3
Tolsta Head: Scotland	10	B1
Tolstoy, Cape: U.S.S.R.	27	S6
Tomakomai: Japan	39	H12
Tomatlán: Mexico	48	A5
Tomaszów Mazowiecki: Poland	20	C2
Tombigbee: r. U.S.A.	51	E3
Tombouctou (Timbuktu): Mali	68	E5
Tombstone: Ariz. U.S.A.	63	E5
Tomelloso: Spain	19	B5
Tomiko Lake: Canada	56	F3
Tomoka: Japan	39	e iii
Tomsk: U.S.S.R.	29	O2
Toms River: town. U.S.A.	55	F5
Tonawanda: U.S.A.	54	B2
Tonbridge: England	15	G3
Tone: r. Japan	39	g iv
TONGA:	44	H8
Tongariro Nat. Park: New Zealand	41	C2
Tonga Trench: Pacific Ocean	45	H9
Tonghing: China	37	A5
Tongue: Scotland	10	D5
Tongue: r. U.S.A.	52	D1
Tongue, Kyle of: sea loch. Scotland	10	D1
Tongue see Tungchow	36	B1
Tonkin: Gulf of S.E. Asia	38	D2
Tonle Sap: l. Kampuchea	38	C4
Tonopah: U.S.A.	63	C4
Tonsberg: Norway	17	B4
Topeka: U.S.A.	58	A4
Topolobampo: Mexico	48	B3
Topozero, Lake: U.S.S.R.	16	F2
Toppenish: U.S.A.	62	B2
Topsham: England	14	C4
Topton: U.S.A.	54	E4
Toowoomba: Australia	43	D4
Torbay Head: Australia	42	b ii
Torbay: England	14	C4
Torbole: Italy	25	C3
Torch: r. Canada	61	E2
Torgau: German D.R.	24	C1
Torhout: Belgium	22	B1
Toride: Japan	39	g iv
Torino see Turin	25	B2
Tornado, Mt.: Canada	60	C3
Torne: r., Fin. /Sweden	16	D2
Torne Lappmark: geog. reg. Sweden	16	D2
Torneträsk Lake: Swed.	16	D2
Tornio: Finland	16	D2
Toronto: Canada	56	F6
Toropi: r. Brazil	66	C2
Tororo: Uganda	70	F7
Torpoint: England	14	B4
Torre Annunziata: Italy	21	B4
Torrens, Lake: Austl	40	F5
Torreón: Mexico	48	B3
Torremolinos: Spain	19	B5
Torres Strait: Australia/Pap.-N.G	40	G3
Torridge: r. England	14	B4
Torridon: & l. Scot.	10	C2
Torrington: Conn., U.S.A.	55	G3
Torrington: Wyo., U.S.A.	53	E2
Tortona: Italy	25	B3
Tortosa: Spain	19	C4
Tortugas: Argentina	66	B3
Torun: Poland	20	C2
Tory I.: Irish Republic	13	C1
Tory Sound: Irish Rep.	13	C1
Tosa-wan: bay. Japan	39	B1
Tostado: Argentina	66	B2
Totnes: England	14	C4
Totoralejos: Argentina	66	B2
Tottenham: Australia	43	B5
Tottenham: Canada	56	F5
Totton: England	14	E3
Touba: Senegal	68	B6
Touggourt: Algeria	68	G2
Toul: France	22	C2
Toulnustouc: r. Can.	57	J1
Toulon: France	23	C3
Toulouse: France	23	B3
Tounan: Taiwan	37	D5
Toungo: Nigeria	67	C2
Toungoo: Burma	38	B3
Touraine: Old Prov. Fr.	23	B2
Tourakom: Laos	38	C3
Tourcoing: France	22	B1
Tournai: France	22	B1
Tours: France	23	B2
Tourville: Canada	57	Q2
Tover: r. England	15	G2
Towada-hachimantai-kokuritsu-kōen: nat. park. Japan	39	D1
Towanda: U.S.A.	54	D2
Towcester: England	15	F2
Tower City: U.S.A.	54	D4
Tow Law: England	12	E2
Townshend I.: Australia	42	C1
Townsville: Australia	42	C1
Towson: U.S.A.	54	D5
Towyn: Wales	14	B2
Toyama: & Pref. Japan	39	C2
Toyama-wan: bay. Japan	39	C2
Toyo: r. Japan	39	d ii
Toyohashi: Japan	39	d ii
Toyokawa: Japan	39	d ii
Toyonaka: Japan	39	b ii
Toyota: Japan	39	d i
Tozeur: Tunisia	68	G2
Trabzon: Turkey	28	D2
Tracy: Canada	57	M3
Tracy: U.S.A.	63	B4
Trail: Canada	62	C2
Tralee: & b. Irish Rep.	13	B4
Tramping Lake: Canada	61	E2
Tramore: Irish Republic	13	E1
Tranås: Sweden	17	C4
Tranent: Scotland	11	F4
Tranqueras: Uruguay	66	C3
Transkei: Bantustan, South Africa	72	D5
Transvaal: Prov., South Africa	72	D3
Transylvanian Alps: mtns. Romania	21	D3
Trapani: Sicily	21	B5
Traralgon: Australia	43	C5
Trat: Thailand	38	C4
Traunstein: Ger F R	25	C2
Travellers Lake: Austl	43	B4
Traverse City: U.S.A.	58	C3
Travesia Puntana: des. Argentina	66	A3
Tredegar: Wales	14	C3
Tregaron: Wales	14	C2
Treherne: Canada	61	F3
Treig, Loch: Scotland	10	D3
Treinta y Tres: Uruguay	66	D3
Trelleborg: Sweden	17	C4
Tremadog Bay: Wales	14	B2
Trenčín: Czechoslovakia	20	C3
Trent: r. Canada	56	H5
Trent: r. England	12	F3
Trente et un Milles. Lac des: Canada	57	K3
Trentino: reg., Italy	25	C2
Trento: Italy	25	C2
Trenton: Canada	56	H5
Trenton: Mo., U.S.A.	58	B3
Tres Arboles: Uruguay	66	C3
Tresco: Scilly Is.	14	c iv
Treshnish Is.: Scotland	10	B3
Três Passos: Brazil	66	D2
Tres Rios: Brazil	66	b i
Trevisto: Italy	25	C2
Trevose Head: England	14	A4
Trident: U.S.A.	62	D2
Trier: German F R	24	C2
Trieste: Italy	25	C2
Trikkala: Greece	21	D5
Trim: Irish Republic	13	E3
Trincomalee: Sri Lanka	32	b ii
Tring: England	15	F3
Trinidad: S. America	53	E4
Trinidad: South Atlantic Ocean	8	G10
TRINIDAD AND TOBAGO:	49	O7
Trinity: r. U.S.A.	50	C3
Trinity B.: Canada	57	R3
Tripoli: Lebanon	28	D1
Tripoli see TARABULUS	68	H2
Tripolis: Greece	21	D5
Tripura: Union Terr. India	33	F4
Tristan da Cunha: i. South Atlantic Ocean	8	J11
Trivandrum: India	32	C7
Trnava: Czechoslovakia	20	C3
Trochu: Canada	60	C2
Trois Rivières: city. Canada	57	N3
Troitsk: U.S.S.R.	29	J3
Trollhättan: Sweden	17	C4
Trollheimen: mtns. Norway	16	A3
Tromsö: Norway	16	C1
Tromsoysund: Norway	16	C2
Trondheim: Norway	16	B3
Trondheimsfjorden: fd. Norway	16	B3
Troon: Scotland	11	D4
Troup: U.S.A.	50	D3
Trout Creek: sett. Canada	56	F4
Trout Lake: N.W.T. Canada	60	L4
Trout Lake: Ont., Can.	56	F3
Trout, Lake: Ont. Can.	61	G2
Trowbridge: England	14	D3
Troy: Turkey	21	E4
Troy: Ala. U.S.A.	51	E3
Troy: N.H. U.S.A.	55	H2
Troy: N.Y. U.S.A.	55	G2
Troy: Pa. U.S.A.	54	D3
Truite, Lac à la: Can.	56	G2
Truk Is.: Caroline Is.	44	E6
Trujillo: Honduras	49	J6
Trujillo: Peru	64	C5
Trumansburg: U.S.A.	54	D2
Truro: Canada	57	X7
Truro: England	14	A4
Truth or Consequences: U.S.A.	52	D4
Tsaidam Swamp: China	34	A3
Tsamai: Nigeria	67	B1
Tsanghsien: China	36	C2
Tsangpo (Brahmaputra): r. China/Angola	33	F3
Tsangwu: China	37	B5
Tsaohsien: China	36	B2
Tsaoyang: China	36	B3
Tsavo Nat. Park: Kenya	71	G8
Tselinograd: U.S.S.R.	29	L3
Tsetserleg: Mongolia	34	C1
Tsiaotso: China	36	B2
Tsimhyansk Reservoir: U.S.S.R.	28	E4
Tsinan (Jinan): China	36	C2
Tsinghai: China	36	A2
Tsing Hai (Koko Nor): r. China	34	B3
Tsinghsien: China	37	C2
Tsingkiang: China	37	B4
Tsingshih: China	37	B4
Tsingtao (Qingdao): China	36	D2
Tsining: Inner Mongolia. China	36	B1
Tsining: Shantung. China	36	C2
Tsingyun: China	37	B5
Tsinkiang (Chuanchow): China	37	C5
Tsinling Shan (Qinlingshan): ra. China	36	A3
Tsitsihar (Lungkiang): China	36	A1
Tsoshui: China	36	G1
Tsowhsien: China	36	C2
Tsoyun: China	36	B2
Tsu: r. China	37	B4
Tsu: Japan	39	c ii
Tsuchiura: Japan	39	g iii
Tsugaru-kaikyo: str. Japan	39	D1
Tsukumi: Japan	39	B1
Tsukuba: Japan	39	g iii
Tsumeb: Namibia	72	B2
Tsuna: Japan	39	a ii
Tsunghua: China	37	B5
Tsuruga: Japan	39	C2
Tsuru: China	37	B4
Tsuru: Japan	39	e iv
Tsuruoka: Japan	39	C2
Tsushima: Japan	39	c i
Tsushima: i. Japan	39	A3
Tsushima-kaikyo: str. Japan	39	A3
Tsuyama: Japan	39	A3
Tuam: Irish Republic	13	C3
Tuamotu Archipelago: Pacific Ocean	45	L8
Tuan: China	37	A4
Tuatapere: N.Z.	41	A4
Tuapse: U.S.S.R.	28	D2
Tuath, Loch: Scotland	10	B3
Tubai: I.: Pacific O.	45	K9
Tuchang: China	36	C2
Tuckerton: U.S.A.	55	F5
Tucson: U.S.A.	63	D5
Tucuman: Prov. Arg	66	B2
Tucuman: Argentina	66	B2
Tucupita: Venezuela	49	O8
Tudela: Spain	19	B4
Tufts Abyssal Plain: Pacific Ocean	45	L2
Tuggsaq: Greenland	47	Z2
Tuktoyaktuk: Canada	60	J3
Tukums: U.S.S.R.	17	D4
Tula: U.S.S.R.	28	D3
Tulare: U.S.A.	63	B4
Tulcan: Colombia	64	C3
Tulcea: Romania	20	E3
Tulear: Malagasy Rep.	71	H12
Tulia: U.S.A.	50	B3
Tullahoma: U.S.A.	51	E2
Tullamore: Australia	43	C5
Tullamore: Irish Rep.	13	D3
Tulle: France	23	B2
Tully: Irish Republic	13	F2
Tulsa: U.S.A.	58	A4
Tumacacon National Monument: U.S.A.	63	D5
Tumaco: Colombia	64	C3
Tumbarumba: Australia	43	C5
Tumbes: Peru	64	B4
Tumbledown Mt.: U.S.A.	57	P5
Tumkur: India	32	C6
Tummel: r. Scotland	10	E3
Tumpat: Malaysia	38	C5
Tumu-Mágurele: Rom.	21	D4
Tumzá: r. Bulgaria	21	E4
Tunceli: Turkey	28	E2
Tunchang: China	38	D2
Tunghwang: Anhwei. China	37	C3
Tungcheng: Hupeh. China	37	C3
Tungchow: China	36	B1
Tungan: Fukien. China	37	D5
Tungan: Hunan. China	37	B4
Tunghai: China	36	C2
Tung-hsin: China	37	B4
Tunghwa: China	36	A1
Tungkan see Penhai	36	C2
Tungkan: Japan	39	B1
Tungkiang: China	37	A3
Tungkou: China	37	B4
Tungku: China	37	B4
Tungkum: Mongolia	34	
Tungkwan: China	36	B3
Tungkwang: China	36	B3
Tung Nghia: Vietnam	38	D4
Tungpeh: China	36	A3
Tungping: China	36	C2
Tungping, Lake: China	37	C5
Tungshan see Suchow	36	C3
Tungsheng: China	36	A2
Tungshih: Taiwan	37	D5
Tungsiang: China	37	A4
Tungtai: China	36	D2
Tungtao: China	37	A4
Tungting, Lake: China	37	B4
Tungtze: China	37	A4
Tungyang: China	37	D4
Tunhua: China	37	A5
Tunis: Tunisia	68	G1
Tunja: Colombia	64	D2
Tunkhannock: U.S.A.	54	E3
Tunki: China	37	C4
Tunliu: China	36	B2
Tunstall: England	14	D1
Tupelo: U.S.A.	51	E3
Tupper Lake: & sett. U.S.A.	57	L5
Tura: r. U.S.S.R.	29	J2
Turanian Plain: U.S.S.R.	29	H5
Turbat: Pakistan	32	c iv
Turbo: Colombia	49	L8
Turda: Romania	20	D3
Tureta: Nigeria	67	F6
Turgai: & r. U.S.S.R.	29	J4
Turgutlu: Turkey	21	E5
Turin (Torino): Italy	25	B3
Turkana, Lake: Kenya	69	N8
Turkestan: U.S.S.R.	29	K5
TURKEY:	28	E5
Turkey: r. U.S.A.	58	B3
Turkmen S.S.R.	29	H6
Turks Islands: W Indies	49	M5
Turku: Finland	17	D3
Turlock: U.S.A.	63	B4
Turnagain, Cape: N.Z.	41	C3
Turner Valley: town. Canada	62	D1
Turnhout: Belgium	22	B1
Turnor Lake: Canada	60	E1
Turnu-Severin: Rom.	21	D4
Turriff: Scotland	10	F2
Turtleford: Canada	60	E1
Turtle Mtn. Provincial Park: Canada	61	F3
Turvo: r. Brazil	66	D1
Tuscaloosa: U.S.A.	51	E3
Tuscany: Reg. Italy	25	C3
Tu Shui: r. China	36	A3
Tuttle Creek Reservoir: U.S.A.	58	A4
Tuttlingen: Ger F R	25	A2
TUVALU:	44	G7
Tuxpan: Mexico	48	C3
Tuyen Quang: Vietnam	38	D2
Tuy Hoa: Vietnam	38	D4
Tuyun: China	37	A4
Tuz, Lake: Turkey	28	C6
Tuzla: Yugoslavia	21	C4
Tweed: r. Scotland/England	11	F4
Tweedsmuir Provincial Park: Canada	62	A1
25 de Mayo: Argentina	66	B4
Twin Bridges: U.S.A.	62	D2
Twin Falls: town. Canada	57	E1
Twin Mountain: U.S.A.	57	P5
Two Harbors: U.S.A.	58	B2
Two Hills: town. Can.	60	D2
Two Rivers: town. Canada	57	E1
Tygda: U.S.S.R.	27	P2
Tyler: U.S.A.	50	C3
Tyndrum: Scotland	10	D3
Tyne: r. England	12	E2
Tyne: r. Scotland	11	F4
Tyne and Wear: Co.	12	E2
Tynemouth: England	12	E1
Tyrone: U.S.A.	54	B4
Tyrone: Co. N Ireland	13	D2
Tyrrell, Lake: Australia	43	B5
Tyrrhenian Sea: Italy	21	B4
Tyumen: U.S.S.R.	29	K2
Tywi: r. Wales	14	B3
Tzepo: China	36	C2
Tzeya: r. China	36	C2
Tzeyang: Shantung. China	36	C2
Ube: Japan	39	B3
Ubeda: Spain	19	B5
Uberaba: Brazil	66	D1
Uberlândia: Brazil	64	J7
Ubon Ratchathani: Thailand	38	C3
Ubsa Nor: l. Mongolia	34	A1
Ubundi: Zaire	71	D8
Ucayali: r. Peru	64	C5
Uchiura-wan: bay. Japan	39	D1
Uckfield: England	15	G3
Udaipur: India	32	B3
Uddevalla: Sweden	17	C4
Udd Lake: Sweden	16	C2
Udine: Italy	25	C2
Udon Thani: Thailand	38	C3
Ueda: Japan	39	C2
Ueno: Japan	39	c ii
Uezerama: Japan	39	f v
Ufa: U.S.S.R.	28	H3
Ufa: r. U.S.S.R.	29	H2
Uffcumne: England	14	C3
UGANDA:	70	F7
Ugie: r. Scotland	10	F2
Uinta Mountains: U.S.A.	63	D3
Uitenhage: S. Africa	72	D5
Uji: & r. Japan	39	b ii
Ujjain: India	32	C4
Ujung Pandang: Indon.	35	F12
Ukene: Nigeria	67	C2
Ukhta: U.S.S.R.	26	G3
Ukiah: U.S.A.	63	B4
Ukmerge: U.S.S.R.	17	D4
Ukpon: Nigeria	67	C2
Ukrainian S.S.R.: U.S.S.R.	28	B4
ULAN BATOR: Mongolia	34	
Ulangom: Mongolia	34	
Ulan-Ude: U.S.S.R.	27	
Ulawa: Solomon Is.	44	
Uldza: Mongolia	34	
Uliastay (Jibhalanta): Mongolia		
Ulladulla: Australia	43	
Ullapool: Scotland	10	
Ullswater: r. England	12	
Ulm: German F R	25	
Ulsan: S. Korea	39	
Ulundi: S. Africa	72	
Ulu-Tau: U.S.S.R.	29	
Ulva: i. Scotland	10	
Ulverston: England	12	
Ul'yanovsk: U.S.S.R.	28	
Ulyungur Nor: l.		
Ulzen: German F R	24	
Uman': U.S.S.R.	20	
Umarkot: Pakistan	32	
Umbagog Lake: U.S.A.	57	
Ume: r. Sweden	16	
Umeå: Sweden	16	
Umfreville, Lake: Can.	61	
Umm Said: Qatar	30	
Umm Urumah: i.		
Umtali: Zimbabwe	72	
Umtata: S. Africa	72	
Umuahia: Nigeria	67	
Unadilla: U.S.A.	54	
Ungava, Baie d': Can.	47	
Ungava, Péninsule d': Canada	47	
União da Vitória: Brazil	66	
Union Beach: town. U.S.A.	55	
Union City: U.S.A.	56	
Uniondale: S. Africa	72	
UNION OF SOVIET SOCIALIST REPUBLICS:	26/7	
Uniontown: U.S.A.	54	
UNITED ARAB EMIRATES:	30	
UNITED KINGDOM:	6	
UNITED STATES OF AMERICA:	48/9	
United States Range: Canada	47	
Unity: Canada	60	
Unst: i. Shetland Is.	10	
Uozu: Japan	39	
Upington: S. Africa	72	
Upper Arrow Lake: Can.	62	
Upper Klamath Lake: U.S.A.	62	
Upper Lough Erne: N. Ireland	13	
Upper Red Lake: U.S.A.	58	
UPPER VOLTA:	68	
Uppingham: England	15	
Uppsala: Sweden	17	
Upton-on-Severn: England	14	
Uqep: Nigeria	67	
Ur: Iraq	30	
Ural: r. U.S.S.R.	28	
Ural Mountains: U.S.S.R.	29	
Uralsk: U.S.S.R.	28	
Uranium City: Canada	60	
Urâwa: Japan	39	
Urbana: U.S.A.	58	
Urdos: France	23	
Ure: r. England	12	
Ureshino: Japan	39	
Urewera Nat. Park: New Zealand	41	
Urfa: Turkey	28	
Urgench: U.S.S.R.	29	
Uri: r. Scotland	10	
Urlingford: Irish Rep.	13	
Urmia, Lake: Iran	30	
Urom: Nigeria	67	
Urr Water: r. Scotland	11	
Uruguai: r. see Uruguay		
Uruguaiana: Brazil	66	
URUGUAY:	66	
Uruguay (Uruguai): r. S. America	66	
Usa: Japan	39	
Usa: r. U.S.S.R.	26	
Usakos: Namibia	72	
Ushant see Ouessant, Île de	22	
Usk: & r. Wales	14	
Usol've: U.S.S.R.	27	
Usongbe: Nigeria	67	
Usoro: Nigeria	67	
Uspallata Pass: Argentina/Chile	65	
Uspenskiy: U.S.S.R.	29	
Ussuri: r. China/U.S.S.R.	27	
Ussunysk: U.S.S.R.	27	
Ustinad Labem: Czech.	24	
Ust'-Kamenogorsk: U.S.S.R.	29	
Ust'-Kut: U.S.S.R.	27	
Ust-Urt Plateau: U.S.S.R.	28/9	
Ust'Usykove: U.S.S.R.	29	
Usuki: Japan	39	
Utah: State. U.S.A.	63	
Utah Lake: U.S.A.	63	
Utashinai: Japan	39	
Ute: r. U.S.A.	53	
Utica: Miss. U.S.A.	51	
Utica: N.Y. U.S.A.	54	
Utiel: Spain	19	
Utik, Lake: Canada	61	
Utikuma Lake: Canada	60	
Utrecht: Netherlands	24	
Utrera: Spain	19	
Utsjoki: Norway	16	
Utsunomiya: Japan	39	
Uttaradit: Thailand	38	
Uttar Pradesh: State. India	32	
Uttoxeter: England	15	
Uvalde: U.S.A.	50	
Uwajima: Japan	39	
Uyet: Nigeria	67	
Uxbridge: Canada	56	
Uxbridge: U.S.A.	55	
Uxmal ruins: Mexico	48	
Uyuni: Bolivia	65	
Uzbek S.S.R.: U.S.S.R.	29	
Uzhgorod: U.S.S.R.	20	
Uzlovaya: U.S.S.R.	28	
Vaal: r. S. Africa	72	
Vaala: Finland	16	
Vaasa: Finland	16	
Vác: Hungary	20	
Vacaria: Brazil	66	
Vadodara: India	32	

Name	Page	ref
Norway	16	E1
Liechtenstein	25	B2
Czech	20	C3
r. ,U.S.A.	29	M1
U.S.A.	55	G2
rette: sett.		
art: Canada	57	K3
Hills: U.S.S.R.	28	C2
enäs: Spain	19	B5
g Penin.: Arg	65	F12
U.S.A.	46	F4
ère: town.		
a: Chile	23	C2
Or: sett.: Can.	65	D11
asta: U.S.A	51	H1
ount: Canada	60	B2
te: France	23	B3
cia: Spain	19	B5
cia: Venezuela	49	N7
cia: Golfo de:	19	B5
iennes: France	22	B1
a: I.: Irish Rep.	13	A5
ine: U.S.A	53	E2
A: Malta	21	B5
U.S.S.R.	17	E4
o: Yugoslavia	21	C4
akoski: Finland	17	D3
olid: Spain	19	B4
Rio del: r.		
ientina	66	B1
Junction: sett.		
ada	57	P3
U.S.A	63	B4
sett.: Wales	14	B1
City: U.S.A	58	A2
field: Canada	57	L4
View: Canada	60	B1
View: U.S.A.	54	D4
cane: Canada	62	E2
aíso: Chile	65	D10
Cape: Indonesia	40	F4
ellina: Italy	25	B2
enosta: valley.	25	C2
ri: Turkey	28	E6
uver: Canada	62	B2
uver: U.S.A	62	B2
uver: Mt.		
ada: U.S.A	46	H4
uver Is.: Canada	62	A2
Lake: Sweden	17	B4
sborg: Sweden	17	B4
U.S.A.	54	D2
anu: i.		
omon Islands	40	K2
Laos	38	C3
ook Hill: sett.		
ada	57	L4
as: Sweden	16	C3
as: France	22	a i
y.: Norway	16	C1
Levu: i.: Fiji	44	G8
gher Pen.: Norway	16	E1
gerfjorden: fd.		
way	16	b ii
ass: India	32	D3
din': Yugoslavia	20	C3
Sweden	17	B4
Reservoir		
Republic	13	E3
a.: Rio da: r.		
zil	66	D2
r.: U.S.A	56	B6
alls: Sweden	17	C4
dal: r.: Sweden	17	B4
gan: U.S.A	29	M2
isay: r.: Scotland	10	A3
nish Pt.: hd.: Scot.	10	B2
okull: ice-cap.		
and	16	b ii
, Lake: Sweden	17	B4
ls: r.: Colombia	64	D3
all: Canada	60	C2
ya: Sri Lanka	32	b ii
Sweden	17	B4
Island		
.S.R.	26	H3
Argentina	66	B3
am: Netherlands	24	B1
.: Norway	16	B2
ville: Canada	60	C2
Denmark	17	A4
Monts du: r.		
quez: Uruguay	66	D4
ya: r.: U.S.S.R.	28	E4
ne: India	32	C6
andois: France	22	B2
eme: Netherlands	24	B3
de Tuerto: Mex	66	B3
eme: France	23	B2
uan Alps: mtns.		
	25	C2
go: reg.: Italy	25	C2
se de Venice	25	C2
ZUELA	64	—
uela: Gulf of: Ven.	49	M7
a: (Venezia): &.g.	25	C2
	25	C2
r.: U.S.S.R.	17	D4
niglia: Italy	25	B3
ls: U.S.S.R.	16	E4
pls: U.S.S.R	17	D4
Argentina	66	B2
Lago: Paraguay	66	C2
ruz: Mexico	48	G6
alt: Italy	25	B2
, Paraguay	66	C1
r.: U.S.A	63	D5
ns: U.S.A	58	A4
n: r.: France	23	C3
n: France	22	C2
iniging: S. Africa	72	D4
iti: Parc de la:		
ada	56/7	H2
ones: U.S.A	57	N5
oyansk: U.S.S.R.	27	Q4
oyansk Range		
.S.R.	27	P4
ion: Canada	60	C2
ion: U.S.A	57	M5
ion Bay: Canada	61	G3
ion Lake: U.S.A	58	B2
ion Range		
.A	58	B2
ion: Ohio.		
.A	56	C8
ion: &.r.: S Dak.		
.A	58	A3

Name	Page	ref
Vermont: State.: U.S.A.	57	N6
Vernal: U.S.A.	63	E3
Verner: Canada	56	E3
Vernon: Canada	62	C1
Vernon: U.S.A.	50	C3
Verona: Greece	21	D4
Verona: Italy	25	C2
Versailles: France	22	B2
Verte: Île: Canada	57	Q1
Verviers: Belgium	22	C1
Vestfjorden: fd.: Nor.	16	C2
Vesle: r.: France	22	B2
Vestmannaeyjar: i.		
Iceland	16	a ii
Vesoul: France	23	C2
Vesuvius: volc.: Italy	21	B4
Veszprem: Hungary	20	C3
Vetlanda: Sweden	17	C4
Vevey: Switzerland	25	B2
Viana do Castelo: Port	19	A4
Viareggio: Italy	25	C2
Viborg: Denmark	17	A4
Vicente Lopez: Arg	66	C3
Vicenza: Italy	25	C2
Vichadero: Uruguay	66	D3
Vichy: France	23	B2
Vicksburg: U.S.A	58	C3
Victor: U.S.A	54	C2
Victor Harbour: Austl	43	A5
Victoria: Argentina	66	B3
Victoria: Cameroun	67	B3
Victoria: Hong Kong	37	B6
Victoria: Malta	21	B5
Victoria: U.S.A.	50	C4
Victoria: Co.Canada	56	G5
Victoria: Lac: Austl	43	B5
Victoria: Grand Lac:		
Canada	56	H2
Victoria: L.: Africa	71	F8
Victoria:West: S Africa	72	C5
Vidin: Bulgaria	21	D3
Vidzeme: hills: U.S.S.R	17	E4
Viejo: r.: Argentina	66	B2
VIENNA: Austria	20	A2
Vienne: r.: France	23	B2
VIENTIANE: Laos	38	C3
Vierzon-Ville: France	23	B2
Vieste: Italy	21	C4
VIETNAM:	38	
Vigevano: Italy	25	B2
Vigia: Spain	19	A4
Vijayawada: India	32	D5
Vikna: i.: Norway	16	B3
VILA: New Hebrides	40	M4
Vilaine: r.: France	22	a i
Vila Nova de Gaia:		
Portugal	19	A4
Vila Real: Portugal	19	A4
Vilhelmina: Sweden	16	C3
Viljandi: U.S.S.R	17	E4
Villa Alberdi: Arg	66	A2
Villa Ángela: Argentina	66	B3
Villa Carlos Paz: Arg	66	B3
Villa Constitución: Arg	66	F1
Villa del Rosario: Arg	66	A3
Villa Dolores: Arg	66	B3
Villa El Alto: Arg	66	A2
Villa Federal: Arg	66	C3
Villaguay: Argentina	66	C3
Villa Hayes: Paraguay	66	C2
Villa Hernandarias:		
Argentina	66	C3
Villa Huidobro: Arg	66	B3
Villalba: Spain	19	A4
Villa María: Argentina	66	B3
Villa Ojo de Agua: Arg	66	B3
Villa Oliva: Paraguay	66	C2
Villa Ocampo: Arg	66	C2
Villarrabledo: Spain	19	B5
Villarrica: Paraguay	66	C2
Villebon: Lac: Canada	56	H2
Villefranche-sur-Saône		
France	23	B2
Villengen: German F R	25	B2
Villengen: German F.R	25	B2
Villeneuve-sur-Lot: Fr	23	B2
Villeurbanne: France	23	B2
Vilnius: U.S.S.R.	17	E5
Vilyuy: r.: U.S.S.R.	27	P5
Viña del Mar: Chile	65	D10
Vinaroz: Spain	19	C4
Vincennes: U.S.A.	58	C4
Vincent: Cape: U.S.A	57	J5
Vinde: r.: Sweden	16	C2
Vindhya Range: India	32	C5
Vineland: U.S.A	54	E5
Vineyard Haven: U.S.A	55	K3
Vinh: Vietnam	38	C4
Vinh Loi: Vietnam	38	D5
Vinh Long: Vietnam	38	D4
Vinkovci: Yugoslavia	21	C3
Vintondale: Canada	54	B4
Virden: Canada	61	B3
Vire: France	22	A2
Virgin Is.: Caribbean		
Sea	49	O6
Virginia: Irish Rep.	13	D3
Virginia: U.S.A.	58	B1
Virginia: State.: U.S.A.	58	D4
Virginatown: Canada	56	F1
Vis: i.: Yugoslavia	21	C4
Visalia: U.S.A.	63	C4
Visby: Sweden	17	C4
Viscount Melville:		
Sound: Canada	46	N2
Viseu: Portugal	19	A4
Vishakhapatnam: India	32	D5
Vistula: r.: Poland	20	C2
Vitebsk: U.S.S.R	17	F4
Viterbo: Italy	21	B4
Viti Levu: i.: Fiji	44	G8
Vitim: &.r.: U.S.S.R	27	O6
Vitória: Brazil	64	K8
Vitoria: Spain	19	B4
Vitry de François: Fr	22	B2
Vittoria: Canada	56	B1
Vittoria Veneto: Italy	25	C2
Vize: i.: see Wiese I		
Vizianagaram: India	32	D5
Vladimir: U.S.S.R	28	E2
(Vladimir Volynsky)		
U.S.S.R	20	D2
Vladivostok: U.S.S.R.	27	Q9
Vlore: Albania	21	C4
Vltava (Moldau): r.:		
Czechoslovakia	20	C2
Vogel Peak: mtn.		
Nigeria	67	C2
Vogelsang Nat Park		
German F R	24	B1
Voghera: Italy	25	B3

Name	Page	ref
Voiron: France	23	C2
Volcán: U.S.A	66	A1
Volcanic Plateau: N.Z.	41	C2
Volga: r. & hills.		
U.S.S.R.	28	F3
Vologda: U.S.S.R	28	D2
Volgograd: U.S.S.R	28	E2
Vólos: Greece	21	D5
Vol'sk: U.S.S.R	28	F3
Volta: l. & dam. Ghana	68	E7
Volta Redonda: Brazil	64	b i
Vom: Nigeria	67	B2
Vouri: r.: Cameroun	67	B3
Voralberg: Prov.: Aust.	25	B2
Vordingborg: Denmark	17	B5
Vorkuta: U.S.S.R	28	J4
Voronezh: U.S.S.R	28	D3
Voroshilovgrad		
U.S.S.R.	28	D4
Võru: U.S.S.R.	17	E4
Vosges: mtns.: France	22	C2
Voss: Norway	17	A3
Voyageurs Nat. Park:		
U.S.A	58	B2
Voynitsa: U.S.S.R	16	E3
Vraca: Bulgaria	21	D4
Vršac: Yugoslavia	21	D4
Vryburg: S Africa	72	C4
Vukovar: Yugoslavia	21	C3
Vulcan: Canada	60	C2
Vung Tau: Vietnam	38	D4
Vyaz ma: U.S.S.R	28	C2
Vyborg: U.S.S.R	17	E3
Vyrnwy: r. & r.: Wales	14	C2
Vyshniy-Volochek:		
U.S.S.R	28	C2

Name	Page	ref
Waal: r.: Netherlands	24	B1
Wabana: Canada	57	Z7
Wabasca: r.: Canada	60	C1
Wabash: r.: U.S.A	58	C4
Wabatongushi Lake:		
Canada	56	A1
Wabowden: Canada	61	F2
Waccasassa Bay:		
U.S.A.	51	F4
Wachusett Reservoir:		
U.S.A.	55	J2
Waco: U.S.A	50	C3
Wada: Japan	39	a iv
Wadden Zee: bay: Neth.	24	B1
Waddington: Mount:		
Canada	62	A1
Waddington: U.S.A	57	K5
Wadebridge: England	14	B4
Wadena: U.S.A	58	A2
Wadi Halfa: town.		
Sudan	69	M4
Wad Hill: Nigeria	67	B2
Wad Medani: Sudan	69	M6
Wagga Wagga: Austl.	43	C5
Wagin: Australia	42	b ii
Waha: Libya	69	J3
Wahpeton: U.S.A	58	A2
Waiau: &.r.: N.Z.	41	B3
Waigeo: r.: Indonesia	35	J11
Waikaremoana, Lake:		
New Zealand	41	C2
Waikato: r.dist.: N.Z.	41	C2
Waikerie: Australia	43	B4
Wainfleet All Saints:		
England	15	G1
Waingapu: Indonesia	35	G12
Wainwright: Canada	60	C2
Waipara: New Zealand	41	B3
Waipawa: New Zealand	41	C2
Wairakei: New Zealand	41	C2
Wairoa: New Zealand	41	C2
Waitaki: r.: N.Z.	41	B3
Waitangi: New Zealand	41	C2
Waitara: New Zealand	41	C2
Waitomo Caves: town.		
New Zealand	41	C2
Wayeung: China	37	B5
Wajima: Japan	39	C2
Wakami Lake: Canada	56	C2
Wakatipu, Lake: N.Z	41	A4
Wakaw: Canada	61	D2
Wakayama: Japan	39	b ii
Wakefield: U.S.A	57	K4
Wakefield: England	12	F4
Wakefield: U.S.A	55	J3
Wake Island: Pacific	44	F5
Wakkanai: Japan	34	L1
Wakomata Lake: Can.	56	B2
Wakwekobi Lake: Can.	56	B2
Wałbrzych: Poland	20	C2
Walchern: i.: Neth.	24	A1
Walcott: U.S.A	57	J6
Walden: U.S.A	55	J1
Waldheim: Canada	60	D2
Waldshut: German F.R	25	B2
Walensee: l.: Switz	25	B2
Wales: principality: U.K	14	C2
Walgett: Australia	43	C3
Walhalla: U.S.A	61	F3
Walker: Lake: U.S.A	63	C4
Walkerton: Canada	56	D3
Wallaceburg: Canada	56	C7
Wallachia: geog.reg.		
Romania	21	D4
Wallaroo: Australia	43	A4
Wallasey: England	12	C3
Walla Walla: U.S.A	63	C3
Wallenpaupack.L.		
U.S.A	54	E3
Wallingford: England	15	F3
Wallingford: U.S.A	55	H3
Wallkill: r.: U.S.A	55	H3
Wallsend: England	12	F2
Walney: i.: England	12	C2
Walsall: England	15	E2
Walsenburg: U.S.A	53	E4
Walton: U.S.A	54	E2
Walton-on-the-Naze:		
England	15	H3
Walvis Bay: town.		
Namibia	72	A4
Walvis Ridge: S Atl.O.	8	L10
Wamba: Nigeria	67	B2
Wanaka, Lake: N.Z	41	B3
Wanapiri: Indonesia	35	J11
Wanapitei Provincial		
Forest: Canada	56	D2
Wanda: Argentina	66	C2
Wandsworth: England	15	F3
Waneta: Canada	62	C2
Wanganui: r.: N.Z.	41	C2
Wangaratta: Australia	43	C4
Wangen: German F.R	25	B2
Wangerooge: i.		
Ger.F.R	24	B1
Wangkiang: China	37	B5
Wanham: Canada	60	B1
Wanhsien: China	37	A3
Wankie Nat.Park: Zamb	72	D3
Wankie: Zimbabwe	72	D3
Wanless: Canada	57	D2
Wanleweyne: Somalia	71	F5
Wansbeck: r.: England	37	E1
Wantage: England	15	E3
Wantsar: China	37	B4
Wanyuan: China	36	A3
Wapawekka Hills: &.l.		
Canada	61	E2
Wapella: Canada	61	E2
Wapiti: r.: Canada	60	B1
Warangal: India	32	C5
Waratah Bay: Australia	43	C5
Warburg: German F R	24	B1
Wardlow: Canada	60	C2
Ware: &.r.: U.S.A	15	H3
Wareham: England	14	D4
Wareham: Canada	55	K3
Warman: Canada	60	D2
Warmbad: Namibia	72	B4
Warminster: England	14	D3
Warner: Canada	60	C3
Warracknabeal: Austl	43	B5
Warragul: Australia	43	C5
Warrego: r.: Australia	42	C3
Warrego Range: Austl.	42	C2
Warren: Idaho: U.S.A	62	C2
Warren: Mass.: U.S.A	55	H2
Warren: Minn.: U.S.A	58	A1
Warren: Ohio: U.S.A	59	D3
Warren: Pa.: U.S.A	54	B3
Warren: R.I.: U.S.A	55	J3
Warren Landing: Can.	61	F2
Warrenpoint: N Ireland	13	E2
Warrensburg: U.S.A	57	M6
Warrington: England	12	D3
Warrnambool: Australia	43	B5
Warroad: U.S.A	58	A2
WARSAW: Poland	20	D2
Warsaw: U.S.A	54	D2
Warta: r.: Poland	20	C2
Warwick: Australia	42	D3
Warwick: England	15	E2
Warwick: N.Y.: U.S.A	55	F3
Warwick: R.I.: U.S.A	55	J3
Warwickshire: Co.		
England	15	E2
Wasaga Beach: town.		
Canada	56	F5
Wasai: Nigeria	67	B1
Wascana Creek: r.: Can.	61	E2
Wase: Nigeria	67	B2
Wasekamio Lake: Can.	60	D1
Washago: Canada	56	F5
Washington: England	12	E2
Washington: Conn.		
U.S.A	55	G3
Washington: Ind.		
U.S.A	58	C4
Washington: N.C.		
U.S.A	51	G2
Washington: State.:		
U.S.A.	62	B2
WASHINGTON D.C.		
U.S.A.	54	C6
Washington: Mount:		
U.S.A	57	O5
Washow Bay: Canada	61	F2
Waskesiu: Canada	60	D2
Watabeag Lake: &.r.		
Canada	56	E1
Watchet: England	14	C3
Waterbury: Vt.: U.S.A	55	N5
Waterbury: L.: Canada	61	E1
Waterford: Canada	56	E3
Waterford: &.Co.		
Irish Republic	13	D4
Waterford: N.Y.: U.S.A	55	H2
Waterford Harbour		
Irish Republic	13	E4
Waterhen: r.: Canada	60	D2
Waterhen: Lake: Can	61	F2
Waterloo: Belgium	22	B1
Waterloo: &.Co.: Ont.		
Canada	56	E3
Waterloo: Canada	57	N4
Waterloo: Iowa: U.S.A	58	B3
Waterloo: Que.	54	D2
Water Mill: U.S.A	55	H4
Waterton Lakes Nat		
Park: Canada	62	D2
Watertown: N.Y.		
U.S.A	57	K6
Watertown: S.Dak.		
U.S.A	58	A3
Watertown: Wis.		
U.S.A	58	C3
Waterville: Maine.		
U.S.A	54	F1
Waterville: Ohio.		
U.S.A	56	B8
Watervliet: U.S.A	55	G2
Watford: England	15	F3
Watkins Glen: U.S.A	54	E1
Watling I.: see San		
Salvador I.	49	M5
Watlington: England	15	F3
Watrous: Canada	61	D2
Watson Lake: town.		
Canada	46	K4
Watsontown: U.S.A	54	C3
Watson: Loch: Scot	10	E1
Watton: England	15	G2
Wau: Sudan	69	L7
Waubaushene: Canada	56	F5
Waukesha: U.S.A	58	C3
Waukegan: U.S.A	58	C3
Wausau: U.S.A	58	C2
Waveney: r.: England	15	H2
Waverly: U.S.A	54	D2
Wawa: Canada	56	A1
Wawatin Falls: Canada	60	D1
Wawota: Canada	61	E2
Waxahachie: U.S.A	50	C3
Waycross: U.S.A	51	F3
Wayland: U.S.A	54	D2
Waymart: U.S.A	54	E3
Waynesboro: Pa.		
U.S.A	54	C5
Waynesboro: U.S.A	59	D4
Waza Nat.Park: Cam.	67	C1
Weald: the: geog.reg:		
England	15	G3
Wear: r.: England	12	E2
Weatherly: U.S.A	54	E3
Weaver: Lake: Canada	61	F2
Weaverville: U.S.A	63	B3
Webbwood: Canada	56	D2
Weber: r.: U.S.A	63	D3
Webster: Mass.: U.S.A	55	J2
Webster: N.Y.: U.S.A	54	D1
Weddell Sea: Antarctica	73	
Wedd: U.S.A	51	G5
Weedon: Canada	57	O4
Weedon Bec: England	15	F2
Weedsport: U.S.A	54	D1

Name	Page	ref
Weggis: Switzerland	25	B2
Wei: r.: Honan/		
Shantung: China	36	C2
Wei: r.: Shantung.		
China	36	C2
Weichang: China	36	C1
Weiden: German F R	24	C2
Weifang: China	36	D2
Weihai: China	36	D2
Weihsien: China	36	C2
Weimar: German D.R	24	C2
Weinan: China	36	A3
Weirton: U.S.A	59	D3
Weiser: U.S.A	62	C3
Weishan, Lake: China	36	C3
Weishih: China	36	B3
Weissenburg: Ger.F R	24	B2
Wessenfels: Ger.D.R	24	C1
Weisshorn: mtn.: Switz	25	B2
Wejherowo: Poland	20	C2
Wekusko: &.l.: Canada	61	F2
Welkom: S Africa	72	D4
Welland: &.canal: Can.	56	F7
Welland: r.: England	15	F2
Wellesley Is.: Austl	40	F4
Wellfleet: U.S.A	55	K3
Wellingborough: Eng	15	F2
Wellington: N.S.W.		
Australia	43	C4
Wellington: S. Austl.		
Australia	42	b ii
Wellington: Canada	56	H6
Wellington: England	14	D3
Wells: England	14	D3
Wells: U.S.A	63	D3
Wellsboro: U.S.A	54	C3
Wells: Austria	25	C2
Wellsburg: U.S.A	54	D2
Wells Gray Provincial		
Park: Canada	62	C1
Wells-next-the-Sea		
England	15	G2
Wellsville: U.S.A	54	B2
Wels: Austria	25	C2
Welshpool: Wales	14	C2
Welwyn Garden City		
England	15	F3
Wem: England	14	D2
Wembley: Canada	60	B1
Wen: r.: China	36	C2
Wenan: China	36	C2
Wenatchee: U.S.A	62	C2
Wenchang: China	37	A3?
Wenchow: China	37	D4
Wendover: England	15	F3
Wendover: U.S.A	63	D3
Wenebegon: l. &.r.		
Canada	56	B2
Weng'an: China	37	A4
Wengen: Switzerland	25	B2
Wengyuan: China	37	B5
Wenham: U.S.A	55	K2
Wenling: China	37	D4
Wenlock Edge: scarp.		
England	14	D2
Wensi: China	36	A3
Wensiang: China	36	B3
Wensleydale: val.: Eng	12	E2
Wensum: r.: England	15	H2
Wentworth: Australia	43	B4
Wentworth: Co.		
Canada	56	E3
Wernigerode: Ger.D R	24	C1
Werribee: Australia	43	B3
Werris Creek: town.		
Australia	43	D4
Weser: r.: German F.R	24	B1
Wesergebirge: mtns.		
Ger.F.R	24	B1
Weslemkoon Lake: Can.	56	H4
West Australian Basin		
Indian Ocean	33	h vi
West Bengal: State.		
India	32	D5
West Branch: sett.		
U.S.A	56	A5
West Branch		
Susquehanna		
r.: U.S.A	54	C3
West Bridgford: Eng	15	E2
West Bromwich: Eng	14	D2
Westbrook: U.S.A	55	H3
West Camden Creek		
U.S.A	57	L6
Westbury: England	14	D3
West Canada Creek		
U.S.A	54	F1
West Caroline Basin		
Pacific Ocean	44	C6
West Chester: U.S.A	54	E4
West Concord: U.S.A	55	J2
Westerhever: Ger F R	18	D2
Westerly: U.S.A	55	J3
Western Australia:		
State: Australia	40	—
Western Isles: Reg.		
Scotland	10	A2
Western Sahara:		
disputed terr.: Africa	68	C3
WESTERN SAMOA	44	H8
Western Sayan Mts		
U.S.S.R.	29	P3
Western Sierra Madre		
Mexico	48	E4
Western Ross: geog.		
Scotland	10	C2
West European Basin		
N Atlantic Ocean	28	J3
Westfield: Mass.		
U.S.A	55	H2
Westfield: r.: U.S.A	55	H2
West Frisian Is.: Neth.	24	b ii
West Glamorgan: Co.		
Wales	14	C3
West Grove: U.S.A	54	E5
Westhope: U.S.A	58	A1
West Indies		
Caribbean Sea	49	—
West Kilbride: Scotland	11	D4
Westland: dist & N P.		
New Zealand	41	B3
West Lebanon: U.S.A	57	N6
West Loch Tarbert		
Scotland	10	B2
Westlock: Canada	60	C2
West Lorne: Canada	56	D3
West Malaysia	35	D9
West Midlands: Co.		
England	15	E2
Westminster: U.S.A	54	D4
West Nicholson: Zimb	72	D3
Weston: Malaysia	35	F9
Weston: U.S.A	59	D4
Weston-super-Mare		
England	14	D3

Name	Page	ref
West Palm Beach: city.		
U.S.A	51	F4
Westphalia: land.		
German F R	24	B1
West Plains: sett.		
U.S.A	58	B4
West Point: sett.		
U.S.A	58	A3
Westport: Canada	57	J5
Westport: Irish Rep	13	B3
Westport: New Zealand	41	B3
Westport: U.S.A	55	G3
Westray: i. & td.		
Orkney Islands	10	e iii
West Scotia Basin:		
S. Atlantic Ocean	8	E13
West Siberian Plain:		
U.S.S.R	26	—
West Stockbridge		
U.S.A	55	G2
West Sussex: Co.: Eng	15	F4
West Swanzey: U.S.A	55	H2
Westville: U.S.A	54	E5
West Virginia: State.		
U.S.A	59	D4
Westview: Canada	62	B2
Westward Ho: England	14	B3
West Warwick: U.S.A	55	J3
Westwood: U.S.A	63	B3
West Yorkshire: Co.		
England	12	E3
Wetabeag: r.: Canada	56	E1
Wetar: i.: Indonesia	35	H12
Wetaskiwin: Canada	60	C2
Wetherby: England	12	E3
Wetzlar: German F.R	24	B1
Wevok: U.S.A	46	B3
Wewak: Pap.-N.G.	40	G1
Wexford: &.Co.:		
Irish Rep	13	E4
Wexford Bay: Irish Rep	13	E4
Wey: r.: England	15	F3
Weybridge: England	15	F3
Weyburn: Canada	61	E3
Weymouth: England	14	D4
Weymouth: U.S.A	55	K2
Whakatane: N.Z	41	C2
Whaley Bridge: England	15	E1
Whalsay: i.: Shet.Is	10	c i
Whangarei: N.Z	41	C1
Wharfe: r.: England	12	D2
Wharfedale: val.: Eng	12	E2
Wharton: Canada	56	G5
Wharton: U.S.A	54	D4
Wharton Basin: Ind.O	33	j vi
Wheatley: Canada	56	C7
Wheatley: England	15	E3
Wheeler: r.: Canada	61	D1
Wheeler Lake: U.S.A	51	E3
Wheeling: U.S.A	59	D3
Whiddy: i.: Irish Rep.	13	B5
Whiskey Lake: Canada	56	C3
Whitby: Canada	56	F6
Whitby: England	12	F2
Whitburn: Scotland	11	E4
Whitchurch: Bucks.		
England	15	F3
Whitchurch: Hants.		
England	15	E3
Whitchurch: Salop.		
England	14	D1
Whitchurch: Scotland	11	D5
Whitley Bay: England	12	E1
Whitman: U.S.A	55	K2
Whitney: Canada	56	G4
Whitney, Mt.: U.S.A	63	C4
Whipsnade: England	15	F3
Whitstable: England	15	H3
Whitsunday I.: Austl	42	C2
Whittlesea: Australia	43	C5
Whittlesey: England	15	F2
Whyalla: Australia	43	A4
White: r.: Canada	56	A2
White: r.: Ark.: U.S.A	50	D3
White: r.: Colo.: U.S.A	63	D4
White: r.: Ind.: U.S.A	58	C4
White: r.: S.Dak.		
U.S.A	53	E2
White: r.: Vt.: U.S.A	55	J2
Whitecourt: Canada	60	B2
White East Fork: r.		
U.S.A	58	C4
Whitefield: U.S.A	55	O5
Whitefish: U.S.A	63	D2
Whitehall: U.S.A	54	C3
Whitehaven: England	12	C2
White Lake: Canada	56	C3
Whitehead: N.Ireland	13	F3
White Lake: town.		
U.S.A	54	C4
White Mountains:		
U.S.A	55	O5
Whitemouth: &.l.: Can	61	F3
Whiten Head: Scotland	10	D1
White Nile: r.: Sudan	69	M6
White Pine: U.S.A	56	B3
White Plains: town.		
U.S.A	55	G3
White River Junction		
U.S.A	57	N6
White Sands National		
Monument: U.S.A	52	D4
Whitesboro: U.S.A	54	E1
White Sea: U.S.S.R	30	C1
Wheshelf Provincial		
Park: Canada	61	F2
White Volta: r.		
Upper Volta	68	E6
Whitewood: Canada	61	E2
Wiay: i.: Scotland	10	A2
Wichita: U.S.A	50	C3
Wichita: r.: U.S.A	50	C3
Wichita Falls: town.		
U.S.A	50	C3
Wick: Scotland	10	E1
Wickenburg: U.S.A	52	C4
Wickham Market: Eng	15	H2
Wicklow: &.Co.		
Irish Republic	13	E4
Wicklow Hd.: Irish Rep	13	E4
Wicklow Mts.		
Irish Republic	13	E4
Widnes: England	12	D3
Wiedenbruck: Ger F.R	24	B1
Wiener Neustadt: Aus	20	B3
Wiesbaden: Ger.F.R	24	B1
Wiese (Vize) I.		
U.S.S.R	27	K2
Wigan: England	12	D3
Wight, Isle of: England	15	E4
Wigton: England	12	C2
Wigtown: &.bay: Scot.	11	D5
Wilhelmina: Canada	57	B4
Wilkawinkong: Canada	56	E1
Wilcannia: Australia	43	B4
Wilcox: U.S.A	54	C3
Wildwood: Canada	60	B2
Wildwood: U.S.A	59	E3
Wilhelmshaven:		
Ger.F.R	24	B1
Wilkes-Barre: U.S.A	54	E3

Page — ref

Wilkie: Canada 60 D2
Willapa Bay: U.S.A. 62 B2
Willamette: r. U.S.A. 62 B3
Willcox: U.S.A. 63 E5
Willemstad: Netherlands Antilles 49 N7
William: r. Canada 60 D1
William, Mt. Australia 43 B5
Williams: Ariz. U.S.A. 63 D4
Williams Minn. U.S.A. 61 G3
Williams Lake: town. Canada 62 B1
Williamsburg Pa.: U.S.A. 54 B4
Williamsburg Va.: U.S.A. 59 E4
Williamson N.Y.: U.S.A. 54 C1
Williamson W.Va.: U.S.A. 59 D4
Williamsport Md.: U.S.A. 54 C5
Williamsport Pa.: U.S.A. 54 C3
Williamstown Mass.: U.S.A. 55 G2
Williamstown N.J.: U.S.A. 54 E5
Williamstown N.Y.: U.S.A. 54 D4
Williamsville U.S.A. 54 B2
Willimantic: U.S.A. 55 H3
Willington: England 12 E2
Williston: U.S.A. 53 E1
Williston Lake: Canada 46 L5
Williton: England 14 C3
Willmar: U.S.A. 58 A2
Willmore Wilderness Prov. Park: Canada 60 B2
Willoughby, Cape: Australia 43 A6
Willowbunch Lake: Can. 61 D3
Willows: U.S.A. 62 B4
Willow South: U.S.A. 46 F4
Will Rogers Turnpike: hwy. U.S.A. 58 A4
Willsboro: U.S.A. 57 M5
Willunga: Australia 43 A6
Wilmington: Mass.: U.S.A. 55 J2
Wilmington N.C.: U.S.A. 51 G3
Wilmington Pa.: U.S.A. 54 E5
Wilmslow: England 14 D1
Wilson: r. Australia 42 B3
Wilson N.C.: U.S.A. 51 G2
Wilson N.Y.: U.S.A. 54 B1
Wilsonville: U.S.A. 55 J2
Wilton: England 15 E3
Wilton: Conn. U.S.A. 55 G3
Wilton Maine. U.S.A. 57 P5
Wilton N.H. U.S.A. 55 J2
Wiltshire: Co. Eng. 14 D/E3
Wiluna: Australia 40 C6
Wimborne Minster: England 15 E4
Wincanton: England 14 D3
Winchcombe: England 15 E3
Winchelsea: England 15 G4
Winchendon: U.S.A. 55 H2
Winchester: Canada 57 K4
Winchester: England 15 E3
Winchester Ky.: U.S.A. 58 D4
Winchester N.H.: U.S.A. 55 H2
Winchester Va.: U.S.A. 54 B5
Wind: r. U.S.A. 62 E3
Windber: U.S.A. 54 B4
Wind Cave Nat. Park: U.S.A. 53 E2
Windermere: & l. Eng. 12 D2
Windermere Lake: Can. 56 B2
Windgap: U.S.A. 54 E4
WINDHOEK: Namibia 72 B3
Wind River Range: U.S.A. 62 E3
Windrush: r. England 15 E3
Windsor: Ont. Canada 56 B7
Windsor Qué. Canada 57 O4
Windsor: England 15 F3
Windsor Conn. U.S.A. 55 H3
Windsor Pa. U.S.A. 54 D5
Windsor Vt. U.S.A. 57 N6
Windsor Locks: town. U.S.A. 55 H3
Windward Is. W. Indies 49 O7
Windward Passage: W. Indies 49 M5
Winefred Lake: Canada 60 C1
Winfield: U.S.A. 55 C2
Wingham: Canada 56 D6
Winfred: U.S.A. 62 E2
Winkler: Canada 61 F3
Winnebago, Lake: U.S.A. 58 C3
Winnemucca: U.S.A. 63 C3

Winnemucca Lake: U.S.A. 63 C3
Winner: U.S.A. 53 F2
Winnipeg: Canada 61 F2
Winnipeg: r. Canada 61 F2
Winnipeg, Lake: Can. 61 F2
Winnipeg Beach: Can. 61 F2
Winnipegosis: & l. Canada 61 E2
Winnipesaukee, Lake: U.S.A. 57 O6
Winona: Minn. U.S.A. 58 B3
Winona Miss. U.S.A. 51 E3
Winooski: U.S.A. 57 M5
Winooski: r. U.S.A. 57 N5
Winsford: England 14 D1
Winslow: England 15 F3
Winslow: U.S.A. 63 D4
Winston-Salem: U.S.A. 51 F2
Winter Haven: U.S.A. 51 F4
Winterset: U.S.A. 58 B3
Winterthur: Switz. 24 C1
Winterton: England 12 F3
Winterton-on-Sea: Eng. 15 H2
Winton: Australia 40 G5
Wirksworth: England 15 E1
Wirral: penin. Eng. 14 D1
Wisbech: England 15 G2
Wiscasset: U.S.A. 57 Q5
Wisconsin: State & r. U.S.A. 58 —
Wisconsin Rapids: town. U.S.A. 58 C3
Wishaw: Scotland 11 E4
Wismar: German D.R. 24 C1
Wissey: r. England 15 G2
Witbank: S. Africa 72 D4
Witdraai: S. Africa 72 C4
Witham: England 15 G3
Witham: r. England 15 F1
Withernsea: England 12 G3
Witney: England 15 E3
Wittenberg: Ger. D.R. 24 C1
Wittenberge: Ger. D.R. 24 C1
Wivenhoe: England 15 G3
Włocławek: Poland 20 C2
Wnion: r. Wales 14 C2
Woking: England 15 F3
Wokingham: England 15 F3
Wolcott: U.S.A. 54 D1
Wolf: r. U.S.A. 58 C2
Wolf Creek: U.S.A. 56 B5
Wolfe Co. Canada 57 O4
Wolfeboro: U.S.A. 57 O6
Wolfe Island: Canada 57 J5
Wolfenbüttel: Ger. F.R. 24 C1
Wolf Point: town. U.S.A. 53 D1
Wolfsburg: Ger. F.R. 24 C1
Wollaston, Lake: Can. 61 E1
Wollongong: Australia 43 D4
Wolseley: Canada 61 E2
Wolverhampton: Eng. 14 D2
Wolverton: England 15 F2
Womdiu: Nigeria 67 C1
Womelsdorf: U.S.A. 54 D4
Wondo: Ethiopia 69 N7
Wonsan: N. Korea 34 H3
Wonthaggi: Australia 43 C5
Wood, Mt.: Canada 60 D3
Woodbine: U.S.A. 54 F5
Woodbridge: England 15 H2
Wood Buffalo Nat. Park: Canada 60 C1
Woodhall Spa: England 15 F1
Woodland: U.S.A. 63 B4
Woods, Lake of the: Canada 61 G3
Woodstock: Canada 56 E6
Woodstock: England 15 E3
Woodstown: U.S.A. 54 E5
Woodville: N.Z. 41 N5
Woodville: U.S.A. 50 C3
Woodward: U.S.A. 50 C2
Wooler: England 11 G4
Woomera: L. Australia 40 F7
Woonsocket: U.S.A. 55 J3
Woosung: China 37 D3
Wootton Bassett: Eng. 15 E3
Worcester: England 14 D2
Worcester: S. Africa 72 B5
Worcester U.S.A. 55 J2
Workington: England 12 C2
Worksop: England 15 E1
Worland: U.S.A. 62 E3
Worms: German F.R. 24 B2
Worms Hd.: c. Wales 14 B3
Worthing: England 15 F4
Worthington: U.S.A. 58 A3
Woy Woy: Australia 43 D4
Wrangel Island: U.S.S.R. 27 U3
Wreake: r. England 15 F2
Wrekin, The: hill. Eng. 14 D2
Wrentham: U.S.A. 55 J2
Wrexham: Wales 14 C1

Wrightsville: U.S.A. 54 D4
Writing on Stone Park: Canada 60 C3
Wrocław: Poland 20 C2
Wrong, Lake: Canada 61 F2
Wrotham: England 15 G2
Wroughton: England 15 E3
Wuchai: China 36 B2
Wuchang: China 37 B3
Wuchiang: China 37 D3
Wuching: China 36 C2
Wuchow: China 37 B5
Wuchuan: China 36 B1
Wuchung: China 36 A2
Wudil: Nigeria 67 B1
Wufeng: China 37 B3
Wuhan: China 37 B3
Wuhsi: China 36 C3
Wuhsiang: China 36 B2
Wuhsuan: China 37 A5
Wuhu: China 37 C3
Wuhua: China 37 C5
Wukang: China 37 B4
Wukari: Nigeria 67 B2
Wuki: China 37 A3
Wukung: China 36 A3
Wukung Shan: mtns. China 37 B4
Wulanhaote: China 34 G1
Wuming: China 37 A5
Wupatki Nat. Monument: U.S.A. 63 D4
Wuping: China 37 C4
Wuppertal: Ger. F.R. 24 B1
Wupu: China 36 B2
Wuqiao: China 36 C2
Würzburg: German F.R. 24 B2
Wuta: China 36 A2
Wutai: China 36 B2
Wuti: China 36 C2
Wuwei: China 37 C3
Wuyi Shan: mtn. China 37 C4
Wuyi Shan: mtns.: China 37 C4
Wuyuan: Inner Mon.: China 36 A1
Wuyuan: Kiangsi, China 37 C4
Wyangala Reservoir: Australia 43 C4
Wyckoff: U.S.A. 55 F3
Wye: r. England 14 D3
Wymondham: England 15 H2
Wyndham: Australia 40 D4
Wynyard: Canada 61 E2
Wyoming: Canada 56 D7
Wyoming: U.S.A. 54 N4
Wyoming: State. U.S.A. 52/3 D2
Wyperfeld Nat. Park: Australia 43 B5

Xai-Xai: Mozambique 72 E4
Xánthi: Greece 21 D4
Xanxerê: Brazil 66 D2
Xi'an see Sian
Xieng Khouang: Laos 38 C3
Xingu: r. Brazil 64 H5
Xisha Is. see Paracel Islands 38 E

Yaan: China 34 C4
Yabassi: Cameroun 67 B3
Yabebyry: r. Paraguay 66 C2
Yabri: Nigeria 67 C1
Yachmata: Japan 39 g iv
Yacuiba: Bolivia 64 F8
Yacyretá, Isla: r. Paraguay 66 C2
Yagoua: Cameroun 67 D1
Yaguari: r. Uruguay 66 C3
Yahagi: r. Japan 39 d ii
Yahk: Canada 60 C2
Yakima: & r. U.S.A. 62 B2
Yakumo: Japan 39 D1
Yakutsk: U.S.S.R. 27 P5
Yale: Mich. U.S.A. 56 C6
Yale: Thailand 38 C5
Yalgoo: Australia 42 b i
Yallourn: Australia 43 C5
Yalta: U.S.S.R. 28 C5
Yama Peninsula: U.S.S.R. 26/7 K4
Yamagata: Japan 39 D2
Yamaska: Co. Canada 57 N4
Yamato: Japan 39 f iv
Yamato-koriyama: Japan 39 b ii
Yamato-takada: Japan 39 b ii
Yamatu: China 39 N4
Yamethin: Burma 38 B2
Yamma Yamma. Lake: Australia 42 B3
Yampa: r. U.S.A. 52 D2
Yampi Sound: Australia 40 C4
Yamuna: r. India 32 D3

Yan: r. China 36 C3
Yanbu: Saudi Arabia 30 C6
Yanchuang: China 36 B2
Yangcheng: China 36 B2
Yangchow: China 36 C3
Yangcho: China 36 A4
Yanghsin: China 37 C4
Yangku: China 36 C2
Yangshuo: China 37 B5
Yangtze (Dre. Kinsha): r. China 34 B4
Yangtze Gorge: China 37 B3
Yangyuan: China 36 B1
Yankan Game Heserve: Nigeria 67 C2
Yankton: U.S.A. 58 A3
Yantic: U.S.A. 55 H3
Yao: Japan 39 b ii
YAOUNDÉ: Cameroun 67 C3
Yar: r. England 15 E4
Yaraka: Australia 40 G5
Yare: r. England 15 H2
Yanga-take: mtn.: Japan 39 C2
Yarkand see Soche 31 L3
Yarker: Canada 57 J5
Yarmouth: Canada 47 W8
Yarmouth: England 15 E4
Yarmouth: U.S.A. 57 P6
Yaroslavl: U.S.S.R. 28 D2
Yarram: Australia 43 C5
Yarraman: Australia 42 D3
Yarrow Water: r. Scot. 11 E4
Yarty: r. England 14 C4
Yashi: Nigeria 67 B1
Yashkera: Nigeria 67 C1
Yasku: Nigeria 67 C1
Yasu: Japan 39 c i
Yatabe: Japan 39 g iii
Yate: England 14 D3
Yatsushiro: Japan 39 B3
Yawatahama: Japan 39 B3
Yazd: Iran 30 F4
Yazoo: r. U.S.A. 50 D3
Yazoo City: U.S.A. 50 D3
Ye: Burma 38 B3
Yeadon: England 12 E3
Yebyu: Burma 38 B4
Yehchiachi: China 36 C3
Yeh-hsien: China 36 B3
Yehsien: China 36 C2
Yell: i. & sd.: Shetland Islands 10 b i
Yellow: r. see Hwang
Yellow Grass: Canada 61 E3
Yellowhead Pass: Can. 60 B2
Yellowknife: Canada 46 N4
Yellowstone: r. U.S.A. 53 D1
Yellowstone Lake: U.S.A. 62 D3
Yellowstone Nat. Park: U.S.A. 62 D3
Yel'nya: U.S.S.R. 28 C3
Yelwa: Nigeria 67 A1
YEMEN, (ARAB REPUBLIC): 30 D7
YEMEN PEOPLE'S DEMOCRATIC REPUBLIC: 30 E7
Yenagoa: Nigeria 65 B3
Yenakiyevo: U.S.S.R. 28 A2
Yenan: China 36 A2
Yencheng: China 36 B2
Yencheng: China 36 D3
Yenho: China 37 A4
Yenisey: r. U.S.S.R. 27 L5
Yenisey, Gulf of: U.S.S.R. 27 K3
Yeniseysk: U.S.S.R. 29 P2
Yenking: China 36 C1
Yenshan: China 36 C2
Yentai: China 36 D2
Yeo: r. England 14 D3
Yeovil: England 14 D3
Yeppoon: Australia 42 D2
Yerevan: U.S.S.R. 28 E5
Yerington: U.S.A. 63 C4
Yermolayevo: U.S.S.R. 28 H3
Yerwa: Nigeria 67 D1
Yes Tor: England 14 B4
Yeu: Burma 38 B2
Yeungchun: China 37 B5
Yeungkong: China 37 B5
Yeungshan: China 37 B5
Yevpatoriya: U.S.S.R. 28 C5
Yeysk: U.S.S.R. 28 D4
Yguazu: r. Paraguay 66 D2
Yi: r. Uruguay 66 C3
Yiannitsá: Greece 21 D4
Yicheng: China 36 D4
Yichun: China 37 C3
Yihsien: China 36 C2
Yinchwan (Ninghsia): China 36 A2
Ying: r. China 36 C3
Yingcheng: China 37 B3
Yinghsien: China 36 B2
Yingkang: China 37 C4
Yingkow: China 36 D1
Yingshan: Hupeh. China 37 C3

Yingshan: Szechwan. China 37 A3
Yingshang: China 36 C3
Yingtak: China 37 B5
Yingtan: China 37 C4
Yinkanie: Australia 43 B4
Yinkiang: China 37 A4
Yin Shan: mtns.: China 36 B1
Yishan: China 37 A5
Yitu: China 36 C2
Yiyang: China 37 B4
Yikitka, Lake: Finland 16 E2
Ylivieska: Finland 16 D3
Yodo: r. Japan 39 b ii
Yoho Nat. Park: Canada 62 C1
Yoichi: Japan 39 D1
Yokaichiba: Japan 39 g iv
Yokkaichi: Japan 39 c ii
Yoko: Cameroun 67 C2
Yokohama: Japan 39 f iv
Yokoshiba: Japan 39 g iv
Yokosuka: Japan 39 f iv
Yokote: Japan 39 D2
Yola: Nigeria 67 C2
Yom: r. Thailand 38 C3
Yonago: Japan 39 B3
Yonkers: U.S.A. 55 G4
Yonne: r. France 22 B2
Yono: Japan 39 f iv
York: Australia 42 b ii
York: Co. Canada 56 F6
York: Nebr. U.S.A. 53 F2
York: Pa. U.S.A. 54 D5
York, Cape: Australia 40 G3
York, Vale of: England 12 E2
York. Beach: town. U.S.A. 55 K1
Yorke Peninsula: Austl. 43 A4
Yorketown: Australia 43 A5
York Factory: Canada 61 G1
York Harbor: U.S.A. 55 K1
Yorkshire Dales Nat. Park: England 12 D2
Yorkshire Wolds. Eng. 12 F2
Yorkton: Canada 61 E2
Yoroi-zaki: cape. Japan 39 c ii
Yosemite Nat. Park: U.S.A. 63 C4
Yoshino: Japan 39 b ii
Yoshkar-Ola: U.S.S.R. 28 F2
Youghal: Irish Rep. 13 D5
Youghal Bay: Irish Rep. 13 D5
Young: Australia 43 C4
Young: Canada 61 D2
Young: Uruguay 66 C3
Youngstown: U.S.A. 59 D3
Youngsville: U.S.A. 56 F8
Yoyang: China 37 B4
Ypacarai: Paraguay 66 C1
Ypané: r. Paraguay 66 C1
Ypres: Belgium 22 B1
Ypsilanti: U.S.A. 56 B7
Yr Efl: pk. Wales 14 B2
Yreka: U.S.A. 63 B3
Ystad: Sweden 17 B4
Ythan: r. Scotland 10 F2
Yu: r. China 37 A5
Yuan: r. China 37 B4
Yuanan: China 37 B3
Yuanping: China 36 B2
Yuba City: U.S.A. 63 B4
Yubari: Japan 39 D1
Yucatan Channel: Cuba/Mexico 49 J5
Yucatan: penin. Mex. 48 J6
Yuch'ang: China 36 C2
Yuching: China 37 A4
Yugashima: Japan 39 e v
Yugawara: Japan 39 f iv
Yuhsien: Hunan. China 37 B4
Yuhsien: Hupeh. China 36 B3
Yuhuan: China 37 D4
Yukagir Plateau: U.S.S.R. 27 S4
Yukan: China 37 C4
Yukon: Terrt. Canada 46 J4
Yukon: r. U.S.A./Can. 46 D4
Yulin: Kwangsi Chuang. China 37 B5
Yulin: Shensi. China 37 A2
Yuma: U.S.A. 63 D5
Yunnan: Prov. China 38 C2

Page

Yunsiao: China 37
Yunting: China 37
Yunting: r. China 37
Yurmala: U.S.S.R. 17
Yushan: China 37
Yushu (Jyekundo): China 34
Yuten: China 34
Yutu: China 37
Yutze: China 36
Yuyang: China 37
Yuyao: China 37
Yuzhno Sakhalinsk: U.S.S.R. 27
Yverdon: Switzerland 25

Zabul: Iran 30
Zacatecas: Mexico 48
Zadar: Yugoslavia 21
Zagora: Morocco 68
Zagora: U.S.S.R. 20
Zagreb: Yugoslavia 20
Zagros Mts.: Iran 30
Zahedán: Iran 30
ZAIRE 71
Zaire (Congo): r. Africa 71
Zakopane: Poland 20
Zalaegerszeg: Hungary 20
Zamboanga: Phil. 35
Zamość: Poland 20
Zamora: Spain 19
Zanesville: U.S.A. 59
Zante: i. Greece 21
Zanthus: Australia 40
Zanzibar: & i. Tan. 71
Zapala: Argentina 65
Zaporozh'ye: U.S.S.R. 28
Zaragoza: Spain 19
Zaranda Hill: Nigeria 67
Zárate: Argentina 66
Zari: Nigeria 67
Zaria: Nigeria 67
Zary: Poland 20
Zaysan: Lake. U.S.S.R. 29
Z Canyon Dam: U.S.A. 62
Zeballos: Canada 62
Zeebrugge: Belgium 22
Zeerust: S. Africa 72
Zehdenick: Ger. D.R. 24
Zeila: Somali Rep. 69
Zeitz: German D.R. 24
Zell am See: Aus. 25
Zella Mehlis: Ger. D.R. 24
Zell am Ziller: Austria 25
Zelten: Libya 69
Zenica: Yugoslavia 21
Zermatt: Switzerland 25
Zetland: Reg. Shetland Islands 10
Zeya: U.S.S.R. 27
Zgierz: Poland 20
Zhangjiakou see Changkiakow 36
Zharma: U.S.S.R. 29
Zhdanov: U.S.S.R. 28
Zhejiang see Chekiang 37
Zhengzhou see Chengchow 36
Zhigalovo: U.S.S.R. 27
Zhitomir: U.S.S.R. 20
Zhmerinka: U.S.S.R. 20
Zielona Góra: Poland 20
Ziguinchor: Senegal 68
Žilina: Czechoslovakia 20
ZIMBABWE (Rhodesia) 72
Zimbabwe: ruins. Zimb. 72
Zinder: Niger 67
Zion Nat. Park: U.S.A. 63
Zipaquira: Colombia 64
Zittau: German D.R. 24
Zlatoust: U.S.S.R. 28
Znojmo: Czech. 20
Zolochev: U.S.S.R. 20
Zomba: Malawi 72
Zone Pt.: U.S.A. 14
Zongo: Zaire 70
Zonguldak: Turkey 28
Zrenjanin: Yugoslavia 21
Zuara: Libya 69
Zug: Switzerland 25
Zugspitze: mtn. Austria 25
Zuidelijk Flevoland: polder. Netherlands 24
Zuider Zee see Ijsselmeer
Zungeru: Nigeria 67
Zuni: r. U.S.A. 52
Zürich: & l. Switz. 25
Zurmi: Nigeria 67
Zuru: Nigeria 67
Zushi: Japan 39
Zwickau: Ger. D.R. 24
Zwolle: Netherlands 24
Żyrardów: Poland 20
Zyryanovsk: U.S.S.R. 29